# The Philosophy of
# William Ellery Channing

Engraved by W.<sup>m</sup> Hoogland, from a picture painted by Chester Harding.

# WILLIAM E. CHANNING, D.D.

# The Philosophy of

# William Ellery Channing

by

## Robert Leet Patterson

Professor of Philosophy, Duke University

Bookman Associates : New York

Manufactured in the United States of America
by Record Press, N. Y. C.

*TO*
Clara

1104870

# Foreword

The purpose of this book is to draw attention to certain aspects of Channing's thought which were, I believe, of fundamental importance in his own eyes, but which do not appear hitherto to have attracted sufficient consideration. In my opinion Channing's status as a thinker has not received adequate recognition; indeed, in my judgment, he is one of the outstanding figures in the history of Christian thought. Whether this estimate be sound the reader will have ample opportunity for deciding in view of the evidence which is placed before him. In any case, I think that he will agree that Channing's constructive work was at least as significant as the destructive polemic which is so widely associated with his name. And the basic principle upon which it rests is the doctrine of *essential sameness* which is the intellectual justification of the mystical interest which so largely dominated his thinking, and became ever more manifest until its close. Such is the thesis which I endeavor to substantiate.

I take great pleasure in acknowledging my obligations to Professors Katherine Gilbert of Duke University, James Luther Adams of the Meadville School of Religion, and Edward D. Myers of Washington and Lee University, who read the typescript of this book in whole or in part, and in thanking them for the numerous valuable suggestions which they so kindly proffered. Needless to say, I alone am responsible for all the interpretations offered and the conclusions advanced, but to them, and to many other friends, too numerous to mention, whose encouragement has been a keen stimulus, my gratitude is as profound as it is ineffaceable.

# Contents

# PART ONE

# Background

# Chapter One

# Calvinism

William Ellery Channing was born on April 7, 1780, just twenty-two years after the death of Jonathan Edwards, America's most eminent theologian and a staunch defender of the Calvinistic orthodoxy whereof Channing was to become an inveterate, although never an uncharitable, opponent. He died on October 2, 1842. Thus his life covered a goodly portion of the two great centuries during which modern civilization made its most spectacular progress, and to which our own period constitutes so disastrous an anti-climax. As in the case of every other thinker, if we are to understand his thought, we must first study the mental environment in which it was formed. The intellectual atmosphere in which Channing was born was the product of two mighty currents of thought. Of these one was, of course, the traditional Calvinism. So much denunciation, much of it just and some of it unjust, has been poured upon Calvinism that we are apt to view it today through eyes unconsciously prejudiced. Our first duty, therefore, if we are to understand Channing's intellectual background, is to try to see Calvinism as it really was in the days of its vigorous youth, and next to discover what it had become in New England at the close of the eighteenth century. And we cannot better begin our inquiry, I believe, than by recalling some observations of James Anthony Froude which come close to the heart of our subject.

"I am going to ask you," said he, in his St. Andrews address, "to consider how it came to pass that if Calvinism is indeed the hard and unreasonable creed which modern enlightenment declares it to be, it has possessed such singular attractions in past times for some of the greatest men that ever lived. And how—being, as we are told, fatal to

morality, because it denies free will—the first symptom of its operation, wherever it established itself, was to obliterate the distinction
between sins and crimes, and to make the moral law the rule of life
for States as well as persons. I shall ask you, again, why, if it be a
creed of intellectual servitude, it was able to inspire and sustain the
bravest efforts ever made by man to break the yoke of unjust authority.
When all else has failed—when patriotism has covered its face and
human courage has broken down—when intellect has yielded, as Gib-
bon says, 'with a smile or a sigh,' content to philosophize in the closet,
and abroad worship with the vulgar—when emotion and sentiment and
tender imaginative piety have become the handmaids of superstition,
and have dreamt themselves into forgetfulness that there is any difference between lies and truth—the slavish form of belief called Calvinism, in one or other of its many forms, has borne ever an inflexible
front to illusion and mendacity, and has preferred rather to be ground
to powder like flint than to bend before violence, or melt under enervat-
ing temptation."

We know what Froude's answer was, elaborated as it is in several of
his "Short Studies." [1] Calvinism, as he saw it, was one of those inevitable outbreaks of moral revolt which occur when corruption, oppression, impurity, and insincerity have become approximately as bad as
they can be, and the soul of man, sickened with iniquity, turns with
relief and yearning toward righteousness. The strength of Calvinism,
in his opinion, was a moral strength. Its theology, on the other hand,
was something of a makeshift, put together in an emergency and con-
structed out of such intellectual material as happened to be immediately
available, but in no sense the genuine and original expression of a new
insight. Thus when the moral impetus declined, as every moral impetus
inevitably does decline in the long run, only this mental lumber
was left, and Calvinism became what we behold it today, a stranded
wreck from which the tide of life has receded.

That there is a certain amount of truth in this theory I have no
doubt. The tendency of human nature to swing from extreme to extreme is well known to us. Every religious movement is born in a
wave of enthusiasm, but as time goes on the wave sooner or later begins to subside; and from this universal tendency Calvinism was not
exempt. So much we may certainly concede to Froude. Nevertheless,
if we try to explain Calvinism as primarily a moral movement, and to
regard its theology as an inert and uninfluential mass of doctrine borne
along with it like a cork floating on a wave, the facts will not bear us out.

That the Calvinist was fired by a zeal for righteousness no one will dispute; yet it is equally clear that from the teachings of his faith he drew inspiration and confidence, that they were his solace in affliction, and that for them he was always ready to do battle and to die a martyr's death. Consequently it is our business to discover if we can what elements in the body of doctrine which he accepted were most closely connected with his religious experience, and provided the nutriment of his devotional life.

It seems obvious, therefore, that we must turn in the first place to the doctrine of predestination which is one of the most famous tenets of his creed, and concerning which Calvin wrote with so much warmth of feeling.[2] If it be true that all events are ordered in accordance with the divine will, if nothing can befall without its sanction, and if "all things work together for good to them that love God," [3] then indeed the believer should face the world with a mighty confidence. Here we touch what is probably one of the chief roots of that heroic courage for which the Calvinists were so conspicuous, and which manifested itself so frequently on the battlefield and at the stake. A single instance must suffice to illustrate the practical consequences of such a belief. When the Vaudois were preparing for their "Glorious Return" and the conquest of their native valleys from which they had been expelled, Javenel, who drew up their plan of operations, strongly advised the seizure of a certain mountain called the Balsille. "You will, of course," he wrote, "be told that you cannot hold it always, and that rather than not succeed in their object, all France and Italy will gather together against you. . . . But were it the whole world, and only yourselves against all, fear ye the Almightly alone, who is your protection." [4] It was in this spirit that the Calvinists won their battles. And a doctrine which proved so potent amidst the dangers of war was doubtless equally consoling to the individual in the trials of daily life. Since nothing occurred by chance, every event was charged with meaning, bearing, as it were, the stamp of divine providence. Such a view must have made God seem very close, and his presence very real to those convinced of its truth. We must not forget the vital significance of this doctrine, and the warmth of emotion which must have surrounded it, when we see Channing entering the lists against it.

Closely connected with predestination are the kindred doctrines of election, the substitutionary atonement, justification by faith alone, irresistible grace, and the perseverance of the saints. It is upon the last two that I desire now to lay the most stress. Whereas Roman

Catholic theology concentrates its attention above all upon man's last end which is the Vision of God, reformed theology is primarily concerned with the initial stages of the spiritual life. Each approach has its peculiar advantages, but, as our present interest is in the religious experience of the Calvinist, it is the dogmas which I have just mentioned that demand our notice.

The Roman Catholic shares, of course, with the Calvinist the belief in election; nevertheless he also believes in free will and in the possibility of meritorious action which makes for salvation. We must not, however, allow ourselves to be misled as to the significance of these beliefs. The ability to perform meritorious actions is imparted to man by God, and not to all men.[5] The aid bestowed by grace is accepted by an act of free will; none the less the man who thus wills freely cannot will otherwise than as God wills that he will, inasmuch as God is the ultimate cause of all action. What God wills to occur of necessity necessarily occurs, and what God wills to occur contingently does occur contingently and cannot fail to do so, otherwise the divine will would be frustrated.[6] The notion of contingency thus invoked applies only to events considered in themselves and in their relations to one another, not to events considered in relation to God. Accordingly, despite his natural desire to have it both ways, the Romanist does not, by appealing to the contradictory notion of a contingent action which cannot fail to occur—in other words, of a necessary contingency— nor yet by resorting to the miserable shift of distinguishing between God's antecedent will whereby he wills all men to be saved and his consequent will whereby he wills some men to be damned,[7] really escape the consequences which are stated with such brutal frankness in the Calvinistic declarations that "those of mankind that are predestined unto life, God, before the foundation of the world was laid, according to his eternal and immutable purpose, and the secret counsel and good pleasure of his will, hath chosen in Christ, unto everlasting glory, out of his mere free grace and love, without any foresight of faith or good works, or perseverance in either of them, or any other thing in the creature, as conditions, or causes moving him thereunto; and all to the praise of his glorious grace," [8] whereas "the rest of mankind God was pleased, according to the unsearchable counsel of his own will, whereby he extendeth or withholdeth mercy as he pleaseth, for the glory of his sovereign power over his creatures, to pass by, and to ordain them to dishonor and wrath for their sin, to the praise of his glorious justice." [9]

There remains, however, this important difference between the two points of view. The Roman Catholic, except in the improbable event of his being favored with a special divine revelation, cannot be sure that he is among the elect. The Calvinist, on the other hand, once he has experienced the process of regeneration, cannot doubt it. This difference follows from the latter's wholsale repudiation of the notion of merit in obedience to the injunction "When ye shall have done all the things that are commanded you, say, We are unprofitable servants; we have done that which it was our duty to do." [10] The Calvinist, accordingly, does not hope to purchase his salvation by good works; he performs good works inevitably because he is a saved and regenerated man. Justification is, if you will, a juristic concept, the accounting righteous of the actual sinner to whom is imputed the righteousness of Christ; but it is accompanied by an act of irresistible grace which makes the sinner into a good man. Thus for him to doubt his own salvation is to mistrust the efficacy of Christ's sacrifice and the power of God which has laid hold upon him. The dogma of the perseverance of the saints assures him that this irresistible grace will never forsake him.

What I have just said, however, holds true only of primitive Calvinism. "The Reformers," Dr. Hodge observes in his commentary on the Westminster Confession of Faith,[11] "went so far as to teach that the special object of justifying faith is the favour of God toward us for Christ's sake. Therefore to believe is to be assured of our own personal salvation. Thus Luther, Melancthon, and Calvin taught. This is the doctrine taught in the Augsburg Confession and Heidelberg Catechism. It is not, however, taught in any other of the Reformed Confessions."

In the Westminster Confession the theory is so far modified as to teach that the infallible assurance of personal salvation "doth not so belong to the essence of faith, but that a true believer may wait long, and conflict with many difficulties before he be partaker of it," [12] and that even after it has been granted it may be "shaken, diminished, and intermitted." [13] In other words a man may confide fully in the promises of God to the elect and yet be uncertain as to whether he himself be one of them. He may even be deceived by "false hopes and carnal presumptions"; [14] nevertheless it is his duty to strive to "make his calling and election sure," and this he may hope to attain to "without extraordinary revelation, in the right use of ordinary means." [15]

Dr. Hodge discusses in some detail[16] the manner in which this infallible assurance is imparted. "Some have maintained," he informs us, "that the passage teaches that the Holy Spirit in some mysterious way directly reveals to our spirits that we are the children of God, as one man immediately conveys information to another man." To this view, which is of course thoroughly mystical, he objects that "Christians are not and cannot be conscious of any such injection of information from without into the mind, and that, as far as such testimony alone is concerned, we should be unable to distinguish certainly the testimony of the Spirit from the conclusions of our own reasons or the suggestions of our own hearts," and that "an expectation of such direct communications would be likely to generate enthusiasm and presumption." His own interpretation of the doctrine, into which we need not enter in any minuteness, involves as its principal feature the belief in a spiritual illumination whereby a man is enabled to "judge truly of the genuineness of his own graces" so that "comparing the outward standard with the inward experience, he may draw correct and unquestionable conclusions." It is evident that here we are far from the warmth and confidence of primitive Calvinism. Even here, however, it is still asserted that the elect are never permitted to fall from grace, and that, with or without subjective assurance, they are irrevocably destined to be saved.

It is clear that the influence of such a theory, whether in its unmodified or modified form, must have been immense. It was this dogma, as a matter of fact, which comforted Cromwell as he lay dying. "I know," he said, "that I was once in grace." The conviction that the believer stands in a direct and unbreakable relationship to a God who will never forsake him could not fail to be powerfully stimulated by such a teaching.

We must now push our investigation further and ask ourselves the twin questions: What, for the Calvinist, is the seat of authority in religion? and: How does he believe that God is known? We shall view his position to best advantage if we remind ourselves that it constitutes in truth one of the concluding stages in the development of mediaeval thought; and that, consequently, to see it aright we must contrast it with the attitudes assumed by his Roman Catholic predecessors and contemporaries.

The seat of authority for the Romanist is, of course, the Church which both guarantees the status of the Scriptures and, under the guidance of the Holy Spirit, interprets them. To the latter question, however, a succession of answers were returned. As Professor Gilson has shown,[17] before the advent of St. Thomas the universal opinion was that the proper point of departure was faith. One believed, then one sought to know. But, having believed, one might fearlessly seek to prove all things—not only the existence of God, but also the doctrines of the Trinity, the Incarnation, and the Atonement—for what one believed one might also know. And in the act of knowledge one was illumined by an intellectual light which streamed forth from God himself and revealed the realm of eternal truths. But the mighty impact of the thought of Aquinas revolutionized the intellectual outlook. Henceforth what one believed one did not know, and what one knew one did not believe.[18] The spheres of reason and faith were now sharply differentiated; the former being that of philosophy and the latter that of theology. One could demonstrate the existence of God by reason alone; but such doctrines as those of the Trinity, the Incarnation, and the Atonement, being mysteries of faith, could not be demonstrated, but only believed. Divine illumination, reduced to a minimum, no longer directly revealed a supersensible world; all knowledge began with and proceeded from sense-experience. Yet, as a good Aristotelian, St. Thomas recognized the presence *in rebus* of universals in the sense that they are susceptible of being abstracted thence, and are capable of providing the philosopher with the *a priori* knowledge which he requires to construct a metaphysic.

The nominalism or conceptualism, however, of William of Occam constituted a second revolution which to the metaphysician was wholly disastrous. The universal vanished entirely from the external world, to become—in so far as it was recognized at all—no more than an entity in the apprehending mind. Only the individual was real. Henceforth the emphasis was on empirical knowledge. Proofs of the unity of God or the immortality of the soul were no longer accounted possible, and with them vanished the possibility of a natural theology. Christianity thus become a system of doctrine wholly supernatural, to be accepted by faith alone.

It is important for us to remember that Occamism constitutes the intellectual background of the Reformation. Luther himself was trained in the thought of Occam's disciple, Biel; hence the frank and hearty contempt which he expressed for the metaphysical powers of human reason. Calvinism, indeed—at least as it finds expression in the work of M. Lecerf, its recent exponent at the Sorbonne—affirms the reality of *universalia in rebus;* [19] but the concession is an unimportant one, inasmuch as Calvin assumes toward reason and revelation an attitude very similar to that of Luther. He does, it is true, appeal to the visible world as testimony to the power, wisdom, and goodness of God,[20] yet rather as a stimulus to pious reflection—which he berates human reason for its unwillingness to indulge in[21]—than as a source whence a solid argument can be derived. In his *Institutes* Calvin explicitly asserts that human reason, since the Fall, is unable to attain to such a knowledge of God as is essential to salvation, but only to so much as will leave it without excuse.[22] The same position, be it observed, is restated in the first chapter of the Westminster Confession.[23] The French Confession—sometimes called the Confession of Rochelle—originally drawn up by Calvin with the aid of De Chandieu, and later revised by a synod at Paris, would seem however to go further,[24] since it roundly asserts that man is unable to approach God by his "intelligence or reason."

Does this latter declaration mean to deny the possibility of demonstrating the divine existence? It is not easy to answer this question, nor is it easy to reconcile the various pronouncements of M. Lecerf as to the attitude of contemporary Calvinism. It may be possible, concedes M. Lecerf, to prove the existence of a god, but not of God, the God of revelation; [25] moreover it is illegitimate to make such an attempt,[26] since God, he tells us, "has a right to be believed," and he has revealed himself. Perhaps we might not unjustly sum up the matter by concluding that, from the Calvinist's standpoint, all philosophical arguments are disputable,[27] uncertain, and inconclusive, and furthermore unnecessary in view of the fact of revelation. Again no philosophical argument can demonstrate the truth of such doctrines as those of the Trinity, the Incarnation, the Atonement, and justification by faith alone.

Whither, then, is the believer, who rejects at once the claims of reason and those of the Church of Rome, to turn in his need? Shall he appeal to the *sensus divinitatis*, implanted in the soul by common grace, which endows him with an intuitive knowledge of God sufficient to leave him without excuse? This is not a very cheerful suggestion. Calvin, however, has his solution ready, and it is one to which too great importance cannot be attached, since it constitutes the very cornerstone of his system. The believer is saved from his desperate condition by the particular grace of the Holy Spirit which bears witness within his soul, at once authenticating the external revelation contained in the Scriptures, and enlightening his mind so that he is able to understand what before appeared to him unintelligible.[28]

Thus the two questions which we previously raised are solved by a single answer. The witness of the Spirit is, for the Calvinist, at once the seat of authority and the knowledge of God. We know God because he speaks to us; his existence is not demonstrated, but the thunder of his voice is heard in the soul. We know that the Bible is his word because he tells us so. Calvinism is thus a religion of first-hand experience. To the individual believer God speaks as directly as he spoke to Amos or Isaiah. No wonder that a movement inspired by such a conviction should have spread over northwestern Europe in a wave of titanic enthusiasm! There could have been nothing like it since the birth of Christianity. In fact, in the eyes of its adherents, it *was* Christianity come alive again.

But, one may well ask, having once appealed to the Spirit, how draw the line between revelation and illusion, between faith and fanaticism? This has been a problem for other teachers than Calvin, and for other religions than Christianity. An amusing instance of its occurrence in the Moslem world is recounted by Professor R. A. Nicholson in his *Studies in Islamic Mysticism,*[29] "Whilst Abu Said was preaching in Nishapur, a learned theologian who was present thought to himself that such doctrine is not to be found in the seven sevenths (i.e. the whole) of the Koran. Abu Said immediately turned towards him and said, "Doctor, thy thought is not hidden from me. The doctrine that I preach is contained in the eighth seventh of the Koran. 'What is that?' the theologian inquired. Abu Said answered: 'The seven sevenths are, *O Apostle, deliver the message that hath been sent down to thee* (Kor. 5, 71), and the eighth seventh is, *He revealed unto His servant that which He revealed* (Kor. 53, 10)." The Zwickau prophets who so disturbed and outraged Luther had similarly claimed an inspiration going beyond the content of Scripture, and the Anabaptist distinction between the written and unwritten word resembles the appeal to the "eighth seventh" of the Koran.

Undoubtedly Calvin was faced by a serious problem, the problem of "trying the spirits." There was a real danger that the Reformation might degenerate into a movement of illiterate ranters. There was also the danger—equally real—that any infringement upon Christian liberty, by checking the outpouring of the Spirit, might transform Protestantism into a legalistic and conventional outward morality. Calvin's solution,[30] whether arbitrary or not, has at least the merit of clarity. The Spirit which bears witness in the soul of the believer is the Spirit which Christ promised to his disciples. The function of the

Spirit, therefore, is not to promulgate a new gospel which Christ did not teach, for his gospel is final and all-sufficient; on the contrary it is to authenticate his teaching, to convince the soul of the divine origin and character of the gospel, and to illuminate it so that it may grasp its meaning.

Such is Calvin's doctrine of the witness of the Spirit. It is re-affirmed, of course, in the French Confession.[31] It is restated in the Belgic Confession,[32] in the First Scotch Confession,[33] and in the Westminster Confession.[34] It is obvious that this doctrine is closely related to the Augustinian theory of illumination, from which indeed it was no doubt partly derived, although it was probably also suggested by various Biblical texts. What is original in it is the confining of the efficacy of the Spirit to the illumination of the Word,[35] and the sacramental function—for it amounts to this—attributed to the Scriptures. It is likewise evident that this doctrine constitutes the very foundation of Calvin's entire system. Whenever it is forgotten, Calvinism becomes transformed into a mere *fidéisme* which is something very far from the intentions of its author. Its seat of authority is destroyed, and it can be accepted, if at all, only upon pragmatic grounds or in consequence of philosophic argumentation, and either line of approach would certainly have been repudiated by its founder.

That the doctrine of the witness of the Spirit was alive in New England in the early eighteenth century we are assured by the testimony of Jonathan Edwards, inasmuch as we have two elaborate statements thereof proceeding from his pen,[36] wherein it is set forth with characteristic clarity and in thoroughly Calvinistic fashion. "There is," he informs us, "if the Scriptures are of any use to teach us anything, a spiritual, supernatural understanding of divine things, *peculiar* to the saints." [37] And, in order to make perfectly clear what he means, he tells us at considerable length what it is not. Such knowledge is not an awareness of new truths, doctrines or propositions, for "*a new meaning*," as Edwards succinctly remarks, is "*a new scripture*"; "It is properly *adding* to the word, which is threatened with so dreadful a curse." [38] Nor does supernatural knowledge consist in impressions made upon the imagination or phantasy. "There is," he points out, "a great difference between these two things, viz. *lively imaginations arising from strong affections,* and *strong affections arising from lively imaginations.*" [39] Such imaginations may be an accidental accompaniment of illumination, but they are not its cause, and are not to be confused with it. Since it has not to do with propositions, supernatural knowledge does not acquaint us with the mystical meaning of parable or allegory. Again, it does not inform us regarding our duty with respect to particular acts, nor does it furnish us with definite guidance as to the affairs of daily life. It is not to be identified with a conviction of sin, and it is to be sharply distinguished from the influence of common grace which merely aids and strengthens man's natural power of apprehension, whereas supernatural knowledge is wholly beyond and above nature. Moreover it is not "notional understanding" or speculative knowledge, and it is not given by natural means.

What, then, is it? "If there be in the saints," says Edwards, "a kind of perception, which is in its nature perfectly diverse from all that natural men can have, it must consist in their having a certain kind of ideas, or sensations of mind, which are simply diverse from all that can be in the minds of natural men. And this is the same thing as to say, that it consists in the sensations of a new spiritual sense, which the souls of natural men have not." [40] It is "a sense of the heart," "a sense of spiritual beauty." [41] "He that sees the beauty of holiness," writes Edwards, "or true moral good, sees the greatest and most important thing in the world, which is the fulness of all things, without which all the world is empty, yea, worse than nothing. Unless this is seen, nothing is seen that is worth the seeing; for there is no other true excellency or beauty. Unless this be understood, nothing is understood worthy the exercise of the noble faculty of understanding. This is the beauty of the Godhead, the divinity of divinity (if I may so speak), the good of the infinite fountain of good. Without this, God himself (if that were possible) would be an infinite evil, we ourselves had better never have been; and there had better have been no being. He therefore in effect knows nothing, that knows not this; his knowledge is but the shadow of knowledge, or the *form of knowledge,* as the apostle calls it. Well therefore may the scripture represent those who are destitute of that spiritual sense, by which is perceived the beauty of holiness, as totally *blind, deaf,* and *senseless,* yea, *dead.* And well may regeneration, in which this divine sense is given to the soul by its Creator, be represented as opening the blind eyes, raising the dead, and bringing a person into a new world." [42]

This perception of the beauty of holiness in the gospel carries with it certainty as to the gospel's truth. In the words of Edwards, "he that truly sees the divine, transcendent, supreme glory of those things which are divine, does as it were know their divinity *intuitively;* he not only *argues,* but *sees* that they are divine." [43]

To say that illumination is not imparted by natural means is not equivalent, according to Edwards, to saying that the natural faculties are quiescent during the process. On the contrary, they are present and active, but the light that lightens them comes immediately from God. Illumination makes use of outward means in that it functions in conjunction with the Word. Yet Scripture is in no sense a mediate or secondary cause of illumination. Its task is to acquaint our minds with the content of doctrine; illumination enables us to see that the doctrine is true. It does this indirectly by removing antecedent prejudice and actively aiding the reason by attracting the mind's attention so that it perceives more clearly, and directly by revealing the presence of the divine beauty. This sense of divine beauty is comparable to a taste for music, for poetry, or for courtesy. No argument can avail against it.

Such a view, observes Edwards in language which reminds one forcibly of Channing, is both scriptural and rational.[44] It is rational to attribute transcendent excellency to divine things, and rational to suppose that such excellency can be seen; not, indeed, by the strength of natural reason—since it is not a matter of speculation—but by the pure and illumined heart. And it is rational to suppose that God does so illumine the rational soul, the nearest of all beings to himself, not by secondary causes but immediately, by imparting to it an emanation of his own beauty. Upon the natural man God operates extrinsically, as upon an external object; but to the soul of the saint God communicates himself, restoring the capacities ruined by the Fall, raising the soul above nature, and making it the habitual abode of his Spirit.

I have thus dwelt at length upon the doctrine of the witness of the Spirit for three reasons. In the first place, it is, as I have said, the corner stone of Calvinism upon which the whole structure is erected. In the second place, it is well that we should see at its best the movement which was first to attract and later to repel Channing, and upon which he was to deliver such telling blows; and it is beyond question that the doctrine of the witness of the Spirit is intimately related to the vital religious experience of Calvin and of his closest followers. Thus it is obvious that Edwards, in the passages which I have just quoted, is attempting to describe a perfectly genuine experience, even though we may suspect that to some degree he unintentionally confuses description with interpretation. And, in the third place, the notion of spiritual illumination, as we shall see, is one which proved extremely attractive to Channing and received his hearty endorsement. Thus, strangely enough, upon this very fundamental issue, Channing had much more in common with Calvin and Edwards than with the majority of his own Unitarian brethren. It is, therefore, of interest that nowhere—so far at least as I can discover—does Channing make any explicit reference to the redoubtable doctrine of the witness of the Spirit; and his failure to do so seems plainly to indicate that the New England Calvinism of the late eighteenth and early nineteenth centuries had—perhaps under the influence of eighteenth century rationalism—become largely biblicist and *fidéiste,* and that the notion of an intuitive, supernatural knowledge had receded into the background.

I do not, of course, intend to suggest that the doctrine of the witness of the Spirit was ever consciously repudiated by any portion of the Calvinistic world, or that it ever failed everywhere to receive formal acknowledgement. What I have in mind is something very different; namely, the thought that for an increasing number of the nominally orthodox it ceased to have any vital meaning. Such an assumption would appear to be inherently plausible. Calvin, indeed, when writing upon this subject, tells us in so many words[45] that every believer has experienced what he is talking about. Those who have been truly regenerated know what regeneration means, and those who have not experienced regeneration are no doubt doomed "to dishonor and wrath." The number of the elect will thus be composed of persons possessed of what today we should term mystical attainments, and those of no mean order.

Edwards appears to realize the magnitude of such a claim, and endeavors to soften it by pointing out that supernatural knowledge need not be, and frequently is not, imparted all at once.[46] But this does not get us over our difficulty. Either a man is regenerate or he is not, he either has or has not this spiritual sense.

Now anyone who has moved in Calvinistic circles at the present day must have met many persons who do not consider themselves in the least unregenerate, but who, if we were to ask them whether they acknowledge the authority of the Scriptures because of the direct attestation of God, would be frankly amazed, and would unhesitatingly disclaim any such supernatural insight. These people accept the Scriptures because they were brought up to do so. In good Roman Catholic fashion, their intellects assent at the command of their wills. There must have been many persons of this type in the New England of Channing's day; in fact we may not unplausibly surmise that they constituted the majority of the orthodox—or nominally orthodox—community.

This probability is increased when we consider the wide-spread influence of the philosophy of Locke, an influence which tended to externalize religion. As we shall return to this topic in the next chapter I shall not further enlarge upon it now except to point out that the fact that the early Unitarians were so greatly affected by the thought of Locke suggests that its influence, if not equally potent, must at least have been far from negligible among the orthodox.

If I be right in thus assuming that the doctrine of supernatural knowledge suffered an eclipse in the period between Edwards and Channing, the question arises: Did any glittering memories of Edwards' religion of beauty shine through the intervening darkness and illumine the soul of Channing? Obviously the answer to such a question must be based to some extent upon conjecture. We know, indeed, that Samuel Hopkins was a living link between Edwards and Channing; and we know also that Channing was inclined[47] to credit Hopkins with having influenced Edwards' thinking in a very important respect, namely, to quote Chadwick's words, in regard to his "development from the idea of virtue as the love of God considered as pure being to the idea of virtue as the love of God considered as morally excellent." [48] Apparently, however, Channing was not very sure of the soundness of his recollections, for he observes, "I consider him (Hopkins) as having contributed largely to the more rational form in which Calvinism is held among us. I cannot judge in what proportions this credit is to be divided between him and President Edwards," [49] and he professes himself anxious to receive further information on the subject.

That Channing had studied Edwards, however, is evident from his references to him. Needless to say, he was profoundly antagonized by Edwards' denial of free will, yet this antagonism was invariably softened by admiration for the mental capacities and religious character of the man. Moreover it is clear that he was attracted by the very aspect of Edwards' thought which we have just mentioned. Thus his nephew informs us that "he spoke with much regard . . . of Edwards, whose energy of intellect he greatly admired, while denying the soundness of his doctrine of necessity, and utterly rejecting its conclusions; many of whose writings he thought suggestive of deeply interesting views of the spiritual relations between the Divine Being and man, while he was horror-struck at the theology of others; and whose sketch of his conversion he once read in part to a friend with a voice trembling in its tenderness and eyes softened with emotion, as being one of the most pathetic and beautiful sketches ever given of the deeper workings of the soul." [50]

In line with this statement is Channing's eulogy of Edwards in his sermon delivered at the ordination of the Rev. J. S. Dwight as pastor of the Second Congregational Church in Northampton. There we find him exclaiming, "Can a minister breathe the atmosphere in which Edwards lived, and content himself with taking passively what others teach? I exhort you to visit the spot where Edwards brought forth his profound works; and let the spiritual presence of that intensest thinker of the New World and of the age in which he lived stir you up to energy of thought. His name has shed a consecration over this place. In many things, indeed, you differ from him; but you will not therefore reverence the less his single-hearted and unwearied devotion of his great powers to the investigation of truth; and in the wide and continued influence of his writings you will learn that secret study, silent thought, is, after all, the mightiest agent in human affairs." [51]

Channing was, then, as we should expect, thoroughly familiar with Edwards' thought. And in precisely that aspect of it which we have been considering he found something extremely congenial. Yet not in Edwards alone did he discover it. The same emphasis upon mystical insight he found in the writings of other great souls of the Church universal. And it does not appear that his own profoundest ideas were immediately suggested by Edwards. If they had been, Channing was the last man to have abstained from acknowledging the debt. The very notion that such might have been the case may, indeed, at first glance seem to verge on the absurd. But that the question is well worth raising will, I trust, become evident when we turn in due course to the examination of Channing's own positive contribution to theology, and in particular his view of intuitive knowledge.

Meanwhile it must be admitted that, although Edwards was capable in a certain mood of presenting Calvinism as a religion of beauty, and of doing so with a magnificent eloquence, this was not his only angle of approach, nor yet the aspect of his thought which has made him most renowned. In later life, when Channing thought of Calvinism, the doctrines which habitually flitted through his mind were those of election, pre-destination, reprobation, inherited guilt, the substitutionary atonement, and everlasting fire. We must, therefore, take note of the fact that there was a period in his early ministry when his own thinking tended in the direction of Calvinism.[52] For this we have his own assurance. "There was a time," he wrote, "when I verged towards Calvinism, for ill health and depression gave me a dark view of things. But the doctrine of the Trinity held me back. When I was studying my profession, and religion was the subject of deepest personal concern with me, I followed Doddridge through his 'Rise and Progress' till he brought me to a prayer to Jesus Christ. There I stopped, and wrote to a friend that my spiritual guide was gone where I could not follow him. I was never in any sense a Trinitarian." [53]

So distasteful does his biographer, Chadwick, find this confession that he cannot forbear from taking the words out of Channing's mouth and substituting his own. Accordingly he proceeds to correct him on this wise; "What is most interesting here is that, in the event, the doctrine of the Trinity was among the least of his objections to the orthodox system. It was the Calvinism of that system that excited his celestial ire; its representation of human nature as totally depraved and of God's nature as much the same, with its doctrines of election and reprobation and of the atonement as a reconciliation of a wrathful God to sinful men." [54]

To substitute our own notions of what a man ought to have felt and thought for what he himself tells us that he actually did feel and think is scarcely the safest course to pursue. We must, I am convinced, take Channing's words at their face value. True enough, the doctrines to which Chadwick refers did subsequently excite his ire, even as they had previously aroused his horror as a boy,[55] and when he thought of Calvinism as distinct from the general mass of traditional doctrines which it shares with Arminianism and Roman Catholicism he did unsparingly denounce these repulsive features; yet at the moment he was prepared to swallow all these dogmas. It *was* the doctrine of the Trinity which he could not stomach. This is, indeed, the all-important fact; and it remains a fact even though it be an inconvenient fact for a certain type of Unitarian apologist.

It is noteworthy that, in the above passage, Channing associates Calvinism with gloom. He did not, then, have in mind Edwards' religion of beauty; he was thinking of the doctrines to which we have just referred. This was natural enough, for the doctrinal skeleton of Calvinism is far more tangible than its mystical soul; yet it indicates with unmistakable clearness the complete absence of any feeling of discipleship toward Edwards.

There was, however, another influence which drew Channing toward Calvinism, and that was the personality of Hopkins for whose character Channing always felt a deep admiration, and whose doctrine of pure disinterestedness—as he himself informs us[56]—profoundly appealed to him. Yet neither in the theology of Edwards nor in that of Hopkins does Channing seem to have found the Ariadne's thread to guide him out of the Calvinistic labyrinth.

It is not, therefore, an idle question to inquire how it came to pass that Channing and the other early Unitarians succeeded in so thoroughly emancipating themselves that they were able to reject without a tremor doctrines which had been accepted for centuries. The answer, it may be urged, is relatively simple. The Reformation had destroyed the authority of the Church, and had put in its place the authority of God, whose attestation to the authenticity of his Word was imparted to the individual believer. With the passage of time the fundamental significance of this spiritual illumination tended to be forgotten, and the Scriptures themselves to be regarded as an ultimate and external authority. Hence the assertion of the right of the individual to interpret them for himself was an inevitable consequence of the rise of Protestantism.

That this statement is true, so far as it goes, I do not question. We are fully entitled to regard the Unitarian movement as the Indian summer of the Reformation, and it is in the thought of Channing that we discern some of the most brilliant tints and hues of that enchanted autumn. The explanation, I repeat, is true so far as it goes; but it does not go far enough, for it omits certain factors which demand recognition.

We have, in the first place, to supplement it by the observation that the ecclesiastical situation in New England was such as to favor the very sort of evolution which actually occurred. This situation was not the result of anyone's planning. The traditional creeds had not been thrust into the background because of any lukewarmness felt in regard to them. On the contrary, it was precisely because in the early days everybody believed in them so completely that it was unnecessary to be always reciting them. The church covenants to which the members of various congregations assented were by no means intended to supplant them; yet what actually happened was that subscription to the creeds ceased to be enforced, and the way was thus left open for the growth of individual thought. It was only when "liberal" ideas had come to be widely held that the orthodox took alarm, and began to agitate for enforcement of subscription to the historic creeds. In so doing they felt themselves fully within their rights, inasmuch as the creeds had never been formally renounced, and had originally been universally accepted. The procedure of the orthodox was not unnatural; in fact in loyalty to their convictions they could hardly have done otherwise. It would be absurd to portray their conduct as characterized by unfairness, or even as aggressively intolerant. They could scarcely have been expected to stand by and see their churches transformed into something which they could no longer recognize as Christian.

The "liberals," on the other hand, were also acting in complete good faith. No one had ever asked them in the past to assent to the creeds, and they resented the unprecedented attempt thus to shackle them. Having been born free, they did not propose to fall into bondage to any man, or any group of men. Hence there was probably never a religious controversy in which there was more to be said on both sides.

Our concern, however, is not at the moment with the rights and wrongs of this historic contest, but with the freedom of thought which made it possible. And there is no doubt that this freedom was greatly favored by the Congregational form of church government. To one who approaches Congregationalism from the standpoint of Episcopacy or Presbyterianism it is apt to appear—with its loose structure of autonomous societies or churches, as they are indifferently called—as an ecclesiastical anomaly, devoid of that solidity which is traditionally associated with the ideal of the Catholic Church. And it was this very looseness of organization which facilitated the infiltration of liberalism. Whenever an individual congregation—such as the Church of the Pilgrims at Plymouth—decided to go over as a body to the Unitarian position, no superior power could call its decision in question. Nor could any minister who avowed his adherence to liberal opinions be silenced so long as he could find a congregation willing to listen to him.

Moreover—and this is an important consideration—when the unavoidable schism between the liberal and orthodox wings at last came about, the emotional strain which accompanied it was reduced to a minimum. In many a Massachusetts village one finds standing in close proximity the Trinitarian and Unitarian churches, and not infrequently it is the Unitarians who have possession of the original parish church. In such a case this means that they were *seceded from* by the Trinitarian minority. But, even where the situation was reversed, the event was of purely local significance. The general effect of the schism was to divide the Congregational denomination into two denominations, one Trinitarian and the other Unitarian, but both were equally lineal descendants of the old Puritan church.

The Unitarians no doubt resented the charge of infidelity advanced against them by the orthodox. Channing more than once gives utterance to their feelings, and deprecates "that intolerance which would exclude us from the church on earth, and from our Father's house in heaven." [57] Nevertheless it was not as though they had been legally ejected from the church of their fathers by a competent ecclesiastical authority. The Unitarian clergy were not unfrocked, nor were the laity denied the right to call themselves by the Congregational name. They were thus spared that most poignant of griefs, the consciousness of being spiritually homeless. Their lot as heretics was cast in pleasant places.

So far, however, we have named only a negative condition—absence of external constraint. But what of internal constraint? What of the power of tradition and hallowed association? Why could not Channing and his associates acquiesce in a conception of God which could command the devotion of Calvin or Edwards? Are we justified in assuming that, as soon as a man refuses to allow his opinions to be dictated by Pope, council, or synod, and insists on thinking for himself, he is sure to drift beyond the confines of orthodoxy? Perhaps we are. Yet we should remember that, although the Unitarians rejected all ecclesiastical authority, they did not reject all authority whatever. On the contrary, there was one authority which they all recognized. The Unitarian aspired to be a Christian, and a better—not a worse—Christian than his orthodox neighbor. And how was he to determine what Christianity was? The Unitarian answered, "By searching the New Testament." Here, and here only, was the seat of authority.

Accordingly, when the claims of any doctrine to his acceptance were advanced, the Unitarian turned to his New Testament to discover whether it was entitled to his allegiance, and, if he could find there no ground for it, the doctrine in question became immediately suspect—at best non-essential, at the worst positively erroneous. When this fact is recalled, Channing's remark that at one time he had "verged towards Calvinism" becomes, I believe, profoundly revelatory. It is notorious that the doctrine of the Trinity is not explicitly taught in the New Testament. It was formulated—as we all know—only after the lapse of centuries. The Trinitarian none the less claimed that it could be inferred from Scriptural texts. To the Unitarian this claim seemed unfounded. Hence to reject the doctrine of the Trinity was a Christian duty.

So far all was plain. But it is precisely the doctrines distinctive of Calvinism—election, predestination, and justification by faith alone, which *do* appear to be taught in the New Testament. So far as their doctrinal content is concerned, the famous eighth and ninth chapters of the epistle to the Romans might have been written by Calvin himself. Or perhaps it is juster to put it the other way, and to say, as an old Presbyterian lady said to me, that "what is called Calvinism is simply what we find in the New Testament." Here, indeed, was something to give Channing pause! That his theology should have been Unitarian is no great wonder, but we may well ask why it was not a Calvinistic Unitarianism.

A hundred and fifty years before Channing's time the gentle soul of Sir Thomas Browne had wrestled with the same problem of predestination and the justice of God. He had dallied, he tells us, with Origen's theory, "That God would not persist in his vengeance for ever, but after a definite time of his wrath, he would release the damned Souls from torture: which error I fell into upon a serious consideration of the great Attribute of God, his Mercy; and did a little cherish it in my self, because I found therein no malice." [58] The history of Christianity offers few more melancholy spectacles than the triumph of orthodoxy over these noble doubts.[59]

Where Sir Thomas Browne had succumbed why were Channing and his fellow-Unitarians victorious? Was it merely because they had more courage in their souls and more warmth in their hearts? Or were they sustained by some force which fostered courage and warmheartedness? The answer must clearly be in the affirmative. One of the most prominent characteristics of the eighteenth and nineteenth centuries was the growth of a practical humanitarianism which manifested itself in multitudinous ways—in the diminution of religious persecution and the increase of tolerance, in the abolition of torture and of slavery, in prison reform, in the organization of charitable institutions, in the advancement of education, and in the mitigation of the brutalities of war. Never before in history had there been such an outpouring of genuine human kindliness. Whether it derived its impetus from a revival of the spirit of primitive Christianity, or, on the contrary, arose in independence of the Christian tradition and subsequently exercised a transforming influence upon it, I shall not stay to inquire. I am not even sure that we possess the data essential to the solution of the problem. But, in any case, we must attribute it to a deepening of moral insight which is an historic fact of the first importance.

It was not to be expected that theology would remain unaffected by this new influence. The repudiation of the Calvinistic scheme of salvation was only a manifestation in the intellectual world of the same spirit which was simultaneously showing itself so potent in the realm of everyday life. When man could be so kind it seemed absurd to attribute to God qualities which even a respectable oriental despot would be anxious to disclaim. Even the youthful Edwards had been conscious of the incongruity.[60] And Channing had the advantage of living in a later age when the progress of the humanitarian movement was more advanced. Interested and active as he was in practically every field in which it displayed itself, he was to become its champion not only in the sphere of practice but in that of thought. To point out that he was not alone in so doing is to deny him neither courage nor originality. It is true that there were Arminians and Socinians before him, and that liberal ideas were spreading in New England while Channing was still inclining toward orthodoxy; none the less, brought up as he was in a conservative household and under the shadow of a yet potent and revered Calvinistic tradition, it required no little resolution to renounce the opinions with which he had been indoctrinated in infancy, and to assume an attitude of intellectual independence. And, once he had adopted the liberal position, he rapidly became its outstanding defender.

To the Unitarians of that era, and above all to Channing himself, we owe a far greater debt than is generally recognized in that they conducted the contest with orthodoxy upon a high intellectual and moral level where the issues involved were those which possess permanent significance. We do well to remember this is an age which is responsible for the Dayton Trial. Among persons superficially acquainted with theology it is frequently assumed that orthodox Christianity is a system of thought fundamentally incompatible with the findings of the physical sciences, and therefore no longer deserving of serious consideration. And, in a similar fashion, it is often taken for granted that orthodoxy has been thoroughly discredited by the results of textual criticism. Both these views I believe to be profoundly mistaken. In Channing's day, however, neither the physical sciences nor textual criticism had developed to such a point as to render assumptions of this sort *prima facie* plausible, and consequently Channing was in no danger of making them.

The statement which I have just made in regard to orthodoxy is, needless to say, open to challenge; hence it is, I believe, incumbent upon me to endeavor to make it good in order that we may not underestimate the strength of the orthodox position and so depreciate Channing's achievement under the impression that he was tilting at windmills. I shall, accordingly, conclude our discussion of the Calvinistic background of Channing's thought by further elaborating it and subjoining certain additional suggestions.

The two assumptions which I have just mentioned are, of course, closely connected. Let us examine them in turn. In what way is orthodoxy incompatible with the findings of science? It is incompatible, we shall inevitably be told, with the theory of evolution. But is it? The God of orthodox Christianity, of Calvinism as well as of Roman Catholicism be it remembered, is a being who exists outside of time in a changeless eternity. He is not related to the world, although the world is related to him. The creation of the universe involves no change in God. By a "timeless act" he brings it into existence. We speak of its coming into existence as its creation, and of its being kept in existence as its conservation; yet these are not two separate divine acts, but merely two ways of regarding a single divine act. The successive events which take place in time—the creation of the soul of Socrates, let us say, at a certain moment on a certain day in a certain year in a certain century, and the subsequent creation of the soul of St. Augustine at another moment on another day in another year in another century—are not willed by separate and successive volitional acts on the part of God, but by a single, changeless, eternal act which is identical with his essence. I do not say that such a view is philosophically sound—I do not think that it is—but, if it be tenable at all, it is surely as compatible with an evolutionary theory of creation through a process involving growth, mutation, and the gradual emergence of higher levels of being, as with the doctrine of a creation in six days of twenty-four hours each.

Again, when we turn to the field of textual criticism, we should realize that the Reformers were by no means wholly ignorant of the type of difficulties which we adduce, and that it was a settled principle of theirs that the purpose of revelation is to impart, not mathematical or scientific, or even chronologically accurate historical knowledge, but religious and doctrinal truths, and that it is from this standpoint that the dogma of the inspiration of the Scriptures must be envisaged.[61] The conservative may plausibly urge that an interpretation of this dogma which insists that accounts of the creation which were compiled many hundreds of years before Christ should have taken into consideration twentieth century theories—possibly not yet too firmly fixed—of physical science is patently wrong-headed. I do not say that the orthodox theologian will have an easy time of it, or that he may not be compelled on occasion to resort to the hoary and obsolete device of allegorizing inconvenient texts, but I do say that his difficulties will be less crucial and less formidable than is often supposed.

What is true of textual criticism is true also of ecclesiastical history and of the history of dogma. Although the latter are less conspicuously in the public eye, the problems which confront the conservative in connection with them are no less vital. To the Unitarian it appears evident that the humanitarian views of Christ's nature which prevailed among the Ebionites, and the Dynamistic Monarchianism of Theodotus, Artemon, and Paul of Samosata, reflect the belief of the primitive Church; and he thinks that he can trace in the Pauline Epistles, and in the subsequent christological controversies the devious process by which the doctrine of the Trinity gradually developed. The effort of the orthodox to account for the maintenance of Unitarian opinions by dismissing them as relapses into Judaism impresses him as an explanation made *ad hoc*. The historical argument is undoubtedly important; yet, persuasive as he finds it, the Unitarian must admit that it is not conclusive, and that to one who is committed on philosphical grounds to the Trinitarian position the facts must unavoidably present themselves in a different light and seem to admit of an alternative explanation. We simply cannot prevent our critical judgment being affected by our metaphysical and dogmatic preconceptions.[62] In this connection it is worth noting that, while Channing states the historical argument briefly and forcibly,[63] he does not dwell upon it overmuch.

During the last century the liberal Protestant movement has drawn increasing support from conclusions derived from the study of comparative religion. All that we know of Channing's temperament assures us that the subject would have awakened his deep interest; unfortunately his life had nearly closed before it had come to occupy a prominent place in the realm of religious thought. Theodore Parker's *Discourse of Religion,* wherein it is treated of at length, was written only a year before Channing's death. But, however much we may regret that we cannot profit by what he might have said and written upon this topic, we must recognize that the significance of the facts gleaned in this field lies chiefly in the philosophical ideas which they tend to suggest or support, and that here again metaphysical presuppositions vitally affect our efforts to interpret and evaluate. Thus, while to the confirmed liberal the discovery that in various religions the same fundamental types of piety, the mystical, the speculative, and the legalistic, tend to manifest themselves, and that similar views and kindred doctrines tend to emerge, suggests Theodore Parker's conclusion that the essence of religion is always and everywhere identical, this same conclusion is rejected today by the Barthians and the Calvinists of the Sorbonne with no less vigor than we might expect to see displayed by Jonathan Edwards were he to rise from the dead. The conflict between liberalism and orthodoxy, which once seemed to have been fought and won, but which the reviving strength of conservativism has caused once more to be renewed, must be fought out on the field of speculative thought. There we find the real issues which divide men most deeply. And, if the contest is ever to be brought to a conclusion, there the final and decisive victory must be won. And it is because Channing conducted the battle upon this *terrain* that his work possesses an abiding significance which will render his thought as fresh a thousand years from now as is that of St. Anselm or Aquinas today.

The basic questions which the liberal must ask himself are these: Is orthodoxy consistent with itself? Is its method sound? Are its arguments cogent? Are its premises certain? Are its inferences valid? And, last but not least, are its value judgments tenable? Judgments of value are, indeed, ultimate; yet they require to be welded together with fact and theory into a consistent whole. Not only to the logical understanding but also to the intuitive apprehension of values quickened by that intensification of moral insight of which I have spoken did Channing make his appeal; and his work—both destructive and constructive—was of a higher order than many, even of his admirers, frequently realize.

We have now surveyed the main outlines of that Calvinistic system of thought which was Channing's intellectual inheritance, and have noticed his fundamental reactions to it. Our next task is to examine the influence exerted upon the thought of New England by the philosophy of Locke.

# CALVINISM

## NOTES

1. See *Calvinism, The Revival of Romanism, The Condition and Prospects of Protestantism.*
2. See the *Institution de la Religion Chrestienne,* ed. by Jacques Pannier, t. III. pp. 123-127.
3. *Romans,* 8:28.
4. Samuel Smiles' *The Hugenots in France after the Revocation of the Edict of Nantes,* p. 415.
5. *Sum. Theol.* I. a. q. 23: a. 3.
6. Ibid., I. a. q. 19: a. 8; q. 22: a. 4. ad $I^m$.; *Con Gen.* lib. III. c. XCIV.
7. *Sum. Theol.* I. a. q. 19: a. 7. ad $I^m$. For a discussion of the subject by a contemporary neothomist see *Predestination* by Father R. Garrigou-Lagrange. O.P., tr. by Dom Bede Rose, O.S.B., D.D.
8. The *Westminster Confession of Faith,* ch. III. V.
9. Ibid., ch. III. VII.
10. Luke, 17:10.
11. Ch. XVIII.
12. Ch. XVIII, III.
13. Ch. XVII, IV.
14. Ibid., I.
15. Ibid., III.
16. *Com.* ch. XVIII.
17. See *La Signification Historique du Thomisme* in his *Etudies de Philosophie Médiévale.*
18. For certain qualifications of this assertion, which do not however affect the present discussinon, see his *Catholicism and Philosophy,* pp. 64-72 (tr. by Ralph MacDonald, C.S.B.).
19. *Introduction à la Dogmatique Reformée,* t. I. pp. 66, 134-135.
20. *Institution,* pp. 52-56; cf., his *Catechism,* ed. *Je Suis,* sec. 4, p. 25.
21. *Institution,* t. I. pp. 58-61.
22. *Institution,* t. I. pp. 122-124.
23. Art. I.
24. Art. IX. Professor Gilson seems to think that the more moderate language of the Westminster Confession is in contrast with the extreme statement of the French Confession, and so with Calvin himself, yet the Westminster Confession merely reproduces Calvin's utterances in the *Institutes.*
25. *Introduction,* t. I. pp. 46, 51.
26. Ibid., t. I. pp. 51-52.
27. *Institution,* loc. cit.
28. *Institution,* t. I. pp. 66-69; *Catechism,* sec. 18, pp. 48-49. For a discussion of intuitive awareness of God from the Calvinistic standpoint see Lecerf's *Introduction,* t. I. pp. 47-50, 126, 150-151, 161-163, 171-174, 183-186, 228, 267-269, 283-284.
29. P. 59. Quoted from the Asráru 'l-tawhíd fí maqámáti 'l-shaykh Abu Sa 'íd by Muhammad ibnu 'l-Munawwar.
30. *Institution,* t. I. pp. 72-76.
31. Arts. IV and V.

32. Art. V.
33. Art. III.
34. Ch. I., arts. IV-VI. for a contemporary statement see Lecerf's *Introduction,* t. II. pp. 173-208, 224-225, 236-239.
35. It is fair to say that the Scriptures play as fundamental a part in the Calvinist's religious experience as does the mass in that of the Roman Catholic, probably even more so.
36. See *A Treatise concerning Religious Affections,* Part III., and the sermon on *A Divine and Supernatural Light, immediately imparted to the Soul by the Spirit of God.*
37. *Treatise,* Part III. sec. iv.
38. *Loc. cit.*
39. *Loc. cit.*
40. *Loc. cit.*
41. *Loc. cit.*
42. *Loc. cit.*
43. Ibid., Part III. sec. v.
44. See the sermon on *A Divine and Supernatural Light.*
45. "Je ne ditz aultre chose que ce qu'un chascun fidèle experémente en soy." *Institution,* t. I. p. 68.
46. "Thus, it plainly appears, that God implanting a spiritual, supernatural sense, makes a great change in a man. And were it not for the very imperfect degree in which this sense is commonly given at first, or the small degree of this glorious light that first dawns upon the soul; the change made by this spiritual opening of the eyes in conversion, would be much greater, and more remarkable every way, than if a man born blind should have the sense of seeing imparted to him at once, in the midst of the clear light of the sun, discovering a world of objects. For though sight be more noble than any of the other external senses, yet this spiritual sense is infinitely more noble, and the object infinitely more important." *Treatise,* Part III. sec. iv.
47. See William Henry Channing's *The Life of William Ellery Channing,* p. 80.
48. *William Ellery Channing,* p. 57.
49. *Life,* p. 84. Perhaps one may be permitted to doubt the accuracy of Channing's judgment. Edwards' sermon on *A Divine and Supernatural Light,* published in 1734—long before he could conceivably have been influenced by Hopkins—stresses the holiness of God.

In his Introductory Remarks to the edition of his writings (*Works,* p. 4) Channing observes, "If Edwards's work on the Will could really answer its end; if it could thoroughly persuade men that they were bound by an irresistible necessity, that their actions were fixed links in the chain of destiny, that there was but one agent, God, in the universe; it would be one of the most pernicious books ever issued from our press. Happily it is a demonstration which no man believes, which the whole consciousness contradicts." On the next page, however, he adds that Edwards was "as eminent for religious as for intellectual power." In his *Remarks on National Literature* (*Works,* p. 128) Channing again refers to Edwards as "one of the greatest men of his age, though unhappily his mind was lost, in a great degree, to literature, and we fear to religion, by vassalage to a false theology. His work on the Will throws, indeed, no light on human nature, and, notwithstanding the nobleness of the subject, gives no great or elevated thoughts; but, as a specimen of logical acuteness and controversial power, it certainly ranks in the very highest class of metaphysical writings."

50. *Life,* pp. 87-88.
51. *Works,* p. 285.
52. See Chadwick's *William Ellery Channing,* pp. 74-76, 118, 122.
53. *Life,* p. 91.
54. *William Ellery Channing,* p. 63.
55. *Ibid.,* pp. 23-24.
56. *Life,* pp. 80-81.
57. *Works,* p. 400.
58. *"The Works of Sir Thomas Browne,* Sayle's ed. vol. I. p. 14.
59. There is no Salvation to those that believe not in *Christ,* that is, say some, since his Nativity, and as Divinity affirmeth, before also; which makes me much apprehend the ends of those honest Worthies and Philosophers which dyed before his Incarnation. It is hard to place those Souls in Hell, whose worthy lives do teach us Virtue on Earth: methinks amongst those many subdivisions of Hell, there might have been one Limbo left for these. What a strange vision will it be to see their Poetical fictions converted into Verities, and their imagined and fancied Furies into real Devils? how strange to them will sound the History of *Adam,* when they shall suffer for him they never heard of? when they who derive their genealogy from the Gods, shall know that they are the unhappy issue of sinful man? It is an insolent part of reason, to controvert the Works of God, or question the Justice of his proceedings. Could Humility teach others, as it hath instructed me, to contemplate the infinite and incomprehensible distance betwixt the Creator and the Creature; or did we seriously perpend that one simile of St. *Paul, Shall the Vessel say to the Potter, Why hast thou made me thus?* it would prevent these arrogant disputes of reason, nor would we argue the definitive sentence of God, either to Heaven or Hell. Men that live according to the right rule and law of reason, live but in their own kind, as beasts do in theirs; who justly obey the prescript of their natures, and therefore cannot reasonably demand a reward of their actions, as only obeying the natural dictates of their reason. It will therefore, and must at last appear, that all salvation is through *Christ;* which verity, I fear, these great examples of virtue must confirm, and make it good, how the perfectest actions of earth have no title or claim unto Heaven." Ibid., vol. I. p. 76.
60. See his account of his conversion.
61. Cf. M. Lecerf's chapter entitled *Examen de la valeur du principe externe et formel de la foi réformée. Theorie de l'inspiration. Introduction,* t. II. ch. VI.
62. As Dr. A. S. Peake truly observes with regard to the Fourth Gospel, "Unfortunately the question of authorship is affected seriously by theological considerations. Those who take a purely humanitarian view of Christ's Person, or disbelieve in the possibility of miracles, naturally find a difficulty in admitting that such a work as the Fourth Gospel can have come from the hand of an apostle. Those for whom the Christology of the Fourth Gospel is untrue, and who consider that Paul started the Church down the fatal slope

of mythology by his doctrine of the Divinity of Christ, will naturally find it difficult, if not impossible, to believe that one who had personally known Jesus should speak of Him as the author does in his prologue; still more, that he should represent Jesus as speaking of Himself as He does in the Gospel. . . . Such a consideration can have no weight with those who believe that the Logos doctrine was true to fact. They will be much readier to admit that Jesus may have spoken of Himself in such language as the Fourth Gospel puts into His mouth. It is necessary to draw attention to this point, since an avowed or unavowed theological presupposition has in some cases not a little to do with the attitude adopted on critical problems in the strict sense of the term." *Introduction to the New Testament*, pp. 212-213.

63. *Works*, p. 372.

# Chapter Two

# Philosophy of Locke

The mention of eighteenth-century empiricism brings to our minds the second of the two great currents of thought which mingled to form the intellectual atmosphere of Channing's youth. Here we have indeed an influence of another sort. If Calvinism at its best was intense, passionate, intuitive, mystical, and at its worst gloomy, oppressive, even terrifying, eighteenth-century empiricism was cold, calm, matter-of-fact, logical, and sensationalist. We are familiar with the phrase "eighteenth-century rationalism," which is primarily applicable to the position of those continental philosophers who depreciated sense-experience and regarded reason as the only organ of knowledge. It is also used in connection with those thinkers who subordinated revelation to reason. When we turn to Locke, whose figure over-shadowed the entire period, we are immediately aware of a pronounced rationalistic element in his thinking. He was, indeed, a firm believer in revelation, and was concerned to defend it and to vindicate its authority. Nevertheless reason was for him the ultimate court of appeal before which revelation must present its credentials; and his habitual attitude is exemplified in the title of one of his well-known works, *The Reasonableness of Christianity*. His thinking, however, displays no sympathy for that whole-hearted reliance upon *a priori* reasoning which characterizes the great speculative systems of the nineteenth century. On the contrary he manifests almost equal antipathy toward mysteries which are esteemed inaccessible to reason and toward all transcendent flights of metaphysical speculation. His own philosophizing is conducted in an empirical manner, and surveys all things from the standpoint of common sense. If we accept, for the nonce, the Hegelian distinction between the reason and the understanding, it is clear that we shall have to classify a philosophy of this type as emphatically an affair of the understanding.

Although all but the last four years of Locke's life fell within the seventeenth century yet his thought breathes the spirit of the century to come. Wearied and disgusted, alike with the fanaticism, intolerance, and—it is to be feared—with the earnestness and devotion of the religious sects and political parties of the period of the Civil Wars and of the Commonwealth, and with the license of the Restoration time, the English people, recoiling from extremes of every kind, yearned in the years following the Revolution of 1688 for tranquility, for individual freedom, and for outward respectability. With its indifferentism, its coldness, its formality, its aspirations after "elegance," the age was an intellectually superficial one. Dr. Johnson's famous refutation of Berkeley, when by kicking the stone he demonstrated the reality of the physical world, is a perfect epitome of the mentality of the time— a mentality which was to endure for a century and more. The secret of Locke's influence is that, to use the Quaker phrase, he "spoke to its condition." For such a period Berkeley was too "fantastical," Hume too shocking. Locke, with his feet on the ground and his head well below the clouds, with his matter-of-fact approach to all problems and his disdain for speculative soarings, was a man after its own heart.

Not only did Locke's influence remain dominent until well into the nineteenth century, it even became intensified in the case of many persons of a religious temperament who had become dissatisfied with traditional orthodoxy. Even as Calvinism seemed to the early New England liberals the Egypt which must be left behind, so the philosophy of Locke was their Promised Land. Hence it is imperative that we should glance for a few moments at the main features of his system.

Locke's well-known point of departure is, of course, his doctrine of ideas. *Idea* is, he tells us, "that term, which, I think, serves best to stand for whatsoever is the object of the understanding when a man thinks; I have used it to express whatever is meant by phantasm, notion, species, or whatever it is which the mind can be employed about in thinking." [1] How does the mind become acquainted with these objects? Locke answers, through sensation and reflection. [2] In the reception of simple ideas, such as color, warmth, or sweetness, the mind is wholly passive; [3] it becomes active in the formation of complex ideas, such as those of substances and relations.

In the case of sensation, however, the ideas or objects which confront us must not be identified with physical entities in the external world. On the contrary, the idea is a *tertium quid,* or, as we should say today, a sense-datum or sensum, produced in some mysterious way by the action of the physical entity upon us. But how stands the case in the mental realm? Are the ideas of reflection similarly generated in intro-spection, and in like manner interposed between subject and object? By analogy we should so conclude. In fact Locke's own way of putting the matter would lead us naturally enough to this conjecture.

"The other fountain," he writes, "from which experience furnisheth the understanding with ideas, is the perception of the operations of our own mind within us, as it is employed about the ideas it has got; which operations when the soul comes to reflect on and consider, do furnish the understanding with another set of ideas, which could not be had from things without; and such are perception, thinking, doubting, believing, reasoning, knowing, willing, and all the different actings of our own minds; which we being conscious of and observing in ourselves, do from these receive into our understandings as distinct ideas, as we do from bodies affecting our senses. This source of ideas every man has wholly within himself: and though it be not sense, as having nothing to do with external objects, yet it is very like it, and might properly enough be called internal sense." [4]

Inasmuch as Locke thus appears to put reflection completely on a par with sensation, it might seem that, in the one case as in the other, our ideas are entities interposed between the apprehending subject and the object. Further consideration, however, can scarcely fail to convince us that such is not the case. For, were it the case, the self would stand upon precisely the same footing as the external object. Since we should not be directly aware of it, we should have to arrive at the knowledge of its existence in some indirect way; and thereby Locke's argument for the existence of God would be threatened.

We must, therefore, carry our investigation further. There are, Locke assures us, two kinds of knowledge.[5] First, there is intuitive knowledge of the agreement or disagreement of our ideas, which yields absolute certainty. Secondly, there is demonstrative knowledge, which Locke, like Descartes, views as merely an expansion of intuitive knowl-edge. It involves the tracing of indirect connections between ideas through intermediate ideas; and in each individual instance of con-nection intuitive apprehension is, of course, necessary. Demonstration yields certainty, "yet the evidence of it," says Locke, is not "so clear and bright, nor the assent so ready," [6] because of the length of the chain of inter-related ideas, the unavoidable reliance upon memory, and the previous presence of doubt concerning the conclusion of the argument, none of which factors are involved in the case of intuitive knowledge.

"There is, indeed," Locke continues, "another perception of the mind, employed about the particular existence of finite beings without us; which going beyond bare probability, and yet not reaching perfectly to either of the foregoing degrees of certainty, passes under the name of knowledge. There can be nothing more certain than that the idea we receive from an external object is in our minds; this is intuitive knowledge. But whether there be anything more than barely that idea in our minds, whether we can thence certainly infer the existence of any thing without us, which corresponds to that idea, is that whereof some men think there may be a question made." [7]

Thus Locke, like certain critical realists of today, wishes to treat the physical world as a certainty while yet admitting that it cannot be a certainty. For how is it to be inferred? In the case of ideas, which are one and all directly apprehended, inference amounts to the following out of intermediate connections between them. But the physical world is not directly apprehended. Hence, if Locke be right in defining knowledge as "nothing but the perception of the connection and agreement, or disagreement and repugnancy, of any of our ideas," [8] it should never come within his purview.

Even if we agree, however, not to press this point, and to permit Locke to think of the physical universe, the question still remains, Upon what principle is its existence to be inferred? Locke's own appeal is to the principle of causality. Yet such an appeal assumes that effect must resemble cause, and how is this contention to be made good? Nor is this the least of the difficulties which confront him. For Locke's philosophy is infected with nominalism.

"The immediate object of all our reasoning and knowledge," he asserts, is nothing but particulars. Every man's reasoning and knowledge is only about the ideas existing in his own mind, which are truly, every one of them, particular existences; and our knowledge and reason about other things is only as they correspond with those of our particular ideas. So that the perception of the agreement or disagreement of our particular ideas is the whole and utmost of all our knowledge. Universality is but accidental to it, and consists only in this, that the particular ideas about which it is are such, as more than one particular thing can correspond with, and be represented by." [9]

How, then, from the awareness of mere particulars is a principle of universal validity to be extracted? Furthermore causality involves relation; and relation, Locke informs us, is "not contained in the real existence of things, but something extraneous and superinduced," [10] "being but by way of considering two things together, and so also an idea of my own making." [11] Hence it would seem that causality is also an idea "of my own making."

This tendency to treat relation as a figment of the mind appears to be an ineradicable characteristic of nominalism. Starting out with a ruthless determination to be true to common sense, to admit only the reality of particulars, and to reject all "metaphysical nonsense," the nominalist is impelled by some strange, but seemingly irresistible, tendency in the direction of subjectivism. [12] Of course Locke is no more consistent in this attitude than other nominalists. [13] He admits that "nature in the production of things makes several of them alike," [14] and that in relation there must be "a ground or occasion for their comparison," [15] although how this can be true if things have nothing in common and are not really related to each other *in rerum natura* we are not told. [16]

The shaky character of Locke's claim to a knowledge of the physical world—for shaky it is, as he himself realizes, despite his equivocations —renders it incapable of serving as a satisfactory foundation for a proof of the existence of God. It is clear from his own words which I have quoted that Locke regarded it, not as genuine knowledge, but as something which "passes under the name of knowledge," and which, since it may be called in question, falls short of certainty.

With the self, however, such is emphatically not the case. In language reminiscent of Descartes, Locke affirms that "we have an intuitive knowledge of our own existence, and an internal infallible perception that we are," so certain as neither to need nor to admit of proof, so that even to doubt one's own existence is to perceive it. [17] "We have," he declares, "the knowledge of our own existence by intuition; of the existence of God by demonstration; and of other things by sensation." [18] From Locke's own words, therefore, as well as from the logic of the situation, we are amply entitled to conclude that the self is known, not inferentially, but directly; and, consequently, that the ideas derived from reflection are not analogous to sense-data interposed between subject and object, but are, on the contrary, identical with states and activities of the mind itself which are directly known in introspection. [19]

Upon this intuitive awareness of the self Locke proceeds to found his proof of the existence of God. It is a causal proof, and is regarded by Locke as yielding complete demonstration. Since nothing can come from nothing, the self must have been produced by a being who always existed; and, since all its powers have likewise proceeded with it from the same source, the being in question is of all beings the most powerful. Consequently, inasmuch as the self is possessed of knowledge, it must have been produced by a "knowing intelligent being." [20]

We have already seen the difficulty of vindicating upon nominalist principles the notion of causality; and, needless to say, the same difficulty arises in connection with the maxim *ex nihilo nihil fit*. Moreover we may ask, How does Locke know that the self began to be? The answer is that he assumes this to be the case. Yet the assumption is wholly gratuitous. To argue that, because a man's memory does not reach back before his birth, therefore he could not have existed before his birth, is like arguing that a man who was striken with aphasia yesterday could not have existed the day before yesterday.

Our task, however, is not to justify Locke's argument, but to grasp the significance of the fact that he made it. By thus claiming to prove the existence of God Locke abandoned the position of the Reformers and went over to that of their Roman Catholic opponents. He was, indeed, not alone in so doing. Various attempts have been made from time to time to build up a system of Protestant theology which shall be a counterpart of Thomism, and wherein reason and faith, like the Scriptural lion and lamb, shall lie down side by side. Such an undertaking is, nevertheless, quite incompatible with genuine Calvinism.[21] The manner in which Locke carries it out is very characteristic of his period. His is a common sense approach, which fails either to raise or to answer the most fundamental difficulties. Still, such as it is, it constitutes an appeal to reason—or perhaps we should say rather an appeal to the logical understanding—as against the theologian's interpretation of religious experience. Of Calvin's God it is true in general to say that he is not demonstrated but encountered, and of Locke's God it is equally true to say that he is not encountered but demonstrated. This intellectual antithesis is the direct and inevitable consequence of Locke's doctrine that all its ideas are imparted to the mind through sensation and reflection, nor is it the only consequence of this doctrine, which powerfully affects Locke's attitude with respect both to ethics and to revelation.

In regard to ethics, as McTaggart used to point out in his lectures, Locke's position is indeed extraordinary, inasmuch as he simultaneously maintains that ethical principles are self-evident and also that they are validated only by rewards and punishments which are not self-evident and are to be known in no other way than through revelation. It is Locke's constant assumption that each physical thing has an essence from which its various properties could be deduced by anyone who knew what the essence was, even as we can deduce from the definition of a triangle the proposition that all its angles are equal to two right angles. But from such a knowledge of the essence we are inhibited by our inability to know the physical object directly. Accordingly all that we can do is to put together the simple ideas which we derive from it through sensation; and these constitute its nominal, as opposed to its real, essence. In the case, however, of complex ideas other than those of substances, inasmuch as these are, as he says, "archetypes of the mind's own making, not intended to be the copies of any thing, nor referred to the existence of any thing, as to their originals," "we cannot but be infallibly certain, that all the knowledge we attain concerning these ideas is real." [22]

Of this sort are mathematical ideas; and it is the general opinion, observes Locke, "that mathematics alone are capable of demonstrative certainty." [23] This, however, he insists, is not the case. Moral ideas are likewise archetypes compounded by the mind out of simple ideas, consequently our knowledge of them is adequate and certain; hence "moral knowledge is as capable of real certainty as mathematics." [24] The contrary view is due to the fact that moral ideas are not susceptible of being "represented by sensible marks," and "are commonly more complex than those of the figures ordinarily considered in mathematics." [25] Accordingly Locke repeatedly calls for the development of a demonstrative science of morality,[26] which would fall under the head of πρακτική, "the skill of right applying our own powers and actions for the attainment of things good and useful." [27]

So far all seems straightforward enough. Yet Locke elsewhere assures us that things are "good or evil only in reference to pleasure or pain," [28] and again tells us even more plainly that "good and evil . . . are nothing but pleasure or pain, or that which occasions or procures pleasure or pain to us. Moral good and evil then is only the conformity or disagreement of our voluntary actions to some law, whereby good or evil is drawn on us by the will and power of the law-maker; which good and evil, pleasure or pain, attending our observance or breach of the law, by the decree of the law-maker, is that we call reward and punishment." [29] Reward and punishment, Locke insists, pertain to "the true nature of all law;" [30] and "the true ground of morality . . . can only be the will and law of a God, who sees men in the dark, has in his hand rewards and punishments, and power enough to call to account the proudest offender." [31]

The reason for this is that, according to Locke, "happiness, and that alone," [32] moves desire. Nor is this, apparently, anything to regret, for Locke lays it down that "the highest perfection of intellectual nature lies in a careful and constant pursuit of true and solid happiness." [33] He is far from the mind of Sir Thomas Browne who considers that "they go the fairest way to Heaven that would serve God without a Hell." [34] Locke, on the other hand, does not serve God for nought. Indeed he informs us that one of the chief purposes of the coming of Christ, in addition to making the true moral code clear and definite so that all men, especially the unlearned, should no more be troubled by uncertainty and distracted by the conflicting opinions of philosophers, was to attract men to it by setting forth future rewards and punishments.

"The philosophers, indeed," he scornfully remarks, "showed the beauty of virtue; they set her off so, as drew men's eyes and approbation to her; but leaving her unendowed, very few were willing to espouse her. The generality could not refuse her their esteem and commendation; but still turned their backs on her, and forsook her, as a match not for their turn. But now there being put into the scales on her side, 'an exceeding and immortal weight of glory;' interest is come about to her, and virtue now is visibly the most enriching purchase, and by much the best bargain. That she is the perfection and excellency of our nature; that she is herself a reward, and will recommend our names to future ages, is not all that can now be said of her. It is not strange that the learned heathens satisfied not many with such airy commendations. It has another relish and efficacy to persuade men, that if they live well here, they shall be happy hereafter. Open their eyes upon the endless, unspeakable joys of another life, and their hearts will find something solid and powerful to move them. The view of heaven and hell will cast a slight upon the short pleasures and pains of this present state, and give attractions and encouragements to virtue, which reason and interest, and the care of ourselves, cannot but allow and prefer. Upon this foundation, and upon this only, morality stands firm, and may defy all competition. This makes it more than a name; a substantial good, worth all our aims and endeavors; and thus the Gospel of Jesus Christ has delivered it to us." [35]

At the present day, when we are sometimes inclined to think that the world is going ever from bad to worse, it is encouraging to reflect that there is no reputable philosopher but would be ashamed to appeal in this bare-faced fashion to self-interest as the sole ground and support of morality.[36] Locke's invocation of the teachings of the Gospel, however, is unfortunately only too well founded. Yet it is not ethical —or perhaps one ought rather to say prudential—considerations alone which impel him in the direction of revelation. Among the truths imparted by revelation there are some of great import for religion apart from ethics. Thus the Fall and redemption of man, the resurrection, and the life to come are of vital significance to us, and of these we could become aware in no other way. Revelation is, therefore, of primary concern to Locke, and his treatment of it we must accordingly proceed to examine.

The first distinction which we must note is that between reason and faith. "Reason," says Locke, "as contradistinguished to faith, I take to be the discovery of the certainty or probability of such propositions or truths, which the mind arrives at by deduction made from such ideas which it has got by the use of its natural faculties, viz. by sensation or reflection." [37] "Faith, on the other side, is the assent to any proposition, not thus made out by the deductions of reason; but upon the credit of the proposer, as coming from God, in some extraordinary way of communication. This way of discovering truths to men we call revelation." [38]

In the second place we must notice Locke's distinction between "original" and "traditional" revelation. "By the one," writes Locke, "I mean that first impression, which is made immediately by God, on the mind of any man, to which we cannot set any bounds; and by the other, those impressions delivered over to others in words, and the ordinary ways of conveying our conceptions one to another." [39]

In the third place there is the distinction drawn by Locke in very scholastic fashion between things "according to, above, and contrary to reason." [40] Propositions according to reason are, of course, those which can be shown to follow from our awareness of the ideas acquired through sensation and reflection. Propositions above reason cannot be thus established. Propositions contrary to reason "are inconsistent with, or irreconcilable to, our clear and distinct ideas." [41] Propositions of this last sort can never be admitted as true, no matter what their claim to be considered as revelation; for such a concession would both "subvert the principles and foundation of all knowledge," and destroy our belief in the goodness and veracity of God.[42] Revelation can, however, communicate to us propositions of either of the first two classes. Yet, in the case of propositions of the first class, it will be unnecessary; furthermore in such instances traditional revelation will always be less certain than the evidence of reason. "For whatsoever truth we come to the clear discovery of, from the knowledge and contemplation of our own ideas, will always be certainer to us than those which are conveyed to us by traditional revelation. For the knowledge we have, that this revelation came at first from God, can never be so sure, as the knowledge we have from the clear and distinct perception of the agreement or disagreement of our own ideas." [43] None the less, where we have not the latter sort of knowledge, our own notions of probability must give way to revelation.[44]

Yet how are we to be sure that there *is* revelation? Beyond doubt we must believe God if he have spoken, but has he spoken? What are the criteria of revelation? What claims has the Christian revelation to our acceptance? Shall the intellect, in medieval fashion, assent at the command of the will? To Locke's credit be it said that the traditional pragmatic attitude is beneath him. Reason, he asserts, must be the judge of what is revelation; [45] and in thus pronouncing he reveals, not only intellectual courage, but psychological acuteness. One may determine by a definite act of the will to live henceforth *as if* certain propositions were true, yet this would be a purely volitional attitude. For genuine belief to enter, the intellect must be appealed to; it must be persuaded, not dragooned; and, to establish even the probability that the propositions in question as a matter of fact *are* true, some evidence must be placed before it upon which it can pronounce.

"Reason," says Locke in a passage of unusually fine feeling, "is natural revelation, whereby the eternal Father of light, and fountain of all knowledge, communicates to mankind that portion of truth which he has laid within the reach of their natural faculties: revelation is natural reason enlarged by a new set of discoveries communicated by

God immediately, which reason vouches the truth of, by the testimony and proofs it gives that they come from God. So that he that takes away reason, to make way for revelation, puts out the light of both." [46] In other words the function of revelation is to provide reason with a set of data which would otherwise be inaccessible to it.

What will be the character of these data? If all ideas be derived from sensation or reflection, and if by reflection is meant what Locke seems clearly to men—introspection—it is clear that revelation cannot take place at all. We must assume, then, that Locke's beloved dogma applies only to the normal and natural process of acquiring knowledge, and that an exception is to be made in the case of inspiration. That this is the correct conclusion seems to be clearly implied by Locke's definition of original revelation. If to "the first impression, which is made by God, on the mind of man," we "cannot set any bounds," it is obvious that these impressions may be whatever God wills them to be. If, however, they be dissimilar to those acquired through sensation or reflection, it follows that they can be shared only with another equally favored, and that no knowledge concerning them can be imparted by the inspired to the uninspired man.[47] "Thus whatever things were discovered to St. Paul," observes Locke, making use of an apropos illustration, "when he was rapt up into the third heaven, whatever new ideas his mind there received, all the description he can make to others of that place is only this, that there are such things, 'as eye hath not seen, nor ear heard, nor hath it entered into the heart of man to conceive.' " [48]

Did Edwards, whom we know to have been a close student of Locke, have these passages in mind as he elaborated his own doctrine of supernatural knowledge? Such may well have been the case, for he so presents his theory that its acceptance does not involve the adoption of his own idealism—so nearly akin to that of Berkeley—but only a willingness to make the most of Locke's concession with regard to the "first impression" or the "new ideas" immediately implanted by God. Edwards' contention, it will be recalled, is that the saints possess "a certain kind of ideas, or sensations of mind, which are simply diverse from all that can be in the minds of natural men." [49] Does this mean that, according to Edwards' view, inspiration is to be identified with first-hand religious experience, so that all the elect are to be regarded as inspired persons? By no means. Inspiration, wherein man functions as an instrument for the transmission of divine revelation, is an extraordinary, whereas supernatural knowledge is an ordinary, gift of the Spirit.

Which of these two, we may inquire, is the more precious gift? Naturally enough we might suppose that inspiration, whereby new truth is imparted, is a nobler gift than the supernatural light whereby the divine character of revelation is apprehended. Such, however, is not Edwards' view. Inspiration, and other extraordinary gifts, he tells us, are characteristics of the infancy of the Church, and may be expected to vanish away as it approaches maturity. "Salvation and the eternal enjoyment of God," he writes, "is promised to divine grace, but not to inspiration. A man may have those extraordinary gifts, and yet be abominable to God, and go to hell. The spiritual and eternal life of the soul consists in the grace of the spirit, which God bestows only on his favourites and dear children. He has sometimes thrown out the other as it were to dogs and swine, as he did to Balaam, Saul, and Judas; and some who in the primitive times of the Christian church, committed the unpardonable sin (Heb. vi.). Many wicked men at the day of judgment will plead, 'Have we not prophesied in thy name, and in thy name cast out devils, and in thy name done many wonderful works.' The greatest privilege of the prophets and apostles, was not their being inspired and working miracles, but their eminent holiness. The grace that was in their hearts, was a thousand times more their dignity and honour, than their miraculous gifts. The things in which we find David comforting himself, are not his being a king, or a prophet, but the holy influences of the spirit of God in his heart, communicating to him divine light, love and joy. The apostle Paul abounded in visions, revelations, and miraculous gifts, above all the apostles; but yet he esteems all things but loss for the excellency of the spiritual knowledge of Christ. It was not the gifts but the grace of the apostles, that was the proper evidence of their names being written in heaven; in which Christ directs them to rejoice, much more than in the devils being subject to them. To have grace in the heart, is a higher privilege than the blessed virgin herself had, in having the body of the second person in the Trinity conceived in her womb." [50] And for his own part Edwards protests that he "had rather enjoy the sweet influences of the spirit . . . one quarter of an hour, than to have prophetical visions and revelations the whole year." [51]

The difference between Edwards and Locke is that between the mystically minded and the unmystically minded man. For the former spiritual illumination is the very process of salvation itself, whereby "the saints are made partakers of the divine nature," [52] and in comparison with which miracles, visions, and inspiration are of relatively little importance. For the latter original revelation is something imparted to a small number of men who serve, as it were, as God's amanuenses; whereas traditional revelation, embodied in the text of Scripture, is something as objective and definite as the constitution of the United States. It is the common property of all men, righteous and sinners alike. And it is all that the average believer has in the way of revelation; let him make the most of it.

The doctrine of illumination has all but faded from the thought of Locke. It is, indeed, quite true that he refers to the promise of the Johannine Christ to send the Spirit to his disciples.[53] Locke does not doubt the promise. Here, then, if anywhere, we should find a *rapprochement* to the Calvinistic point of view. Locke, however, seems to interpret the promise in terms of moral support rather than in those of intellectual illumination.[54] And if we turn to the chapter on "enthusiasm"—by which, of course, he meant fanaticism—in the fourth book of the *Essay*, we shall see with unmistakable clearness how far removed is Locke from both Calvin and Edwards. There we shall discover how he really believes that revelation is authenticated, and what is his substitute for the Calvinistic doctrine of the witness of the Spirit.

"Immediate revelation," writes Locke, "being a much easier way for men to establish their opinions, and regulate their conduct, than the tedious and not always successful labour of strict reasoning, it is no wonder that some have been very apt to pretend to revelation, and to persuade themselves that they are under the peculiar guidance of heaven in their actions and opinions, especially in those of them which they cannot account for by the ordinary methods of knowledge, and principles of reason. Hence we see that in all ages men, in whom melancholy has mixed with devotion, or whose conceit of themselves has raised them into an opinion of a greater familiarity with God, and a nearer admittance to his favour than is afforded to others, have often flattered themselves with the persuasion of an immediate intercourse with the Deity, and frequent communications from the Divine Spirit. God, I own, cannot be denied to be able to enlighten the understanding by a ray darted into the mind immediately from the fountain of light; this they understand he has promised to do, and who then has so good a title to expect it as those who are his peculiar people, chosen by him, and depending on him?

"Their minds being thus prepared, whatever groundless opinion comes to settle itself strongly upon their fancies, is an illumination from the spirit of God, and presently of divine authority; and whatsoever odd action they find in themselves a strong inclination to do, that impulse is concluded to be a call or direction from heaven, and must be obeyed; it is a commission from above, and they cannot err in executing it.

"This I take to be properly enthusiasm, which, though founded neither on reason nor divine revelation, but rising from the conceits of a warmed or over-weening brain, works yet, where it once gets footing, more powerfully on the persuasions and actions of men than either of these two, or both together." [55]

In this passage Locke functions as the very mouthpiece of the spirit of the eighteenth century. We are not wrong, surely, if we conjecture that, as he wrote these words, memories of the violent extravagances of the early Quakers, of the Fifth Monarchy men, and of the other strange sects of the Commonwealth period flitted through his mind. How justly his description applies to many of the cults which arise from time to time among uneducated people, we in America realize full well. Enthusiasm is for Locke a real and permanent danger which he is resolved to do his best to expose, and, in performing his task, he expresses himself so forcefully that his reader may well wonder how he can admit even the possibility of revelation.

We must distinguish, Locke points out, between the perception of the truth of a proposition, and the perception that it is a revelation.[56] "Where a proposition is known to be true," he observes, "revelation is needless: and it is hard to conceive that there can be a revelation to any one of what he knows already." [57] Plausible as this sounds, it is nevertheless inconsistent with his previous admission that the same truth can be both revealed and knowable by reason.[58] Locke, however, continues, "if therefore it be a proposition which they are persuaded, but do not know, to be true, whatever they may call it, it is not seeing, but believing." [59] "What I believe," he declares, "I take to be so upon the testimony of another: but this testimony I must know to be given, or else what ground have I of believing? I must see that it is God that reveals this to me, or else I see nothing." [60] Very true, but how can I possibly see this? The strength of the emotional response awakened by any pronouncement is, as Locke repeatedly observes, no guarantee of its truth. Upon this ground, as he remarks, contradictory propositions are propounded.[61] Moreover there is another possibility, that I may have genuine knowledge at which I am conscious of not having arrived "in a natural way," and that I may owe it, not to God, but to inferior spirits who excited in me the necessary ideas and enabled me to trace the connections between them.[62]

Here Locke touches, whether consciously or not, upon a crucial weakness of the Calvinist's position. It is quite true that, as Edwards points out, illumination does not consist in the formulation of propositions unknown before. The propositions already confront us, set forth in the Scriptures where all men may read them. None the less it is the supernatural light which shines into the believer's soul that enables him to understand and believe them; and, in making such a claim, Edwards appears to be in perfect harmony with the position of Calvin. The essential purport of Locke's question is, however, still germane. How does the individual know whence the supernatural illumination proceeds unless he perceive its source? Plainly he does not know. He may believe that God is its source because of the emotions which it arouses, because of the moral stimulus which accompanies it, or because such a supposition is in accord with the convictions which he already holds. But this is belief, not knowledge. If he is to be certain, he must perceive the source; he must have, in other words, a vision of God himself. Yet this is precisely what Calvin denies that he can have; for, even as the vast majority of medieval Christians, Calvin maintains that man cannot directly perceive the divine essence.[63] True enough, both Calvin and his modern disciple, M. Lecerf, talk of intuition; but, whatever they mean by it, they certainly do not mean direct awareness of God's essence. I will not undertake to say what they do mean, but I fear that Locke's phrase "firmness of persuasion" [64] comes close to the mark.

It is clear that to base one's entire system, in haughty disdain alike of the powers of human reason and of ecclesiastical authority, upon the soul's direct experience of God is an impressive attitude; but the effect is hopelessly spoiled as soon as one begins to hedge upon the question of the directness of this experience. No doubt the moral and emotional transformation which introspection discloses may be so profound as to give rise to the conviction that it *must* be due to divine agency. It is the ardor and strength of this conviction which gives a certain majesty to the thought of Calvin and Edwards. Yet conviction, when all is said, is only conviction. It rests upon inference—if you will, upon an irresistible inference—but not upon direct awareness.

It may plausibly be urged that perception is never purely immediate, but inevitably involves upon the part of the apprehending subject various mental activities—discrimination, comparison, and recollection. This is doubtless the case. Yet there is a difference, and a vastly important difference, between grasping the nature of what is presented to us, and arguing from what is presented to what is not presented. If that which is presented be only certain states of the self observed in introspection, and if the cause which has produced these states be not presented, it is obvious that this cause can be known only indirectly. It is all very well for Calvin to say that the experience of divine illumination is equivalent to contemplating "with the eye the Essence of God in itself." [65] This is mere rhetoric. Inference from the observed to the unobserved can never be equivalent to direct awareness. The enthusiasm engendered by his claim is understandable; no doubt it was productive of confidence and exhilaration in minds disposed to accept it without critical examination; but his position is logically indefensible. It may be said that the experience of illumination yields a practical certainty, in other words that the inference in question possesses an extremely high degree of probability; yet what is this but an appeal to that "firmness of persuasion" concerning which Locke is so justifiably sceptical?

It is of interest to observe that the step which Calvin failed to take was, as a matter of fact, taken by those thinkers, found chiefly although not exclusively in Roman Catholic circles, who are known to neoscholastic writers as ontologists. Ontologism, condemned in the last century as a heterodoxy, attributes to man a direct, although confused awareness of the divine essence, an awareness which is of nature and not of grace. Had Calvin dared to say as much, his own system would have acquired a logical consistency which it lacks. This reference to ontologism, I may remark, is not intended merely in the nature of an interesting aside. We shall find an aspect of Channing's thought which looks in this direction, and which will challenge us to conjecture what was his own attitude toward this problem, and how far he had thought the matter out.

It would seem then, to return to Locke, that, if all immediately self-evident or rationally demonstrable propositions are to be received for

themselves and not as accredited by revelation, and if no other propositions can be so far guaranteed by interior illumination as to place them
beyond reasonable doubt, there is no place left for revelation at all.
And, as I have said, the forcefulness of the language which Locke at
times uses would suggest as much. "Light, true light, in the mind is or
can be nothing else but the evidence of the truth of any proposition;
and if it be not a self-evident proposition, all the light it has, or can
have, is from the clearness and validity of those proofs upon which it
is received. To talk of any other light in the understanding, is to put
ourselves in the dark, or in the power of the Prince of darkness, and by
our own consent to give ourselves up to delusion, to believe a lie. For
if strength of persuasion be the light, which must guide us; I ask how
shall any one distinguish between the delusions of Satan and the inspirations of the Holy Ghost." [66]

Thus there is definitely no illumination upon which we may rely
without inquiry or examination. "God, when he makes the prophet,"
writes Locke, "does not unmake the man. He leaves all his faculties
in the natural state, to enable him to judge of his inspirations, whether
they be of divine original or no. When he illuminates the mind with
supernatural light, he does not extinguish that which is natural. If
he would have us assent to the truth of any proposition, he either evidences that truth by the usual methods of natural reason, or else
makes it known to be a truth which he would have us assent to, by his
authority; and convinces us that it is from him, by some marks which
reason cannot be mistaken in. Reason must be our last judge and guide
in every thing." [67]

What are these outward marks which will command the assent of
reason? They, obviously, are the real criteria of revelation, beside which
illumination sinks into relative insignificance. "The holy men of old,"
asserts Locke, "who had revelations from God, had something else beside that internal light of assurance in their own minds, to testify to
them that it was from God. They were not left to their own persuasions
alone, that those persuasions were from God; but had outward signs to
convince them of the author of those revelations. And when they were
to convince others, they had a power given them to justify the truth
of their commission from heaven, and by visible signs to assert the
divine authority of a message they were sent with. Moses saw the bush
burn without being consumed, and heard a voice out of it. This was
something beside finding an impulse upon his mind to go to Pharaoh,

that he might bring his brethren out of Egypt: and yet he thought not this enough to authorise him to go with that message, till God, by another miracle of his rod turned into a serpent, had assured him of a power to testify his mission, by the same miracle repeated before them, whom he was sent to. Gideon was sent by an angel to deliver Israel from the Midianites, and yet he desired a sign to convince him that this commission was from God. These, and several the like instances to be found among the prophets of old, are enough to show that they thought not an inward seeing or persuasion of their own minds, without any other proof, a sufficient evidence that it was from God; though," admits Locke truthfully, "the scripture does not every where mention their demanding or having such proofs." [68]

This, then, is the conclusion of the whole matter. Miracle is the only guarantee of revelation. Any illumination not thus authenticated must be tried by reason and Scripture.[69] But the outward sign, affecting the senses of the beholder, is in Locke's eyes an evidence not to be gainsaid. Thus miracle is his substitute for the Calvinistic doctrine of the witness of the Spirit. It is miracle which induces conviction.

The influence of this doctrine is momentous. Religion thereby becomes externalized. It is an affair of the senses and the logical understanding in contact with the external world. Supernatural knowledge is contained in a book, and its genuineness is guaranteed by events of a physical nature. Man is practically denied any direct access to the spiritual world.

We have seen the courageous attempt made by Jonathan Edwards to turn the tide of thought, and to emphasize the mystical element in religion. Nor were his efforts wholly unavailing. The tremendous stress laid by certain sects in America upon the notion of conversion owes much to him. Unfortunately, however, it was the more emotional and the less cultivated who felt its attraction. In the intellectual world the influence of Locke continued to predominate.

It is, therefore, essential for us to seek for Locke's definition of miracle. In his *Discourse of Miracles* we find it. "A miracle," he informs us, "I take to be a sensible operation, which, being above the comprehension of the spectator, and in his opinion contrary to the established course of nature, is taken by him to be divine." Were we to define miracle, Locke points out, as an event contrary to the established laws of nature, the question would at once arise as to what these laws are; and this question "philosophers alone, if at least they, can pretend to determine." Consequently, "it is unavoidable, that that should be a miracle to one, which is not so to another."

It might appear at first sight that this concession will prove a fatal one for Locke, since, if men can differ as to what constitutes a miracle, what becomes of the certitude which it is the function of miracles to inspire? But such is not Locke's opinion. His own theory, however, rests upon certain presuppositions which require to be stated. In the first place, as we have seen, no man can be known to be a messenger from God who does not perform miracles. This proposition of itself, suffices, it would seem, to dispose of Mohammed, who, as Locke reminds us, had no miracles to produce. In the second place, the only miracles that are significant are those wrought to authenticate a prophet's mission. This does not tell us very much, since practically all the miracles reported to have occurred can be regarded as authenticating the divine mission of some prophetic figure or of God's chosen people or of the Church of Christ.[70] In the third place, the notion of miracle can be entertained only upon a basis of monotheism; for it is inconceivable that one of a number of deities should perform miracles in order to support his claim to be the sole god, and to abolish the cult of other gods. In the fourth place, the more miracles the better; "two supernatural operations showing more power than one, and three more than two."

No miracles, indeed, can authenticate any teaching "derogating from the honour" of God or "inconsistent with natural religion and the rules of morality;" nor, again, of any frivolous or unimportant pronouncement. A revelation miraculously guaranteed must have to do with "supernatural truths relating to the glory of God, and some great concern of men."

But how if miracles be performed by the proponents of conflicting and contradictory doctrines? It is difficult to be sure, since our notions of the divine power are so vague, that any particular event contrary to the order of nature may not be due to some supernatural agent other than God. Nevertheless there is a sure test. For it concerns the goodness and honor of God, once he has undertaken to guarantee the truth of a revelation, not to permit himself to be vanquished by any subordinate power. When Aaron's rod became a serpent, and the rods of the Egyptian sorcerers also became serpents, no man could tell where the truth lay; but, once Aaron's rod had swallowed up their rods, the decision was clear. God will always be on the side of the greater wonder-worker.

Furthermore, Locke assures us that there have been only two revelations—namely, those of Moses and of Jesus—which have claimed miraculous authentication, and that they are mutually confirmatory. The self-consistency of revelation is thus indicative of its inherent rationality.

We now understand what a miracle is, and how it is to be appraised. That Jesus performed miracles and appealed to them in proof of his messiahship is a point upon which Locke lays great stress both in his *Discourse of Miracles* and also in his *Reasonableness of Christianity*. They are evidences of Christ's divine authority which do not transcend the humblest apprehension. "He that can distinguish between sick and well, lame and sound, dead and alive, is capable of this doctrine. To one who is once persuaded that Jesus Christ was sent by God to be a King, and a Saviour of those who do believe in him, all his commands become principles; there needs no other proof for the truth of what he says, but that he said it." [71]

This insistence upon the absolute authority of Christ demands especial attention. It sounds a relatively new note in the ears of the modern Christian. In the very beginning of our era men did, indeed, at times appeal directly to the teachings of Jesus, but his authority soon came to be confused with that of the Church which was supposed to be inspired by his Spirit. The reformers, rejecting the claims of the Church, invoked instead the Scriptures and the witness of the Spirit in the soul of the individual believer; none the less they persistently insisted that they were not heretics, and not only accepted the historic creeds as embodying the content of revealed truth, but proceeded to amplify them by confessions of faith which were made binding upon the various Protestant churches. It was inevitable, however, that in the course of time the individual Protestant would claim the right to interpret the Bible for himself. Since the authority of the creeds was now purely derivative, depending upon the accuracy with which the propositions contained in them were inferred from the text of the Scriptures, since general councils might err and had erred,[72] the creeds themselves could not escape being called in question. The fundamental principles of the Reformation seemed clearly to imply that every individual who acknowledged the divine authority of the Scriptures was entitled to appeal to them against the teachings of men, and to refuse to accept any dogma which did not seem to him to be adequately supported by the inspired text.

It is in this spirit that Locke asserts that in the New Testament "are contained all the articles of the Christian faith," [73] and denies the right of any ecclesiastical authority to impose upon us any beliefs other than those set forth by Jesus and the Apostles as essential for salvation, and for membership in the Christian Church.[74] What are these beliefs? In the first place we are required to acknowledge Jesus as the Messiah. In fact this acknowledgement is frequently presented as though it were the single requirement for discipleship. So, in a sense, it is; yet only if its presuppositions be fully realized and accepted. To believe in Jesus as the Messiah we must believe in the God who sent him,[75] and in his resurrection which is a proof of his messiahship.[76]

In his *Reasonableness of Christianity* Locke makes clear his own conception of the fundamentals of the Christian faith. The orthodox theory that

> "In Adam's fall
> We sinned all,"

and are consequently liable to eternal damnation for our inherited guilt even before we have committed any additional sins of our own is repudiated by Locke with a heartiness which leaves nothing to be desired. Such a doctrine he holds to be utterly irreconcilable with the goodness and justice of God. Even the wicked, he asserts, will be condemned at the Last Day, not for want of faith, but for sins actually committed. What Adam lost through the Fall was bliss and immortality. These are the reward of righteousness and perfect obedience; because of his transgression Adam was no longer entitled to them, nor is any of his posterity unless he be able to live without sin.

The law of works, which seems a hard law, is unavoidably so. It is the law of reason which, because of his very nature, God must impose upon a rational creature. "If rational creatures," says Locke, "will not live up to the rule of their reason, who shall excuse them? If you will admit them to forsake reason in one point, why not in another?" The law is "such as it ought to be, and could not otherwise be."

Moreover, with the exception of the ceremonial and political injunctions laid upon the Hebrews, it is still in force. "Nor can it be otherwise," affirms Locke, "for, were there no law of works, there could be no law of faith." It is our failure to keep the law of works which is the occasion for the promulgation of the law of faith, given of God's free grace. By the law of faith God offers salvation to men on two conditions: (1) that they believe what he commands them to believe —namely, that Jesus is the Messiah, and (2) that they repent of their sins. Locke's definition of repentence is thoroughly Jewish. "Repentence is an hearty sorrow for our past misdeeds, and a sincere resolution and endeavour, to the utmost of our power, to conform all our actions to the law of God. So that repentence does not consist in one single act of sorrow, (though that being the first and leading act, gives denomination to the whole) but in 'doing works meet for repentence;' in a sincere obedience to the law of Christ, the remainder of our lives."

Thus it is clear that Locke is of the mind of St. James who maintains that "by works a man is justified, and not only by faith." [77] Here, again, he deserts the position of the reformers, and embraces a theory approximating to that of the Church of Rome.

Those to whom the gospel is preached must, not only repent, but also believe in Christ, if they are to be entitled to salvation, for not to believe what God has commanded is a sin; the heathen, however, who have not had the gospel preached to them, are nevertheless enlightened by the light of reason, and, if they make use of that light and truly repent of their sins, will be among the saved. "This way of reconciliation, this hope of atonement, the light of nature revealed to them: and the revelation of the Gospel, having said nothing to the contrary, leaves them to stand or fall to their own Father and Master, whose goodness and mercy is over all his works." Here we note another departure from the Calvinistic faith which, as set forth in the Westminister Confession, denies that those who do not profess Christianity can "be saved in any other way whatsoever, be they never so diligent to frame their lives according to the light of nature and the law of that religion they do profess." [78]

Locke's conception of the relation of Christ to God is reminiscent of that of Paul of Samosata. It is "such an union with God, that God operates in him and by him." Through his miraculous birth Jesus is "properly the Son of God." By nature, therefore, he is immortal, and not subject to the power of death. All men who believe in him become the sons of God by adoption. All mankind will be restored to life by Christ at the resurrection, when he will function as judge and will assign to every man his lot in accordance with the above principles which he has himself disclosed to us.

We have now reviewed in its main outlines the thought of Locke in so far as it was directed upon the subject of religion. It is easy to see why it was so welcomed by the New England liberals. Its calm, dispassionate spirit appeared to them a wholesome corrective to the excesses of evangelical revivals. Its common-sense outlook, its thorough-going empiricism, were not only in accord with the temper of their day, but seemed to offer a new avenue of approach to ancient problems. Locke's minimization of essentials impressed favorably those already restive under orthodox restraint, and dissatisfied with the elaborate structure of traditional dogma. His externalization of religion seemed to bring it out into the light of day where all men could judge of it by the common standard of reason, and to undermine the position of those who endeavored to sustain irrational dogmas by an appeal to religious experience.

Locke's persistent disregard of the Trinity, his insistence upon the recognition of Jesus' messiahship as the essential condition of Christian discipleship, and his direct appeal to the text of Scripture without reference to the historic creeds had inevitably exposed him to the charge of Socinianism; and, although Locke cannily refused to be drawn, the logical consequence of his assertions was patent. Thus Channing repeatedly hails him as a great Unitarian.[79] He admits, indeed, that Locke's Unitarianism has been called in question, but attributes this to the fact that his name has "been found useful to the Unitarian cause," and pronounces all attempts to dispel "the long and general belief"[80] in his Unitarianism unsuccessful.

In all probability the influence of Locke upon Channing's thought is nowhere to be discerned more clearly than in the latter's emphasis upon the rational character of revealed religion. His words, indeed, are a very echo of Locke's pronouncements. "Christianity," declares Channing, "is a rational religion. Were it not so, I should be ashamed to profess it. I am aware that with some it is the fashion to decry reason, and to set up revelation as an opposite authority. This error, though countenanced by good men, and honestly maintained for the defence of the Christian cause, ought to be earnestly withstood; for it virtually surrenders our religion into the hands of the unbeliever." And in the succeeding paragraph he continues, "Revelation is but a means, and is designed to concur with nature, providence, and God's Spirit, in carrying forward reason to perfection. I glory in Christianity because it enlarges, invigorates, exalts my rational nature. If I could not be a Christian without ceasing to be rational, I should not hesitate as to my choice. I feel myself bound to sacrifice to Christianity property, reputation, life; but I ought not to sacrifice to any religion that reason which lifts me above the brute and constitutes me a man." [81]

As we shall see in due course Channing's conception of reason is more inclusive than that of Locke, in that it embraces not only the logical understanding but also an intuitive power concerning which he sometimes speaks in language which reminds one of Plato, Plotinus, or St. Augustine. At the moment, however, our concern is with similarities rather than with differences; and we can scarcely be wrong in seeing in these passages one of the high water-marks of Locke's influence.

The most important consequence of Locke's externalization of religion was, of course, his theory of miracles as the essential evidence of divine revelation; and in no respect was his influence upon the New England Unitarians more profound. They welcomed this doctrine with practically unanimous assent. Even Channing, who tells us that his study of Price's *Dissertations* "saved" him "from Locke's philosophy," [82] and who was in any case too much of mystic ever to feel thoroughly at home in such a system, was powerfully affected by it; and the average Unitarian far more so. Hence the furor raised by Theodore Parker, when he denied that the belief in miracles is an essential part of Christianity, [83] is quite understandable. His fellow-Unitarians at once loudly denounced him as not a Christian; and we can clearly see, upon their own principles, how entirely right they were.

Channing's attitude toward the issue raised by Theodore Parker is a matter which will later occupy our attention; but, as a present indication of the importance which he attached to miracles, I may point to his challenge to the orthodox in the opening sentences of his letter on creeds. "Work some miracle," he cries. "Utter some prophecy. Show me something divine in you, which other men do not possess. Is it possible that you are unaided men like myself, having no more right to interpret the New Testament than myself, and that you yet exalt your interpretations as infallible standards of truth, and the necessary conditions of salvation? Stand out of my path. I wish to go to the Master." [84]

Perhaps no feature of Locke's thought was more congenial to the Unitarian mind than his identification of the seat of authority with the New Testament—that is with the teaching of Jesus and his Apostles.

Its consequences are truly momentous. The man who adopts this position acknowledges, indeed, an external authority; but he becomes at the same time the interpreter of that authority. Neither Pope, priest, nor presbyter has any more dominion over him. The Unitarians who followed Locke's example felt that they had come out of a house of bondage, and looked with proud disdain upon the "man-made" creeds of orthodoxy. Theirs was the liberty with which Christ had made them free. In Channing's famous Baltimore sermon we find a forceful and succinct statement of their position, which we may regard as a Unitarian declaration of independence. "Jesus Christ," he asserts, "is the only master of Christians, and whatever he taught, either during his personal ministry or by his inspired Apostles, we regard as of divine authority, and profess to make the rule of our lives." [85]

It was natural enough that Channing, living as he did at a period when textual criticism was in its infancy, should not distinguish between the teachings of Jesus himself and the beliefs of the early Church. Leaving this consideration on one side, however, as too obvious to require comment, I wish to call attention to the fact that Channing here takes one side of an issue which still divides thinking men. Whenever the question is raised, What is Christianity?, two conflicting answers are returned. The term Christianity, we are sometimes told, should be taken to mean the Christian religion as a historic phenomenon with its history extending over twenty centuries; and Christian doctrines are those which have been developed by Christian men and have been received by the Christian Church. Since Christians have unfortunately disagreed so violently among themselves, this definition engenders considerable difficulties when we seek to apply it. Are we, for instance, to call transubstantiation and consubstantiation both Christian doctrines? Yet, if we deny the Christian name to one of these doctrines, do we not arrogate to ourselves the right to make Christianity what we wish it to be, and so perhaps imitate the example of those who

> "compound for sins they are inclined to
> by damning those they have no mind to?"[86]

The opposing view has been well stated by the French scholar, Jean Reville. "True Christianity," he asserts, "is the religion of Christ, the religion which Jesus taught and lived, not the one which, later on, His disciples built around His person and work. One feels some reluctance in pressing so elementary a truth; and yet one cannot choose but do so, since it has continually been disregarded by the Churches.

"No one would dream of identifying the philosophy of Socrates with that of the Neo-Platonists, although the latter is, in the history of ancient thought, the final embodiment of the spiritual evolution initiated by Socrates. Now, to be a Christian, is to be a disciple of Christ; and in order to ascertain in what measure one is really and faithfully a disciple of Christ, one must know what Christ taught, did, and required of His hearers that they might become His disciples." [87]

Such is essentially the position of Channing. "The great doctrine of the Reformation," he tells us, "was this,—that Jesus Christ is the only infallible teacher of his church, and that to him, as he speaks in his word, and not to human guides, we are all bound to listen. It is the character of the consistent Protestant, and of the enlightened Christian, that he calls no man master, and bows his faith and conscience to no human tribunal. He is not intimidated by positive assertion, anathemas, and cries of heresy. He goes to no infallible head, whether at Rome, Geneva, or Wittenberg; borrows no creed from Trent or Westminster; takes no name from Luther, Calvin, or Arminius; intrenches himself behind no traditions of forefathers and ancient saints. He, indeed, avails himself of the lights and arguments of good and great men of present and former times. But Jesus is the only *authority* to whom he submits." [88]

In the same spirit he writes, "By a liberal Christian, I understand one who is disposed to receive as his brethren in Christ all who, in the judgment of charity, sincerely profess to receive Jesus Christ as their Lord and Master. He rejects all tests or standards of Christian faith and of Christian character, but the word of Jesus Christ and his inspired apostles. He thinks it an act of disloyalty to his Master to introduce into the church creeds of fallible men as bonds of union, or terms of Christian fellowship. He calls himself by no name derived from human leaders, disclaims all exclusive connection with any sect or party, professes himself a member of the Church Universal on earth and in heaven, and cheerfully extends the hand of brotherhood to every man of every name who discovers the spirit of Jesus Christ." [89]

Thus, for Channing, Christian liberty is rooted in the recognition of the unique and infallible authority of Jesus. It is the unqualified character of that recognition, and the unchallenged, absolute, and intimate nature of that authority, which render every attempt to impose a creedal standard upon believers an act of *lese-majeste*. It is important that we should grasp this fact, and realize at the outset that the Unitarian notion of spiritual freedom was originally derived from that of a single and universally acknowledged authority, an authority too sacred to permit the toleration of any rival.

How vivid and intense was this sense of Christian discipleship is brought out by Channing's declaration that "whilst we deny the Christian name to none who acknowledge Jesus as their Saviour and Lord, we do deliberately believe that, by many who confess him, his religion is mournfully disfigured. We believe that piety at present is robbed in no small degree of its singleness, energy, and happiness, by the multiplication in the church of objects of supreme worship; by the division of the One God into three persons, who sustain different relations to mankind; and above all, by the dishonorable views formed of the moral character and administration of the Deity. Errors relating to God seem to us among the most pernicious that can grow up among Christians; for they darken, and, in the strong language of Scripture, 'turn into blood' the Sun of the Spiritual Universe." [90]

Had Channing's anti-Trinitarianism been the purely negative thing which it is frequently represented to have been, a mere protest without any corresponding positive affirmation, we should not be astonished to find him thus affirming his nearness to Trinitarian disciples of the common Master. But, when we have examined the roots of Channing's Unitarianism and seen how it springs from the very depths of his devotional life, and how intensely positive it was, we shall be in a position to appreciate the strength of that loyalty to Jesus which made him feel closer to a Trinitarian who denied the unity of God than to a Jew or a Moslem who acknowledged it, but who did not also acknowledge the Lordship of Christ.

Unitarianism was thus, in its origin, essentially a back-to-Jesus movement. And it was precisely this feature of it which must most have annoyed its detractors. In their efforts to represent it, in Channing's satirical words, as "the most cunning weapon ever forged in the fires of hell," its orthodox opponents must have been uncomfortably conscious that, in challenging the Christianity of men who acknowledged no master but Jesus, and recognized no authority—beyond that of human reason—other than his teachings, they could not but run the risk of making themselves ridiculous.

We have now surveyed the two currents of thought, the teaching of Calvin and that of Locke, which mingled to form the intellectual atmosphere in which Channing grew to maturity, and to indicate in some measure their influence upon him. Other influences there were of a more personal nature which proceeded, not out of this general atmosphere, but from his individual study of great thinkers and great minds of the Church. But it is time for us to turn to the detailed examination of Channing's thought, in the course of which these various influences will appear.

## NOTES

1. *Essay*, bk. I. ch. I. sec. 8.
2. *Ibid.*, bk. II. ch. I. secs. 2-3.
3. *Ibid.*, bk. II. ch. I. sec. 25; ch. XII. sec. 1.
4. *Essay*, bk. II. ch. I. sec. 4.
5. *Ibid.*, bk. IV. ch. II.
6. *Loc. cit.* sec. 4.
7. *Loc. cit.* sec. 14.
8. *Ibid.*, bk. IV. ch. I. sec. 2.
9. *Ibid.*, bk. IV. ch. 17. sec. 8. It may be objected that, although in this particular passage Locke seems to anticipate Berkeley's nominalism, yet, inasmuch as he admits general terms, his philosophy should rather be classed as conceptualism. But in what sense does he admit general ideas? "General and universal," he says, "belong not to the real existence of things, but are the inventions and creatures of the understanding, made by it for its own use, and concern only signs, whether words or ideas" (*Ibid.*, bk. III. ch. III. sec. 11). This may sound like conceptualism, but Locke continues, "Words are general, as has been said, when used for signs of general ideas, and so are applicable indifferently to many particular things: and ideas are general, when they are set up as the representatives of many particular things; but universality belongs not to things themselves, which are all of them particular in their existence; *even those words and ideas which in their signification are general. When therefore we quit particulars, the generals that rest are only creatures of our own making, their general nature being nothing but the capacity they are put into by the understanding, of signifying or representing many particulars. For the signification they have is nothing but a relation, that by the mind of man is added to them.*" (*Loc. cit.* Italics mine.) It seems clear, I think, that this is nominalism.
10. *Ibid.*, bk. II. ch. XXV. sec. 8.
11. *Ibid.*, bk. III. ch. X. sec. 33.
12. A contemporary illustration of this tendency is to be found in the thought of Professor Sellars. "Ontologically," he tells us, "similarity signifies that things are individually *such that* a knower must consider them alike in nature. And yet there is no peculiar relation of similarity between them" (*The Philosophy of Physical Realism*, p. 126). "Resemblance," he affirms once

more, "is a fact about things which is discoverable *under the condition that a mind thinks them together.* This togetherness, when achieved, is external and expressive of an operation of the mind. Mind is a kind of spectator capable of a ghostly supervenience. Thinking together is not a real relation between the things. It is a mental kind of relating which is unique and must be so regarded. And things can be said to be similar if they would be judged similar were they to be thought of together. This is an important point, for it shows that similarity is not a relation but a fact about things due to their natures" (*Ibid.*, p. 174).

13. For a discussion of Locke's inconsistencies see Professor R. I. Aaron's *John Locke*, pp. 182-206.

14. *Ibid.*, bk. III. ch. III. sec. 13.

15. *Ibid.*, bk. II. ch. XXV. sec. 6.

16. Professor Sellars' statement in the passage just cited (p. 45. n. 3) that "similarity is not a relation but a fact about things due to their natures" is plainly a restatement of Locke's contention. The point is made again (pp. 172-173 of the same work) when he declares that "the relating, or the possible relating, is external to the objects. It is supervenient (cf. Locke's "super-induced") and presupposes a prior act of knowing. Neither the knowing nor the comparing made possible by it affects the nature of the object. *That* things are similar is, accordingly, a fact about them resting on their respective natures and independent of our knowing and comparing. But I do think that we are always haunted in addition by a sense of the mind as a spectator which *could* know and compare. This is not strange since any actual *discovery* of similarity is mediated by knowledge and comparison."

17. *Ibid.*, bk. IV. ch. IX. sec. 3; cf. ch. X. sec. 2.

18. *Ibid.*, bk. IV. ch. IX. sec. 2.

19. When Locke writes, "Since the things the mind contemplates are none of them, besides itself, present to the understanding, it is necessary that something else, as a sign or representative of the thing it considers, should be present to it: and these are ideas" (*Ibid.*, bk. IV. ch. XXI. sec. 4), it seems clear that he is thinking only of the ideas of sensation whereby physical objects, which are not present to the understanding, are known. The mind, which is so present, is directly known; hence the ideas or objects of reflection can be nothing else than states, parts, aspects, or activities of the mind itself.

20. *Ibid.*, bk. IV. ch. X. sec. 5.

21. See Lecerf's *Introduction*, t. I. pp. 44, 288-289.

22. *Essay*, bk. IV. ch. IV. sec. 5.

23. *Ibid.*, bk. IV. ch. II. sec. 9.

24. *Ibid.*, bk. IV. ch. IV. sec. 7.

25. *Ibid.*, bk. IV. ch. III. sec. 19; cf. ch. II. sec. 10.

26. *Ibid.*, bk. IV. ch. III. sec. 18.

27. *Ibid.*, bk. IV. ch. XXI. sec. 3.

28. *Ibid.*, bk. II. ch. XX. sec. 2.

29. *Ibid.*, bk. II. ch. XXVIII. sec. 5.

30. *Ibid.*, bk. II. ch. XXVIII sec. 6.

31. *Ibid.*, bk. I. ch. III. sec. 6. "Without such a knowledge as this," remarks Locke, "a man can never be certain that any thing is his duty. Ignorance,

or doubt of the law, hopes to escape the knowledge or power of the law-maker, or the like, may make men give way to a present appetite; but let any one see the fault, and the rod by it, and with the transgression a fire ready to punish it; a pleasure tempting, and the hand of the Almightly visibly held up, and prepared to take vengeance (for this must be the case, where any duty is imprinted on the mind); and then tell me whether it be possible for people, with such a prospect, such a certain knowledge as this, wantonly, and without scruple, to offend against a law, which they carry about them in indelible characters, and that stares them in the face whilst they are break-ing it" (*Ibid.*, bk. I. ch. III. sec. 13).

32. *Ibid.*, bk. II. ch. XXI. sec. 41.

33. *Ibid.*, bk. II. ch. XXI. sec. 51.

34. *Works*, vol. I. p. 74.

35. *The Reasonableness of Christianity*.

36. In the *Essay* Locke argues in a similar vein that the preference of vice to virtue is always an instance of wrong judgment. "When infinite happiness is put into one scale against infinite misery in the other, if the worst that comes to the pious man, if he mistakes, be the best that the wicked can attain to, if he be in the right, who can without madness run the venture? Who in his wits would choose to come within a possibility of infinite misery, which if he miss, there is yet nothing to be got by that hazard? Whereas, on the other side, the sober man ventures nothing against infinite happiness to be got, if his expectation comes to pass. If the good man be in the right, he is eternally happy; if he mistakes, he is not miserable, he feels nothing. On the other side, if the wicked be in the right, he is not happy; if he mistakes, he is infinitely miserable. Must it not be a most manifest wrong judgment that does not presently see to which side, in this case, the preference is to be given? I have forborn to mention any thing of the certainty or probability of a future state, designing here to show the wrong judgment that any one must allow he makes upon his own principles, laid how he pleases, who prefers the short pleasures of a vicious life upon any consideration, whilst he knows, and cannot but be certain, that a future life is at least possible" (*Essay*, bk. II. ch. XXI. sec. 70).

37. *Essay*, bk. IV. ch. XVIII. sec. 2.

38. *Loc. cit.*

39. *Ibid.*, bk. IV. ch. XVIII. sec. 3.

40. *Ibid.*, bk. IV. ch. XVII. sec. 23.

41. *Loc. cit.*

42. *Ibid.*, bk. IV. ch. XVIII. sec. 5.

43. *Ibid.*, bk. IV. ch. XVIII. sec. 4.

44. "Revelation, where God has been pleased to give it, must carry it against the probable conjectures of reason" (*Ibid.*, bk. IV. ch. XVIII. sec. 8).

45. *Ibid.*, bk. IV. ch. XVIII. sec. 10; ch. XIX. sec. 14.

46. *Ibid.*, bk. IV. ch. XIX. sec. 4. There is, I would suggest, a ring of noble con-fidence about this passage which makes Kant's *dictum* concerning the neces-sity "to deny knowledge, in order to make room for faith" seem rather cheap (See *The Critique of Pure Reason*, Professor Norman Kemp Smith's tr., p. 29).

47. "I say," declares Locke, "that no man inspired by God can by any revelation communicate to others any new simple ideas, which they had not before from sensation or reflection. For whatsoever impressions he himself may have from the immediate hand of God, this revelation, if it be of new simple ideas, cannot be conveyed to another, either by words or any other signs. Because words, by their immediate operation on us, cause no other ideas but of their natural sounds: and it is by the custom of using them for signs, that they excite and revive in our minds latent ideas; but yet only such ideas as were there before." (*Ibid.*, bk. IV. ch. XVIII. sec. 3.)

48. *Loc. cit.*

49. See above p. 16.

50. *Distinguishing Marks of a Work of the Spirit of God*, sec. 111. 111.

51. *Loc. cit.*

52. *Loc. cit.*

53. *The Reasonableness of Christianity.*

54. "If we do what we can," writes Locke, "he will give us his Spirit to help us to do what, and how we should. It will be idle for us, who know not how our own spirits move and act us, to ask in what manner the Spirit of God shall work upon us." The devout man, it appears, should be content to know "that he is from a sure hand, and an Almighty arm, promised assistance to support and carry him through."

55. *Essay*, bk. IV. ch. XIX. secs. 5-7.

56. *Ibid.*, bk. IV. ch. XIX. sec. 10.

57. *Loc. cit.*

58. Bk. IV, ch. XVIII. sec. 4.

59. Bk. IV. ch. XIX. sec. 10.

60. *Loc. cit.*

61. See above p. 54.

62. "I may perceive the truth of a proposition in Euclid, without its being, or my perceiving it to be, a revelation: nay, I may perceive I came not by this knowledge in a natural way, and so may conclude it revealed, without perceiving that it is a revelation from God; because there be spirits, which, without being divinely commissioned, may excite those ideas in me, and lay them in such order before my mind, that I perceive their connexion. So that the knowledge of any proposition coming into my mind, I know not how, is not a perception that it is from God." (*Ibid.*, bk. IV. ch. XIX. sec. 10.)

63. Calvin tells us that the divine essence is known "not as it is in itself, but as it is with respect to us"—*non pas quel il est en soymesme, mais tel qu'il est envers nous (Institution*, t. I. p. 77. *Cf.* Lecerf's *Introduction*, t. I. p. 228).

64. *Ibid.*, bk. IV. ch. XIX. sec. 12.

65. "*Tout ainsi que si nous contemplions à l'oeil l'Essnce de Dieu en icelle*" (*Institution*, t. I. p. 67).

66. *Ibid.*, bk. IV. ch. XIX. sec. 13.

67. *Ibid.*, bk. IV. ch. XIX. sec. 14.

68. *Ibid.*, bk. IV. ch. XIX. sec. 15.

69. *Ibid.*, bk. IV. ch. XIX. sec. 16.

70. Locke appears to realize this himself, for, in *The Reasonableness of Christianity*, he remarks, "His wisdom is not usually at the expense of miracles, (if I may

so say) but only in cases that require them, for the evidencing of some revelation or mission to be from him. He does constantly (unless where the confirmation of some truth requires it otherwise) bring about his purposes by means operating according to their natures. If it were not so, the course and evidence of things would be confounded, miracles would lose their name and force, and there could be no distinction between natural and supernatural."

71. *The Reasonableness of Christianity.*
72. See the *Thirty-Nine Articles of the Church of England*, art. XXI.
73. See his third letter to the bishop of Worcester.
74. See *The Reasonableness of Christianity.*
75. *Ibid.*
76. *Ibid.*
77. James, 2:24.
78. Cap. X. art. IV.
79. *Works*, pp. 392, 406, 513.
80. *Ibid.*, p. 406.
81. *Ibid.*, p. 233.
82. *Life*, p. 34.
83. See his sermon on *The Transient and Permanent in Christianity.*
84. *Works*, p. 286.
85. *Ibid.*, p. 367.
86. *Hudibras.*
87. *Liberal Christianity*, Victor Leuliette's tr. pp. 38-39.
88. *Life*, p. 217.
89. *Life*, p. 195. n. 1.
90. *Works*, p. 274.

PART TWO

The Thought of
William Ellery Channing

# Chapter Three

# God

As we take up the systematic investigation of Channing's views, two alternative courses present themselves for our choice. On the one hand we may approach his thought from the periphery, as it were, by examining first of all its relations to the work of other men—that is, by carrying further considerations of the type with which we closed the last chapter—and so gradually converge upon the central element in it which is original and new. Or, on the other hand, we may plunge at once *in medias res* and seek to grasp at the outset Channing's dominant ideas, and thus gain a perspective which will enable us to see his thought as a whole, and subsequently to survey from this standpoint the environment in which it is situated. In following the former course, we should proceed from the circumference to the center; in pursuing the latter, we should go from the center to the circumference. It is this latter course which seems to me to offer the greater advantages, and which I have accordingly decided to adopt.

First of all, however, a word of warning. Unitarians have always been prone to conceive of Channing after their own image. Sometimes he has been identified with the early Unitarianism of the nineteenth century with its Lockian background, its Arian christology, its precritical approach to the New Testament, its miracles, and its somewhat mechanical notion of inspiration. Again, the exponents of the idealistic monism which was the dominant force in later nineteenth and earlier twentieth century Unitarianism, have pointed to features of his thought which are undeniably akin to views entertained by the transcendentalists, have hailed him as a precursor of their movement, and have maintained that, had he lived a generation later, he would have thought as they thought. And, last of all, the so-called "humanists" have so earnestly appealed to the social aspects of his thinking, to his emphasis upon the dignity of man and upon freedom of thought, that one is sometimes inclined to believe that it would scarcely do them injustice to represent them as contending that, if he had lived today, his gospel would have been limited to a demand for education for all, a chicken in every pot, a playground in every school, and good sewer pipes in every street.

This is the sort of tendency of which we are to beware. Channing was not a typical Unitarian in his own day, and I, for one, do not believe that he would have been a typical Unitarian in any other day. He was too individual, too many-sided, a thinker. He was not typical of the Unitarians of the early nineteenth century in that he was unable to accept without reservation the purely empirical, common-sense, and external method of approach to religious problems which commended itself to them. That he could ever have been a typical transcendental-ist we shall see reason to doubt when we have examined his criticism of the position of Theodore Parker, and have allowed for the intense personalism which was a basic element in his thought. And, to believe that he could ever have sympathized with "humanism," is to blind ourselves to the fact that despite—or, perhaps, because of—all his emphasis upon the dignity and worth of the human being, Channing did not conceive of man as the humanist conceives of him. To Channing man was a creature of divine origin, capable of divine perfection, and with an infinite future before him in which that perfection could be realized. Channing habitually conceived of God and man in conjunction, of God as revealing himself in man, and of man as becoming perfected in God. God and man were the two poles about which his thinking revolved, and the removal of either would transform it beyond all recognition. What we have to do, then, is to try to sweep all preconceptions from our minds and to see the man as he was, if we would learn anything from him.

That Channing was not a typical Unitarian of his own day is a fact for which we have his own assurance. "Let none listen to me," he exclaims, "for the purpose of learning what others think. I indeed belong to that class of Christians who are distinguished by believing that there is one God, even the Father, and that Jesus Christ is not this one God, but his dependent and obedient Son. But my accord with these is far from universal, nor have I any desire to extend it. What other men believe is to me of little moment. Their arguments I gratefully hear. Their conclusions I am free to receive or reject. I have no anxiety to wear the livery of any party. I indeed take cheerfully the name of Unitarian, because unwearied efforts are used to raise against it a popular cry; and I have not so learned Christ as to shrink from reproaches cast on what I deem his truth. Were the name more honored I should be glad to throw it off, for I fear the shackles which a party connection imposes. I wish to regard myself as belonging not to a sect, but to the community of free minds, of lovers of truth, of followers of Christ, both on earth and in heaven." [1]

Again he asserts, "I have little or no interest in Unitarians *as a sect*. I have hardly anything to do with them. I can endure no sectarian bonds. With Dr. Priestley, a good and great man, who had most to do in producing the late Unitarian movement, I have less sympathy than with many of the 'Orthodox.' " [2] "I distrust sectarian influence," he wrote in 1841, "more and more. I am more detached from a denomination, and strive to feel more my connection with the Universal Church, with all good and holy men. I am little of a Unitarian, have little sympathy with the system of Priestley and Belsham, and stand aloof from all but those who strive and pray for clearer light, who look for a purer and more effectual manifestation of Christian truth." [3]

Channing, then—we have his own word for it—was not interested in Unitarianism as a sect. What, precisely, does this imply? It implies at least that he was not concerned about its future as an organized movement, as an ecclesiastical entity as one denominational body among others. Yet it probably implies more than this. In another letter written in 1841,[4] twenty-two years after he had himself preached the sermon which had as its immediate result the formation of the new denomination, we find him deprecating the rise of a "Unitarian orthodoxy." It is, he thinks, possibly a necessary evil involved in keeping the ground already gained, but none the less lamentable as an indication of arrested progress. "Old Unitarianism," as he can already call it at that early day, "must undergo," he declares, "important modifications or developments. This I have felt for years. Though an advance on previous systems, and bearing some better fruits, it does not work deeply, it does not strike living springs in the soul. This is perfectly consistent with the profound piety of individuals of the body. But it cannot quicken and regenerate the world. No matter how reasonable it may be, if it is without *power*."

It seems clear, accordingly, that Channing, despite his confirmed distaste for sectarian ties, chivalrously attached himself to the Unitarian movement because he regarded it as the bearer of certain ideas of such importance that he could refer to them as Christ's truth, and that he was subsequently disappointed by its failure to develop these ideas, and by its tendency towards a crystallization of thought. That Channing believed that there was a definite, positive, Unitarian gospel is a fact which admits of no doubt at all, for he assures us of it in so many words. In his New York sermon entitled *Unitarian Christianity Most Favorable to Piety* he affirms[5] that he would "rejoice to spread it through this great city, to carry it into every dwelling, and to send it far and wide to the remotest settlements of our country," and he carefully distinguishes the truths which constitute it from other truths, "historical, metaphysical, scientific, literary," which, he states, "we have no anxiety to propagate," as "the highest, most important, most efficient truths, and therefore demanding a firm testimony and earnest efforts to make them known."

What these truths are it is our business, if we can, to discover. There is one suggestion, doubtless, which comes instantly to mind. We shall be referred to the wonderful event in Channing's fifteenth year under the clump of willows when, as his nephew informs us, he had a "view of the dignity of human nature," "the glory of the Divine disinterestedness, the privilege of existing in a universe of progressive order and beauty, the possibilities of spiritual destiny, the sublimity of devotedness to the will of Infinite Love." [6] Here emerge in significant connection the two poles of Channing's thought, God and man, of which I have already spoken.

No doubt this exalted moment was, as we are told, frequently recalled and forever cherished in memory. Nevertheless we must beware lest we exaggerate it out of due proportion. "This holy hour, however," says William Henry Channing, "was but the first wildflower of the spring, the opening of a long series of experiences by which he was led up to perfect consecration." [7] As a matter of fact, in a letter written from Richmond to his uncle some five years later about the turn of the century, we encounter the following statement: "I believe that I never experienced that *change of heart* which is necessary to constitute a Christian till within a few months past. The worldling would laugh ut me; he would call conversion a farce. But the man who has felt the influences of the Holy Spirit can oppose fact and experience to empty declaration and contemptuous sneers. You remember the language of the blind man whom Jesus healed—'This I know, that whereas I was blind, now I see.' " [8]

It might seem that this experience, followed as it was by a written declaration of self-dedication to God, must be regarded as the crucial moment of Channing's life. Yet here, once more, the nephew interposes, and tells us that "at a later period of his life, when asked by a most estimable Orthodox acquaintance 'whether he had not at some time experienced conversion,' he answered, 'I should say not, unless the whole of my life may be called, as it truly has been, a *process* of conversion.' " [9]

The reply is significant. We are not to infer that these two experiences were ever regarded by Channing as unimportant, but that they took their relative places among a multitude of others, of most of which in all probability no account has been given us, in the life of this man whose last words were, "I have received many messages from the Spirit." [10]

To these experiences we must return when we examine Channing's views as to the nature of religious knowledge, but at present our concern is with the intellectual formulation of those ideas which to his mind constituted the Unitarian gospel; hence we must turn to his controversial utterances. In his great Baltimore sermon Channing sets forth first among the beliefs characteristic of Unitarians one which, he tells us, is of "infinite importance." It is "the doctrine of God's UNITY, or that there is one God, and one only," and he cautions us to "take heed lest any man spoil us of it by vain philosophy." [11] In this doctrine all Christians, indeed, profess to believe, yet few of them would acquiesce in Channing's interpretation of it. "We understand by it," he announces, "that there is one being, one mind, one person, one intelligent agent, and one only, to whom underived and infinite perfection and dominion belong."

In his Baltimore sermon, after stating his doctrine of the divine unity, Channing contents himself with a little more than a hint of its positive implications,[12] and proceeds thereafter to refute the doctrine of the Trinity. Accordingly, inasmuch as we wish to grasp these implications, we shall do well to turn to a later sermon, namely, that delivered in New York in 1826 and entitled *Unitarian Christianity Most Favorable to Piety.*

The title itself may raise a question in our minds. The assumption seems to be that the doctrine most favorable to the growth of piety is to be preferred. But why is it to be preferred? Is it because it works better than any other? Does Channing, in other words, here anticipate the pragmatists, and does he identify the workableness of a doctrine with its truth? Or does he, on the other hand, see in its workableness only an evidence of its truth, an indication that it does as a matter of fact correspond to reality? All that we know of Channing's thought would lead us to embrace the latter suggestion, and to acquit him of the charge—or, if one prefer—to deny him the glory of being the first pragmatist. Undoubtedly Channing believed that his doctrine was true in the sense that it corresponded to objective fact. But it was entirely in keeping with his unstated premises—premises which include, needless to say, the existence of God and the capacity of man to attain union with God—that he should assume that the true doctrine will have the greatest efficacy, and consequently that its superior efficacy is a witness to its truth.

The sermon to which I refer is, indeed, one of Channing's greatest; for there we see, with transparent clearness, the intimate relation between his thinking and his devotional life, and are thereby enabled to appreciate how each in turn nourished and stimulated the other. Never was there a theologian in whom the rational and the mystical powers were more happily blended, nor more harmonious in their productivity. This it is, indeed, which gives its chief fascination to the study of Channing.

"Unitarianism," he writes, "is a system most favorable to piety because it presents to the mind one, and only one, Infinite Person to whom supreme homage is to be paid. It does not weaken the energy of religious sentiment by dividing it among various objects. It collects and concentrates the soul on one Father of unbounded, undivided, unrivalled glory. To him it teaches the mind to rise through all beings. Around him it gathers all the splendors of the universe. To him it teaches us to ascribe whatever good we receive or behold, the beauty and magnificence of nature, the liberal gifts of Providence, the capacities of the soul, the bonds of society, and especially the riches of grace and redemption, the mission, and powers, and beneficent influences of Jesus Christ. All happiness it traces up to the Father, as the sole source; and the mind, which these views have penetrated, through this intimate association of everything exciting and exalting in the universe with one Infinite Parent, can and does offer itself up to him with the intensest and profoundest love of which human nature is susceptible. . . . The more strict and absolute the unity of God, the more easily and intimately all the impressions and emotions of piety flow together and are condensed into one glowing thought, one thrilling love. No language can express the absorbing energy of the thought of one Infinite Father. When vitally implanted in the soul, it grows and gains strength for ever." [13]

Such is the opening note of Channing's systematic exposition of Unitarian doctrine, and the same spirit animates his closing paragraphs. "We prize and would spread our views," he declares, "because we believe that they reveal God to us in greater glory, and bring us nearer to him, than any other. We are conscious of a deep want, which the creation cannot supply,—the want of a Perfect Being, on whom the strength of our love may be centered, and of an Almighty Father, in whom our weaknesses, imperfections, and sorrows may find resource; and such a Being and Father Unitarian Christianity sets before us. For this we prize it above all price. We can part with every other good. We can endure the darkening of life's fairest prospects. But this bright, consoling doctrine of one God, even the Father, is dearer than life, and we cannot let it go. Through this faith, everything grows brighter to our view. Born of such a Parent, we esteem our existence an inestimable gift. We meet everywhere our Father, and his presence is as a sun shining on our path. We see him in his works, and hear his praise rising from every spot which we tread. We feel him near in our solitudes, and sometimes enjoy communion with him more tender than human friendship. We see him in our duties, and perform them more gladly, because they are the best tribute we can offer our Heavenly Benefactor. Even the consciousness of sin, mournful as it is, does not subvert our peace: for, in the mercy of God, as made manifest in Jesus Christ, we see an inexhaustible fountain of strength, purity, and pardon, for all who in spiritual reliance, seek these heavenly gifts. Through this faith, we are conscious of a new benevolence springing up to our fellow creatures, purer and more enlarged than natural affection. Towards all mankind we see a rich and free love flowing from the common Parent, and, touched by this love, we are the friends of all. We compassionate the most guilty, and would win them back to God. Through this faith, we receive the happiness of an ever-enlarging hope. There is no good too vast for us to anticipate for the universe or for ourselves, from such a Father as we believe in." [14]

In these eloquent words Channing is obviously speaking from the very depths of his soul. There is nothing negative about this form of Unitarianism! On the contrary, we have here an emphatic affirmation of what Channing takes to be the fundamental principle of Christianity. In the above passages the emotional element clearly predominates. But the balance is redressed by Channing's claim that "Unitarianism is the system most favorable to piety, because it presents a distinct and intelligible object of worship,—a Being whose nature, whilst inexpressibly sublime, is yet simple and suited to human apprehension. An Infinite Father is the most exalted of all conceptions and yet the least perplexing. It involves no incongruous ideas. It is illustrated by analogies from our own nature. It coincides with that fundamental law of the intellect through which we demand a cause proportional to effects. It is also as interesting as it is rational; so that it is peculiarly congenial with the improved mind. The sublime simplicity of God, as He is taught in Unitarianism, by relieving the understanding from perplexity, and by placing him within the reach of thought and affection, gives him peculiar power over the soul." [15]

The concluding sentence is important. The doctrine is said to place God "within reach of thought and affection." This two-fold emphasis is highly characteristic of Channing. It is precisely because God is intelligible, he contends, that he can be loved with an intensity and depth of emotion which no unintelligible and mysterious entity could possibly excite. Intelligence and heart alike find ultimate satisfaction in their divine object. This is a theme to which we shall frequently return, and which must constantly be kept in mind.

Furthermore, it will be observed that, in the passages just quoted, Channing speaks both of the divine unity and of the divine simplicity. These are familiar terms in scholastic philosophy, but there they bear a very different meaning from that which they have in the pages of Channing. In the thought of St. Thomas Aquinas and his followers the divine essence is simple unity utterly devoid of multiplicity. It possesses, indeed, in itself all perfections. Yet these perfections are not separate entities, qualities, or characteristics, but are by some mysterious alchemy identified with the divine essence, and *ipso facto* with one another. The universe in all its multiplicity imitates in various ways different aspects of this fecund simplicity.

Plainly a doctrine such as this hovers on the very edge of the perilous abyss of self-contradiction. In an attempt to anchor it on the *terra firma* of rationality, scholastic theologians have made use of the doctrine of degrees of being, which needs to be carefully distinguished from the theory known to defenders and critics of contemporary absolute idealism as that of degrees of reality. According to the latter view, the real is the whole, the all-encircling Absolute. Whatever falls within that circle is not wholly real, and the further we penetrate from the circumference the less degree of reality do we find; for the more inclusive is always more real than that which it includes. Accordingly we may conveniently symbolize the universe by a series of concentric circles, the innermost circle including the lowest degree of reality which is only one remove from unreality, and the outermost circle enclosing the whole which is complete or absolute reality. But, in addition, we must realize that any segment of the universe, viewed from the standpoint of the Absolute, will fall into its proper place as an element in a perfectly unified whole, whereas to any finite intelligence it will appear distorted. Thus degrees of reality are also degrees of truth, and the absolutely true is the absolutely real.

The doctrine of degrees of being, on the other hand, suggests a different symbol—that of a pyramid, at the apex of which is the undifferentiated and simple unity of the divine essence, and at the base of which we find the lowest degree of being and the highest degree of multiplicity. The pyramid is stratified in different levels of being. We ascend from accidents to substance, from the material to the spiritual, from incarnate to discarnate spirit, from angel to archangel, and always from less to greater unity and simplicity. What is manifold at a lower level, becomes, according to what I have ventured to term the *principle of fusion*, progressively unified at a higher, until at last we arrive at God, where multiplicity vanishes altogether and only unity is left.

Now in the light of this doctrine Unitarianism has not infrequently been caricatured as an attempt, by suppressing the doctrine of the Trinity—which is itself adventitious to this whole scheme—to conceive of God as a stark unit, an utterly undifferentiated unity, something as remote from human imagination and as unfit to be the object of religious emotion as could well be found. How far removed is this travesty from Channing's conception of God should now, I trust, be fully apparent.[16] When Channing talks of the unity and simplicity of God, he is thinking of that integration of manifoldness in oneness which we call personality. Channing's God is a Person. He is one as a person is one, and consequently he can be manifold as a person is manifold. But he cannot be many persons, any more than a man can be so. A plurality of persons would be a plurality of gods.

I will even venture the suggestion, which may be taken for what it it worth, but is—I should maintain—thoroughly consonant with Channing's way of thinking, that he would have proved sympathetic to the Hegelian view that the highest degree of unity is characterized by the highest degree of differentiation, so that God would be at once the most fully differentiated and the most completely unified of beings. For how else are we to conceive of a personal God? A living intelligence which surveys the entire universe and feels for all its creatures must surely be characterized by a vast plurality of psychic states which, so far from disrupting, are actually constitutive of the unity in which they are harmonized.

However this may be, it is essential, if we are adequately to appreciate the originality of Channing's thought, that we linger for a few moments over the contrast between his position and the teachings of orthodoxy. The issue is one of fundamental importance, for what Channing is about to say has never been said before in the history of Christendom with such clarity and impressiveness. He is about to challenge the almost unbroken tradition of two millennia. But, if we are to estimate aright the revolutionary character of his utterances, we must first recall what that tradition is.

It is the basic contention of orthodoxy that the infinite essence of God cannot be grasped by the human intellect. All our concepts are derived by abstraction from the objects which we experience, and the existence of these objects is not necessary but contingent; whereas it is impossible that God, in whom essence and existence are identical, should not exist. Again, each of these objects is a substance possessed of qualities, and thus involved in multiplicity and complexity: whereas God is neither a quality nor, *à la rigeur*, a substance, but absolute unity, absolute simplicity, the fulness of Pure Being. Hence the divine essence lies altogether beyond the limits of our experience, and evades all the categories of human thought. It is, therefore, in the strict sense of the word, *unknowable*. We can know only *that* God is, not *what* he is. Consequently the only assertions that we can make with respect to God which will be adequate to the requirements of genuine knowledge will be negative statements. If, for instance, we say that God is immaterial, that he is unchanging, or that he is not a member of any genus, these statements are literally true, and fall within the field of negative theology which thus proceeds *per viam remotionis*.

Were we to content ourselves with such negations, we should stop where Maimonides stopped, and where today the Barthians stop, with the notion of a God who is "wholly other" and "utterly utter." But Christian theologians of the traditional type have never been content to stop here. They have felt that something more is essential to a true theism, that some positive information must be procurable which, however imperfect and partial it may be, however it may fall short of what in strictness can be termed knowledge, is nevertheless genuine so far as it goes. And there is every reason why they should think so. For a God of whose nature we were wholly ignorant would be as otiose as the Kantian thing-in-itself. To form a conception of him would be as impossible as to describe a substance without mentioning any of its characteristics. If God is to be more than a name, knowledge, in some sense, of his nature—however meager that knowledge may be—must be attainable. And the famous five proofs of St. Thomas clearly presuppose as much. Unless God be the source of motion, the efficient cause of the created universe, the permanent reality which sustains all that is transient and contingent, ultimate being, goodness, and truth, and the intelligence which stamps upon its works the marks of design and purpose, these five proofs are of no avail. For it is by professing to show that God is all this that they profess to show also that he exists.

How, then, is such positive knowledge to be obtained? In answer to this question theologians refer us to the distinction between univocal, equivocal, and analogous terms. A univocal term is one which is applicable in the same sense to a plurality of entities. In the case of an equivocal term, however—as in Spinoza's illustration of the dog and the constellation which bears its name—there is nothing in common except the word. Analogous terms are a mean between these two extremes. They signify that there is something in common but also a difference, that there is at once similarity and dissimilarity. And it is by invoking the principle of analogy that we arrive at a positive knowledge of God *per viam affirmativam.*

Having thus answered, however, theologians are by no means of one mind as to how the principle of analogy is to be employed. In the writings of St. Thomas, as is well known, two forms of analogy are to be found; one of which he terms the analogy of proportion, and the other that of proportionality. His successors, unfortunately, have needlessly complicated the situation by altering his terminology; and have rechristened his analogy of proportion the analogy of attribution, and his analogy of proportionality the analogy of proportion.

Accommodating ourselves to this modern usage, let us proceed to distinguish between them. The analogy of proportion is based upon similarity of relations.[17] Thus, although we have no adequate notion of what the divine intelligence is, we can formulate an equation, and assert that, as the human intelligence stands to the finite human being, so does the divine intelligence stand to the infinite being, God.[18] The analogy of attribution, on the other hand, proceeds directly from the creature to the Creator. Although no definite proportion can be established between the finite and the infinite, still—it is argued—there must be genuine similarity. We know that human intelligence is superior to the instinct of brutes. So, even though the divine intelligence infinitely surpass our own, we know at least that it is above and not below our own. We know which way to look, even if we do not know what to look for. Accordingly, when we say, God is wise, we are making a statement which is true so far as it goes. It is not an adequate statement; for our concept of wisdom, derived from our experience, is other than our concept of goodness and other than our concept of beauty, whereas in God wisdom, goodness, and beauty are all one. Still the statement expresses the uttermost degree of truth to which we can attain, and does yield positive information.

Each of these forms of analogy has its own partisans, and theorists of various schools debate with earnestness, and even with acrimony, concerning their respective validity and their relative advantages.[19] What is important, however, for us to keep in mind is the fact that, not only Roman Catholic, but also Calvinist theologians[20] are agreed as to the soundness of the general theory of the negative and affirmative ways, and unite in regarding the principle of analogy as the basis of man's positive knowledge of God.

Now it is precisely this ancient theory which Channing, in effect, sets out to demolish. In saying this I do not mean to make any assertion as to the extent to which Channing had familiarized himself with its historic foundations or the classical terminology in which it is expressed, a matter concerning which I am in ignorance. But it is quite clear that he grasped the fundamental idea upon which it is based; namely, the incapacity of the human mind to attain to any definite knowledge of the divine nature, or to ascribe any qualities to God in the same sense in which they are ascribed to creatures; and that he regarded it as an error of the first magnitude.

That Channing should view it with such seriousness, and bend every effort to counteracting it, is typical of his whole point of view. For him theological speculation is no merely academic activity; it stands in the most vital relation to man's spiritual development. "Errors relating to God," he assures us, "seem to us the most pernicious that can grow up among Christians; for they darken, and, in the strong language of Scripture, 'turn into blood' the Sun of the Spiritual Universe. Around just views of the Divine character all truths and all virtues naturally gather; and although some minds of native irrepressible vigor may rise to greatness in spite of dishonorable conceptions of God, yet, as a general rule, human nature cannot spread to its just proportions under their appalling, enslaving, heart-withering control." [21]

The fear of dishonorable views of God arising in the minds of Christians was certainly no idle one, as the history of orthodoxy has shown. For, if all we know of the divine goodness is that it infinitely transcends our own goodness, so that we can form no clear conception of it, how can we be sure that it may not manifest itself in ways which will outrage all our ethical judgments? This line of defense constituted, indeed, the standing *apologia* of Channing's Calvinistic opponents; and upon it, therefore, he directs a concentrated attack. In so doing he does not explicity distinguish between equivocal and analogous predication; and, were we to take certain of his statements in isolation from their general context, we might be tempted to think that he had in mind only the former. Were this, indeed, the case, we should be compelled to charge Channing with having misunderstood the position of orthodox Calvinism which, as we have seen, is committed to the principle of analogy. A detailed examination of his argument, however, makes it abundantly clear, as I shall now try to show, that—whatever his degree of familiarity or unfamiliarity with scholastic terminology—he was in fact concerned to maintain that we have a knowledge of God of a type consistent neither with equivocal nor analogous predication, and which is in truth univocal.

Channing's principal utterances on this subject are to be found in his essay entitled *The Moral Argument against Calvinism* and in his sermon on *Likeness to God*. Because of the great importance of the subject I shall endeavor to present in ordered sequence, and as far as possible in his own words, the fundamental contentions there set forth.

Growth in likeness to God is, as Channing sees it, the very essence of religion. It is, consequently, a subject the importance of which cannot be exaggerated, and Channing begins his treatment of it in good mediaeval fashion with a preliminary prayer. "Such is the topic now to be discussed; and I implore Him whose glory I seek to aid me in unfolding and enforcing it with simplicity and clearness, with a calm and pure zeal, and with unfeigned charity." [22] Man's likeness to God, he then goes on to observe, is a spiritual likeness.[23] This may seem too obvious to some to be worth mentioning, yet there is wisdom in making this explicit assertion; for few things, perhaps, are more amazing than the frequency with which the objection is raised whenever one speaks—as Channing was wont to do—of a personal God, "Ah, then you mean that God has a body!" Crudely anthropomorphic views of this kind were, of course, actually held by certain mediaeval Jewish and Moslem theologians, and are still maintained by the Wahabis at the present day. It may have been as well, therefore, that Channing should make it evident that he was not of this group. Man resembles God, not by reason of the fact that he has arms and legs, but because he is a mind; and through moral progress he can become increasingly like his Creator.

"Likeness to God," writes Channing, "is the true and only preparation for the enjoyment of the universe. In proportion as we approach and resemble God, we are brought into harmony with the creation; for in that proportion we possess the principles from which the creation sprung; [24] we carry within ourselves the perfections of which its beauty, magnificence, order, benevolent adaptations, and boundless purposes are the results and manifestations. God unfolds himself in his works to a kindred mind. It is possible that the brevity of these hints may expose to the charge of mysticism what seems to me the calmest and clearest truth. I think, however, that every reflecting man will feel that likeness to God must be a principle of sympathy or accordance with his creation; for the creation is a birth and shining forth of the Divine Mind, a work through which his spirit breathes." [25]

Now it is sure to be objected, Channing observes, that to stress man's likeness to God is to interpret the Scriptures too literally, to forget that God is unapproachable, "that we and all things illustrate the Creator by contrast, not by resemblance," [26] that it is human worthlessness which ought to be emphasized, that God is infinite and incomprehensible, and that we cannot presume to judge of his administration by human standards.[27]

To these objections Channing replies, in the first place, that God is in truth incomprehensible, but that in this he is not alone, for so is everything else. Nothing is fully understood; everything possesses unknown properties.[28] But, although we cannot know everything about

God, it does not follow that we cannot know anything. The range of the human intellect is relatively narrow, but what falls within that range is as truly knowledge as that which is included within the wider purview of an angel. Thus Channing, unlike the traditional theologian, conceives of the limitation to which our knowledge is subjected as quantitative rather than qualitative. "We grant," he writes, "that our understandings cannot stretch beyond a very narrow sphere. But still the lessons which we learn within this sphere are just as sure as if it were indefinitely enlarged. Because much is unexplored, we are not to suspect what we have actually discovered. Knowledge is not the less real because confined." [29]

Thus it will be seen that for Channing there are no degrees of truth. It is evident that he would dissent from the theory that the knowledge of a finite being, because fragmentary, is infected with falsehood, and that from the point of view of the whole everything would wear a different aspect. "No extent of observation," he affirms, "can unsettle those primary and fundamental principles of moral truth which we derive from our highest faculties operating in the relations in which God has fixed us. In every region and period of the universe, it will be as true as it is now on the earth that knowledge and power are the measures of responsibility, and that natural incapacity absolves from guilt. These and other moral verities, which are among our clearest perceptions, would, if possible, be strengthened, in proportion as our powers should be enlarged; because harmony and consistency are the characters of God's administration, and all our researches into the universe only serve to manifest its unity, and to show a wider operation of the laws which we witness and experience on earth." [30]

Furthermore, from the fact that God is incomprehensible, it does not follow that he is unintelligible. "This distinction," observes Channing, "we conceive to be important. We do not pretend to know the *whole* nature and properties of God, but still we can form some *clear ideas* of him, and can reason from these ideas as justly as from any other. . . . God's goodness, because infinite, does not cease to be goodness, or essentially differ from the same attribute in man; nor does justice change its nature, so that it cannot be understood, because it is seated in an unbounded mind." [31] In opposition alike to "philosophers falsely socalled" and to "the mistaken Christian," Channing declares "that God's attributes are intelligible, and that we can conceive as truly of his goodness and Justice as of these qualities in men. In fact these qualities are essentially the same in God and man, though differing in degree, in purity, and in extent of operation. We know not and we cannot conceive of any other justice or goodness than we learn from our own nature; and if God have not these, He is altogether unknown to us as a moral being; He offers nothing for esteem and love to rest upon; the objection of the infidel is just, that worship is wasted; 'we worship we know not what.' " [32]

It is evident that in these passages Channing means by *essential sameness* what the scholastics, Romanist and Calvinist, mean by univocacy. God's attributes, as he says, differ from man's "in degree, in purity, and in extent of operation," that is, they enjoy a higher degree of intensity and are unmixed with evil and imperfection, but they are not different attributes. This essential sameness follows, according to Channing, from the doctrine of the divinity of human nature which is taught in the New Testament.[33]

The correctness of this identification of essential sameness with univocacy would seem to be established beyond dispute by the following rhetorical question. "It is asked," says Channing, "On what authority do we ascribe to God goodness and rectitude *in the same sense in which these attributes belong to men*,[34] or how can we judge of the nature of attributes in the mind of the Creator?" In reply Channing asks, "How is it that we become acquainted with the mind of a fellow-creature? The last is as invisible, as removed from *immediate* inspection, as the first. Still we do not hesitate to speak of the justice and goodness of a neighbor; and how do we gain our knowledge? We answer, by witnessing the effects, operations, and expressions of these attributes. It is a law of our nature to argue from the effect to the cause, from the action to the agent, from the ends proposed and from the means of pursuing them, to the character and disposition of the being in whom we observe them. By these processes we learn the invisible mind and character of man; and by the same we ascend to the mind of God, whose works, effects, operations, and ends are as expressive and significant of justice and goodness as the best and most decisive actions of men. If this reasoning be sound (and all religion rests upon it), then God's justice and goodness are intelligible attributes, agreeing essentially with the same qualities in ourselves. Their operation, indeed, is infinitely wider, and they are employed in accomplishing not only immediate but remote and unknown ends. Of consequence, we must expect that many parts of the divine administration will be *obscure*, that is, will not produce *immediate* good, and an *immediate* distinction between virtue and vice. But still the unbounded operation of these attributes does not change their nature. They are still the same as if they acted in the narrowest sphere." [35]

Putting the same point in another way,[36] Channing inquires, "Whence do we derive our knowledge of the attributes and perfections which constitute the Supreme Being? I answer, we derive them from our own souls. The divine attributes are first developed in ourselves, and thence transferred to our Creator. The idea of God, sublime and awful as it is, is the idea of our own spiritual nature, purified and enlarged to infinity. In ourselves are the elements of the Divinity. God, then, does not sustain a figurative resemblance to man. It is the resemblance of a parent to a child, the likeness of a kindred nature.[37]

"We call God a mind," continues Channing. "He has revealed himself as a Spirit. But what do we know of mind but through the unfolding of this principle in our own breasts? That unbounded spiritual energy which we call God is conceived by us only through consciousness. . . . God is another name for human intelligence raised above all error and imperfection, and extended to all possible truth." [38] Similarly, with regard to the divine goodness, Channing asks, "How do we understand this, but by the principle of love implanted in the human breast?" [39] "The same is true," he asserts, "of all the moral perfections of the Deity. These are comprehended by us only through our own moral nature." [40]

The objection may, however, be raised, Channing observes, "that we receive our idea of God from the universe, from his works, and not so exclusively from our own souls." [41] Indeed it may, and indeed it has been. This is the very point which a scholastic philosopher would at once stress. And, in so doing, he would be wholly loyal to St. Thomas, who calmly rejects all arguments based exclusively upon mental, moral, or religious experience. Few things, perhaps, are more impressive than the widespread assent with which this decision has been welcomed in Roman Catholic circles, or the heartiness with which the vast majority of neo-scholastic writers repudiate an appeal to the *argumentum ex experientia religiosa*. Their attitude in this matter has doubtless been confirmed by theological developments subsequent to the time of St. Thomas; for the self-authenticating character of religious experience constitutes the very cornerstone of Calvinism, and the assertion that the human mind is endowed with a natural and direct awareness of God has been condemned as the chief error of the heterodox Ontologist.[42] Accordingly it is a settled principle of genuine Thomism that neither religious, moral, or any other form of psychological experience provides a satisfactory basis for a proof of the existence of God, and that the worth of such experiences can be estimated aright only in the light of a previously established rational demonstration of the divine existence founded upon the general characteristics of the external world.

Channing, however, in words which have an almost Augustinian ring, boldly declares, "The effects and signs of power, wisdom, and goodness are apparent through the whole creation. But apparent to what? Not to the outward eye; not to the acutest organs of sense; but to a kindred mind, which interprets the universe by itself. It is only through that energy of thought by which we adapt various and complicated means to distant ends, and give harmony and a common bearing to multiplied exertions, that we understand the creative intelligence which has established the order, dependencies, and harmony of nature. We see God around us because He dwells within us. It is by a kindred wisdom that we discover his wisdom in his works. The brute, with an eye as piercing as ours, looks on the universe; and the page, which to us is radiant with characters of greatness and goodness, is to him a blank. In truth, the beauty and glory of God's works are revealed to the mind by a light beaming from itself. We discern the impress of God's attributes in the universe by accordance of nature, and enjoy them through sympathy."[43]

There remains, nevertheless, the objection that essential sameness of divine and human attributes carries with it the corollary that man is competent to judge concerning the rectitude of the divine administration, and the ensuing charge that such an attitude involves presumption. With characteristic manliness Channing does not attempt to evade the issue, but frankly accepts the inference, and replies to the accusation with a direct denial. "We answer confidently, No; for in many cases we are competent and even bound to judge. And we plead first in our defence the Scriptures. How continually does God in his word appeal to the understanding and moral judgment of man! 'O inhabitants of Jerusalem and men of Judah, judge, I pray you, between me and my vineyard. What could have been done more to my vineyard, that I have not done in it?' " [44]

In the second place, "all religion," declares Channing, "supposes and is built on judgments passed by us on God and on his operations. Is it not, for example, our duty and a leading part of piety to *praise* God? And what is praising a being, but to adjudge and ascribe to him just and generous deeds and motives? And of what value is praise, except from those who are capable of distinguishing between actions which exalt and actions which degrade the character? Is it presumptuous to call God *excellent?* And what is this, but to refer his character to a standard of excellence, to try it by the established principles of rectitude, and to pronounce its conformity to them; that is, to judge of God and his operations?" [45]

"This is the religion," asserts Channing, "which most truly honors God. To honor him is not to tremble before him as an unapproachable sovereign, not to utter barren praise which leaves us as it found us. It is to become what we praise. It is to approach God as an inexhaustible fountain of light, power, and purity. It is to feel the quickening and transforming energy of his perfections." [46]

"This view of religion," Channing maintains, is "infinitely important." [47] "You cannot," he tells his hearers, "think too highly of the majesty of God. But let not this majesty sever him from you. Remember that his greatness is the infinity of attributes which you yourselves possess. . . . It is through such views that religion raises up the soul, and binds man by ennobling bonds to his Maker." [48]

In the third place, Channing holds that to judge of God is the duty of an intellectual nature. "God, in giving us conscience, has implanted a principle within us which forbids us to prostrate ourselves before mere power, or to offer praise where we do not discover worth,—a principle which challenges our supreme homage for supreme goodness, and which absolves us from guilt, when we abhor a severe and unjust administration. Our Creator has consequently waived his own claims on our veneration and obedience, any further than He discovers himself to us in characters of benevolence, equity, and righteousness. He rests his authority on the perfect coincidence of his will and government with those great and fundamental principles of morality written on our souls. He desires no worship but that which springs from the exercise of our moral faculties upon his character, from our discernment and persuasion of his rectitude and goodness. He askes, he accepts, no love or admiration but from those who can understand the nature and the proofs of moral excellence." [49]

In the fourth place, Channing points to the general esteem in which Christians have always held those who have endeavored to demonstrate the divine perfections.[50] This involves judging concerning those attributes, concerning what is consonant with them or indicative of them. But, if it be true that "what seems unjust to man may be in the Creator the perfection of rectitude" [51] —and this, as we have seen, is quite possible upon the theory of analogy—a disastrous consequence follows. "If the strongest marks and expressions of injustice do not prove God unjust, then the strongest marks of the opposite character do not prove him righteous. If the first do not reserve our confidence, because of our narrow views of God, neither do the last. If, when more shall be known, the first may be found consistent with perfect rectitude, so, when more shall be known, the last may be found consistent with infinite malignity and oppression." [52]

In the fifth place, Channing calls attention to the fact that Christians have commonly attached great importance to the internal evidence of their religion, that they have lauded its doctrines as manifesting the perfections of God and indicative of its origin, and have freely criticised other religions on the ground that these instill unworthy conceptions of the Deity. Such a line of argumentation, he observes, would be rendered worthless if man's capacity for making judgments concerning God could be successfully impugned. And, lastly, he refers us to the habitual practice on the part of theologians of all denominations of basing upon the divine perfections arguments in support of their various doctrines. "Theological writings," he observes, "are filled with such arguments; and yet *we*, it seems, are guilty of awful presumption when we deny of God principles of administration against which every pure and good sentiment in our breasts rises in abhorence." [53]

If, however, it still be maintained that the sheer infinite immensity of God renders a finite intelligence incapable of grasping him, Channing boldly meets the objector on his own ground. "I affirm, and trust that I do not speak too strongly, that there are traces of infinity in the human mind; and that, in this very respect, it bears a likeness to God. The very conception of infinity is the mark of a nature to which no limit can be prescribed. This thought, indeed, comes to us not so much from abroad as from our own souls. We ascribe this attribute to God, because we possess capacities and wants which only an unbounded being can fill, and because we are conscious of a tendency in spiritual faculties to unlimited expansion. We believe in the divine infinity through something congenial with it in our own breasts. I hope I speak clearly, and if not, I would ask those to whom I am obscure to pause before they condemn. To me it seems that the soul, in all its higher actions, in original thought, in the creations of genius, in the soarings of imagination, in its love of beauty and grandeur, in its aspirations after a pure and unknown joy, and especially in disinterestedness, in the spirit of self-sacrifice, and in enlightened devotion, has a character of infinity. There is often a depth in human love which may strictly be called unfathomable. There is sometimes a lofty strength in moral principle which all the power of the outward universe cannot overcome. There seems a might within which can more than balance the might without. There is, too, a piety which swells into a transport too vast for utterance, and into an immeasurable joy. I am speaking, indeed, of what is uncommon, but still of realities. We see, however, the tendency of the soul to the infinite in more familiar and ordinary forms. Take, for example, the delight which we find in the vast scenes of nature, in prospects which spread around us without limits, in the immensity of the heavens and the ocean, and especially in the rush and roar of mighty winds, waves, and torrents, when, amidst our deep awe, a power within seems to respond to the omnipotence around us. The same principle is seen in the delight ministered to us by works of fiction or of imaginative art, in which our own nature is set before us in more than human beauty and power. In truth, the soul is always bursting its limits. It thirsts continually for wider knowledge. It rushes forward to untried happiness. It has deep wants, which nothing limited can appease. Its true element and end is an unbounded good. Thus, God's infinity has its image in the soul; and through the soul, much more than through the universe, we arrive at this conception of the Deity." [54]

Such is Channing's teaching with regard to man's knowledge of God. So far as I know, nothing comparable to it had ever before appeared in the history of Christian thought. For this reason I have striven, with perhaps wearisome persistence, to make clear from his own words its nature and the grounds upon which it is based, the more so because its significance and importance have been strangely disregarded. The fundamental convictions upon which it is based are plainly these: that man's true blessedness consists in the love of God; that God can be loved as a person is loved only if he can be conceived of as a Person; and that, if he can be so conceived of, univocal predication with respect to God and man must be possible.

"Are you not making," I may nevertheless be asked, "an unsupportable claim with respect to the uniqueness and originality of Channing's position? Have you not forgotten that the Subtle Doctor, Duns Scotus, was himself the proponent of a doctrine of univocal knowledge, and, in placing Channing's roughly adumbrated theory by the side of his carefully worked out formulation, are you not comparing the small with the great?" This is a pertinent question, and demands a straight answer.

In reply I should in the first place concede that there is a distinct, although partial, resemblance between the attitudes of the two men.

We do not, indeed, find in Scotus that balance of intellect and emotion which is so characteristic of the mind of Channing, and which is productive of a theology so adequately expressive of his spiritual experience; yet this may be due less to difference of temperament than to difference of intellectual climate and historic background. It is impossible, I would suggest, that we should find such an intimate unity of thought and emotion in the writings of a theologian who is committed to the theory that God, although essentially intelligible *in se,* is not essentially intelligible *quoad nos.* For such a man the realm of feeling will inevitably extend far beyond the domain of reason, and find its nutriment in doctrines which are professedly incomprehensible.

None the less Scotus shares with Channing the conviction that, if we are to have any knowledge whatsoever of God, there must be in our conceptions of Creator and creature some common element upon which such knowledge is based. And we find in his pages many vigorous statements of this conviction to which, I feel sure, Channing could have heartily subscribed. Thus Scotus roundly declares, "All comparison is to some extent univocal; for when it is said, This is more perfect than that, if it be asked, In what is it more perfect?, it is needful here to assign to each something common; so that in all comparison there is a common determinable in each of the terms compared. For a man is not more perfectly man than an ass, but more perfectly animal." [55]

Again Scotus explicitly states that in metaphysical inquiry concerning God the proper procedure is to take some formal concept which does not essentially involve any imperfection, such as that of wisdom, intellect, or will, and, having removed from it those imperfections with which we find it actually associated in the creatures, to attribute it in its highest perfection to God.[56] Now this is precisely what Channing does. So far, therefore, they are at one.

We come now to the point where they differ. Scotus is concerned, it appears, not with objective entities as they actually exist *in rerum natura,* but with the concepts to which these entities give rise. He is desirous of showing that we do and must apply in the same sense to God and man such concepts as those of being, intellect, and will. But it does not follow, according to Scotus, that these concepts adequately represent the divine reality, or that God and man actually do have anything in common. So, at least, he is understood by his devoted disciple, Hieronymus de Montefortino, who sums up the matter in these words, "The diversity in all modes of God and the creature in *reality* a *parte rei* being thus admitted, they agree *univocally* in *inadequate* and *imperfect* concepts." [57] So, also, he is interpreted by our contemporaries, Professors De Wulf[58] and Belmond.[59] And they can point in support of their view to Scotus' own words which appear to be conclusive: "God and the creatures are not *primarily diverse* as *conceived*; yet they are primarily diverse in *reality*, because in no reality do they agree." [60]

It is only fair to add that this interpretation is contested, and that by no less a person than Professor Gilson, who protests that the Scotist doctrine of univocacy does not mean "that being is a universal concept logically attributable both to God and creatures, for this everyone would admit," but that, on the contrary, "what the doctrine really means is that the quiddity, the very essence of the act of existing, taken apart from the modalities which determine the different modes of existence, is apprehended by the intellect as identical." [61] I confess that I am not very clear as to just what this means, nor yet as to how this interpretation of the doctrine is to be applied in the case of the other transcendentals. I must also point out, however, that Father Van de Woestyne, perhaps the most eminent of living Scotists, maintains that the doctrine in question is not one of logic but of metaphysics, and that it actually does envisage an *ens-realitas* common to Creator and creature.[62]

In view of this uncertainty as to what Scotus' position really was, it is difficult to compare or to contrast his teaching with that of Channing. Of one thing, however, we can be sure. Channing is primarily concerned, not with how we think but with what we think about, not with the psychological or logical processes whereby we conceive of God but with God himself. It is, of course, quite true—it is in fact the merest tautology—to say that we can know God only by thinking about him, but it does not follow that we cannot think of him as he is. If Channing had been asked how we can know that our thought does not distort its object, he would have replied, I conjecture, as Locke would have replied, that our ideas are derived from contact with reality and correspond to reality. Accordingly, when Channing says that God is good, he does not mean merely that we conceive of God as if he were characterised by the same quality which characterises a good man; he means that God really is good, and good in the same sense in which a man is good. This is what he tries to make clear by his use of the phrase "essentially the same."

Let us now look a little more closely at the Scotist position. What does Hieronymus de Montefortino mean by "inadequate concepts?"

Let us take his own illustration.[63] Let us conceive of an entity which is characterised by intense whiteness. To conceive of it adequately, we must conceive of it as possessing the precise degree of brilliance which does in fact characterise it; such a concept would be proper to it, and could not be applied to another object which is qualified by whiteness of an inferior degree of brilliance. Yet by abstraction we can form the general but inadequate concept of whiteness which can legitimately be applied to both. In this concept, then, they agree; whereas in reality the "two whitenesses," [64] so Hieronymus tells us, have nothing in common.

This last assertion, indeed, gives one pause. We should not, unless we were inclined toward nominalism, speak of two whitenesses; and concerning the two white objects we should certainly say that they had something in common, namely, whiteness. But we should also admit that they differ with respect to the purity or brilliance of their color. If this be, in truth, the way in which Scotus conceived that God and man differ, his view does resemble that of Channing. For never does Channing dream of asserting that man can be as good as God. What he means is that God and man are both good in the sense in which the two objects are both white. But from this it follows that, while God is numerically wholly other than man, he is by no means qualitatively wholly other than man; there must, indeed, be many qualities which God and man possess in common.

It is important to observe, however, that Hieronymus' illustration from degrees of whiteness does not really bear upon the principle of analogy as the Thomist conceives it, but only—as Father Garrigou-Lagrange has pointed out—upon analogy "quite improperly so-called." [65] By invoking degrees of intensity one does not escape from univocacy; true analogy is concerned, with differences, not of degree, but of kind. Now it seems clear that Scotus accepted the theory of analogy,[66] and regarded his doctrine of univocacy as thoroughly compatible with it; which is understandable if the former have to do with objective reality, and the latter only with concepts. Here, then, we find a fundamental disagreement between Scotus and Channing.[67]

Furthermore, although Channing would undoubtedly agree with Scotus in his contention that all negative knowledge of God must be rooted in positive knowledge, and that in the absence of such positive knowledge we should have no more justification for calling God wise than for calling him a stone,[68] he does not stop here. On the contrary, he carries this way of thinking to its logical conclusion, which is the complete repudiation of the negative theology. In so saying, I do not, of course, wish to imply that Channing would have contended that *no* negative statements can be made with respect to God, for this would be sheer absurdity. It is obvious that, if we can say that God is perfect, we can also say that he is not evil; that, if we can say that God is a mind, we can also affirm that he is not a stone. But the negative theology involves much more than this. It rests upon the assertion that no knowledge at all, in the strict sense of the word *knowledge,* is possible with regard to the divine essence. Thus our good Scotist, Hieronymus de Montefortino, is content to echo St. Thomas' pronouncement "that we cannot know what God it, but what he is not; that we cannot consider how God is, but rather how he is not." [69]

Now it is plain that Channing's doctrine of the essential sameness of divine and human attributes is developed in direct opposition to this very theory. And it is equally evident that the theory of analogous predication, which is intended to mitigate the rigor of the negative theology—and is, in fact, inconsistent with it—seems to Channing a miserable subterfuge which yields us no genuine knowledge of God, and which is compatible with the ascription to him of deeds and motives which from the human point of view can only be described as evil.

"If God's justice and goodness," asks Channing, "are consistent with those operations and modes of government which Calvinism"—and he might well have added Romanism—"ascribes to him, of what use is our belief in these perfections? . . . If it consist with divine rectitude to consign to everlasting misery beings who have come guilty and impotent from his hand, we beg to know what interest we have in this rectitude, what pledge of good it contains, or what evil may be imagined which may not be its natural result? If justice and goodness, when stretched to infinity, take such strange forms and appear in such unexpected and apparently inconsistent operations, how are we sure that they will not give up the best men to ruin, and leave the universe to the powers of darkness?" [70] "Is it said," exclaims Channing, "that the divine faithfulness is pledged in the Scriptures to a happier issue of things? But why should not divine faithfulness transcend our poor understandings as much as divine goodness and justice, and why may not God, consistently with this attribute, crush every hope which his word has raised? Thus all the divine perfections are lost to us as grounds of encouragement and consolation, if we maintain that their infinity places them beyond our judgment." [71]

The *Via Negativa* and the *Via Eminentiae* are, then, alike rejected by Channing, whose theology is nothing else than an unqualified and consistent exposition of the *Via Affirmativa*. It is, consequently, through and through a positive theology, founded upon a theory of univocal knowledge.

It may be remarked that Channing's position would appear to possess a peculiar advantage when we come to consider the arguments for the existence of God. To these I have not hitherto adverted, for the reason that he nowhere enters upon a detailed examination of them. His reference to "that fundamental law of the intellect through which we demand a cause proportioned to effects" [72] suggests that he accepted the causal argument, probably in its Lockian form. Yet, as presented by Channing, this argument is habitually fused with the argument from design, which is itself an argument from a special kind of effects to a special kind of cause. Upon this type or argumentation, Channing tells us, "all religion rests;" [73] hence it is evident that, unlike the Calvinist, he attached great importance to it.

The Thomist also appeals to the principle of causality when he would demonstrate the existence of God.[74] Yet his theory of analogy places him under a serious disadvantage, since, if no predicate can be attributed univocally to creature and Creator, we cannot say that God is a cause in the same sense in which anything else is a cause. Hence the cogency of the argument appears to be in danger of seeping away through the ambiguity of its middle term. The Thomists, indeed, contest the justice of this criticism,[75] and unblushingly maintain that the analogical character of the middle term does not impugn the validity of a syllogism. Nevertheless the difficulty is a serious one,[76] for cause and effect are correlative terms, and, if we have no definite notion of what we mean by *cause* when the term is applied to God, it follows that we have an equally indefinite notion of what would constitute the divine effects.

All this is made very manifest by St. Thomas' treatment of the argument from design. He employs it, in the first place, to demonstrate the existence of God. But, inasmuch as he is committed to the negative theology, he is compelled to regard it as proving nothing with respect to the divine *nature* and as establishing only the divine *existence*. When, however, the negative theology has been developed to such a point that its potentialities have become exhausted, and—the principle of analogy having been introduced—we enter upon the affirmative way, it becomes necessary to show that God is possessed of intelligence; and here St. Thomas shamelessly resorts a second time to the argument from design.[77]

Clearly this is philosophical malpractice. If the argument hold good at all it proves the first time precisely what it proves the second time. If it prove anything, it proves the existence of God by showing that he is a cosmic intelligence; thus it yields at the same time knowledge both of his existence and of his essence. In no way, therefore, can this argument be made consistent with the principle of the *Via Negativa*. Channing himself brings out this point very clearly. "Let me ask," he writes, "what we mean when we say that we discern the marks of intelligence in the universe? We mean that we meet there the proofs of a mind like our own. We certainly discern proofs of no other; so that to deny this doctrine would be to deny the evidences of a God." [78] Precisely so. Whether the teleological argument be conclusive is a question upon which I shall not attempt to pronounce; but that it presupposes the theory of univocal knowledge is as evident as anything can well be.

Thus Channing's position is the very opposite of that of the anonymous author of *The Cloud of Unknowing*. Never did the *Via Negativa* receive a more eloquent endorsement than in the famous utterance of that nameless mystic, "By love may He be gotten and holden; but by thought never." [79] Can we love without knowing whom we love? Channing did not think so. Perhaps, however, we shall do well to recall Professor Pratt's antithesis [80] between the moral and the mystical interests, which he deems so fundamental in the religious life. The former, he tells us, leads to the concept of a finite, personal God; the latter to a pantheistic Absolute. In Channing and the author of *The Cloud of Unknowing* do we find two representatives of these contrasted and conflicting interests? And, if so, must we conclude that the word *love* does not mean to one what it means to the other?

Whatever be our answer to the last question, it is clear that Channing's love for God is an emotion which can be felt only for a person. But it is for a Person whom, rightly or wrongly, Channing conceives of as infinite. Moreover it would certainly be unfair to term it a moral, as distinct from a mystical urge; for it is both. If by mysticism we mean what Dr. Rufus Jones means, namely, "immediate awareness of relation with God," "direct and intimate consciousness of the Divine Presence," "religion in its most acute, intense, and living stage," [81] then there is no doubt that we must class Channing as a mystic. A personalistic mysticism, if I may so phrase it, was his native air; hence for him the vital connection between thought and emotion, between conceiving of God and loving him.

We are now in a position to appreciate, as before we had done justice to the positive and affirmative character of his thinking we should not have been in a position to appreciate, the real ground for Channing's whole-souled detestation of the doctrine of the Trinity. This doctrine negates all that he deems most precious. By disrupting the personality of God, it at once renders him unintelligible, and strikes at the very root our love for him. As Channing indignantly declares: "One God, consisting of three equal persons or agents, is so strange a being, so unlike our own minds, and all others with whom we hold intercourse,—is so misty, so incongruous, so contradictory, that He cannot be apprehended with that distinctness and that feeling of reality which belong to the opposite system. Such a heterogeneous being, who is at the same moment one and many; who includes in his own nature the relations of Father and Son, or, in other words, is Father and Son to himself; who, in one of his persons, is at the same moment the Supreme God and a mortal man, omniscient and ignorant, almighty and impotent; such a being is certainly the most puzzling and distracting object ever presented to human thought. . . . To commune with such a being must be as hard as to converse with a man of three different countenances, speaking with three different tongues. The believer in this system must forget it when he prays, or he could find no repose in devotion." [82] "He whose mind is thoroughly and practically possessed by this system, can hardly conceive the effulgence of glory in which the one God offers himself to a pious believer in his strict unity." [83]

It is all very well for Trinitarian theologians to assure us—as they sometimes do—that Father, Son, and Holy Spirit are not to be conceived as persons in the sense in which we are persons, but the logic of the situation is too strong for them. No other interpretation can avail to make sense of what they tell us, for the relations of these three entities to one another are emphatically personal relations.[84] While the Father and the Holy Spirit remain discarnate, the Son becomes incarnate and is identified with an actual historic personality. The Father sends, and the Son is sent, and himself again sends the Spirit. The Son is obedient to the Father, and offers himself to allay his wrath, and the Father is appeased by the offering. "When we attempt to conceive of three Gods," says Channing, "we can do nothing more than represent to ourselves three agents, distinguished from each other by similar marks and peculiarities to those which separate the persons of the Trinity." [85]

The practical effect of this doctrine seems to Channing deplorable. Instead of concentrating our devotion, it disperses it among the three Persons who are equally entitled to share it.[86] The significance of this objection is profound. It is Channing the mystic, even more than Channing the rationalist, who revolts against the doctrine of the Trinity. It is not a fondness for dry and arid negation which leads him to dissent; he is impelled to do so by the whole force of his being, and in behalf of the mighty affirmation of the divine unipersonality which he takes to be the very quintessence of the Christian gospel. Moreover it is evident that the theory of univocal knowledge leaves us no choice between Unitarianism and tritheism, for, if personality be ascribed to God and man in a sense "essentially the same," three divine Persons must constitute three gods.

The most exalted of God's characteristics is his moral perfection. Upon this too great emphasis cannot be laid. Unfortunately, however, most Christians have tended to think of God "as if He were raised, by his greatness and sovereignty, above the principles of morality, above those eternal laws of equity and rectitude to which all other beings are subjected." [87] This, to Channing's mind, is a disastrous error; whence it is of the highest importance to maintain the contrary. "We believe," states Channing, "that his almighty power is entirely submitted to his perceptions of rectitude; and this is the ground of our piety. It is not because He is our Creator merely, but because He created us for good and holy purposes; it is not because his will is irresistible, but because his will is the perfection of virtue, that we pay him allegiance. We cannot bow before a being, however great and powerful, who governs tyrannically. We respect nothing but excellence, whether on earth or in heaven. We venerate not the loftiness of God's throne, but the equity and goodness in which it is established." [88]

This is bold and manly language, which would no doubt have shocked St. Paul to the core of his being, and which is as refreshing as it was novel at the time when these words were spoken. One cannot refrain from asking, however, precisely what are its implications. Are God's perceptions of rectitude directed upon something external to himself, upon a Platonic Idea of the Good which serves him as a standard? Such would seem to be the obvious inference.[89] But it is an inference which Channing himself does not explicitly draw; and which, therefore, one hesitates to attribute to him. Are we, then, to locate the standard within the divine reason? This is one of the fundamental problems which confront the theist, and it is one which Channing nowhere attempts to solve for us.

None the less he insists that the love of God is identical with the love of virtue.[90] Since God and man are alike persons, and possess attributes in common, their likeness of nature constitutes a ground of union. They are, indeed, related as the infinite to the finite, yet it is the very infinity of God which brings him near to man,[91] and renders the union of creature and Creator superior to "all other bonds in strength and intimacy."[92] "The connection of all other beings with us, when compared with this," announces Channing, "is foreign and remote. The nearest friend, the most loving parent, is but a stranger to us, when contrasted with God."[93] And "this living fellowship with the Father," he assures us, is "the one end of existence."[94]

As in Calvinism the sovereignty of God is the dominant idea, so, in the theology of Channing, the fatherhood of God is the central and controlling thought. It is one to which he is never tired of returning. And, as fatherhood and sonship are correlative terms, so the assertion of the fatherhood of God proclaims the divine sonship of man. The critic who exclaims that Channing has given us too human a God would do well, before he condemns, to inquire what Channing thinks of humanity. And it is to this question that we must next direct our attention.

## NOTES

1. *Works*, pp. 246-247.
2. *Life*, p. 427.
3. *Life*, p. 427.
4. *Ibid.*, p. 435.
5. *Works*, p. 385.
6. *Life*, p. 32.
7. *Ibid.*, p. 33.
8. *Ibid.*, p. 74.
9. *Ibid.*, p. 75.
10. *Ibid.*, p. 698.
11. *Works*, p. 371.
12. The passage in question reads as follows: "It is a great excellence of the doctrine of God's unity, that it offers to us ONE OBJECT of supreme homage, adoration, and love, . . . one original and fountain, to whom we may refer all

good, in whom all our powers and affections may be concentrated, and whose lovely and venerable nature may pervade all our thoughts. True piety, when directed to an undivided Deity, has a chasteness, a singleness, most favorable to religious awe and love." *Ibid.,* p. 372.

13. *Ibid.,* p. 387.
14. *Ibid.,* p. 400.
15. *Ibid.,* pp. 389-390.
16. "Of what avail would be the notion of an Absolute, Infinite existence, an Uncaused Unity, if stripped of all those intellectual and moral attributes which we learn only from our own souls? What but a vague shadow, a sounding name, is the metaphysical Deity, the substance without modes, the being without properties, the naked unity, which performs such a part in some of our philosophical systems? The only God whom our thoughts can rest on, and our hearts can cling to, and our consciences can recognize, is the God whose image dwells in our own souls. The grand ideas of Power, Reason, Wisdom, Love, Rectitude, Holiness, Blessedness, that is, of all God's attributes, come from within, from the action of our own spiritual nature." (*Ibid.,* pp. 6-7.)
17. In the case of mathematical proportions univocal relations are to be found. Thus the relation of 2 to 4 is the same as that of 50 to 100. But, where we have to deal with various modes or levels of being, the relations—so the scholastics inform us—will not be univocal, but only similar. See the Abbé M. T.-L. Penido's *Le rôle de l'analogie en théologie dogmatique,* pp. 24-25.
18. The situation is further complicated by the fact that, if the divine essence be utterly simple, there can be no real distinction between God and his intelligence, so that there can be no relation *in re* but merely a "relation of reason."
19. For a detailed discussion of the whole subject, and a spirited defence of the analogy of proportion see Abbé Penido's *Le rôle de l'analogie.* For an elaborate vindication of the analogy of attribution see Father Pedro Descoqs' *Institutiones Metaphysicae Generalis,* t. I. cc. III-IV; also his *Praelectiones Theologiae Naturalis,* t. II. Pars. Secunda.
20. See M. Auguste Lecerf's *Introduction à la Dogmatique Réformée,* t. I. pp. 189, 222-225. M. Lecerf clearly favors the analogy of proportion; see p. 223.
21. *Works,* p. 274.
22. *Ibid.,* p. 291.
23. *Loc. cit.*
24. *Cf.* Boehme's admonition, "Son, when thou are quiet and silent, then art thou as God was before nature and creature; thou art that which God then was; thou art that whereof he made nature and creature: Then thou hearest and seest even with that wherewith God himself saw and heard in thee, before ever thine own willing or thine own seeing began." *Of the Supersensual Life,* Dialogue I.
25. *Ibid.,* p. 292.
26. *Loc. cit.*
27. *Loc. cit., cf.* pp. 461-462.
28. *Ibid.,* p. 463.
29. *Ibid.,* p. 463.
30. *Loc. cit.*

31. *Loc. cit.*
32. *Ibid.,* p. 404.
33. *Ibid.,* pp. 292-293.
34. Italics mine.
35. *Ibid.,* p. 464.
36. *Cf.* "Whence come my conceptions of the intelligence, and justice, and goodness, and power of God? It is because my own spirit contains the germs of these attributes." *Ibid.,* p. 47.
37. *Ibid.,* p. 293.
38. *Loc. cit.*
39. *Loc. cit.*
40. *Loc. cit.*
41. *Ibid.,* p. 294.
42. This also explains the suspicion excited by the philosophies of such neo-Thomists as M. Blondel and Fathers Rousselot, De Broglie, and Maréchal.
43. *Ibid.,* p. 294.
44. *Ibid.,* p. 464. See Isaiah 5:3-4.
45. *Ibid.,* pp. 464-465.
46. *Ibid.,* p. 296.
47. *Loc. cit.*
48. *Ibid.,* p. 297. col. 1.
49. *Ibid.,* p. 465.
50. *Ibid.,* p. 465. col. 2; p. 466. col. 1.
51. *Ibid.,* p. 466. col. 1.
52. *Loc. cit.*
53. *Ibid.,* p. 466. col. 2.
54. *Ibid.,* pp. 294-295; *cf.* p. 511. col. 2.
55. Omnis comparatio est in aliqualiter univoco; quando enim dicitur *hoc est perfectius illo,* si quaeretur in *quo* est quid perfectius, oportet ibi assignare aliquid *commune* utrique; ita quod omnis comparationis determinabile commune est utrique extremo comparationis; non enim homo est perfectior *homo* quam asinus, sed perfectius *animal. Opus Oxoniense,* Lib. I. Dist. VIII. q. III. a. 1.
56. *Ibid.,* Lib. I. Dist. III. qq. I et II. a. 4.
57. "Stante igitur omnimoda diversitate Dei et creaturae in *realitate a parte rei,* conveniunt *univoce* in conceptibus *inadequatis* et *imperfectis. Sum. Theol.* Lib. I. q. IV. a. III. p. 129.
58. *History of Mediaeval Philosophy* (3rd English ed.), vol. II. p. 305.
59. Professor S. Belmond's book *Etudes sur la Philosophie de Duns Scot. I. Dieu. Existence et Cognocibilité,* contains a detailed defence of this view.
60. Deus et creaturs non sunt *primo diversa* in *conceptibus;* tamen sunt primo diversa in *realitate,* quia in nulla realitate conveniunt. *Ibid.,* Lib. I. Dist. VIII. q. III. a. I.
61. *The Spirit of Mediaeval Philosophy,* p. 264.
62. See his *Cursus Philosophicus,* t. II. Pars. II. lib. III. cap. III.
63. *Sum. Theol.* Lib. I. q. IV. a. III. ad3.
64. Etsi duae albedines in nullo a parte rei conveniunt. *Loc. cit.*

55. *Dieu, son existence et sa nature,* p. 543. n. I.; Dom Bede Rose's tr., vol. II. p. 210. n. 10.

56. See Van de Woestyne's *Cursus Philosophicus,* t. II. Lib. III. pp. 189. n. 7., 204. n. 2.; *cf.* Gilson's article, *Avicenne et le point de départ de Duns Scot, Archives d'Histoire Doctrinale et Littéraire du Moyen Age,* t. II. pp. 110-111.

57. It might, perhaps, be contended in opposition to this interpretation of his teaching that what Channing objects to is, not the theory of analogous predication, but the view of Maimonides and Spinoza that only equivocal predication with respect to God and man is possible. Undoubtedly Channing was opposed to this view, and possibly it is to it that he refers when he speaks of " 'philosophers falsely so-called' who have argued, from the unlimited nature of God, that we cannot ascribe to him justice and other moral attributes in any proper or definite sense of these words." With these he associates the "mistaken Christian" who teaches something "not very different"—is this the theory of analogy?—and "shrouds the Creator in utter darkness" (*Works,* p. 464). Again, he takes cognizance of the assertion "that God's infinity places him beyond the resemblance and approach of man" (*Ibid.,* p. 294). This seems, however, intended to be a restatement of an objection formulated in the preceding paragraph "that these various attributes of which I have spoken exist in God in infinite perfection, and that this destroys all affinity between the human and the divine mind." This statement appears to involve some confusion of thought, for, if there be no "affinity between the human and the divine mind," we cannot know of any attributes which exist in the Deity "in infinite perfection," and, if we do know of any, analogous predication at least must be possible.

There are, however, two observations to be made. In the first place, Channing's repeated assertion that predicates can be ascribed to God and man "in the same sense" can be nothing else than an affirmation of the possibility of univocal knowledge, for this is what univocal knowledge is. And, in the second place, we should realize that what Channing is trying to do is to demolish the claims of orthodoxy—especially those of Calvinism. Now both Calvinism and Romanism agree in rejecting the view that only equivocal predication with respect to God and man is possible, and in accepting the theory of analogy. Hence Channing's criticism would have been pointless, had he also accepted the same theory. And it is this theory which he seems clearly to envisage when he speaks of the divine attributes as "stretched to infinity" (*Ibid.,* p. 467), and of divine faithfulness, goodness, and justice as—in the view of his opponents—"transcending our poor understandings." One must not attribute to Channing too great a knowledge of scholastic thought, but it seems evident that he thoroughly grasped the basic issues; and his main point, if I understand him aright, is that, if univocal predication be illegitimate, analogous predication will prove a broken reed, and we shall be left with nothing better than equivocacy.

68. *Opus Oxoniense,* Lib. I. Dist. VIII. q. III. a. 1.

69. Quia de Deo scire non possumus quid sit, sed quid non sit: non possumus considerare de Deo quomodo sit, sed potius quomodo non sit. *Sum. Theol.* Lib. I. q. III.

70. *Ibid.,* pp. 466-467.

71. *Ibid.*, p. 467.
72. *Ibid.*, p. 390.
73. *Ibid.*, p. 464. col. 2.; *cf.* pp. 932-933.
74. The first, second, third, and fifth of Aquinas' classic proofs are all dependent upon this principle. The causal character of the fourth proof has been contested. In my *Conception of God in the Philosophy of St. Thomas Aquinas* (pp. 81-90) I have argued in the affirmative.
75. See Garrigou-Lagrange's *Dieu, son existence et sa nature*, pp. 569. n. I. and 572. n. 2.; Rose's tr., vol. II. pp. 247. n. 49. and 250. n. 53.
76. For a discussion of the problem involved see Miss Dorothy M. Emmet's paper on *The Use of Analogy in Metaphysics, Proceedings of the Aristotelian Society*, New Series, vol. XVI. 1921.
77. See the *Contra Gentes*, Lib. I. cap. XLIV.; *cf.* the *Commentary on Peter Lombard's Sentences*, Lib. I. Dist. XXXV. q. I. a. 1 sol.
78. *Ibid.*, p. 294. col. 2.
79. Ch. 6.
80. See his presidential address to the American Theological Association entitled *God and the Moral Law, Harvard Theological Review*, July, 1936.
81. *Studies in Mystical Religion*, p. XV.
82. *Ibid.*, p. 390. col. 1.
83. *Ibid.*, p. 391. col. 1.
84. *Ibid.*, pp. 371, 387. col. 2.
85. *Ibid.*, p. 371. col. 2.
86. *Ibid.*, pp. 372. col. 2. and 387. col. 2.—388. col. 1.
87. *Ibid.*, p. 376. col. 1.
88. *Ibid.*, p. 376.
89. It is an inference which appears to be confirmed by Ezra Styles Gannett's criticism. See William C. Gannett's *Ezra Styles Gannett*, p. 217.
90. *Ibid.*, p. 572. col. 1.
91. *Ibid.*, p. 511. col. 2.
92. *Ibid.*, p. 295. col. 2.
93. *Ibid.*, p. 957. col. 2.
94. *Ibid.*, p. 974. col. 2.

# Chapter Four

# Man

We turn now to the second of the two poles of Channing's thought —namely, man. Not for a moment, however, must we forget the vital connection which subsists between them. As it is impossible, according to Channing, to think of God aright except in terms of man, so the converse holds good, that it is impossible to think of man aright except in terms of God. So much the doctrine of *essential sameness* has made clear. As God is man in the large, so is man, as it were, God in the little. He is a form of divinity. This is a thought which one encounters again and again, expressed in varied phraseology, in Channing's writings. But we must be careful not to read into it the pantheistic implications attributed to it by certain varieties of Transcendentalism. The finite consciousness is not included within the absolute mind, nor is it destined to final absorption into the divine essence. Such a view is wholly incompatible with Channing's robust personalism. Man is definitely a creature, and a creature he will forever remain. Moreover he is a creature capable, not only of progress, but also of retrogression. In language of the deepest feeling Channing warns his auditors against the "folly" of "thinking lightly of sin." [1] To be conquered by it is the worst evil that can befall one, an evil so horrible that it may, indeed, culminate in irretrievable ruin.[2]

This sombre possibility however, is but the inevitable consequence of man's capacity for spiritual progress, a progress to which no limits can be set. It is an advance which can continue without end.[3] The limitless capacities of the human spirit constitute the "impress" of God's infinity.[4] "The soul," Channing insists, "viewed in these lights, should fill us with awe. It is an immortal germ, which may be said to contain now within itself what endless ages are to unfold. It is truly an image of the infinity of God, and no words can do justice to its grandeur." [5]

Thus to stress the greatness and worth of human nature is, Channing recognizes, to lay oneself open to the charge of propagating a doctrine which is apt to impress the hearer as strange and heterodox. As a matter of fact he is sounding a chord which has perpetually vibrated throughout the history of Christian thought, but only to produce perpetual discord. Frequently the teachings of the mystics, and occasionally even the utterances of orthodox theologians, strike the same note. Nevertheless Channing is quite right in asserting that the characteristic tendency of the theological mind has been "to establish striking contrasts between man and God, and not to see and rejoice in the likeness between them." [6] This we have found abundantly illustrated in the theory of the *analogia entis*. It is, Channing thinks, a natural tendency. The habitual contemplation of the infinity and power of the Deity has led men to prostrate themselves in abject, and even slavish adoration. But, though a natural tendency, it is an unfortunate one and has resulted in the serious error of underestimating the potentialities of man and of acquiescing in his present imperfections. The pressing task of theology, he maintains, is to reconcile the finite and the infinite, man's free will and the boundlessness of divine power, human rights and God's sovereignty. [7]

To accomplish this, Channing concedes, is "no very easy work. "But," he urges, "it must be done. Man's free activity is as important to religion as God's infinity. In the Kingdom of Heaven, the moral power of the subject is as essential as the omnipotence of the sovereign. The rights of both have the same sacredness. To rob man of his dignity is as truly to subvert religion as to strip God of his perfection. We must believe in man's agency as truly as in the Divine, in his freedom as truly as in his dependence, in his individual being as truly as in the great doctrine of living in God. Just as far as the desire of exalting the Divinity obscures these conceptions, our religion is sublimated into mysticism or degraded into servility." [8]

In the Orient, Channing believes, a monistic philosophy which denies the reality of the individual soul has been the seed of political despotism. [9] It is interesting that he should reason so, for the opposite point of view has also been maintained, namely, that the rise of absolute monarchy profoundly influenced the conception of God. This is, it would seem, an instance in which Sir Roger de Coverley's verdict, that "there is much to be said on both sides," assent to which by a philosopher so often proves ruinous to clear and cogent thinking, may well be admitted, inasmuch as the mutual influence of political and religious ideas is a psychological probability.

In the case of the Greeks and Romans, Channing continues, their extremely anthropomorphic polytheism was unfavorable to religious reverence; yet, on the other hand, their assertion of individual independence and responsibility was highly beneficial.[10] Turning next to the Christian Church, he observes that among Roman Catholics the mystical impulse has perpetually manifested itself; and its effect, he believes, has been the encouragement of a point of view approximating that of the Oriental pantheists. Fenelon's quietism, he observes, amounted to a "disease." [11] The Quakers, too, in their effort to bring the soul into a state of concentrated attention in which it could hear the voice of God,[12] have tended in the same direction. Lastly, Calvinism, with its denial of free will, has also trodden this well-worn path.

The Calvinist, Channing recognizes, does not intentionally associate himself with the pantheist. On the contrary, he explicitly affirms the distinction between the divine and the human consciousness; yet, by his refusal to concede genuine efficacy to human will, he has landed himself in a position which is to all intents and purposes identical with the pantheist's.[13] The motive which has stimulated this unfortunate development has been the Calvinist's loyalty to his fundamental principle, *Soli Deo Gloria*. In itself this loyalty is highly commendable. Where the Calvinist has gone astray has been in his identification of God's glory with unlimited and arbitrary power. He has failed to see that in the creation of free, morally responsible agents, capable of voluntary obedience and of genuine progress toward perfection, consists the true glory of God.[14] The fear that, by acknowledging the freedom of the creature, one minimizes or denies his dependence upon God is groundless. "On the contrary, the greater the creature, the more extensive is his dependence; the more he has to give thanks for, the more he owes to the free gift of his Creator." [15]

Moreover the notion that absolute dependence is the root of religion and the basic doctrine of Christianity is erroneous. The fundamental question, Channing contends, is, What kind of universe did God create, and for what purpose did he create it? [16] To answer this question we must approach it from the side of creation. To begin with the idea of an Absolute and Indefinite Being is to go about it the wrong way. "What but a vague shadow, a sounding name, is the metaphysical Deity, the substance without modes, the being without properties, the naked unity, which performs such a part in some of our philosophical systems? The only God whom our thoughts can rest on, and our hearts can cling to, and our consciences can recognize, is the God whose image dwells in our own souls. The grand ideas of Power, Reason, Wisdom, Love, Rectitude, Holiness, Blessedness, that is, of all God's attributes come from within, from the action of our spiritual nature. Many indeed think they learn God from the works of design and skill in the outward world; but our ideas of design and skill, of a determining cause, of an end or purpose, are derived from consciousness, from our own souls. Thus the soul is the spring of the knowledge of God." [17]

Here again, we have the re-assertion of the doctrine of *essential sameness* of divine and human attributes so fundamental in Channing's thought. The idea of God which he so emphatically repudiates is that of scholastic philosophy; and this repudiation carries with it that of the *analogia entis* by the aid of which the idea in question is developed. It is because God is in reality a being like man, a person in the full sense of the word, that we can revere his character, discern, admire and approve his purposes, and endeavor to cooperate with those purposes.

We must not suppose, however, because Channing affirms with such vehemence and conviction the freedom of the human will, that he feels that no difficulties are involved in the assertion, or believes that he himself has said the last word upon the problem which it raises. On the contrary, we find him, in his essay upon Milton, clamoring for more light.[18] What he is concerned to insist upon is that the consciousness of free choice and of moral responsibility is not something which can be explained away, but a hard, indubitable fact which must be recognized, and the implications of which must be examined by and incorporated within, any philosophy which professes to offer a coherent and integrated world view.

From what has been said it is clear that the status of man in the universe is a relatively exalted one. For Channing, as for the Psalmist, he is "a little lower than the angels." And from this follow conclusions of the greatest import, not only in the spheres of religion and ethics, but also in those of politics and the social sciences. For it is precisely because man is a creature of divine origin and potentialities that each individual of the species can make upon his fellows claims of the most sacred character. "The spiritual principle in man," says Channing, "is what entitles him to our brotherly regard." [19] What he is justified in expecting of us above all else is interest in him as an intellectual, moral, and religious being. Upon this point Channing is most explicit and emphatic, and his emphasis merits our attention; for nowhere do we find him at a farther remove from those twentieth century "humanists" who invoke the *aegis* of his memory with an enthusiasm equal to that wherewith they repudiate his basic teachings.

The issue comes out clearly in Channing's lecture *On the Elevation of the Laboring Classes* when he tells us wherein the desired elevation consists. "It is not an outward change of condition. It is not release from labor. It is not struggling for another rank. It is not political power. I understand something deeper. I know but one elevation of a human being, and that is elevation of soul. Without this it matters nothing where a man stands or what he possesses; and with it, he towers, he is one of God's nobility, no matter what place he holds in the social scale. There is but one elevation for a laborer and for all other men. There are not different kinds of dignity for different orders of men, but one and the same to all." [20] Such elevation, he fully concedes, can be greatly assisted by the betterment of the external environment, and will itself in turn stimulate such a process of amelioration; nevertheless we find this devoted philanthropist asserting with regard to such material development that "supposing it to exist in separation from inward growth and life, it would be nothing worth, nor would I raise a finger to promote it." [21]

Moral worth, then, is the only source of human dignity, and the only ultimate end to be striven for. From this it does not follow that material goods are unimportant, but that they are instrumental, and that their importance is therefore secondary. Moral perfection, Channing tells us, is man's "only true and enduring good." [22] Were we to take these words in their literal sense, we should be forced to conclude that virtue is the only intrinsic value. Yet can they be so taken? The frequent references to what seem obviously to be other intrinsic values suggest that the phrase "moral perfection" is to be equated with the Good, that it is a general term intended to apply not only to virtue but also to these other intrinsic values.

Beauty, for instance, is the recipient of an enthusiastic homage; [23] and, although we are left in some uncertainty as to its precise relationship to the Good, there can be no question that it is an intrinsic, and not an instrumental, value.[24] God himself is the All-Beautiful, and the beauty of the created universe is a revelation of him.

Truth, again, is accorded an almost unbounded reverence. It is "the light of the Infinite Mind, and the image of God in his creatures. Nothing endures but truth. . . . The love of truth, a deep thirst for it, a deliberate purpose to seek it and hold it fast, may be considered as the very foundation of human culture and dignity." [25] Was not moral worth, we may ask, allotted this high place? There is no inconsistency here, Channing would reply, for the general tendency to distinguish between intellect and conscience, thought and virtue, is, he holds, a mistaken one. The ego cannot be thus divided into separate faculties. "We mutilate our nature," he asserts with an earnestness which would enlist the sympathy of a twentieth-century psychologist, "by thus drawing lines between actions or energies of the soul, which are intimately, indissolubly, bound together. The head and the heart are not more vitally connected than thought and virtue. Does not conscience include, as a part of itself, the noblest action of intellect or reason? Do we not degrade it by making it a mere feeling? Is it not something more? Is it not a wise discernment of the right, the holy, the good? Take away thought from virtue, and what remains worthy of a man? Is not high virtue more than blind instinct? Is it not founded on, and does it not include clear, bright perceptions of what is lovely and grand in character and action?" [26] By denying the rational character of moral judgment, he insists, we should deliver conscience over to become the prey of fanaticism and delusion.

The reason is thus, in Channing's view, capable not only of logical ratiocination, but also of direct apprehension of values. His ethics, therefore, will clearly be of an intuitionist cast. And, when we come to examine more closely his conception of the nature of religious experience, we shall find intuitive awareness present there also.

In his possession of reason, we may repeat, lies man's true greatness, and the development of his intellectual capacity is his first duty.[27] But while all knowledge is good, Channing insists in language reminiscent of St. Augustine, of Calvin, and of Descartes, that what is of greatest import to man is the knowledge of himself and of his relation to God.[28]

The emotions of benevolence, love, reverence,[29] too are good; but what is true of reason is true of emotion also, that it finds its highest object and its chief end in God.[30] And, last of all, happiness is a value, which in the most exalted form accompanies the attainment of the other intrinsic values, and which reaches its highest degree of intensity in the experience of fellowship with the Divine.[31]

The "supreme good" and the "chief end" of man, Channing tells us, "is to bring out, cultivate, and perfect our highest powers, to become wise, holy, disinterested, noble beings, to unite ourselves to God by love and adoration, and to revere his image in his children." [32] It is evident, therefore, that his ethical position is practically identical with that of the school which today we term eudaemonist, or perfectionist.[33] And this fact must be kept in mind as we approach his formulation of the doctrine of natural rights which occupies so important a place in his philosophy of politics. For such a philosophy Channing does give us, at least in outline, and his theory of natural rights has been thought out with unusual thoroughness as a consequence of his preoccupation with the issue of slavery.

It is a commonplace in the world of political thinking to say that the doctrine of natural rights may be defended in either of two ways, (a) by attributing these rights, as did our Founding Fathers, to the beneficence of the Creator, or (b) by showing that they are essential pre-requirements to the attainment of the *summum bonum*. They may thus be referred either to man's origin or to his end. Channing is in the fortunate position of being able simultaneously to adopt both courses. He is, indeed, logically compelled to do so, since for him the two theories mutually imply one another. Natural rights are "the gifts of God," [34] but they are bestowed in order that they may be exercised, and that through the exercise of them man may advance toward moral perfection and toward union with his Creator. Inasmuch as they proceed from God they are, of course, dependent upon the divine volition; yet that volition, as we have seen, is never arbitrary; it invariably accords with a moral standard, and, in the present instance, it is called forth by a recognition of human capacities,[35] which are themselves due to the divine creativity.

Scholastic philosophers tell us that, although it is legitimate for us to speak of *creation*, if we contemplate the world-process as having a beginning, and equally legitimate to speak of *conservation*, if we envisage the same process as continuing; yet the terms *creation* and *conservation* do not refer to two distinct acts on the part of God, but to two different aspects of the same act. In somewhat analogous fashion, in the case of the theory before us, we may regard natural rights as imparted to man by his Creator or as implicated in his capacity to attain to God, the *summum bonum;* yet it is the same God who is at once Creator and *summum bonum,* origin and end. Any attempt, therefore, to isolate origin from end will inevitably result in a mutilation of the entire theory. If man had not the ability to attain to the knowledge of God and to enjoy fellowship with him, he would not have the rights which he has; but, if he had not the rights which he has, he would not be the creature that he is. He was created such as he is that he might become what he is capable of becoming. To make Channing's notion of natural rights intelligible we must recognize the identity of man's origin and his end.

Such being the case, it is inevitable that we should ask, Does Channing's doctrine of natural rights presuppose the immortality of the soul? The question is even more important than it appears at first sight because of the intimate relation which, in Channing's view, subsists between rights and duties. "The sense of duty," Channing declares, "is the fountain of human rights. In other words, the same inward principle which teaches the former bears witness to the latter. Duties and rights must stand or fall together. It has been too common to oppose them to one another; but they are indissolubly bound together. That same inward principle which teaches a man what he is bound to do to others, teaches equally, and at the same instant, what others are bound to do to *him.* That same voice which forbids him to harm a single fellow-creature, forbids every fellow-creature to do *him* harm. His conscience, in revealing the moral law, does not reveal a law for himself only, but speaks as a universal legislator. He has an intuitive conviction that the obligations of this divine code press on others as truly as on himself. That principle which teaches him that he sustains the relation of brotherhood to all human beings, teaches him that this relation is reciprocal, that it gives indestructible claims, as well as imposes solemn duties, and that what he owes to the numbers of this vast family, they owe to him in return. Thus the word nature involves rights." [36]

From this interdependence of rights and duties it would seem to follow that, if the former presuppose the doctrine of the immortality of the soul, so do the latter. Such an admission is only what we should expect in the case of a disciple of Locke. That philosopher, be it recalled, insisted that the belief in future rewards and punishments is the only secure basis of morality. From the point of view of the modern "liberal" thinker who is prepared to champion the claims of religion such a position is unsatisfactory, not merely because of its frankly hedonistic appeal, but also because it precludes any attempt to found an argument for immortality, in Kantian fashion, upon the moral nature of man. For, clearly, we cannot simultaneously assert that man must be immortal because he is a moral being, and that man ought to be a moral being because he is immortal. Nevertheless the hedonistic outlook was an extremely common one in the eighteenth century; accordingly, it should be no cause for astonishment were we to discover that it was shared by Channing.

As a matter of fact, however, Channing does explicitly affirm as we have already noticed, that moral judgments based upon intuitive insight, are ultimate and self-evident. In so doing he is, of course, inconsistently enough supported by Locke. But we must not forget that he has recorded the profound impression made upon him by a thinker whose attitude in regard to this subject was very different from that of Locke, namely by Samuel Hopkins, whose doctrine of pure disinterestedness Channing found so intensely appealing.[37] Yet even Hopkins, despite his emphasis upon disinterestedness, regarded "happiness in the simple sense of enjoyment as the ultimate good, and made moral good the means." [38] But Channing himself is of another mind.

"An inward voice," he declares, "has told men, even in heathen countries, that excellence of character is the supreme good, and that baseness of soul and action involves something worse than suffering." "Is there anyone here," he inquires of his auditors, "who does not feel that what the divine faculty of conscience enjoins as right has stronger claims upon him than what is recommended as merely agreeable or advantageous; that duty is something more sacred than interest or pleasure; that virtue is a good of a higher order than gratification; that crime is something worse than outward loss? What means the admiration with which we follow the conscientious and disinterested man, and which grows strong in proportion to his sacrifices to duty? Is it not the testimony of our whole souls to the truth and greatness of the good he has chosen?" [39]

These words obviously voice a complete repudiation of ethical hedonism. Can we, then, at once conclude that there is no close connection between Channing's ethics and his belief in immortality? Were we to do so, we should be very much mistaken. For Channing immortality—which he, of course, regards as inextricably linked to theism—is a truth of the greatest practical importance for the moral life.

"Confidence in God," he writes, "alone gives the hope of reaching perfection. Hope inspires energy. But without trust in God I have no sufficient hope to excite and sustain persevering efforts after excellence. True, there are other aids of virtue besides religion,—the approbation and rebukes of conscience, the esteem and honor of fellow-beings, the present recompenses of uprightness and charity. But that watchful discipline over the inmost thoughts and motives, that aspiration after disinterestedness and inward purity, that scorn of suffering in the way of well-doing, that preference of the soul's health and progress to outward interests, that conflict with absorbing self-love,—all of which are so essential to eminence and permanence of rectitude,—come not from ourselves. They demand continual, fresh supplies of divine inspiration. So tremendous is the power of passion, so subtle is temptation, so contagious is the influence of example, that a man, conscious of no higher power than his own, and expecting no improvement but such as he can compass by his unaided will, might well despair of resisting the combined powers of evil. An infinite motive is needed to quicken us in this never-ending war with selfishness and the world. And where is such a motive to be found, if we believe in no everlasting friend of goodness, and in no future life where our present spiritual growth will be crowned with perfection.

Take away the prophetic hopes of religion, and my nature is full of discouraging contradictions. I see and approve the good, and resolve on amendment and progress. I have conceptions of excellence, which I burn to make real in character and deed. But the weight of mortality depresses the spirit to the dust; resistless currents are hurrying down my nature to indulgence; there is a tendency to excess in every passion and impulse; and sensuality and sloth perpetually thwart the upward efforts of the moral nature. Is there in the universe no power of good to overcome evil higher than I am conscious of in my own breast? How then can I ever realize that ideal of excellence which shines before me? Then can I attain at best but to a low virtue. When I consider, too,—as without religious faith I must,—that even this low virtue will soon pass from me, and that I have no power to preserve it beyond the grave, that every high aspiration, benevolent sympathy, and upright energy is to perish with the body, what motive remains sufficient to quicken me in becoming better. Hope is the gift of religion." [40]

Whether or not we be inclined to think that Channing has overstated his case,[41] we can scarcely deny that there is a case to be stated. If before each of us there stretches a limitless future, then, indeed, are we provided with "an infinite motive" to strive for our own and our fellows' moral improvement.[42] Were we to become convinced, on the other hand, that there is no life beyond the grave, our ethical judgments would no doubt remain very much what they were before in the sense that we should still judge the same actions to be right and the same actions to be wrong, but the motive which leads us to act in accordance with these judgments would be definitely weakened. The good would still be the good, but it would have become to a very great degree unrealizable. The noblest sacrifice could result only in transitory gains, no permanent benefit would ever accrue to anyone, and, with the extinction of life upon this planet, all would become as it had been before the first amoeba initiated the entire evolutionary process. Lord Russell, in recommending to his fellow-naturalists "a foundation of unyielding despair"[43] as the most satisfactory basis for a philosophy which, in his estimation, they are likely to find, has shown a profundity of insight rare indeed among thinkers of that school.

It may be urged, however, that in his emphasis upon future rewards and punishments, Channing has, after all, reverted to the position of Locke. "Religion," he insists, "has threatenings, and it *must* have them; for evil, misery, is necessarily and unchangeably bound up with wrongdoing, with the abuse of moral power,"[44] but the purpose of these threatenings, he adds, is to liberate us from the domination of the passions, and "to make us spiritually free."[45]

How are these statements to be interpreted? That the fear of the painful consequences of evil conduct causes many men to abstain from such conduct is a familiar fact. But it does not help us to answer the question, Is the good man one who acts for the sake of the pleasure which accompanies a right action, or is he one who acts in complete disregard of the accompanying pleasure solely because of the rightness of the act? Despite Channing's admiration for the Hopkinsian doctrine of disinterestedness we must not attribute to him a Kantian disregard of consequences. It seems evident, in other words, that it is the good rather than the right which is primary, and that the good includes, not only virtue, but pleasure. Pleasure, although an end, is not the sole end; virtue is not merely a means, but is likewise an end. The pleasure of which Channing so often and so emphatically speaks is intimately connected therewith; it is that delight in moral health and communion with the Divine which theologians term blessedness; and, conversely, the suffering which accompanies and follows wrong-doing is, in its intensest form remorse—that consciousness of moral degeneration which is the extreme of evil.

So much having been said, we now return to Channing's doctrine of natural rights. These, he tells us, are all comprised in, and may all be deduced from,[46] one "great fundamental right"—namely, "the right which belongs to every rational being, to exercise his powers for the promotion of his own and others' happiness and virtue." [47] The close connection of this right with a eudaemonist ethics is obvious.[48]

As to particular rights Channing observes that, "perhaps they do not admit very accurate definition any more than human duties; for the spiritual cannot be weighed and measured like the material." [49] This raises the question whether they may not vary with attending circumstances, whether, in other words, applications of general principles will not vary with differing environments. If the response be in the affirmative, then one of the great objections to the doctrine of natural rights—that it makes no allowance for cultural, intellectual, and moral dissimilarities, and for the changing states of social transformation and evolution—will have been answered in advance.

Before we attempt to reply to this question, however, let us see what the natural rights are. Of the particular rights which, he has told us, are deducible from the one, fundamental right Channing mentions eight, but it is clear that by so doing he does not intend to provide a complete enumeration, inasmuch as he concludes by observing that these are "a few of human rights," [50] thus by implication affirming that there are a great many more. The eight rights mentioned are the following:[51]

1. "Every man has a right to exercise and invigorate his intellect."

2. "Every man has a right to inquire into his duty, and to conform himself to what he learns of it."

3. "Every man has a right to use the means given by God and sanctioned by virtue for bettering his condition."

4. Every man "has a right to be respected according to his moral worth."

5. Every man "has a right to be regarded as a member of the community to which he belongs, and to be protected by impartial laws."

6. Every man has "a right to be exempted from coercion, stripes, and punishment, as long as he respects the rights of others."

7. Every man "has a right to an equivalent for his labor."

8. Every man "has a right to sustain domestic relations, to discharge their duties, and to enjoy the happiness which flows from fidelity to these and other domestic relations." [52]

The derivation of all specific rights from one fundamental right rooted in the nature of man as a moral being capable of limitless progress is obviously a great improvement upon the theory of natural rights as previously expounded, even if we regard it as only the making explicit of what earlier theorists had implicitly assumed. Although Channing assures us that these particular rights are "comprised in," and "may easily be deduced" from, the one fundamental right, no formal deduction of the particular rights is attempted. Perhaps we should do no violence to his thought were we to assume that he regarded it as self-evident that particular rights are only abstractions from the concrete fundamental right, or—to put the same point in another way—as applications of the general principle in varying circumstances.

There is, however, a right not explicitly included in the foregoing enumeration—although it may plausibly be classified as a particular application of right number three—to which Channing nevertheless attaches great importance, namely, the right to property. "Property," he asserts, "is not an arbitrary thing, dependent wholly on man's will. It has its foundations and great laws in nature, and these cannot be violated without crime. It is plainly the intention of Providence that certain things should be owned,—should be held as property. They fulfill their end only by such appropriation. The material world was plainly made to be subjected to human labor, and its products to be moulded by skill to human use. He who wins them by honest toil has a right to them, and is wronged when others seize and consume them." [53] The vindication of this right, be it observed, seems to involve an appeal to the argument from design.

It is in recognition of this right that whatever a man rightfully owns in the state wherein he resides is accounted his when he travels into the territory of another state. It is true that the northern states do not acknowledge the slaveholder's right to his property in his slaves, and, if he bring them north, pronounce them free. But their justification for so doing rests upon reason's intuitive perception of the truth that man may not rightfully be owned anywhere, and that all laws permitting such ownership are iniquitous.[54]

The state, indeed, does take away a man's property in the form of taxation; yet it does so that it may provide security for what remains, and thus implicitly recognizes his right to it. He is entitled to demand that the state equalize, so far as it can, the burden of taxation, and that for whatever portion of his property it finds need to confiscate, it shall, if it can, make adequate compensation. It is, of course, possible that the right of property may under certain conditions come into conflict with other human rights, and it will then be the function of the state to adjudicate the matter. Then the state may, in case of genuine necessity, confiscate that for which it cannot provide compensation. It may alter the tenure of property, it may abolish entails and break up huge estates, and it may so legislate as to prevent the acquisition of property by any individual to such an extent that it may interfere with his fellow-citizens' ability to earn their living, or render him politically dangerous through the power which it confers. But, in so acting, it must not violate the basic principles of property, the preservation of which is one of the reasons for its existence.[55]

Is this emphasis upon the right to property indicative of the influence of Locke? The conjecture is a natural one, and it well nigh becomes transformed into a certainty when we observe how the right in question is rooted in that thoroughly Lockian notion[56]—the right to property in oneself. "If there be property in anything," declares Channing, "it is that of a man in his own person, mind, and strength. All other rights are weak, unmeaning, compared with this, and in denying this all right is denied." [57] This vigorous phraseology suggests that we are to take the present pronouncement as a re-statement of the "great fundamental right." "Whatever he (man) may be denied by man," writes Channing, "he holds, from nature the most valuable property, and that from which all other is derived,—I mean his strength. His labor is his own, by the gift of that God who nerved his arm, and gave him intelligence and conscience to direct the use of it to his own and others' happiness. No possession is so precious as a man's force of body and mind. The exertion of this in labor is the great foundation and source of property in outward things." [58]

Not only is this language reminiscent of the Lockian justification of private property by occupancy and use; it clearly reveals that the right to private property, like other particular rights, is merely an application of the basic principle that man is entitled "to exercise his powers for the promotion of his own and others' happiness and virtue." [59]

Inasmuch as human rights are rooted in the very nature of man, it is clear that, while government can and must recognize them, it is powerless to abolish them. It can only violate them. "They belong," asserts Channing, "as we have seen, to man as a moral being, and nothing can divest him of them but the destruction of his nature." [60] A contempt for the rights of the individual has been fostered, Channing believes, by the theory that man, upon his entrance into society, surrendered some of his natural rights. When the question is once raised as to how many of them he surrendered, it is easy to answer that he yielded all of them. What Channing makes reference to is, of course, the notions, so familiar to the thought of the eighteenth century, of a state of nature and a social compact.

In this connection it is important to observe that these same notions have since incurred a quite unjustified degree of obloquy as a result of the progress of human knowledge. Anthropologists assure us that the idea that men at some prehistoric time, lived in a state of isolated self-sufficiency, and that government originated in consequence of a voluntary and considered compact, is a baseless one; on the contrary, the transition from the herd to the tribe is represented as a process of undesigned and natural evolution. Nevertheless it is evident that the conceptions so loudly discredited are possessed of a philosophical significance independent of such considerations.

The state of nature, as Hobbes describes it, is nothing else than the low-water mark of social relationship, a condition wherein law is found to be inoperative, a state of anarchy or "unlaw," as our Anglo-Saxon ancestors termed it. Such, as he points out, is the relation in which all nations stand to each other.[61] Such, again, is the condition which recurs whenever organized government collapses, and the individual is thrown upon his own resources and becomes his own protector and avenger. And such, once more, is the state in which every man finds himself when he meets a robber, or when he locks his door at night.[62]

The "social compact" is likewise far from being a mere theorist's dream, for instances of the formation of such compacts by the mutual consent of contracting individuals who were beyond the control and protection of any existing government have actually taken place. The foundation of the state of Franklin by the Tennessean pioneers, and the formation of the early Boer republics, are cases in point. It seems probable that Channing, in common with so many other thinkers of his time, believed that all government had originated in similar fashion. But it is also clear that, whether he did so or not, his fundamental position with regard to national rights and to the relation of the individual to the state remains unaffected, depending, as it does, solely upon his metaphysical views, and in no sense upon the historicity of any alleged happening in the past. Regardless of how government may have originated, it is as much the concern of any individual today as it was of Socrates in the past, when, upon arriving at adulthood, he is about to assume the obligations and privileges of citizenship, to know in what relation he stands to the state and to consider whether it is such as to merit his approval as a moral being. Are the rights which he legally enjoys with respect to his fellow-citizens recognized by the state as holding good in relation to itself? Is he a free man, or a slave of his government? The relative worth of the individual and the state is the fundamental question, and Channing's answer to it is obviously dictated solely by his estimate of the status of man in the universe; in other words, it is a metaphysical and not an historical problem.

"We are sometimes taught," writes Channing, "that society is the creature of compact and selfish calculation; that men agree to live together for the protection of private interests. But no. Society is of earlier and higher origin. It is God's ordinance, and answers to what is most godlike in ourselves. The chief ties that hold men together in communities are not self-interests, or compacts, or positive institutions, or force. They are invisible, refined, spiritual ties, the bonds of mind and heart. Our best powers and affections crave instinctively for society as the sphere in which they are to find their life and happiness." [63]

"I consider the freedom or moral strength of the individual mind," writes Channing, "as the supreme good, and the highest end of government. I am aware that other views are often taken. It is said that government is intended for the public, for the community, not for the individual. The idea of a national interest prevails in the minds of statesmen, and to this it is thought that the individual may be sacrificed. But I would maintain, that the individual is not made for the state so much as the state for the individual. A man is not created for political relations as his highest end, but for indefinite spiritual progress, and is placed in political relations as the means of his progress. The human soul is greater, more sacred, than the state, and must never be sacrificed to it. The human soul is to outlive all earthly institutions. The distinction of nations is to pass away. Thrones, which have stood for ages, are to meet the doom pronounced upon all man's works. But the individual mind survives, and the obscurest subject, if true to God, will rise to a power never wielded by earthly potentates." [64]

From this what follows? "Nothing seems to me so needful," declares Channing, "as to give the mind the consciousness, which governments have done so much to suppress, of its own separate worth. Let the individual feel that, through his immortality, he may concentrate in his own being a greater good than that of nations. Let him feel that he is placed in the community, not to part with his individuality or to become a tool, but that he should find a sphere for his various powers, and a preparation for immortal glory. To me, the progress of society consists in nothing more than in bringing out the individual, in giving him a consciousness of his own being and in quickening him to strengthen and elevate his own mind." [65]

In saying all this, Channing insists, he has no intent to disparage the state. It provides a magnificent opportunity for mutual service. There is, he maintains, "a beautiful harmony between the good of the state and the moral freedom and dignity of the individual." [66] The best service the individual can render is to develop his own character through the performance of those duties upon the fulfillment of which his own rights depend. For the state he is bound, if need be, to sacrifice life, property, and happiness; but never can it require him to injure his own character or to commit an immoral act. [67]

What, then, of the contention that, by assenting to the social compact, a man waives some or all of his rights? The proper answer, returns Channing, in the spirit of Locke, is that he "adopts new modes of securing them." [68] Thus he submits to the rule of law that he may obtain justice, to taxation that he may safely enjoy the remainder of his property. The theory that "a man derives all his rights from the nation to which he belongs" is, Channing affirms, "a terrible doctrine" for "it makes man nothing in himself." Moreover "it is as false as it is terrible. Man is not the mere creature of the state. Man is older than nations, and he is to survive nations. There is a law of humanity more primitive and divine than the law of the land. He has higher claims than those of a citizen. He has rights which date before all charters and communities; not conventional, not repealable, but as eternal as the powers and laws of his being." [69]

May no eventualities, however, conceivably occur in which the suspension or abrogation of natural rights would be justified? Is it never permissible to proclaim martial law or to resort to the establishment of a dictatorship? Such a situation, Channing admits, may develop in a period of civil convulsion in which drastic measures of the type contemplated may be unavoidable. But their justification inheres in their transiency, in their character of being purely temporary expedients. "In these cases," observes Channing, "the great idea of rights predominates amidst their apparent subversion. A power above all laws is conferred, only that the empire of law may be restored. Despotic restraints are imposed, only that liberty may be rescued from ruin. All rights are involved in the safety of the state; [70] and hence, in the cases referred to, the safety of the state becomes the supreme law. The individual is bound for a time to forego his freedom, for the salvation of institutions without which liberty is but a name." [71] "If, in an emergency," he declares, "its (the state's) safety, which is the interest of each and all, may demand the imposition of peculiar restraints on one or many, it is bound to limit these restrictions to the precise point which its safety prescribes, to remove the necessity of them as far and as fast as possible, to compensate by peculiar protection such as it deprives of the ordinary means of protecting themselves, and, in general, to respect and provide for liberty in the very acts which for a time restrain it." [72]

In the same spirit Channing makes it plain that, in advocating the abolition of slavery, he does not contemplate the immediate removal of all restraints upon the slave. He is to be confined to the plantation on which he lives, and, if unwilling to work, he must be compelled to do so "on the same principles on which the vagrant in other communities is confined and compelled to earn his bread." [73] What are these principles? They appear to be two in number. In the first place there is the safety of the community. Not all its members are slaves and those who are not have a right to be protected from the abuse of newly given freedom on the part of those who are. In the second place, there is the well-being of the slave himself. He is ignorant of his duties and unwilling to perform them. Left to himself, he will pass from idleness to crime, he will become a social menace, and must eventually be dealt with as such, so that his last lot will be worse than his first.

Can these concessions be reconciled with Channing's theory? How do they bear upon our previous question as to whether rights, as general principles, must be modified by differences of environment and circumstance? Is his view sufficiently elastic? Or does he make it seem to be so only by a fundamental inconsistency?

Let us consider first the admission that the safety of the state may involve the temporary disregard of natural rights. It is important to realize that the emergency must be one of the first magnitude, so that the very existence of the state actually trembles in the balance. This is made abundantly evident by Channing's own attitude toward the declaration of war against Great Britain in 1812, an act of which, like many New Englanders, he highly disapproved. We find Channing reminding his congregation that the republican form of government secures to them "two most important rights—the right of suffrage, and the right of discussing with freedom the conduct of rulers." [74] Neither of these rights is mentioned in the enumeration of natural rights cited above. It is true that this enumeration does not profess to be complete; yet it is also true, as we shall see, that suffrage—at least universal suffrage—is elsewhere asserted by Channing not to be a natural right.[75] As for free discussion, it may possibly be taken to be directly implied by the great fundamental right, or perhaps to follow from particular rights, one, two, three, or five; yet none of these various possibilities is anywhere explicitly discussed. It is, nevertheless, a right which many persons today would assume might well be waived in time of national danger.

On the occasion in question, however, Channing informs his hearers that "the duty of maintaining" these two rights, and "of never surrendering them, cannot be too strongly urged. Resign either of these, and no way of escape from oppression will be left you but civil commotion." [76] "The cry has been that war is declared, and that all opposition should therefore be hushed. A sentiment more unworthy of a free country can hardly be propagated. If this doctrine be admitted, rulers have only to declare war and they are screened at once from scrutiny." [77] Without freedom of discussion, "the right of election is not worth possessing." [78] "In war, then, as in peace," he concludes, "assert the freedom of speech and of the press. Cling to this as the bulwark of all your rights and privileges." [79]

Is this spirited defence of the right of free speech in time of war inconsistent with Channing's later recognition that the temporary waiving of natural rights may be inevitable in times of crisis, and must we therefore, postulate a change of view on his part? It does not appear so. For the justification for the transient disregard of rights is that the exercise of them will imperil the survival of the state, and it can be nothing less than this. And it is evident that Channing felt that freedom of speech in time of war did not so imperil the state, and that its suppression would constitute a far greater danger.

In the world of today, where the powers of destruction have been so immensely enhanced, and where the military security essential to national preservation involves industrial development, abundance of labor, and facility of transportation, one may well inquire whether an "emergency" of the type which Channing contemplated has not become "chronic," and, consequently, whether the waiving of individual rights has not been transformed into a necessity equally "chronic." If Professor Toynbee be right, if "the time of troubles" in which we may become, or perhaps, have become involved can terminate only with the establishment of a "universal state," may not the formation of the state be accomplished only at the price of the sacrifice of the liberties of its subjects? Channing would undoubtedly reply, and Professor Toynbee would presumably agree with him, that the stability thus acquired cannot be permanent, and that the solution will possess only a transitory efficacy. Plato maintained, as Whitehead has reminded us, that persuasion, and not force, is alone genuinely productive. "Civilization," observes the latter philosopher, "is the maintenance of social order, by its own inherent persuasiveness as embodying the nobler alternative. The recourse to force, however inevitable, is a disclosure of the failure of civilization, either in the general society or in a remnant of individuals.[80] This, I think, is the sum and substance of Channing's contention, although it is highly improbable that in his wildest dreams he ever anticipated how severely his theory of natural rights would be put to the test.

In regard to the second concession with respect to the necessity of control over slave and vagrant, the most important principle involved is that of the mutual implication of rights and duties. Capacity and readiness to perform the latter are what entitle a man to the enjoyment of the former; ignorance and unwillingness disqualify him until they be removed. Is this admission only a shift to conceal the inevitable modification of natural rights as a consequence of environmental and cultural differences? I do not believe that it is, for the following reason. If one concede that rights may be modified by circumstances, how is one to determine which modifications are legitimate and which are not? And upon what principle is one to pronounce one state of society less admirable than another? If, on the contrary, one assert that the rights are always there, as the duties are always there, whether recognized or not, and are always the same, one is thereby justified in condemning any society where any element of the population is disqualified by ignorance or defect of character from claiming those rights, and in agitating for intellectual and moral improvement. And the principle of the mutual implication of rights and duties is, in its turn, sustained, as Channing points out, by the universality of the moral law, which decrees that what a man may rightfully claim from his neighbors they may with equal right demand from him in return.

Moreover, Channing insists, it is important to recognize "that sacrifices which may be demanded for the safety are not due from the individual to the prosperity of the state. The great end of society is to secure rights, not to accumulate wealth." [81] The notion of the general good has been interpreted in a materialistic sense; and to the general good as thus conceived it is urged that the rights of the individual must give way. Thus the notion of the general good plays in republics the same part as that played in monarchies by the doctrine of the divine right of kings. "It is a shelter for the abuses and usurpations of government, for the profligacies of statesmen, for the vices of parties, for the wrongs of slavery." [82] So to argue is to subordinate moral to material interest. Furthermore it is fatuous, for, "public prosperity, general good, regarded by itself, or apart from the moral law, is something vague, unsettled, and uncertain, and will infallibly be so construed by the selfish and grasping as to secure their own aggrandizement. It may be made to wear a thousand forms, according to men's interests and passions. . . . The best concerted schemes of policy often fail; whilst a rash and profligate administration may, by unexpected concurrences of events, seem to advance a nation's glory. In regard to the means of national prosperity, the wisest are weak judges. For example, the present rapid growth of this country, carrying, as it does, vast multitudes beyond the institutions of religion and education, may be working ruin, whilst the people exult in it as a pledge of greatness. We are too short-sighted to find our law in outward interests." [83]

It is possible and legitimate, Channing recognizes, to interpret the phrase, "the general good," so as to include, instead of exclude, man's moral elevation. But then it will not undermine, but sustain, the theory of natural rights for which he has been contending.[84]

Does this doctrine, which constitutes the fundamental principle in Channing's philosophy of politics, entitle him to, or disqualify him for, the name of *democrat*? The question cannot, of course, be answered, until the word *democracy* be defined. Is a democratic state one in which individual rights are safe-guarded, individual initiative encouraged, and the functions of government reduced to a minimum, or is it one in which the will of the majority is absolute and unchecked by any restraints? These two interpretations are antithetical, and no man can be a democrat in both senses of the word. In view of this ambiguity Channing takes pains to make clear where he stands.

"I am not anxious," he writes, "to bear any name into which government enters as the great idea. I want as little government as consists with safety to the rights of all. I wish the people to govern no further than they must. I wish them to place all checks on the legislature which consist with its efficiency. I honor the passion for power and rule as little in the people as in a king. It is a vicious principle, exist where it may. If by democracy be meant the exercise of sovereignty by the people under all those provisions and self-imposed restraints which tend most to secure equal laws and the rights of each and all, then I shall be proud to bear its name. But the unfettered multitude is not dearer to me than the unfettered king." [85]

Needless to say, no other answer could consistently be returned by a man who believed in absolute moral standards. The term *democracy*, however, may properly be applied to a government which has been formed under the inspiration of these ideals. "By democracy," explains Channing, "we understand that a people governs itself; and the primary, fundamental act required of a people is, that it shall lay such restraints on its own powers as will give the best security against their abuse. This is the highest purpose of a popular constitution. A constitution is not merely a machine for ascertaining and expressing a people's will, but much more a provision for keeping that will within righteous bounds. It is the act of a people imposing limits on itself, setting guard on its own passions, and throwing obstruction in the way of legislation, so as to compel itself to pause, to deliberate, to hear all remonstrances, to weigh all rights and interests before it acts. A constitution not framed in these principles must fail of its end." [86] "Democracy, considered in itself," he asserts, "is the noblest form of government, and the only one to satisfy a man who respects himself and his fellow-creatures. But if its actual operation be regarded, we are compelled to say that it works very imperfectly. It is true of people, as it is of kings and nobles, that they have no great capacity for government." [87]

It is evident that Channing's theory of government is identical with that which inspired the great majority of our founding fathers, and that his effort has been to reinforce it by making explicit the philosophical principles which it implies and upon which it depends. Nevertheless, were we to leave the matter so, it is not improbable that his attitude might be grievously misjudged, and that the reader might conclude that Channing, like a mediaeval inquisitor, was concerned, not at all for the earthly welfare and happiness of men, but merely for their souls. Such a conclusion, however, would do him great injustice. Consequently we shall proceed to scrutinize more closely his position in regard to the "average man."

The doctrine of the essential equality of all men "so venerable in the eyes of our fathers," has, he tells us,[88] "lately been denied" upon the ground that men obviously differ with respect to their physical and intellectual endowments. This awkward fact, which many twentieth-century theorists still find it easier to disregard than frankly to face, Channing explicitly recognizes; but, he insists, the recognition of it does not discredit the doctrine in question.

"It is freely granted that there are innumerable diversities among men; but be it remembered, they are ordained to bind men together, not to subdue one to the other; ordained to give means and occasions of mutual aid, and to carry forward each and all, so that the good of all is equally intended in this distribution of various gifts. Be it also remembered, that these diversities among men are as nothing in comparison with the attributes in which they agree; and it is this which constitutes their essential equality. All men have the same rational nature and the same power of conscience, and all are equally made for indefinite improvement of these divine faculties, and for the happiness to be found in their virtuous use. Who, that comprehends these gifts, does not see that the diversities of the race vanish before them." [89]

In view of all this, the notion that a stratified society with a graduation of social ranks is essential to a civilized state cannot be countenanced for a moment. "It is a libel on social order to suppose that it requires for its support the reduction of the multitude to ignorance and servility," and "it is a libel on the Creator to suppose that He requires, as the foundation of communities, the systematic depression of the majority of his intelligent offspring. The supposition is too grossly unreasonable, too monstrous, to require labored refutation." [90]

Moreover such a policy of repression is no longer feasible. The people have begun to think, and to demand the amelioration of their lot. "It is plain that in the actual state of the world, nothing can avail us but a real improvement of the mass of the people. No stable foundation can be laid for us but in men's minds. Alarming as the truth is, it should be told that, outward institutions cannot now secure us. Mightier powers than institutions have come into play among us,— the judgment, the opinions, the feelings of the many; and all hopes of stability which do not rest on the progress of the many shall perish." [91] And, in ringing accents Channing declares that "it is the great mission of this country to forward this revolution, and never was a sublimer work committed to a nation. Our mission is to elevate society through all its conditions, to secure every human being the means of progress, to substitute the government of equal laws for that of irresponsible individuals, to prove that, under popular institutions, the people may be carried forward, that the multitude who toil are capable of enjoying the noblest blessings of the social state." [92]

This is, indeed, an inspiring announcement; yet obviously the realization of such a program can be accomplished—if at all—only by a nation animated by a noble enthusiasm. Does the American people give evidence of being thus uplifted? As Channing looks about him, he feels obliged to confess that a growing materialism is manifesting itself in an increasing "worship of wealth;" and against this tendency we find him frequently inveighing. [93] Moreover the fact that civilization has increased, rather than diminished, the labors of men indicates "a deep defect in what we call the progress of society." "One thing," he concludes, "seems plain, that there is no tendency in our present institutions and habits to bring relief. On the contrary, rich and poor seem to be more and more oppressed with incessant toil, exhausting forethought, anxious struggles, feverish competitions. Some look to legislation to lighten the burden of the laboring class. But equal laws and civil liberty have no power to remove the shocking contrast of condition which all civilized communities present." [94] "Our whole social fabric," he insists, "needs thorough, searching, complete reform." [95] And he even confesses that he sometimes feels "as if a great social revolution were necessary to break up our present mercenary civilization, in order that Christianity, now repelled by the almost universal worldliness, may come into new contact with the soul, and may reconstruct society after its own pure and disinterested principles." [96] "What a country most needs," he contends, "is the well-being of all classes of its population, and especially of the most numerous class."

The revolution which Channing thus intermittently hopes for, however, has nothing in common with the Socialists' Utopia. "The laboring class," he writes, "are sometimes stimulated to seek power as a class, and this it is thought will raise them. But no class, as such, should bear rule among us. All conditions of society should be represented in the government, and alike protected by it; nor can any thing be expected but disgrace to the individual and the country from the success of any class in grasping at a monopoly of political power." [97] This declaration is not only in accord with the doctrine of individual rights which he has so forcefully stated; it is also inspired by two other convictions which are fundamental in Channing's thought.

In the first place he is deeply impressed by the limited efficacy of government. His pages bristle with pronouncements to this effect. "To leave a people to themselves," he asserts, "is generally the best service that their rulers can render." [98] "A good government," he maintains, "is one of the slowest fruits of civilization. In truth a good government exists nowhere." [99] "The very vices of men," he assures us, "which make government needful unfit them to govern. Government is only to be endured on account of the greater evils of anarchy which it prevents." [100]

This is not to say that a good government is not essential to the happiness of a people; it is so essential. But a good government is one which knows its proper business, and is content to mind its own business; and that business is to repress crime, give security, protect property, and safeguard liberty.[101] The highest function of government is negative because "the highest political good, liberty, is negative. It is the removal of obstructions. It is security from wrong. It confers no positive happiness, but opens a field in which the individual may achieve his happiness by his own unfettered powers." [102]

Wherever government has trespassed beyond its proper bounds, it has done more harm than good. Wherever, for example, it has taken charge of religion and education, it has given its people the kind of religion and education which it desired them to have, namely, the kind which would render them docile and obedient, and destroy their individual initiative.[103] Our own happiness and prosperity must be the work of our own brains and hands.[104]

The great interests of a community, from Channing's point of view, are virtue and intelligence,[105] and these government can do little to aid.[106] Again beside "the rights of property and person," the protection of which is the proper function of government, are other rights no less sacred. The individual "has a right to be regarded and treated as a man, as a being who has excellent powers and a high destiny. He has a right to sympathy and deference, a right to be helped in the improvement of his nature, a right to share in the intelligence of the community, a right to the means, not only of bodily, but of spiritual well-being. These rights a government can do little to protect or aid. Yet on these human progress chiefly rests." [107] The reason for the importance of government in this field is that legislation rests on force, and force is not an agency which can act efficiently upon a man's character or his intellect. Hence "government does little more than place society in a condition which favors the action of higher powers than its own." [108]

Consequently, Channing believes that the discovery "must sooner or later be made that the importance of government is enormously over-rated, that it does not deserve all this stir, that there are vastly more effectual means of human happiness." [109] What are these means? We think naturally of the church, of colleges and universities, of voluntary associations. But "the spirit of society, not an outward institution, is the mighty power by which the hard lot of men is to be meliorated. The great idea, that every human being has a right to the means of exercising and improving his highest powers, must pass from a cold speculation into a living conviction, and then society will begin in earnest to accomplish its end. This great idea exists as yet only as a germ, in the most advanced communities, and is working faintly. But it cannot die. . . . It is, indeed, possible that this country may sink beneath the work imposed on it by Providence, and, instead of bring-ing the world into its debt, may throw new darkness over human hope. But great ideas, once brought to light, do not die. The multitude of men through the civilized world are catching some glimpses, however indistinct, of a higher lot; are waking up to something higher than animal good. There is springing up an aspiration among them, which, however dreaded as a dangerous restlessness, is the natural working of the human spirit, wherever it emerges from gross ignorance, and seizes on some vague idea of its rights. Thank God! it is natural for man to aspire; and this aspiration ceases to be dangerous just in propor-tion as the intelligent members of society interpret it aright, and respond to it, and give themselves to the work of raising their brethren." [110]

In the second place Channing regards with the utmost detestation the passion for domination. In the spirit of a modern psychologist he is careful to discriminate between power in the sense of moral and in-tellectual energy which leads a man to develop his own highest poten-tialities and to aid his neighbors to develop theirs, and to extend the dominion of man over physical nature, and power in the sense of a craving to subdue, to control, and to tyrannize over others. The former is "vivifying" and "productive," the latter, as he acutely observes, "if tried by the only fair test, that is, by its effects, seems to have more affinity with weakness than with strength. It enfeebles and narrows what it acts upon." [111] To its baleful consequences all history bears eloquent testimony. "Power trampling on right, whether in the per-son of king or priest, or in the shape of democracies, majorities, and republican slaveholders, is the saddest sight to him who honors human nature and desires its enlargement and happiness." [112]

Now it is an unfortunate characteristic of republican institutions that they pander to this degrading lust for domination. Although they do indeed limit the possibility of its exercise in the case of any individual, yet, by rendering all men eligible for office, they tend to infect the multitude with this unholy desire. Men value their own independence and their individual rights less than the prospect of coercing their fellows. "The despot's great crime is thought to be that he keeps the delight of dominion to himself, that he makes a monopoly of it, whilst our more generous institutions, by breaking it into parcels, and inviting the multitude to scramble for it, spread this joy more widely." [113] The sovereign people likes to be flattered and republican statesmen become its courtiers.[114] "So fearful is the principle of which I have spoken," says Channing, "that I have thought it right to recommend restrictions on power, and a simplicity in government, beyond what most approve. Power, I apprehend, should not be suffered to run into great masses. No more of it should be confided to rulers than is absolutely necessary to repress crime and preserve public order." [115]

Thus these are three reasons for Channing's distrust of government; it is prone to trample upon human rights which it exists to safeguard, it is incapable—inasmuch as it can appeal only to physical force—to contribute effectively to the development of intelligence and virtue, and it tends to stimulate the craving for domination. Still, government one must have, for without it human rights have no protection; and a government which understands, and limits itself to the performance of, its negative function is a blessing. Such a government should be a democracy, in the sense in which Channing has defined the term; that is, it should be a government which affords impartial protection to all classes and individuals, and which, by a self-denying ordinance, prohibits itself from exceeding its proper bounds. Republican statesmen should be like the Gilbertian peers in *Iolanthe*, who

> "do not itch
> To interfere in matters which
> They do not understand."

Such being the case, we may inquire what specific suggestions Channing was prepared to advocate with a view to improving the American form of government as it existed in his own day.

In the first place we find him frankly opposed to the principle of universal suffrage.[116] This disapproval, he explains, must not be taken to imply that he considers the laboring classes "unfit depositaries of political power." [117] Nevertheless he is definitely of the opinion that "the elective franchise is extended too far in this country." [118] And his reason for holding it is that suffrage amounts to "the *participation* of SOVEREIGNTY, of the supreme power of the state." [119] "The levity with which this dignity is conferred," he remarks, "the thoughtlessness with which it has been extended, constitutes one of our great political dangers. Were the proper qualifications for it required, they would not exclude one class rather than another. The aim should be to exclude the unworthy of all classes. A community is bound to provide for itself the best possible government, and this implies the obligation to withhold political power from those who are palpably disqualified by gross ignorance or by profligacy for comprehending or consulting the general welfare,—who cannot exercise the sovereignty, without injuring the commonwealth." [120]

What, then, are the qualifications which should be required? "No man, I think," Channing answers, "should be intrusted with this high privilege, who has not been instructed in the principles of our government and in the duties of a good citizen, and who cannot afford evidence of respectibility in regard to morals. One of the principal objects of our public schools should be, to train the young of all conditions for the duties of good citizens, to furnish them with the necessary knowledge of principles for the judicious use of political power. The admission of the young to the privilege of voting would be the most solemn public act, the grand national festival. It should be preceded by an examination of the candidates. It should be accompanied by the most imposing forms, fitted to impress the young and the whole community with the great responsibility and honorableness of this trust." [121]

That the practical difficulty of introducing such a reform would be very great, and perhaps insuperable, Channing clearly recognized. Well he might, for one can easily imagine the dismay with which every political boss would contemplate a measure which would exclude the ignorant and immoral from the polls! "Still," continues Channing, "it is useful to hold up to a people what it owes to itself. At least these remarks will prevent my fellow-citizens from considering me as an advocate of universal suffrage, in the present state of society. I think, however, that a system of education should be established in a republic for the very purpose of making suffrage universal,—that is, for the purpose of qualifying every man to be a voter. But in the case of those who will not avail themselves of the natural means of improvement, political power should be withheld." [122]

This last qualification makes it plain that universal suffrage is a goal which may be approached, but which one must not anticipate will be attained so long as human nature remains what it is. We must observe, however, that Channing's advocacy of a limited franchise is not inconsistent with his theory of natural rights. Liberty, be it remembered, is "negative," "a freedom from obstructions," whereas suffrage is something positive, and therefore in no sense a natural right.

In the second place we discover that Channing warmly approves of the United States senate as then constituted, namely, as a body elected, not by the people at large, but by the legislatures of the various states, every member of which enjoys a term of office three times as long as that of members of the lower house. "It has," he tells us, "two grand functions,—one to watch the rights of the several States, and the other, not less important, to resist the fluctuations of the popular branch. The Senate is a power raised for a time by the people above their own passions, that it may secure stability to the administration of affairs." [123]

The performance of these two functions on the part of the Senate has, however, been grossly interfered with by the vicious theory of "Instructions," according to which the individual senator is to be regarded merely as the spokesman of the wishes of the majority. He is expected to have his ear to the ground in order to detect the passing trends of public opinion, and to act in compliance therewith. The very contrary is the course which he ought to pursue. He should respect himself and his responsibilities, to cultivate an open mind, and to act according to the dictates of his reason and conscience. "Yet," asks Channing prophetically, "were new institutions to be framed at this moment, would not the people forget the restraint which they should impose on themselves, and the respect due to their delegates? and, from attaching a foolish self-importance to the act of governing, would they not give to their momentary feelings more and more the conduct of public affairs?" [124]

What Channing thus advocates is, of course, a return to the original conception of the senate as established by the Founding Fathers, and it is wholly in keeping with his theory of government. With regard to the presidency we find Channing, after emphasizing the importance of the chief executive as the representation of national unity, commending, as we should expect, the power of veto with which the constitution has entrusted him. It is "a negative not simply designed to guard his own power from encroachment, but to correct partial legislation, and to be a barrier against invasions of the Constitution by extensive combinations of interest or ambition. Every department should be a check on legislation; but this salutary power there is a disposition to wrest from the executive, and it would hardly find a place in a new confederacy." [125]

The political excitement into which the country is recurrently plunged upon the eve of a presidential election seems to Channing, however, "too solemn and fearful to be overlooked. A remedy must be found, or the country will be thrown into perpetual convulsions, and split into factions devoted each to a chief. We shall waste ourselves in struggles for a few leaders, who, by their prominence, will become dearer to a people than their institutions, and in fighting for our favorites we may become their slaves." [126] There is no indispensable man. The people should have "no idols, no favorites. It should annihilate with its frown those who would monopolize its power, or bring it into subserviency to their own glory. No man's name should be much on its lips. It should bind up in no man its prosperity and honor." [127]

It is true that "to the President are confided important functions, but not such functions as can be discharged by one or two individuals in the country, not such as ought to make him the object of idolatry or dread, not such as should draw to him any extraordinary homage, not such as to justify intense desire in the candidate, or intense excitement in the people. Under institutions really free, no office can exist which deserves the struggles of ambition." [128] That the highest office is too exalted to be made the object of political ambition and exposed to conflicts of faction and party, and should therefore be hereditary, is, he reminds us, "the grand argument in favor of monarchy"; and "as a people," he acknowledges, "we have done too much to confirm it." [129]

This degradation of the president's office until it has become the prize of insensate ambition is only the supreme example of that lust for power which republican institutions have done so much to encourage. Yet, as a matter of fact, many presidents have been men who wielded comparatively little influence. An individual senator or congressman has often done more to shape our policies. "This," says Channing, "is as it should be." [130] What is the remedy for this undue exaltation of the presidency in the popular mind? There is no remedy but a moral one, a growth in self-respect and in the understanding of what genuine freedom involves. Failing this, it were better, Channing desperately suggests, "to choose a President by lot from a hundred names to which each state shall contribute its fair proportion." [131]

There is, however, a department of the government of more importance than the senate, and an office more exalted than that of the president. The department is the judiciary, and the office is that of the chief justice. Their importance far exceeds that accorded them in general estimation. The impartial administration of justice is the noblest function of government. The judiciary "is worth more to the people than any other department." "The chief justice should rank before king or president. The pomp of a palace may be dispensed with; but every imposing solemnity consistent with the simplicity of our manners should be combined in the hall where the laws which secure every man's rights are administered. To accomplish the great end of government, nothing is so important as to secure the impartiality and moral independence of judges; and for this end they should be appointed for life, subject to removal only for violation of duty. This is essential. A judge should not hang on the smiles of king or people. In him the people should erect a power above their own temporary will. There ought to be in the state something to represent the majesty of that stable, everlasting law to which all alike should bow; some power above the sordid interests, and aloof from the struggles and intrigues of ordinary life. The dependence of the judge on the breath of party or the fleeting passions of the people is a deformity in the state, for which no other excellence in popular institutions can make compensation." [132] "Yet it is seriously proposed," exclaims Channing indignantly, "to destroy the independence of the judiciary power, to make the judge a pensioner on party, by making the office elective for a limited time; and it is not improbable that this pernicious feature might be impressed on new institutions which might spring up at the present time." [133] The intimate relation between this exaltation of the judiciary and the doctrine of natural rights is too obvious to require elaboration.

One of the most prominent features of the American constitution is, of course, its division of political power, in obedience to the teaching of Montesquieu, between the legislative, executive, and judicial branches of the government, with the object of forestalling the attempt of any would-be despot to concentrate it all in his own hands. One would naturally expect that such a measure, evidently inspired by the ideal of liberty which is Channing's own, would have called forth his enthusiastic approval. It is with some astonishment, therefore, that one finds him expressing a profound distrust of it.[134] He does so, not upon the ground that it is wrong, but that it has proved inefficacious. Our history has shown, what intelligence might have foreseen, that a dominant party will possess itself of all branches of the government, and is thus able to act without restraint.[135] The measure in question constitutes nothing more than a vain effort to secure freedom by outward forms; [136] but all forms and institutions are bound to fail a people unworthy of freedom.[137] "There is no substitute," he reminds us, "for virtue." To encourage virtue should be the first effort of a statesman, and this he can do, not, as we have seen, by positive action, but by concentrating upon the prevention of crime.

To this end Channing calls for few and simple laws.[138] "An extensive and obscure code multiplies occasions of offense, and brings the citizen unnecessarily into collision with the state." [139] Again, "arbitrary and offensive laws invite offense, and take from disobedience the consciousness of guilt." [140] The utmost care should be taken that all laws should be impartial, and bear with equal severity upon rich and poor.[141]

Moreover the punishment of crime should aim at the reformation of the criminal. Such efforts, it is true, are frequently unsuccessful, but they are not always so; and the reflection that society and the state bear their share of responsibility for crime should intensify our efforts in this direction.[142]

There is another source of danger to liberty beside the tendency of government to invade individual rights which Channing discovers, and that is the growth of voluntary associations, and their proneness to concentrate power in the hands of a few leaders, and to breed in their members habits of docility and obedience.[143] Such associations are capable of accomplishing great good, but their success is to be judged by the degree in which they are productive of moral energy and freedom in others.[144] Nevertheless, Channing maintains, "They are perilous instruments. They ought to be suspected. They are a kind of irregular government created within our constitutional government. Let them be watched closely. As soon as we find them resolved or disposed to bear down a respectable man or set of men, or to force on the community measures about which wise and good men differ, let us feel that a dangerous engine is at work among us, and oppose to it our steady and stern disapprobation." [145]

It was the intolerance and fanaticism of the Abolitionists, and their efforts to stir up popular excitement which made Channing reluctant to associate himself with them, even as the violence directed against them attracted him to them.[146] Another case in point was the temperance movement. With this Channing deeply sympathized. The effect of ardent spirits is, he assures us, extremely harmful, and any man who makes use of them "virtually arrays himself against the cause of temperance and humanity." [147] "He forsakes the standard of social reform, and throws himself into the ranks of its foes." [148] Some of the advocates of temperance, however, have gone too far. They have discouraged the drinking of wine, "an innocent and often salutary beverage;" a custom which is not only harmless in itself but enjoyed in addition the sanction of Jesus, who, at Cana of Galilee, miraculously increased the amount.[149] Channing, indeed, looks forward to a time when the sale of spirits will be forbidden by law, yet he warns the supporters of the movement that public opinion must be educated to bear on temperance, "rationally, generously, not passionately, tyrannically, and with the spirit of persecution." "Men cannot," he prophetically remarks, "be driven into temperance. Let the temperate become a party, and breathe the violence of a party, and they will raise up a party as violent as their own." [150]

In regard to the right of insurrection against a government, Channing's view is very much the same as Locke's. In the first place, a justifiable insurrection must be able to appeal to moral principle. A people merely impatient of necessary restraint, "need and deserve an arbitrary government." In the second place, every other method of relief must have been shown to be futile. It is not true, however, that a bad government may rightfully invoke the Scriptures in support of its authority. The "higher powers," to which obedience is enjoined, are described as "ministers of God for good," and this description does not apply to rulers, who have become oppressors.[151]

The relation of the individual to the state becomes especially difficult, however, in the case of war. The contention of the extreme pacifist that war is always wrong is, indeed, explicitly repudiated by Channing. [152] The principle, "Resist not evil" cannot be literally applied, for "the very end and office of government is to *resist* evil men. For this, the civil magistrate bears the sword; and he should beware of interpretations of the Scriptures which would lead him to bear it in vain." [153] Next to the martyr for religion, "happy is the martyr to the cause of his country." [154]

Nevertheless, in all cases war is a tremendous evil. And "the presumption is always against the justice and necessity of war." [155] we know too much of the corruption of governments, monarchial and republican, to think otherwise.[156] The appeal will always be made to national honor, but in what does national honor consist? It is a compound of three elements, justice, philanthropy, and "institutions which tend and are designed to elevate all classes of its citizens." [157] A nation guilty of injustice has no honor to fight for.[158] Nor can the contention that the decision of the government to engage in war binds the conscience of the citizen be for a moment admitted. The individual cannot shuffle off his moral responsibility on his rulers He must examine and decide for himself.[159] This is, indeed, a severe requirement, but it is one, Channing maintains, which the Christian cannot evade. "Let him bear witness against unholy wars, as his country's greatest crimes. If called to take part in them, let him deliberately refuse. If martial law seizes him, let him submit. If hurried to prison, let him submit. If brought thence to be shot, let him submit. There must be martyrs to peace as truly as to other principles of our religion. The first Christians chose to die rather than obey the laws of the state which commanded them to renounce their Lord. 'Death rather than crime,' such is the good man's watchword such the Christian's vow. Let him be faithful unto death." [160]

Patriotism, for Channing, is a noble emotion, yet not the noblest "Just in proportion as you sever a man from his country and race,' he asserts, "he ceases to be a man;" [161] and to this saying the most ardent of nationalists would subscribe. But it must be balanced by the declaration that "our attachment to our country must be very much proportioned to what we deem its tendency to form a generous race of man. We pretend not to have thrown off all national feeling; but we have some stronger feelings. We love our country much, but mankind more." [162] And, in the same vein, Channing urges that "it is of the highest importance that the prevalent notion of a man's relation to the state should be rectified. The idea of this relation is so exaggerated and perverted as to impair the force of every other A man's country is more thought of than his nature. His connection with a particular community is more respected than his connection with God. His alliance with his race[163] is reduced to a nullity by his alliance with the state. He must be ready to give up his race, to sacrifice all its rights and interests, that the little spot where he was born may triumph or prosper. The history of nations is very much the history of the immolation of the individual to the country. His nationality stands out before all his other attributes. The nation, represented by one or a few individuals, has arrogated to itself the dignity of being the fountain of all his rights. It has made his religion for him. Its will, called law, has taken the place of all other laws. It has seized on the individual as its tool, and doomed him to live and die for its most selfish purposes. . . . But . . . the nation is not the fountain of right. Our first duties are not to our country. Our first allegiance is not due to its laws. We belong first to God, and next to our race. We were, indeed, made for partial, domestic, and national ties and affections, and these are essential means of our education and happiness in this first stage of our being; but all these are to be kept in subjection to the laws of universal justice and humanity. They are intended to train us up to these. In these consists our likeness to the Divinity." [164]

With an optimism characteristic of the nineteenth century Channing believed that international relations were improving and destined to continue to improve. And in the hope of accelerating this improvement he has two suggestions to make. One is the establishment of an "impartial umpire" for the adjudication of international disputes;[165] the other is the establishment of free trade, which, he believes, would do much to lessen international friction.[166]

In conclusion we may inquire what kind of life the individual will lead in a state regulated in accordance with Channing's ideals. It will be an earnest and serious life, that goes without saying; but it will not be a gloomy one. Channing himself, as we know, in his youth practiced an asceticism so severe as permanently to undermine his health and this he frankly acknowledged to be a mistake. "It is a false idea," he maintains, "that religion requires the extermination of any principle, desire, appetite, or passion which our Creator has implanted. Our nature is a whole, a beautiful whole, and no part can be spared. You might as properly and innocently lop off a limb from the body as eradicate any natural desire from the mind. All our appetites are in themselves innocent and useful, ministering to the general meal of the soul. They are like elements of the natural world, parts of a wise and beneficent system, but, like the elements, are beneficent only when restrained.[167]

This need for restraint is due to the fact that appetites contain in themselves no principle of measure, and therefore tend to expand without limit.[168] Reason and conscience, the two, as we have seen, in reality constituting a single principle, must impose order upon these appetites, and assign every one its due sphere. The result, frequently, is internal conflict, but it is a healthy conflict, and rightly conducted, is conducive to strength of moral purpose.[169] The wise and good man, accordingly, will seek to develop those capacities and to satisfy those desires most worthy of being fostered, and society will do the same.

How shall we go about it? We do not desire a monotonous existence; monotony is already too characteristic of life. While a system of castes or classes is obnoxious, a multiplicity and variety of occupations is desirable.[170] Yet all men have at bottom the same needs and are entitled to the same means of satisfying them. One of the great evils of society is the hours of toil which deny the laboring man the opportunity for self-development.[171] An improved efficiency of industry, Channing believed, would ultimately result in an increased amount of leisure; [172] yet, should this expectation be disappointed, the same end, he believed, could be reached if only the desire for gain could be moderated. "Sacrifice the wealth," he urged, "and not the mind of a people." [173]

What, then, are the chief means to self-development and moral and spiritual improvement which deserve to be encouraged? In the first place, we should desire the growth of a national literature. What we wish for our country is neither "a dead level of intellect," [174] even if it be a higher level than that which obtains elsewhere, nor yet the production of "a race of pedants." [175] "We want great minds to be formed among us,—minds which shall be felt afar, and through which we shall act on the world. We want the human intellect to do its utmost here. We want this people to obtain a claim on the gratitude of the human race, by adding strength to the foundation, and fulness and splendor to the development, of moral and religious truth; by originality of thought, by discoveries of science, and by contributions to the refining pleasures of taste and imagination." [176]

It is a noble ideal, and a catholic one. He is aware, Channing remarks, that the term *literature* "is often confined to compositions which relate to human nature and human life; that it is not generally extended to physical science; that mind, not matter, is regarded as its main subject and sphere. But the worlds of matter and mind are too intimately connected to admit of exact partition. All the objects of human thought flow into one another." [177] Hence all contributions of superior minds, whether they are found in the fields of poetry, fiction, history, jurisprudence, ethics, metaphysics, or physical science, constitute a nation's literature.[178] Hence, he concludes, "it is plainly among the most powerful methods of exalting the character of a nation, of forming a better race of men; in truth, we apprehend that it may claim the first rank among the means of improvement." [179]

By this assertion, Channing realizes, he will incur the reproach of deprecating the importance of revealed religion. But the charge is based upon a misapprehension of the relation between revelation and human reason, it is a consequence of the failure to understand that the two are not antithetical but complimentary. The function of Christianity, in particular, is to stimulate and inspire, and by so doing to dominate, the human intellect. "It admits of endless development. It is the last truth which should remain stationary. It ought to be so explored and so expressed as to take the highest place in a nation's literature, as to exalt and purify all other literature." [180] In this respect Channing's hope for his country was destined to a magnificent, if partial fulfillment, for before his death, the literary "flowering of New England" was nearly in full-bloom; and the ideals which inspired it were in great measure his own, even as the great majority of those writers who contributed to it were men and women of his own faith.

In spite of his catholic conception of literature, however, Channing does not look upon all forms of it as equally efficacious in improving the national character. Any form of knowledge is so to some extent; but physical science, while it increases man's power over nature, has the disadvantage that it concentrates his attention upon what is below himself. "Miserably narrow," exclaims Channing, "is the culture which confines the soul to matter, which turns it to the outward as to something nobler than itself. I fear the spirit of science at the present day is too often a degradation rather than the true culture of the soul. It is the bowing down of the heaven-born spirit before unthinking mechanism. It seeks knowledge rather for animal transitory purposes, than for the nutriment of the imperishable inward life." [181] He looks rather to history which "reveals the causes and means by which the happiness and virtue of the race may be enlarged," [182] to poetry which utters the feelings of the heart, expresses the sympathy between man and nature, and creates "beautiful forms of manifestation for great moral truths;" [183] and to that "higher philosophy" which is concerned with the nature of man, the problems of knowledge, of value, and of man's relation to God.[184] "The true cultivation of a human being," writes Channing, "consists in the development of great moral ideas; that is, the ideas of God, of duty, of right, of justice, of love, of self-sacrifice, of moral perfection as manifested in Christ, of happiness, of immortality, of Heaven." [185]

In the second place we should encourage the love of music. Music is not only the strengthener of all exalted emotions, but is a "refined taste" which is beneficial to public morals, and cannot fail to elevate both public and domestic life.[186]

In the third place, dancing should be encouraged. Its end "is to realize perfect grace in motion." [187] This is highly desirable; and, accordingly, we should encourage it so heartily that it will no longer be associated with wealth and luxury, but will become "an every day amusement" in the hope that our own people will thus acquire an appreciation of grace and refinement comparable to that of the French.[188] This desire has been satisfied to the extent that dancing is now in high favor with all classes of the population, but whether our modern dancing has done much to increase the general appreciation of grace is a question which we may leave to aesthetes and sociologists to answer.

In the fourth place there is the theater. Of the drama of his own day Channing thought so poorly as to pronounce that it merited "no encouragement," [189] and even to denounce it as positively vicious.[190] Nevertheless the drama ought to furnish "the noblest of all amusements." It "answers a high purpose when it places us in the presence of the most solemn and striking events of human history, and lays bare to us the human heart in its most powerful, appalling, glorious workings." [191] As an immediate measure of relief he advocates the cultivation of the art of recitation. "It is not easy," he urges, "to conceive of a more effectual way of spreading a refined taste through a community. The drama, undoubtedly, appeals more strongly to the passions than recitation; but the latter brings out the meaning of an author more. Shakespeare, worthily recited, would be better understood than on the stage. Then, in recitation, we escape the weariness of listening to poor performers, who, after all," he remarks, "fill up most of the time at the theatre. Recitation, sufficiently varied, so as to include pieces of chaste wit, as well as of pathos, beauty, and sublimity is adapted to our present intellectual progress as much as the drama falls below it." [192] Whatever we think of this project, and however we may regard his estimate of the drama of his own time, it is clear that, in a society moulded according to Channing's ideas, the individual will not have a dull time, so long as native talent can be found. What he obviously desired was a forcing house of genius, such as the ancient Greek or the Mediaeval Italian republics actually were, and what his own New England, wherein his own ideals were to some extent genuinely operative, was showing signs of becoming.

We have now seen, as from a bird's eye view, indeed, what Channing thinks of man, both as an individual and in the group. And we have done so because such an inspection is essential to place his thought in its proper perspective. For Channing was more than a preacher and a theologian; he was an ethical, a social, and a political thinker as well. And his chief achievement in this latter field has been to give us a philosophy of the American Constitution. He has taken its presuppositions, explicit and implicit, has coordinated them, and has sought to supply them with an adequate metaphysical foundation. The task, you may say, was an easy one, inasmuch as Channing and the Founding Fathers were alike disciples of Locke. But Channing is not a mere disciple. He has contributed to the philosophic structure elements which are original with himself, and these elements are basic.

As we glance back over the outlines of Channing's system, so far as we have hitherto been able to trace them, we cannot fail to be struck by the closely interwoven texture of his thought. It is sustained by a few all-important ideas, the influence of which is everywhere apparent. In his ethical and in his political theories, all follows from his doctrine of the divinity of man. Upon this rights, duties, the function of government, the means and goals of education, the conception of civilization, alike depend. The divinity of man, the objector may urge, is an ancient and well-worn doctrine. I answer, Not as Channing conceives of it. If the essential nature of God be unknown, as for orthodoxy it is unknown, then, to assert that man is a child of God is nearly equivalent to saying that he is a creature, and to declare that he is destined to become like God is only to affirm, with the Sufi mystic that he is to become "what no heart e'er conceived." [193] But, for Channing, the divine nature *is* known. The principle of essential sameness is the common basis of his conceptions of God and man. Both are *Persons*, one uncreated and infinite, the other created and finite; the one possessing eternally in unmixed purity and infinite extension those attributes which the other possesses only partially and imperfectly; yet the second is destined to grow forever into the likeness of the first.

Upon this principle depend equally Channing's theology, his ethics, and his politics. He dissents with equal vehemence both from the absolutist, pantheistic, or scholastic type of thinking which would shroud the divine nature in a "cloud of unknowing," and from the view of naturalistic humanism which looks upon man as an ephemeral being whose destiny is fulfilled in a brief and transitory existence upon this tiny planet.

Does not Channing, however, we may ask, expect too much of men? His theories may seem plausible when presented to an audience of earnest New Englanders; but all the world, as he himself would be the first to admit, is not like Massachusetts. Is there not something unreal and fantastic in this continuous harping upon the divinity of man— man who so often behaves rather like a devil than an angel? In reply Channing, I feel sure, would have appealed to the evidence of history, he would have asked us to take a long view, to consider what man was and what he has already become, to weigh his actual accomplishments in the scales with his errors and shortcomings and then to pronounce our verdict.[194] It is an argument which he might have presented with even greater force today, when man's past is no longer reckoned in the brief term of six thousand years. Perchance he would find many who would still agree with him that "if there be one striking fact in human nature, it is its susceptibleness of improvement." [195]

Undoubtedly, however, he would have urged upon us a second consideration. How is it possible, he would have asked, not to hope all things of man when one remembers his origin. "There is no good," he would repeat, "too vast for us to anticipate for the universe or for ourselves, from such a Father as we believe in." [196] The Father in whom Channing believes is not one who has doomed the majority of his offspring to everlasting torment, but one who, like the Good Shepherd, is concerned "to seek and to save that which was lost." And against the will of this mighty being the forces of evil cannot prevail. This outlook is today a familiar one, characterizing as it does practically all liberal Protestant thinkers, but Channing was one of the first to envisage it, and none has ever expounded it more earnestly or eloquently than he.

Lastly we may ask, Is Channing's attitude not too otherworldly? The thought of immortality is ever in his mind, and the word is ever on his lips. It dominates his ethical and political, no less than his theological, thinking.

The answer is that his attitude is no doubt too otherworldly for the the materialist or the naturalist, for they are concerned precisely to deny what Channing thinks it of the greatest importance to affirm. The reasons for his belief we are not yet ready to discuss, but, if the soundness of that belief be granted, it is difficult to see how Channing could be accused of making too much of it.

One consideration, however, may well be emphasized. Channing's otherworldliness is not antithetical, but rather complementary, to a rational this-worldliness. This life is not everything, but the other life is not all. A single day in a man's life is not rendered unimportant by the fact that he is to live through other days. On the contrary, almost all its importance is due to its relation to them. Much may be done in a day to make or mar one's fortune in the future; a single event may exert its beneficent or malign influence throughout the entire remainder of one's life.

These general considerations are reinforced for Channing by the conviction which he derives from the Scriptures that this life is designed to constitute a state of probation, wherein the consequences of one's deeds do not become fully apparent. "In this respect," he writes, "the future will differ from the present world. After death, character will produce its full effect. According to the Scriptures, the color of our future existence will be wholly determined by the habits and principles which we carry into it." [197] The importance of this present life is, then, not diminished, but enhanced, by its relationship to the life to come.

After all this world and the other world are in reality not two worlds, but one. They form a single universe. Consequently the attempt to distinguish between spiritual and material interests is bound to fail. "There is a unity in our whole being. There is one great end for which body and mind were created, and all the relations of life were ordained; one central aim, to which our whole being should tend; and this is the unfolding of our intellectual and moral nature." [198] Channing's first and last word is thus, moral improvement. What his views in detail are of the connection between these two provinces of the universe is a topic which we shall explore in due time. But before we turn to examine it, we must first turn our eyes to behold, with Channing, a colossal figure of superhuman proportions standing between man and the throne of Deity, Jesus Christ, the Son of God. What did Channing think of Christ? This must constitute the next subject of our investigation.

## NOTES

1. *Works,* p. 347. col. 1.
2. *Ibid.,* p. 353.
3. The Christian revelation, Channing declares, carries with it the assumance "that our highest attainments here are but the beginning of our everlasting progress; and that there is no height of intelligence, power, beneficence, and bliss to which we are not destined to ascend!" (*Works,* p. 1000. col. 1). "Its (Christianity's) greatest doctrine," he tells us, "is, that the most lost are recoverable, that the most fallen may rise, and that there is no height of purity, power, felicity in the universe, to which the guiltiest may not, through penitence, attain." (*Ibid.,* p. 70).
4. See *Ibid.,* p. 1001. col. 1.
5. *Ibid.,* pp. 1-2.
6. *Ibid.,* p. 2. col. 1.
7. "Let it not be imagined from these remarks, that I would turn the mind from God's Infinity. This is the grand truth; but it must not stand alone in the mind. The finite is something real as well as the infinite. We must reconcile the two in our theology. It is as dangerous to exclude the former as the latter. God surpasses all human thought; yet human thought, mysterious, unbounded, 'wandering through eternity,' is not to be contemned. God's sovereignty is limitless; still man has rights. God's power is irresistible; still man is free. On God we entirely depend; yet we can and do act from ourselves, and determine our own characters. These antagonist ideas, if so they may be called, are equally true, and neither can be spared. It will not do for an impassioned or an abject piety to wink one class of them out of sight. In a healthy mind they live together; and the worst error in religion has arisen from throwing a part of them into obscurity." (*Ibid.,* pp. 2-3.)
8. *Ibid.,* p. 3, col. 1. Notice the use, so characteristic of the early nineteenth century, of the word *mysticism* to signify pantheistic absorption.
9. *Ibid.,* p. 3. col. 2.
10. "As far as they thus severed themselves from God, they did themselves great harm; but in their recognition, however imperfect, of the grandeur of the soul, lay the secret of their vast influence on human affairs." (*Ibid.,* p. 4. col. 1.)
11. *Loc. cit.*
12. *Loc. cit.*
13. "The doctrine that God is the only Substance, which is Pantheism, differs little from the doctrine that God is the only active power of the Universe. For what is substance without power? It is a striking fact that the philosophy which teaches that matter is an inert substance, and that God is the force which pervades it, has led men to question whether any such thing as matter exists; whether the powers of attraction and repulsion, which are regarded as the indwelling Deity, be not its whole essence. Take away force, and substance is a shadow, and might as well vanish from the universe. Without a free power in man, he is nothing. The divine agent within him is every thing. Man acts only in show. He is a phenomenal existence, under

which the One Infinite Power is manifested; and is this much better than Pantheism?" (*Ibid.*, p. 4.)

14. *Ibid.*, pp. 5-6.
15. *Ibid.*, p. 6. col. 1.
16. "On this, and on the relations growing out of this, religion wholly rests. True we depend on the Creator; and so does the animal; so does the clod; and were this the only relation, we should be no more bound to worship than they. We sustain a grander relation, that of rational, moral, free beings to a Spiritual Father. We are not mere material substances, subjected to an irresistible physical law, or mere animals subjected to resistless instincts; but are souls, on which a moral law is written, in which a divine oracle is heard. Take away the moral relation of the created spirit to the universal spirit, and that of entire dependence would remain as it is now, but no ground and no capacity of religion would remain; and the splendor of the universe would fade away." (*Ibid.*, p. 6. col. 2.)
17. *Ibid.*, pp. 6-7.
18. "We wish that we could add that he had thrown new light on free agency. This great subject has indeed baffled as yet the deepest thinkers, and seems now to be consigned, with other sublime topics, under the sweeping denomination of 'metaphysics,' to general neglect. But let it not be given up in despair. The time is coming when the human intellect is to strike into new fields, and to view itself and its Creator and the universe from new positions, and we trust that the darkness which has so long hung over our moral nature will be gradually dispersed. This attribute of free agency, through which an intelligent being is strictly and properly a cause, an agent, an originator of moral good or moral evil, and not a mere machine, determined by outward influences, or by a secret, yet resistless efficiency of God, which virtually makes him the author and sole author of all human actions, —this moral freedom, which is the best image of the creative energy of Deity, seems to us the noblest object of philosophical investigation. However questioned and darkened by a host of metaphysicians, it is recognized in the common consciousness of every human being. It is the ground of responsibility, the fountain of moral feeling. It is involved in all moral judgments and affections, and thus gives to social life its whole interest; whilst it is the chief tie between the soul and its Creator. The fact that philosophers have attempted to discard free agency from their explanations or moral phenomena, and to subject all human action to necessity, to mechanical causes, or other extraneous influences, is proof enough that the science of mind has as yet penetrated little beneath the surface, that the depths of the soul are still unexplored." (*Works*, pp. 511-512.)
19. *Ibid.*, p. 691. col. 1.
20. *Ibid.*, p. 42. col. 1.
21. *Ibid.*, p. 42. col. 2.
22. *Works,* p. 1001. col. 2. *cf. Ibid.*, p. 1012. col. 1.
23. *Ibid.*, pp. 18-19, 129, 934, 981-982.
24. "What beauty is, is a question which the most penetrating minds have not satisfactorily answered; nor, were I able, is this the place for discussing it. But one thing I would say; the beauty of the outward creation is inti-

mately related to the lovely, grand, interesting attributes of the soul. It is the emblem or expression of these. Matter becomes beautiful to us when it seems to lose its material aspect, its inertness, finiteness, and grossness, and by the ethereal lightness of it forms and motions seems to approach spirit; when it images to us pure and gentle affections; when it spreads out into a vastness which is a shadow of the Infinite; or when in more awful shapes and movements it speaks of the Omnipotent. Thus outward beauty is akin to something deeper and unseen, is the reflection of spiritual attributes; and of consequence the way to see and feel it more keenly is to cultivate those moral, religious, intellectual and social principles of which I have already spoken, and which are the glory of the spiritual nature." (*Ibid.*, p. 19. col. 1.)

25. *Ibid.*, p. 45. col. 1.

26. *Ibid.*, p. 43. col. 2. "This disinterested principle in human nature," observes Channing in his essay on *Self-Culture*, "we sometimes call reason, sometimes conscience, sometimes the moral sense or faculty. But, be its name what it may, it is a real principle in each of us, and it is the supreme power within us, to be cultivated above all others, for on its culture the right development of all others depends." (*Ibid.*, pp. 15-16.)

27. *Ibid.*, p. 264. col. 2.

28. "We regard nothing so important to a human being as the knowledge of his own mind, and of its intimate connection with the infinite Mind." (*Ibid.*, p. 572. col. 1.)

    "Religion, if it be true, is the central truth, and any knowledge, which is not gathered round it, and quickened and illuminated by it, is hardly worth the name." (*Ibid.*, p. 575.)

29. *Ibid.*, pp. 933-934.

30. To this subject, because of its great importance, we shall subsequently return.

31. *Ibid.*, pp. 358, 364-366, 934, 956-957.

32. *Ibid.*, p. 170. col. 2.; *cf.* pp. 698. col. 1, 855. col. 2.

33. To admit this is not inconsistent with what was said on page 140 with regard to an "intuitive cast" in his thought upon ethics, for eudaemonism endeavors to make a place for a theory of intuition, even though that place may not be as extensive as Channing might desire. See Professor W. K. Wright's *General Introduction to Ethics*, p. 352.

34. *Ibid.*, p. 697. col. 1. *cf. loc. cit.* col. 2. "The gifts of the Creator."

35. "Man's rights belong to him as a moral being capable of perceiving moral distinctions, as a subject of moral obligations." (*Ibid.*, p. 697. col. 2.) "They belong, as we have seen, to man as a moral being, and nothing can divest him of them but the destruction of his nature." (*Ibid.*, p. 699. col. 1.)

36. *Ibid.*, p. 698. col. 1. The reader of Mazzini's *Duties of Man* will remember that he found there the same emphasis upon the interdependence of rights and duties. Is it possible that this is due to the influence of the New England thinker upon the Italian, perhaps through the mediation of Margaret Fuller?

37. *Ibid.*, p. 424. col. 1.

38. *Ibid.*, p. 427. col. 2.

39. *Ibid.*, pp. 348-349.

40. *Ibid.*, pp. 986-987.

41. Channing is firmly convinced that, deprived of the support of religion, the entire structure of society would collapse. "We hope, perhaps," he writes, "that human laws and natural sympathy would hold society together. As reasonably might we believe that, were the sun quenched in the heavens, our torches could illuminate and our fires quicken and fertilize the earth. What is there in human nature to awaken respect and tenderness, if man is the unprotected insect of a day? and what is he more, if atheism be true? Erase all thought and fear of God from a community, and selfishness and sensuality would absorb the whole man. Appetite knowing no restraint, and poverty and suffering having no solace or hope, would trample in scorn on the restraints of human laws. Virtue, duty, principle, would be mocked and spurned as unmeaning sounds. A sordid self-interest would supplant every other feeling, and man would become in fact, what the theory of atheism declares him to be, a companion for brutes." (*Ibid.*, p. 187.)

42. Needless to say, the possibility of moral development is a genuine one only if man's will be free, and—Channing would certainly add—only if it can confidently rely upon divine grace.

43. See *A Free Man's Worship*.

44. *Ibid.*, p. 178. col. 1.

45. *Loc. cit.*

46. *Ibid.*, p. 698.

47. *Loc. cit.* col. 1.

48. It would appear to be equally compatible with the theory presented by Professor G. E. Moore in his *Principia Ethica*.

49. *Loc. cit.* col. 1.

50. *Ibid.*, p. 699. col. 1.

51. *Ibid.*, pp. 698-699.

52. There is a verbal confusion here. It seems probable that, in his first reference to domestic relations, Channing was thinking of the relations of husband and wife, parent and child, mentioned on page 855.

53. *Ibid.*, p. 866.

54. *Ibid.*, p. 867.

55. *Ibid.*, p. 799. col. 1. "I always hear with pain," writes Channing, "the doctrine too common among lawyers that property is the creature of the law; as if it had no natural foundation, as if it were not a natural right, as if it did not precede all laws, and were not their ground instead of being their effect. Government is ordained, not to create so much as to protect and regulate property; and the chief strength of government lies in the sanction which the moral sense, the natural idea of right, gives to honestly earned possessions. The notion which I am combating is essentially revolutionary and destructive. We hear much of radicalism, of agrarianism, at the present day. But of all radicals, the most dangerous, perhaps, is he who makes property the 'creature of law'; because what law creates it can destroy. If we of this Commonwealth have no right in our persons, houses, ships, farms, but what a vote of the legislature or the majority confers, then a vote of the same masses may strip us of them all, and transfer them to others; and the right will go with the law. According to this doctrine, I see not why the majority, who are always comparatively poor, may not step into the

mansions and estates of the rich. I see not why the law cannot make some idle neighbor the rightful owner of your fortune or mine. What better support can radicalism ask than this?" (*Ibid.*, p. 798. col. 2.)

56. See the Treatise, *Of Civil Government.*

57. *Works,* p. 694. col. 1.

58. *Ibid.*, p. 703. col. 2; p. 704. col. 1.

59. See above, page 107.

60. *Ibid.*, p. 699. col. 1.

61. "The League of Nations" and the U.N.O. are attempts, hitherto unsuccessful, to abolish this state of affairs.

62. As a matter of fact the American frontiersmen who penetrated westward beyond the limits of the Thirteen Colonies, and the Boer Foretrekkers when they crossed the boundaries of Cape Colony, were in a condition approximating to "the state of nature." I say *approximating,* because of the inveterate tendency of every little group of pioneers to treat itself as a sovereign commonwealth entitled to control, at least to some extent, the actions of its members, and to punish crime. But the more isolated individuals upon both continents were at times quite literally in "the state of nature."

63. *Ibid.*, p. 182. col. 1.

64. *Ibid.*, p. 176. col. 1.

65. *Ibid.*, p. 176. col. 2.

66. *Ibid.*, p. 177. col. 1.

67. *Loc. cit.*

68. *Ibid.*, p. 699. col. 1.

69. *Ibid.*, pp. 857-858.

70. By this utterance Channing obviously means, not that rights are derived from the state, but that the actual exercise of them depends upon the protection, and thus upon the preservation, of the state.

71. *Ibid.*, p. 702. col. 2.

72. *Ibid.*, p. 699. col. 2.

73. *Ibid.*, p. 726. col. 2.

74. *Ibid.*, p. 682. col. 1.

75. This raises the possibility that Channing, on this occasion, was thinking primarily of legal, rather than of natural, rights.

76. *Loc. cit.*

77. *Ibid.*, p. 682. col. 2.

78. *Ibid.*, p. 682. col. 1.

79. *Ibid.*, p. 683. col. 1.

80. *Adventures of Ideas,* p. 105. The second comma in the last sentence is obviously a misprint.

81. *Ibid.*, pp. 702-703.

82. *Ibid.*, p. 700. cols. 1-2.

83. *Ibid.*, p. 701. cols. 1-2. *Cf.*, p. 774. col. 2.

84. *Ibid.*, p. 701. col. 2.

85. *Ibid.*, p. 897. col. 1. "If I am to be hedged in on every side," observes Channing, "to be fettered by the perpetual presence of arbitrary will, to be denied the exercise of my powers, it matters nothing to me whether the chain

is laid on me by one or many, by king or people. A despot is not more tolerable for his many heads." *Ibid.*, p. 895. col. 1.

86. *Ibid.*, p. 895. col. 2. "That men may greatly strengthen and improve society by written constitutions," observes Channing, "I readily grant. There is, however, a constitution which precedes all of men's making, and after which all others are to be formed; a constitution, the great lines of which are drawn in our very nature; a primitive law of justice, rectitude, and philanthropy, which all other laws are bound to enforce, and from which all others derive their validity and worth." *Ibid.*, p. 182. col. 1.

87. *Ibid.*, p. 895. col. 1.

88. *Ibid.*, p. 693. col. 2.

89. "Let it be added," Channing continues, "that the natural advantages which distinguish one man from another, are so bestowed as to counterbalance one another, and bestowed without regard to rank or condition in life. Whoever surpasses in one endowment is inferior in others. Even genius, the greatest gift, is found in union with strange infirmities, and often places its possessor below ordinary men in the conduct of life. Great learning is often put to shame by the mother-wit and keen good sense of uneducated men. Nature, indeed, pays no heed to birth or condition in bestowing her favors. The noblest spirits sometimes grow up in the obscurest spheres. Thus equal are men; and among these equals, who can substantiate his claim to make others his property, his tools, the mere instruments of his private interest and gratification." *Ibid.*, pp. 693. col. 2—694, col. 1.

90. *Ibid.*, p. 54. col. 1.

91. *Ibid.*, p. 56. "Whoever studies modern history with any care," observes Channing, "must discern in it a steady, growing movement towards one most interesting result,—I mean towards the elevation of the laboring class of society. This is not a recent, accidental turn of human affairs. We can trace its beginnings in the feudal times, and its slow advances in subsequent periods, until it has become the master movement of our age. Is it not plain that those who toil with their hands, and whose productive industry is the spring of all wealth, are rising from the condition of beasts of burden, to which they were once reduced, to the consciousness, intelligence, self-respect, and proper happiness of men. Is it not the strong tendency of our times to diffuse among the many the improvements once confined to the few? He who overlooks this has no comprehension of the great work of Providence." *Ibid.*, p. 767. col. 2.

92. *Ibid.*, p. 768. col. 2.

93. *Cf. Works*, pp. 75, 166-167, 749, 890.

94. *Ibid.*, pp. 103-104.

95. *Ibid.*, p. 943. col. 1.

96. *Ibid.*, p. 749.

97. *Ibid.*, p. 41. col. 2.

98. *Ibid.*, p. 557. col. 2.

99. *Ibid.*, p. 756. col. 1.

100. *Ibid.*, p. 891. col. 2.

101. *Ibid.*, p. 556. col. 1; 630.

102. *Ibid.*, p. 630. This holds true, not only of the state government in relation to to the individual, but of the national government in relation to the states. "We ask nothing of the General Government but to hold us together, to establish among the different States relations of friendship and peace; and we are sure that our State Governments and individual energies will work out for us a happiness such as no other people have yet secured" (*Loc. cit.*). In this respect Channing is much more of a Jeffersonian democrat than a Federalist.

103. *Ibid.*, p. 556. col. 1.

104. In this connection it is interesting to find Channing explaining the futility of price fixing (*Ibid.*, p. 558. col. 1).

105. *Loc. cit.*

106. It can aid the work of education financially, by the establishment of schools and the paying of teachers. Pp. 30, 557.

107. *Ibid.*, p. 890. col. 1.

108. *Ibid.*, p. 890. col. 2.

109. *Ibid.*, p. 42.

110. *Ibid.*, p. 890. col. 2.

111. *Ibid.*, p. 551. col. 1.

112. *Ibid.*, p. 8. col. 2.

113. *Ibid.*, p. 554. col. 2.

114. *Ibid.*, p. 555. col. 1.

115. *Ibid.*, p. 8. col. 2.

116. His remarks on this topic were called forth by the abortive insurrection, known as Dorr's Rebellion, which took place in his native state of Rhode Island in 1842. In this connection Channing explicitly acknowledges that the system of representation which there prevailed constituted a serious injustice. "The existence of these wrongs in the established system," he writes, "has always made me look with great tenderness on the rash steps of the revolutionists. I believe that the idea of right has been present to their minds, and has done much to hide from them their own violence and wrong-doing. And I insist on this, because I am most desirous that a system of great lenity should be adopted towards these misguided men. I know that the State does not need severity for its own safety, and I hope that it will not fall into cruelty from revenge." *Life*, p. 580.

117. *Life*, p. 580. The wording here is ambiguous, and, at first glance, may appear to contradict the assertion explicitly made elsewhere that "No class, as such, should bear rule among us." But the contradiction is only apparent. Suffrage, Channing insists, should be based, not upon class, but upon character and intelligence.

118. *Ibid.*, pp. 580-581.

119. *Ibid.*, p. 581.

120. *Loc. cit.*

121. *Loc. cit.*

122. *Loc. cit. Cf.*, p. 598.

123. *Works*, p. 896. col. 1.

124. *Loc. cit.*

125. In writing these words Channing was contemplating the possible dissolution of the Union over the issue of slavery.
126. *Ibid.,* p. 637. col. 2.
127. *Loc. cit.*
128. *Ibid.,* p. 638.
129. *Ibid.,* p. 639.
130. *Ibid.,* p. 638. col. 2.
131. *Ibid.,* p. 639. col. 1.
132. *Ibid.,* p. 896. col. 2. *Cf.,* pp. 558, 637.
133. *Ibid.,* p. 897. col. 1.
134. *Ibid.,* p. 183. col. 2.
135. *Ibid.,* p. 184. col. 1.
136. *Ibid.,* p. 183. col. 2.
137. "We need to learn that the forms of liberty are not its essence; that whilst the letter of a free constitution is preserved its spirit may be lost; that even its wisest provisions and most guarded powers may be made weapons of tyranny. In a country called free, a majority may become a faction, and a proscribed minority may be insulted, robbed, and oppressed. Under elective governments, a dominant party may become as truly a usurper, and as treasonably conspire against the state, as an individual who forces his way by arms to the throne." *Loc. cit.*
138. *Ibid.,* p. 184. col. 2.
139. *Loc. cit.*
140. *Loc. cit.*
141. *Loc. cit.* Imprisonment for debt is pronounced shocking and barbarous, a judgment with which no one at the present day is likely to disagree.
142. *Ibid.,* p. 185.
143. *Ibid.,* pp. 148-149.
144. *Ibid.,* p. 147. col. 1.
145. *Ibid.,* p. 149. col. 1.
146. *Ibid.,* pp. 731-737, 743-752, 812-818, 845-846.
147. *Ibid.,* p. 113. col. 2.
148. *Ibid.,* p. 114. col. 1.
149. *Ibid.,* p. 150. col. 1.
150. *Ibid.,* p. 116. col. 1.
151. *Ibid.,* pp. 680-681, 649. col. 1.
152. *Ibid.,* pp. 648-649, 661-662, 679.
153. *Ibid,* p. 649. col. 1. *Cf.* pp. 661. col. 2.—662. col. 1.
154. *Ibid.,* p. 687. col. 2.
155. *Ibid.,* p. 676. col. 2.
156. *Ibid.,* p. 677.
157. *Ibid.,* pp. 660-661.
158. *Ibid.,* p. 660. col. 1.
159. "I maintain that the citizen, before fighting, is bound to enquire into the justice of the cause which he is called to maintain with blood, and bound to withhold his hand if his conscience condemn the cause. On this point he is able to judge. No political question, indeed, can be determined so easily as this of war. War can be justified only by plain palpable necessity; by un-

questionable wrong, which, as patient trial has proved, can in no other way be redressed; by the obstinate, persevering invasion of solemn and unquestionable rights. The justice of war is not a mystery for cabinets to solve. It is not a state-secret which he must take on trust. It lies within our reach. We are bound to examine it." *Ibid.*, p. 676. col. 1.

160. *Ibid.*, p. 677. col. 2: So wrote Channing in 1835. It is interesting to compare this declaration, which is in complete accord with his general principle that the state must never require the individual to transgress the moral law, with his attitude in 1814, when during the war with Great Britain, of which he thoroughly disapproved. Boston was threatened with attack. On this occasion Channing addressed his auditors as follows:

"The question now is, not whether we will carry invasion, slaughter, and desolation into an unoffending province, not whether we will give our strength and wealth to the prosecution of unprincipled plans of conquest, but whether we will defend our firesides and altars, whether we will repel from our shores a hostile army. On this question our duty is clear. However unjustifiable may have been the measures by which we have been reduced to this mournful extremity, our right to our soil and our possessions remains unimpaired; the right of defence can never be wrested from us; and never, whilst God gives means of resistance, ought we to resign our country to the clemency of a foe. Our duties as patriots and Christians are plain. Whilst we disclaim all share in the guilt of that war which is bursting on our shores, we should resolve that we shall be true to ourselves, to our fathers, and to posterity, that we will maintain the inheritance which we have received, that whilst God gives us power we will not receive law as a conquered people." (*Ibid.*, p. 686. col. 2.)

If we are to attempt to reconcile these two pronouncements, we can only assume that the Christian may rightfully fight on behalf of his country, after it has engaged in an unjust war, when that war has gone against it so far as to threaten it with invasion. But this is to distinguish between offensive and defensive war in a wholly artifical and impracticable manner. We can only conclude that Channing has left the ethical problem unsolved. In this connection it may be observed that his suggestion, called forth by a disgust with the pomp and parade of war with which many would sympathize, that the soldier, like the hangman, be dressed as becomes his craft (*Ibid.*, p. 678) seems to betray a touch of fanaticism rare indeed in his writings. His demand for full and free discussion before engaging in war (*Ibid.*, pp. 682-683), if advanced today, would deserve the same censure, but it is fair to remember that in his day our relative isolation was such as to render such a measure perhaps not impracticable.

161. *Ibid.*, p. 910. col. 2. "Race," here obviously means a particular race, such as the Anglo-Saxon.

162. *Ibid.*, p. 125. col. 2.

163. In this instance *race* clearly stands for "the human race."

164. *Ibid.*, pp. 872. col. 2.—873. col. 1. Channing's attitude, it will be seen, is equally opposed to that of the early Christians, to whom the state was an alien and hostile power, and to that of the modern nationalist of the Nazi type, for whom the state is everything and religion and humanity nothing. (It is interesting to observe that the same exaltation of patriotism within

limits, coupled with a stern determination to keep it within those limits, which is Channing's consistent attitude, is also characteristic of the thought of Mazzini.) "In our survey of our own and other countries," he writes, "the great question which comes to us is this, "Where and under what institutions are men most likely to advance? Where are the soundest minds and the purest hearts formed? What nation possesses, in its history, its traditions, its government, its religion, its manners, its pursuits, its relations to other communities, and especially in its private and public means of education, the instruments and pledges of a more resolute virtue and devotion to truth, than we now witness? Such a nation, be it where it may, will engage our warmest interest. We love our country, but not blindly. In all nations we recognize one great family, and our dearest wish for our native land is, that it may take the first rank among the lights and benefactors of the human race." (*Ibid.*, p. 125. col. 2.)

165. *Ibid.*, p. 652. col. 2. *Cf.* p. 663. col. 1.
166. "Free trade!—this is the plain duty and plain interest of the human race. To level all barriers to free exchange; to cut up the system of restriction, root and branch; to open every port on earth to every product; this is the office of enlightened humanity. To this a free nation should especially pledge itself. Freedom of the seas; freedom of harbors; an intercourse of nations, free as the winds; this is not a dream of philanthropists. We are tending towards it, and let us hasten it." (*Ibid.*, p. 166. col. 2; *Cf.* pp. 635-636.)
167. *Ibid.*, p. 340. col. 1.
168. *Ibid.*, p. 340.
169. *Ibid.*, pp. 341-342.
170. *Ibid.*, p. 54.
171. *Ibid.*, pp. 56-58, 103-104.
172. *Ibid.*, p. 58. col. 1.
173. *Loc. cit.*
174. *Ibid.*, p. 128. col. 1.
175. *Ibid.*, p. 130. col. 2.
176. *Ibid.*, p. 128. col. 1.
177. *Ibid.*, p. 124.
178. *Ibid.*, p. 124.
179. *Ibid.*, p. 126. col. 1.
180. *Ibid.*, p. 127. col. 1.
181. *Ibid.*, p. 81. col. 2.
182. *Ibid.*, p. 129. col. 2.
183. *Loc. cit.*
184. *Ibid.*, pp. 129. col. 2.—130. col. 1.
185. *Ibid.*, p. 80. col. 1.
186. *Ibid.*, p. 110. col. 2.
187. *Ibid.*, p. 111. col. 1.
188. *Loc. cit.*
189. *Ibid.*, p. 111. col. 1.
190. *Ibid.*, p. 111. col. 2.
191. *Loc. cit.*
192. *Ibid.*, pp. 111. col. 2.—112. col. 1.; p. 34. col. 2.

193. See R. A. Nicholson's *The Mystics of Islam*, p. 168.

194. "How any man can read ancient history," writes Channing, "and not perceive the immense advance of the human race, amazes me." *Ibid.*, p. 997. col. 2.

195. *Ibid.*, p. 277. col. 1.

196. *Ibid.*, p. 400. col. 2.

197. *Ibid.*, p. 352. col. 1.

198. *Ibid.*, p. 181. col. 2.

# Chapter Five

# Christ

As we have already seen, the root of the controversy between the early Unitarians and their Trinitarian opponents with regard to the seat of authority in religion was due to the extreme emphasis placed by the former upon the centrality of Christ. In thus stressing the unique and absolute supremacy of Jesus, they were, of course, faithful to their master, Locke. Yet, by adopting this position, they sundered themselves from every branch of orthodoxy.

For the Eastern Church the source of authority is to be found in the decisions of the ecumenical councils of the "ancient and undivided" church. It is a purely historical authority, for, since the schism between East and West, the Holy Spirit has declined to function through a divided church. According to the mediaeval Roman Catholic, however, the Spirit continued to function through the ecumenical councils of his own church, thus providing him with a living and contemporary authority. According to the modern Roman Catholic the Spirit now functions, as it always has functioned, through the mouth of the Pope presiding over an ecumenical council. The Calvinist, on the other hand, regards all councils as liable to error, and appeals to the authority of the *testimonium Spiritus Sancti internum* as it speaks to the soul of the individual believer; yet the office of the Spirit thus addressing him is to authenticate the revelation recorded in the Scriptures, and ancient creeds and modern confessions are authoritative only because they correctly interpret the essential teaching therein contained. For the Unitarian, however, all creeds and confessions were but "the commandments of men." They were wrong in principle, and to acknowledge their claims to submission on the part of the individual Christian constituted, as Channing expressly says, a kind of disloyalty.[1] The Christian knows but one Lord, Jesus Christ, and his allegiance should be whole-hearted and undivided.

"To whom am I to go," asks Channing, "for my knowledge of the Christian religion but to the Great Teacher, to the Son of God, to him in whom the fulness of the Divinity dwelt? This is my great privilege as a Christian, that I may sit at the feet not of a human but divine Master; that I may repair to him in whom truth lived and spoke without a mixture of error; who was eminently the wisdom of God and the light of the world. And shall man dare to interpose between me and my heavenly guide and Saviour, and prescribe to me the articles of my Christian faith? What is the state of mind in which I shall best learn the truth? It is that in which I forsake all other teachers for Christ. . . . Let me go to Jesus with a human voice sounding in my ears, and telling me what I must hear from the Great Teacher, and how can I listen to him in singleness of heart? . . . . This is what shocks me in the creed-maker. He interposes himself between me and my Saviour. He dares not trust me alone with Jesus. He dares not leave me to the word of God. This I cannot endure. The nearest possible communication with the mind of Christ is my great privilege as a Christian. I must learn Christ's truth from Christ himself, as he speaks in the records of his life, and in the men whom he trained up and supernaturally prepared to be his witnesses to the world." [2]

Here we have a conception of authority as purely historical as that of the Eastern Christian. Its importance, however, can scarcely be over estimated, for it functions as a sort of Occam's Razor in the domain of theology. What a multiplicity of dogmas are pared away by its unsparing application! The Trinity, the Incarnation, the Substitutionary Atonement, to name no others, fall immediate victims to its keen edge. Yet it is not an instrument to be applied carelessly or unintelligently. Reason, as we have seen, is required for the understanding of revelation.[3] The two can never be in conflict, for was not Christ the *wisdom* of God. Hence any irrational doctrine *must* be unchristian. "Whenever doctrines are taught you from the Christian records," Channing admonishes, "opposing any clear conviction of reason and conscience, be assured that it is not the teaching of Christ which you hear. Some rash human expounder is substituting his own weak, discordant tones for the voice of God, which they no more resemble than the rattling chariot-wheel does heaven's awful thunder." [4]

Is not such a position vitiated by the fatal defect that it provides an opportunity for reading one's own ideas into the words of Scripture? Certainly it is, if Channing's fundamental assumption that the Scriptures contain the record of an infallible teaching he rejected. But we must provisionally accept this assumption if we are to understand him. In this respect Channing shares the outlook of Locke, not that of his younger contemporary Theodore Parker, upon whom the initial achievements of the higher criticism produced so profound an impression. He is untroubled by the doubts and uncertainties which disturb the judgment of the modern scholar. He is sure that the four Gospels were written by the men whose names they bear, and that they embody a firsthand account of a teaching which contained no "mixture of error." [5] If this presupposition be granted, there are evidently only two ways of interpreting this teaching. One is to take it *au pied de la lettre,* with the most slavish literalness. But this is fatal, for it lands one in confusion, absurdity, and self-contradiction. "Allow me," writes Channing, "to prove doctrines in the same way,[6]—that is, by detaching texts from their connection and interpreting them without reference to the general current of Scripture, and I can prove anything and everything from the Bible. I can prove that God has human passions.[7] I can prove transubstantiation, which is taught much more explicitly than the Trinity. Detached texts prove nothing." [8] The only alternative, then, is to use one's own reason in interpreting a document which, one knows beforehand, contains a rational teaching. This conclusion is thoroughly in harmony with Channing's general theory of the relation between reason and revelation, for, as we shall discover when we come to examine in detail this aspect of his doctrine, he regards them as mutually interpenetrating one another, so that, in effect, they fuse together into a single whole.

At present, however, there are two points which need to be emphasized. One is that in thus insisting upon the unique authority and lordship of Christ, Channing was at one with his fellow-Unitarians. The second is that he is concerned to emphasize that this allegiance which the Christian owes to Christ involves no element of mental or moral servility and imposes no restraint upon intellectual freedom. There is no taint, he assures us, either in the character of Christ or in his teaching of the lust for spiritual domination. Christianity, he asserts, "has but one aim, which is, not to exalt its teacher, but to improve the disciple; not to fasten Christ's name on mankind, but to breathe into them his spirit of universal love." [9] "As far as I am Christian," he exclaims, "I am free. My religion lays on me not one chain. It does not prescribe a certain range for my mind beyond which nothing can be learned." [10] "Inward spiritual liberty, this," he affirms, "is the great gift of Jesus Christ." [11] And in accordance with this conviction he proclaims that mind free "which jealously guards its intellectual rights and powers, which calls no man master, which does not content itself with a passive or hereditary faith, which opens itself to light whencesoever it may come, which receives new truth as an angel from heaven, which, whilst consulting others, inquires still more of the oracle within itself, and uses instructions from abroad not to supersede but to quicken and exalt its own energies." [12] "Such," he observes, "is the spiritual freedom which Christ came to give." [13]

One wonders how the early Fathers of the Church would have regarded this interpretation of Christian discipleship. But there is no doubt that for Channing it is absolutely fundamental. Christ is the great Liberator from bondage of every kind. To follow him is to become free, and to become truly free is to follow him. Such is Channing's unchanging conviction. In the next to the last year of his life [14] he writes in the same strain, "As to Christ's *authority*, there is a sense in which I think it important, and reliance on it most natural and reasonable. I never meet a superior mind without some degree of reliance on it. From such a mind as Christ's, I am sure I can hear nothing but truth. Whatever he says, I am sure will, when fully understood, be found in harmony with God's perfection. This leads me to a reverential study of his words, as of no other man. If in the course of such study I meet anything which seems inconsistent with any known truth, and especially with the pure, liberal conceptions which Jesus has given me, I feel that I have not reached his meaning. I wait for further light, I examine the dark passage again and again, and the probability is that light will at length shine. If not, I cannot suffer for my ignorance." [15]

One must thoroughly grasp this conception of Christian discipleship if one is to appreciate the basis for a certain conservatism which, while it showed some signs of modification, yet in great measure continued to characterize Channing's outlook to the last day of his life. Only thus will one understand the reason for his dislike of the humanitarian view of Christ's nature, and his charitable condemnation of the position of Theodore Parker.

We must now examine Channing's application of the principle of Christ's unique and unrivalled authority—the Unitarian razor, as we may well term it—to the traditional doctrine of the nature of Christ himself. The rational and religious grounds for Channing's onslaught upon the doctrine of the Trinity we have already scrutinized, and in this connection it remains only to add that he supported his attack by wielding with dexterity the Unitarian razor, by pointing out that the New Testament habitually applies the term *God* to the Father, and by challenging his opponents "to adduce one passage in the New Testament where the word God means three persons, where it is not limited to one person, and where, unless turned from its usual sense by the connection, it does not mean the Father." [16]

When we turn to the doctrine of the deity of Christ, we see the same razor operating with devastating results. Here his task is facilitated by the large number of texts of a positive character which he is able to cite on behalf of the contrary view. "If we examine the passages in which Jesus is distinguished from God," maintains Channing, "we shall see that they not only speak of him as another being, but seem to labor to express his inferiority. He is continually spoken of as the Son of God, sent of God, receiving all his powers from God, working miracles because God was with him, judging justly because God taught him, having claims on our belief because he was annointed and sealed by God, and as able of himself to do nothing. The New Testament is filled with this language. Now we ask what impression this language was fitted and intended to make? Could any who heard it have imagined that Jesus was the very God to whom he was so industriously declared to be inferior; the very Being by whom he was sent, and from whom he professed to have received his message and power." [17]

As in the case of the doctrine of the Trinity, however, the argument from silence is also efficacious. Jesus, Channing points out, was to all appearances a human being, with a body sensitive to pain; and, moreover, a human being in "humble circumstances." The natural tendency, therefore, must have been to regard him as such. Hence, "we should expect to find in the New Testament perpetual care and effort to counteract this tendency, to hold him forth as the same being with his Father, if this doctrine were, as is pretended, the soul and centre of his religion. We should expect to find the phraseology of Scripture cast into the mould of this doctrine, to hear familiarly of God the Son, of our Lord God Jesus, and to be told that to us there is one God, even Jesus. But instead of this, the inferiority of Christ pervades the New Testament. It is not only implied in the general phraseology, but repeatedly and decidedly expressed, and unaccompanied with any admonition to prevent its application to his whole nature. Could it, then, have been the great design of the sacred writers to exhibit Jesus as the Supreme God." [18]

The above passages illustrate with sufficient clarity the manner in which Channing invokes the Scriptures to establish the Unitarian view of the subordinate nature of Christ. But the New Testament is not his only weapon. The doctrine of the Incarnation is stigmatized by Channing not only as unscriptural, but also as irrational. And here lies our chief interest. For it is evident from the space which he devotes to the subject and from the earnestness with which he presses his attack, that Channing is opposing something which he takes to be more than a mere intellectual confusion. A vital issue is involved, one fraught with practical significance for the spiritual life. Nor is this due merely to the close connection between the dogma in question and that of the Trinity. The doctrine of the Incarnation includes some element obnoxious in itself, from which Channing's whole soul recoils. That this is the case must be due to the fact that in his eyes the dogma negates some positive truth or truths which he regards as of the highest importance, and which we must clearly grasp if we are to understand him.

The issue has, moreover, been beclouded by the wearisome persistence with which for nearly a century Unitarian thinkers have reiterated that the Arian christology is more intolerable than that of Athanasius, and that the error of the latter resides, not in the positive but rather in the negative aspect of his doctrine, not in his assertion that God became incarnate in Christ but in his restriction of the Incarnation to Christ alone. Such a pronouncement, it is obvious, presupposes the acceptance of monistic idealism, upon the basis of which alone it becomes intelligible. The Absolute Mind is thus conceived as differentiating itself into a multiplicity of individual minds which remain included within it. Each of these individual minds is finite, and, as finite, imperfect, and subject to ignorance and error, to sin and self-condemnation. To speak, therefore, of such a mind as an incarnation of God is to use the term *incarnation* in a sense which is clearly metaphorical. The individual mind is not identical with the Absolute, it is only an appearance or manifestation, or at best a part, thereof. Such is not the theory against which Channing is in arms, nor does it even enter his purview.

In the field of comparative religion the notion of a divine incarnation is a thoroughly familiar one, descending as it does from remote antiquity. It may roughly be defined as the identification of an actual, individual human being with a god who dwells within him. As such it made its appearance at an early date in the history of Christian doctrine under the form of Patripassianism. According to this view, Jesus Christ was the human embodiment of the Father, who actually was born, and who lived, suffered, died, and rose again in his person. Patripassianism was thus an incarnationist Unitarianism, and as such, it was condemned as a heresy. With it neither Channing nor his orthodox opponents are to be credited with any sympathy.

According to the traditional doctrine it is not the Father, but the Son, the second Person of the eternal Trinity, who becomes incarnate. Yet even this phrase "became incarnate," innocent as it sounds, is likely to lead us astray, unless we use due caution. When we examine the doctrine as expounded, for instance, by that champion of orthodoxy, St. Thomas Aquinas, we discern that the Incarnation produced no change in God. Indeed it was impossible that it should do so, since God is eternal and, therefore, unchangeable. What happened was that the human soul and body of the man Jesus became so closely united to the second Person of the Trinity as to coalesce with it into a single Person. This is the mystery of the hypostatic union, an experience which is unique in the case of Jesus, and which is shared by none of his followers. Christ has thus a human nature and a divine nature, a human will and a divine will, yet he constitutes but a single person, and that person is not human but divine. His humanity is absorbed into his Godhead.

Such a view requires only to be stated for us to grasp in some measure how offensive it must inevitably have been to Channing. His own outlook is emphatically one which we should term today *personalistic*. A person, according to Channing, is an ultimate entity which cannot be resolved into, or compounded out of, antecedently or independently existing elements. To assert that it can is to subvert his whole philosophy, and to blast alike his conceptions of God and man.

Accordingly we find him remonstrating on behalf of himself and his fellow-Unitarians as follows: "We believe in the unity of Jesus Christ. We believe that Jesus is one mind, one soul, one being, as truly one as we are, and equally distinct from the one God. We complain of the doctrine of the Trinity, that, not satisfied with making God three beings, it makes Jesus Christ two beings, and thus introduces infinite confusion into our conceptions of his character. This corruption of Christianity, alike repugnant to common sense and to the general strain of Scripture, is a remarkable proof of the power of a false philosophy in disfiguring the simple truth of Jesus.

According to this doctrine, Jesus Christ, instead of being one mind, one conscious, intelligent principle, whom we can understand, consists of two souls, two minds; the one divine, the other human; the one weak, the other almighty; the one ignorant, the other omniscient. Now we maintain that this is to make Christ two beings. To denominate him one person, one being, and yet to suppose him made up of two minds, infinitely different from each other, is to abuse and confound language, and throw darkness over all our conceptions of intelligent natures. According to the common doctrine, each of these two minds in Christ has its own consciousness, its own will, its own perceptions. They have, in fact, no common properties. The divine mind feels none of the wants and sorrows of the human, and the human is infinitely removed from the perfection of the divine. Can you conceive of two beings in the universe more distinct? We have always thought that one person was constituted and distinguished by one consciousness. The doctrine that one and the same person should have two consciousnesses, two wills, two souls, infinitely different from each other, this we think an enormous tax on human credulity." [19]

Expressed in theological terms the burden of Channing's accusation is that in reality orthodoxy is nothing more than a disguised Nestorianism.[20] What is of especial importance, however, in the passage just cited is the emphasis upon the intelligibility of Christ as viewed by Unitarianism. This is a consideration which we find stressed elsewhere. "According to Unitarianism," declares Channing in his great sermon in New York,[21] "he is a being who may be understood, for he is one mind, one conscious nature. According to the opposite faith, he is an inconceivable compound of two most dissimilar minds, joining in one person a finite and infinite nature, a soul weak and ignorant, and a soul almighty and omniscient. And is such a being a proper object for human thought and affection." [22]

Now we are getting to the root of the matter. As in the case of God, so in the case of Christ, reason and emotion must function in harmony. We can love only a being whom we can understand.[23] Make Christ unintelligible, and you make him unlovable.[24] The principle of essential sameness holds true in this instance as inevitably as it holds true of God and man. Its vital significance is thus even more apparent. We have not yet got out of it all that Channing will draw from it, but we are now in a position to see that it constitutes the bedrock upon which all his thinking rests.

Channing has not yet finished, however, with the Incarnation. The Trinitarian does not realize, he thinks, all that is included in this doctrine. It makes God a material being in the same sense that man is a material being, "for man is material only by the union of the mind with the body; and the very meaning of incarnation is that God took a body, through which he acted and spoke, as the human soul operates through its corporeal organs." [25] "Every bodily affection," he continues, "may thus be ascribed to God. Accordingly the Trinitarian, in his most solemn act of adoration, is heard to pray in these appalling words: 'Good Lord, deliver us; by the mystery of thy holy incarnation, by thy holy nativity and circumcision, by thy baptism, fasting, and temptation, by thine agony and bloody sweat, by thy cross and passion, good Lord, deliver us.' Now I ask you to judge, from the principles of human nature, whether to worshippers who adore their God for his wounds and tears, his agony, and blood, and sweat, the ideas of corporeal existence and human suffering will not predominate over the conceptions of a purely spiritual essence; whether the mind, in clinging to the man, will not lose the God; whether a surer method for depressing and adulterating the pure thought of the Divinity could have been devised." [26]

The results of such a teaching, Channing points out, are what one might have anticipated. The worshippers are fascinated by, and attracted to, the incarnate member of the Trinity, as man is drawn to man, and the other divine Persons are treated with comparative disregard.[27] He does not question that intense emotions may thus be excited, but he does question their value.[28] They seem to him too earthly and too transitory, lacking in the vastness and spiritual exaltation which are awakened by the thought of the Father.

Moreover to materialize God is to externalize him, and thus to shut oneself off from the possibility of intimate communion with him. It is Channing the mystic who here raises his voice in protest. "My friends," he exclaims, "hold fast the doctrine of a purely spiritual Divinity. It is one of the great supports and instruments of a vital piety. It brings God near as no other doctrine can. One of the leading purposes of Christianity is to give us an ever-growing sense of God's immediate presence,—a consciousness of him in our souls. Now, just as far as corporeal or limited attributes enter into our conception of him, we remove him from us. He becomes an outward, distant being, instead of being viewed and felt as dwelling in the soul itself. It is an unspeakable benefit of the doctrine of a purely spiritual God, that He can be regarded as inhabiting, filling our spiritual nature; and, through this union with our minds, He can and does become the object of an intimacy and friendship such as no embodied being can call forth." [29]

When contrasted with the teaching of the Fourth Gospel, that "God is a spirit, and they that worship him must worship him in spirit and in truth," the dogma of the Incarnation constitutes in Channing's opinion, "a relapse into the error of the rudest and earliest ages," it is "a doctrine which, in earthliness reminds us of the mythology of the rudest pagans, and which a pious Jew, in the twilight of the Mosaic religion, would have shrunk from with horror." [30]

Furthermore, the doctrine in question becomes increasingly incredible when viewed in its historic setting. The timing is all wrong. If the ancient Jew and the ancient Greek could grasp the concept of a purely spiritual Deity, it is absurd to suppose that the Christian cannot do the same, and that the Godhead must become flesh in order that he may know it. "It is plain," remarks Channing, "that such a manifestation, if needed at all, was peculiarly required in the infancy of the race." [31]

Moreover, acceptance of the doctrine of the Incarnation logically invalidates the Biblical prohibition of image-worship, for the reason assigned for that prohibition is "that ye saw no manner of similitude on the day that the Lord spake unto you in Horeb out of the midst of the fire." "If, since that period, God has taken a body, then," urges Channing, "the reason of the prohibition has ceased; and, if he took a body, among other purposes, that He might assist the weakness of the intellect, which needs a material form, then a statue, which lends so great an aid to the conception of an absent friend, is not only justified, but seems to be required." [32] In other words, the Romanist is right, and the consistent Trinitarian ought also to be an idolator.

Channing's attack upon the doctrine of the Incarnation is, in the opinion of the writer, the most powerful which has ever been delivered; and this power is due, not only to the sincerity which rings true in every line of it, and to the cogency of the reasoning, but also to the spiritual outlook which inspires it. As reason and revelation mutually involve each other, so intellect and emotion in the soul of the Christian must fuse together in an *amor intellectualis,* and this is as true when the object is Christ as when the object is God. The doctrine of the Incarnation has given us an unintelligible, and therefore an unlovable, Christ. Moreover, it violates the fundamental principle of *essential sameness,* in accordance with which God and Christ are conceived to be persons in the same sense in which a man is a person; and, since only persons can—in the strict sense of the word—be loved, it thereby strikes at the very root of Christian piety. Here, as always, Channing's destructive effort is not indulged in for its own sake. He is striving to remove what he considers to be an obnoxious and harmful error, because he has a positive end in view. What is this positive end? What is the positive significance of Channing's christology?

In seeking an answer to this question we cannot do better than to view the problem in the light of the basic principle of *essential sameness* which we have found so illuminating in our examination of Channing's conception of God. And, once we have placed ourselves at this standpoint, we can see clearly how relatively unimportant the issue between Arianism and Humanitarianism must have seemed to the mature mind of Channing, and also, why the former theory must have impressed him as inherently the more plausible.

For Channing the primary significance of Christ is the perfection of his character, a perfection the reality of which he never dreams of questioning, and with regard to which he assumes that all other Christians will be of the same mind as himself.[33] This perfection he habitually speaks of as "moral," but it is important to remember that he uses the term in the broader rather than in the narrower sense; that Channing conceives of it as including, not only ethical impeccability, but also perfect rationality and boundless devotion both to God and man. In Christ Channing sees the complete integration of intellect, emotion, and volition which constitutes the actualization of that ideal toward which every disciple must aspire. Here we behold the living likeness of the divine character. This is the point of fundamental importance. Moral perfection *can* be achieved, for Christ *has* achieved it. We know that he has achieved it, for he has actually lived on this earth, united to a human body as the souls of men are united to their bodies, and has thereby shown us what a perfect personality is. Thus we know that our ideal is not a sentimental dream or the impracticable projection of irresponsible fancy but a practicable goal, inasmuch as it has actually been realized.

Are not all these reflections, nevertheless, rendered nugatory by the acceptance of the Arian hypothesis? This is the stock objection, advanced with ceaseless reiteration by Unitarians of the Humanitarian persuasion. If Christ be neither God nor man, is it not evident, they urge, that his character, however exalted, and his achievements, however magnificent, reveal to us nothing with respect to the nature of God, on the one hand, or to the potentialities of man, on the other? And the admission which we are expected immediately to make is that Arianism is a theory so totally unsatisfactory as to be not worth discussing. Yet there is a further question which we may well ask of them in return. If the bankruptcy of Arianism be so potently, even blatantly, obvious, is it not remarkable that this fact should have entirely escaped the attention of Channing, which, however limited in its purview, was of singular penetration when directed upon things of the spirit? How are we to account for this extraordinary and deplorable blindness? Was Channing merely the victim of an irrational prejudice in favor of conservatism and tradition? Was he deceived in regard to his own boasted independence of thought?

We may, of course, seek to explain the unwelcome fact by invoking Channing's profound reverence for the letter of the New Testament, a reverence natural enough in the case of an intellect which had matured before the impact of the higher criticism had been experienced by the thought of New England. Yet one may point out that Channing's eminent contemporary, Andrews Norton, was able to cast off this restraining influence. It is possible, needless to say, that Channing nodded when Norton was awake. Yet we should do well, before assuming that this is a sufficient explanation, to examine more carefully

Channing's own position, for it may be that we shall discover there certain considerations which will alter our perspective.

Let us, then, begin with a phrase which Channing was fond of repeating. "All minds are of one family." [34] By "minds" we are to understand the hierarchy of rational intelligences, human, angelic, and seraphic.[35] Is God to be included within this hierarchy? In a sense, yes, and in a sense, no. The principle of *essential sameness* assures us that God is a person in the same sense in which an angel or a man is a person. Yet there remains an important difference. God is an uncreated and a creative intelligence; all other minds are creatures; hence, for Channing, the tremendous importance of the conviction that Christ is not God. This is the one conclusion with regard to his "rank" in the universe which is of really vital significance for the Christian; since, if Christ be God, the perfection of his character, while it does, indeed, reveal the divine nature, constitutes for man neither stimulus nor promise. If, on the contrary, Christ stand on the side of the creatures, and yet hold a unique rank in the universe, subordinate only to that of God, he is in a position to fulfill both functions. He is at once above us and of us; he simultaneously manifests the actuality of the divine perfection and the divine potentiality of man.

The principle of *essential sameness* is thus once again the ground of human hope. It is the personality, rather than the humanity or the superhumanity of Christ, that is of vital import. It is because we are minds in the same sense that Christ is a mind, and persons in the same sense that he is a person, that his perfection has a meaning for us and that he is fitted to be an examplar to us.[36] It is upon Christ's moral perfection and upon his godlikeness that Channing loves to dwell, and it is for this reason that we find him, not discouraging inquiry into, yet resolutely excluding from the focus of interest the question of Christ's ontological status in the universe. It is the perfection of his personality that is the central truth, and the Humanitarian who recognizes this has a saving faith.[37]

Furthermore, it requires to be stressed that Channing insists, with an emphasis in no way inferior to that of the Humanitarian, that Jesus, during his earthy existence, was *very man*.[38] His soul was united to his body in the same way in which all men's souls are united to their bodies, and, if this is to be human, Christ was human as anybody could be. "Jesus," asserts Channing, "by his birth, was truly a *human being*; and in this we should rejoice. He was flesh of our flesh. He had our wants and desires, our hunger and thirst, our sensations of pleasure and pain, our natural passions. He was born of woman, was folded in a mother's arms, was nourished from a mother's breast; and he felt the gratitude, the tenderness of a son. He bore the relations of life toward kindred, neighbors, and friends. He grew up amidst the labors of mortal men, ate the bread of his own earnings, and was acquainted by experience with the hardships to which the multitudes of men are exposed. He was thus actually one of our race, a brother of the great human family." [39] The ancient formula, then, holds true. "He became what we are that we might become what he is." [40]

That the saviour of the human race should also be a member of the human race seems to Channing indicative of a wisdom worthy of divine providence. That a superangelic being could not fully sympathize with men without himself becoming man is an assertion which he regards with deep suspicion, but he is nonetheless confident that only another human being could call forth from men the fullest understanding, appreciation, sympathy, and devotion. His reservation with regard to the former point is worthy of notice, for it carries with it social and political, as well as christological, implications, and throws light, moreover, upon his conception of the communion of saints.

"I am not prepared to say," he remarks, "that a superangelic being, continuing such, might not have entered into all our wants and feelings as truly as one of our race. Our ideas of higher orders of beings are very much perverted by the habit of comparing them with the higher ranks of men on earth. We are apt to conceive of angels as separated from us immeasurably, as filled with the consciousness of their superiority, as looking down upon us with feelings not unlike those with which the aristocracy of this world regard the lower classes of men. The true doctrine, I believe, is, that just in proportion as a being rises in the scale of intelligence and virtue, he becomes knit by tenderer sympathy with inferior orders of being. In truth he rises above the conception of different orders. He regards all beings who possess thought, conscience, and the power of knowing God, as his brethren. He respects them as essentially his equals, in consequence of their capacity of indefinite improvement. He recognizes his own nature in the lowest human creature, and is most solicitous to raise the most fallen. Yes! My belief is, that the beings who sympathize most with human infirmity and sorrow, and who feel most deeply for human guilt, are the beings who are *above* us." [41]

Even with regard to his subsequent admission, that only the appeal of another man could call forth the deepest response from men, Channing's enthusiastic personalism, and his loyalty to the principle of *essential sameness,* cause him some misgivings. "I feel indeed," he admits, "as if, with my present views of the heavenly world, I should not shrink before an archangel. But these views I owe to Christianity. They were unknown before Jesus appeared. And perhaps I deceive myself. Perhaps with an archangel's form I could not associate the idea of *fraternal* sympathy. But with Jesus, who was born at Bethlehem, I can form this association. He wore our nature; and therefore I know that our nature is honored by him, and is precious to him. . . . He was a man. I see in him a brother and a friend. I feel the reality of that large, loving, *human* sympathy, which so gloriously distinguished his whole character and life. Let us rejoice then that Christ the Saviour was *born.*" [42]

We are now in a position to see how and why Channing's earlier hostile attitude toward the Humanitarian view underwent a change, and how that hostility evaporated. We have yet to enquire, however, why he still professed himself unable to accept it. What were the considerations which led him to prefer the Arian Theory?

In the first place, of course, there was the testimony of the Scriptures, and that this exercised a constraining influence upon the mind of Channing there is no denying. Despite his rejection of the notion of verbal inspiration, his reverence for the letter was profound. And it is easy to understand why such was the case. His approach to the Bible—need we repeat?—was utterly different from that of the modern scholar. Convinced that Jesus had proceeded with the definite intention of founding a religious association—the church[43]—and of promulgating a system of doctrine which he had "supernaturally prepared" his immediate followers to expound, he could scarcely have regarded the silence of the synoptics as of any significance at all in the light of the positive statements of the Epistles and the Fourth Gospel.[44] Yet, were this the only ground for his conviction, his attitude would have for us today only a psychological interest, as indicative of his conservatism and literal-mindedness. But, as we shall see, it constituted, almost certainly, the weakest of the considerations which impressed him as so weighty.

It is to the perfection of Christ's character, which was of such supreme importance to Channing, that we must return, if we are to appreciate the attraction which Arianism held for him. The Humanitarian theory seemed to him totally incapable of accounting for it; hence, in his eyes, Humanitarian was, not, indeed, morally obnoxious, but intellectually jejune.

Had Channing been a determinist, of the type of Edwards, for instance, he would have experienced little or no difficulty in subscribing to the Humanitarian doctrine. If a man's character be only the expression of the divine will, if there be in reality only one will operative in the universe, then we can find in that will the sufficient explanation of any man's character—be it what it may. It will be no more difficult for God to create a saint than a sinner, or an archangel than a man. But determinism was, for Channing, an utterly incredible position, one completely irreconcilable with the reality of the moral life. Moral perfection is not something ready-made; something that can be assumed, as a man might put on a coat. It is something that must be developed, that must be fought for. This is as true of Christ as it is of anyone else. His perfection must have been reached by effort; and, if in his earthly life there be no trace of such development, that development must have taken place previously, that is, before his birth, during an earlier life.

There is yet a further consideration which powerfully reinforces this conclusion, and that is the moral character of God. If Christ occupy, as the Scriptures state that he does, the most exalted position in the universe under God, he must owe his rank to one of two causes; either to his own worth or to divine favor. But the latter hypothesis is wholly inadmissible; for it amounts to asserting that God plays favorites. Nearness to a just and righteous God can be attained in only one way, by becoming like him. Hence Jesus' rank cannot be the mere consequence of an arbitrary divine fiat. Its bestowal must have constituted the coronation of a moral conqueror who had emerged victorious from the most tremendous combat which a rational being can wage, that for the realization of the divine potentiality within him.

Among Channing's unpublished papers[45] there is an essay or sermon, which either was never finished or the concluding portion of which has been lost or misplaced, which is devoted to the elaboration of this view. "I fear," writes Channing, "that the example of Christ loses its power, through the idea, that his nature and circumstances were so peculiar, as to make his virtue something necessary, inevitable.

It is thought, that a being so connected with God, clothed with such powers, illumined by such revelation, could not but be spotless, sinless; that no moral effort was necessary to his purity; that his character owed its excellence to a necessity as irresistible as that by which a plant in a fine climate, and under the mingled and happiest influences of sunshine and rain, unfolds the beauty of its leaves and flowers.

"Freedom, freedom," he continues, "is the condition and element of all greatness. Make the mind of Jesus a machine—i.e., suppose it placed under influences which it could not resist, suppose it to be visited with such continual instruction and suggestion from God as to render its own exertions needless—suppose it to have motives urged upon it by omnipotence, which it could not withstand, and though faultless, he could have no moral worth, no virtue, no greatness.

Christ's peculiar powers, revelations, and connections with God, instead of causing, determining, and fixing his character, were on the contrary the effects, results, and recompenses of his character. Instead of making him pure, they were founded upon his purity. He was clothed with all his high office, because he was endued with high virtue. He won this glory by his goodness. In saying this, I say of Jesus what I conceive to be true of all beings in all worlds. . . . Christ was no exception to the universal principle of divine government. Nothing but moral goodness, the settled purpose of duty, manifested in an obedient life, can gain the approving love of God."

If, now, we turn to Channing's published works we find the same idea briefly stated in "The Perfect Life," [46] "What is it that endears Jesus Christ to his Father? You may learn it from the following passage: 'Jesus said to his disciples, If ye keep my commandments, ye shall abide in my love, even as I have kept my Father's commandments, and abide in his love.' I beg you to weigh these words. Jesus owed the peculiar love with which he was regarded by God,—he owed his office as the Messiah, and all the power with which he was invested,— to his obedience, to his moral and religious integrity, to his unfailing reverence for goodness. Why was it that he enjoyed such peculiar communion with God? He says: 'The Father hath not left me alone, because I do always those things which please him.' *This* was the bond of union between him and his Father. To this perfect rectitude of his will, his reason, and his life he owed not only his mission on earth, but his crown in heaven."

Thus Channing's Arianism reposes upon two fundamental convictions—the moral perfection of Christ and the freedom of the will.

Not only, therefore, is it easy to see why he adopted this position; it is also difficult to believe that he ever abandoned it. And, as a matter of fact—despite second-hand testimony to the contrary—we can point to Ezra Styles Gannett's considered opinion that he never did abandon it.[47]

In Theodore Parker's contention that the simple humanity of Christ involved his imperfection, Channing must have seen the logical opposite of his own view. But we can be quite sure that he would not have sympathized with James Freeman Clark's objection that Parker's assertion was a piece of unjustifiable dogmatism; on the contrary, he would surely have agreed that Parker's conclusion followed logically from his premises. Deny Christ's pre-existence, he would have urged, and you are confronted with a perfection which is incredible. That perfection, however, Channing was never prepared to call in question. It appeared to him to be too well authenticated by historic records. Not only is it impossible, he maintained,[48] to excise the miracles from the life of Jesus without impugning the historicity of the entire account; the whole life itself constituted one tremendous miracle. Accordingly we must either take it for what it is, or seek to explain it away as a fiction. But such a character as that of Christ could never have been invented; it must, therefore, have been real.[49]

Furthermore we can see that Channing must have regarded the stock objection to Arianism—that the perfection of a superhuman being is of no significance for us—as constituting the grossest travesty of his position; for the principle of *essential sameness* which assures us that Christ is a person in the same sense in which we are persons, renders his perfection of the greatest significance for us.[50] "All souls," asserts Channing, in a familiar strain, "are one in nature, approach one another, and have grounds and bonds of communion with one another. I am not only one of the human race; I am one of the great intellectual family of God. There is no spirit so exalted with which I have not common thoughts and feelings. That conception which I have gained of One Universal Father, whose love is the fountain and centre of all things, is the dawn of the highest and most magnificent views in the universe; and if I look up to this Being with filial love, I have the spring and beginning of the noblest sentiments and joys which are known in the universe. No greatness, therefore, of a being separates me from him or makes him unapproachable by me. The mind of Jesus Christ, my hearer, and your mind are of one family; nor was there anything in his of which you have not the principle, the capacity, the promise in yourself." [51]

This community of nature in which God, man, and Christ alike participate is, in Channing's eyes, the presupposition of the Gospel, the denial of which deprives it of all its meaning. Only in the light of this principle, he insists, can Christ's activity be understood.[52] "In the most fallen and depraved man he saw a being who might become an angel of light. Still more, he felt that there was nothing in himself to which men might not ascend. His own lofty consciousness did not sever him from the multitude; for he saw in his own greatness the model of what men might become. So deeply was he thus impressed, that again and again, in speaking of his future glories, he announced that in these his true followers were to share. They were to sit on his throne and partake of his beneficent power." [53] "We are thus admitted," asserts Channing, "to a fellowship with Jesus Christ, whose highest end was that he might act with a new and celestial energy on the human mind. We rejoice to think that he did not come to monopolize this divine sway, to enjoy a solitary grandeur, but to receive others, even all who should obey his religion, into the partnership of this honor and happiness. Every Christian, in proportion to his progress, acquires a measure of this divine agency." [54]

In all this there is undeniably much that is old, so old that it tends perpetually to be forgotten, yet there is also unmistakably something that is new. The tremendous emphasis upon the future exaltation and divinization of the faithful believer is only an echo, albeit a thrilling echo, of the promises set forth in the Gospel of John, in the Pauline Epistles, and in the Apocalypse; although no doubt the significance of these promises has been largely obscured for the average believer by the dogma of the Hypostatic Union. Yet in Channing's conception of a God who not only encourages, but actually commands us, to try his character by moral standards which he did not himself create, in his portrait of a Christ who is consumed by a reverence for human nature, in his perpetual insistence upon the dignity of man, there breathes the distinctive spirit of the eighteenth century. To what extent the ideals of the century derived respectively from Christian or Hellenic sources is a question into which we need not enter. Yet we have only to compare the picture of the exalted Christ in the book of Revelation with Channing's description of the character of Christ's reign in heaven to recognize that there is a profound difference.

"Jesus is, indeed, sometimes spoken of as reigning in the future world, and sometimes imagination places him on a real and elevated throne. Strange that such conceptions can enter the minds of Christians. Jesus will indeed reign in heaven, and so he reigned on earth. He reigned in the fishing-boat, from which he taught; in the humble dwelling, where he gathered round him listening and confiding disciples. His reign is not the vulgar dominion of this world. It is the empire of a great, godlike, disinterested being over minds capable of comprehending and loving him. In heaven, nothing like what we call government on earth can exist, for government here is founded in human weakness and guilt. The voice of command is never heard among the spirits of the just." [55] Whether Channing may not have penetrated more deeply into the mind of Christ than did those who portrayed him as a magnified oriental monarch is a question which, perhaps, the wisest New Testament scholar might hesitate to answer; yet one cannot help but wonder what form St. Paul's comments on the above passage would have taken.

In view of Channing's constant emphasis upon the moral excellence of Christ, his conception of Christ's mission should now be clear to us. It was, in a word, to win others to virtue and piety.[56] "The truth is," declares Channing, "the love of Christ is but another name for the love of virtue." [57] "Others may love Christ for mysterious attributes," he exclaims upon another occasion, "I love him for the rectitude of his soul and his life." [58] "I love him, I have said, for his moral excellence; I know nothing else to love." [59] Were these sentences to be taken in isolation from their context, they might well be deemed indicative of an appallingly impersonal attitude. Needless to say, however, they cannot be so taken without misrepresenting their author's thought. On the contrary, we find Channing protesting against any attempt to sunder Christian revelation from its revealer. "Jesus is his religion embodied and made visible. The connection between him and his system is peculiar. It differs altogether from that which ancient philosophers bore to their teachings. An ancient sage wrote a book, and the book is of equal value to us whether we know its author or not. But there is no such thing as Christianity without Christ. We cannot know it separately from him. It is not a book which Jesus wrote. It is his conversation, his character, his history, his life, his death, his resurrection. He pervades it throughout. In loving him, we love his religion; and a just interest in this cannot be awakened, but by contemplating it as it shone forth in himself." [60] God and Christ can no more be loved apart from their qualities than a substance can be conceived apart from its attributes; hence the importance of understanding what those qualities are. "Nothing," Channing insists, "has wrought so powerfully on the human soul as the mind and character of Jesus Christ. Among all means of civilization and improvement, I can find nothing to be compared in energy with this. The great impulse which is to carry forward the human race is the character of Jesus, understood ever more clearly, and ever more deeply felt." [61]

What is probably the best exposition of Channing's conception of the work of Christ is to be found in the discourse entitled, *Jesus Christ the Brother, Friend, and Saviour*, in *The Perfect Life*. There Jesus is portrayed as "the great emancipator." He came, Channing tells us, in the first place to free the intellect.[62] He came "to inspire an earnest love of truth, and to animate men in its pursuit,—unfettered by their own passions, prejudices, and interests, and by the customs, traditions, and authority of others. Christianity is the charter of intellectual liberty, authorizing and commanding every man to use freely his own faculties in discovering truth, and especially religious truth. This is a liberty which Christians have thus far too little prized, though it lies at the root of all other liberty, and is indispensable for the development of the human mind." [63]

In the second place, Jesus came to liberate the human conscience from the domination of passion and sloth, and to inspire men with an enthusiasm for noble living.[64] With this thought we are already familiar.

In the third place, Jesus came to "set free our imprisoned energy for love. Man was made for love; he lives by love; and the measure of his life is the largeness and liberty of his love." [65] By "love" Channing seems here clearly to mean both the personal devotion which binds us to a relatively few individuals and also the more impersonal altruism which units the good man to his race. The affections of the home, he tells us, are intended to overflow until they embrace the entire human race. Few will contest the soundness of this interpretation of Christ's mission.

Lastly, Channing concludes, Jesus came to bring "a yet nobler salvation, by delivering the soul from the enthralling sway of creation, and lifting it into communion with the Creator. No man knows human nature, till he discerns in it that central principle, which might well be called the love of the infinite. The profoundest, sublimest, grandest emotion in man is the longing for an unbounded good, the aspiration to be one with the All-Good. We grow weary of whatever is limited. Forever and everywhere we overpass all bounds. The infinite Creator quickens in the inmost essence of the soul this insatiable desire, for which he only is the sufficing object, which he alone by his own overflowing fulness can gratify. The diverse and multiplied forms of good in creation may for a time bewilder, oppress, and imprison this divine principle; but they cannot destroy it. For ever it awaits the deliverer. Now Jesus came to set this love of the perfect free." [66]

Such, in its broad outlines, is Channing's view of the significance of Jesus' life. But what of his death? For orthodoxy, with its doctrine of the blood-atonement, the death of Christ is vastly more important than his life, since it was his sufferings on the cross which purchased man's salvation. The nature of Channing's onslaught upon this famous doctrine is too well known to require a detailed examination. Upon its legitimacy christocentric, theocentric, and humanistic Unitarians are agreed, and the echoes which it awakened have been resounding in "liberal" pulpits all over the land for more than a century. It is the incorporation of this dogma which rendered the various forms of orthodoxy ethically abhorrent to the modern man. It is these systems which make the gospel "the saddest news ever told on earth," [67] which "take from us our Father in heaven, and substitute for him a being whom we cannot love if we would, and whom we ought not to love if we could." [68] The doctrine of the blood-atonement "obscures the mercy of God" [69] in that it teaches that man's pardon is payed for by the blood of Christ. But, when payment is rendered and satisfaction made, there is no genuine forgiveness; [70] for the essence of forgiveness is that it be an act of free grace, unbought, unpayed for, and unmerited. [71] The notion that to sin against an infinite being is to incur infinite guilt deserving of infinite punishment, "overlooks the obvious maxim that the guilt of a being must be proportioned to his nature and powers." [72] "With such a Creator," Channing indignantly affirms, "the idea of mercy cannot coalesce; and I will say more, that under such a government man would need no mercy; for he would owe no allegiance to such a Maker, and could not, of course, contract the guilt of violating it; and, without guilt, no grace or pardon would be wanted." [73]

Moreover, intellectual insult is added to the moral injury already inflicted when we discover that all the suffering is supposed to have been borne by the human soul and body of Christ. The much-vaunted "infinite satisfaction" thus turns out to be a sham. The doctrine of the Hypostatic Union constitutes an ineffectual attempt to mask the unacknowledged, yet unvanquished, Nestorianism which has controlled the formulation of the dogma.[74]

With the justice of Channing's structures the vast majority of liberal thinkers would concur. Nonetheless there remains a further question which it is instructive to ask. Granted that the doctrine of the substitutionary atonement be as morally obnoxious and intellectually self-contradictory as Channing maintains, is this all that can be said about it? Does it contain nothing of value? Does it not present the idea, however grotesquely mutilated, of divine chivalry? The Jewish thinker, Montefiore, has answered this query with an emphatic affirmative. That God sympathizes and suffers with man is, he maintains, an important truth which must be rescued from the wreck of this doctrine, and which, he hopes, will be incorporated in liberal Judaism. To these considerations Channing is the last man whom we should expect to be blind. Yet he shows no sign of being influenced by them. The horror which he more than once evinces in speaking of the notion of the supreme God undergoing physical suffering and death is obviously genuine and unqualified. In a worshipper of power—and more theologians have worshipped power than one likes to admit—this would be natural enough, but in the case of Channing, whose primary reverence is for God's goodness, such an attitude appears incongruous.

Perhaps we shall find the explanation in the comparatively depreciatory manner in which Channing speaks of compassion as divorced from moral considerations. "To be touched by suffering," he tells us, "is a light thing." [75] Yet this is the emotion which ordinary men attribute in the fullest measure to Jesus, and thereby "ascribe to him a low and commonplace character." [76] "Now this overpowering compassion," observes Channing, "called forth by the view of exquisite misery, is a very ordinary virtue; and yet, I apprehend, it is the character ascribed above all others to Jesus. It certainly argues no extraordinary goodness, for it is an almost necessary impulse of nature. Were you, my friends, to see millions and millions of the human race on the edge of a fiery gulf, where ages after ages of torture awaited them, and were the shrieks of millions who had already been plunged into the abyss to reach your ear, could you refrain from an overpowering compassion, and would you not willingly endure hours and days of exquisite pain to give these wretched millions release? Is there any man who has not virtue enough for this? I have known men of ordinary character hazard their lives under the impulse of compassion, for the rescue of their fellow-beings from infinitely lighter evils than are here supposed." [77]

Had Channing lived in the days of the Holy Inquisition, or in a century in which Nazis, Fascists, and Communists were masters of whole countries, he might have arrived at the conclusion that compassion is by no means so common a characteristic, or of so little worth, as he here supposes it to be. Putting this consideration aside, we may proceed to note the unfortunate consequences—as Channing esteems them—of this tendency.

In the first place, men are naturally led to contrast the compassionate Jesus with his unmerciful Father, whose wrath can be appeased only by blood and death. The divine mercy is thus "obscured." In the second place, human compassion for Christ's physical sufferings is the feeling most naturally aroused; and this Channing, with Kantian severity, pronounces destitute of moral value.[78] And, in the third place, it awakens in the soul an irrational, selfish gratitude to Jesus for having rescued it from pain and suffering, such gratitude as would naturally be felt toward a man who had saved one from being carried down a cataract. "Is not this," asks Channing, "a necessary working of nature, a fruit of terror changed into joy." "I mean not to condemn it," he continues, "I only say it is not virtue. It is a poor tribute to Jesus; he deserves something far purer and nobler." [79] It is the greatness of Christ's spirit which one ought to admire.[80]

Nowhere is the influence of eighteenth century thought more evident in Channing's writings than in those lines where he attempts to show that Jesus was not an "enthusiast." [81] There he emphasizes the practicality of Jesus, his good sense, his knowledge of human nature, his restraint, his composure, his constancy, the soundness of his judgement, the absence of vehemence, precipitancy, of any sign of fanaticism. "Does the Lord's Prayer," he asks, "breathe a feverish enthusiasm." "The habitual style of Jesus on the subject of religion," he continues, "if introduced into many churches of his followers at the present day, would be charged with coldness." Consequently Channing can affirm, "I see nothing in Jesus of the overpouring compassion which is often ascribed to him. His character rarely exhibited strong emotion. It was distinquished by calmness, firmness, and conscious dignity. Jesus had a mind too elevated to be absorbed and borne away by pity, or any other passion. He felt, indeed, deeply for human suffering and grief; but his chief sympathy was with the mind, with its sins and moral diseases, and especially with its capacity of improvement and everlasting greatness and glory. He felt himself commissioned to quicken and exalt immortal beings. The thought which kindled and sustained him was that of an immeasurable virtue to be conferred on the mind, even of the most depraved,—a good, the very conception of which implies a lofty character; a good, which as yet has only dawned on his most improved disciples. It is his consecration to this sublime end which constitutes his glory; and no further than we understand this, can we yield him the love which his character claims and deserves." [82]

We can not, I believe, better understand how Channing could be indifferent even to that aspect of the orthodox theory of the Atonement which could favorably impress a Montefiore. The Scriptural statement that, "God so loved the world that he gave his only begotten Son that whosoever believeth on him should not perish, but should have everlasting life" seemed to him to express a doctrine sounder in every way, and to indicate just what one might expect of a good and merciful heavenly Father, and of his benevolent interest in his human children. But what of the fear of the orthodox believer that, if he cannot plead the merits of Christ in extenuation of his guilt, he will be left naked and defenceless with his sins upon his head before the vengeful wrath of an omnipotent Deity? To Channing's mind this fear does indeed argue an appalling lack of understanding of, and trust in, the divine goodness. In an outburst of passionate eloquence he exclaims, "The essential and unbounded mercy of my Creator is the foundation of my hope, and a broader and surer the universe cannot give me." [83]

Does the death of Christ, then, have no profound significance for Channing? Let him answer for himself. "I prize the cross and blood of Christ as highly as any Christian can. In view of that cross I desire ever to live; and of that blood, in the *spiritual sense,* I desire ever to drink. I hope, as truly as any Christian ever did or could, to be saved by the cross of Christ. But what do I mean by such language? Do I expect that the *wood* to which Christ was nailed is to save me? Do I expect that the *material* blood which trickled from his wounds is to save me? Or do I expect this boon from his bodily agonies? No! By the cross and blood of Christ I mean nothing outward, nothing material. I mean the spirit, the character, the love of Jesus, which his death made manifest, and which are pre-eminently fitted to bind me to him, and to make me a partaker of his virtues. I mean his religion, which was sealed by his blood, and the spirit of which shone forth most gloriously from his cross. I mean the great principles for which he died, and which have for their sole end to purify human nature." [84]

In other words, the crucifixion affects Channing very much as the burning of Jeanne d'Arc affects those convinced of her divine inspiration. It constitutes the culmination, at once tragic and triumphant, of a life of utter abnegation and devotion to the will of God, an example which thrills the believing heart with the sheer magnificence of its consecration.[85] Is this the conclusion of the whole matter? In his Baltimore sermon Channing refers to a divergence of opinion among the Unitarians of his day with respect to Christ's death in the following words: "Many suppose that this event contributes to our pardon, as it was a principal means of confirming his religion, and of giving it a power over the mind; in other words, that it procures forgiveness by leading to that repentence and virtue which is the great and only condition on which forgiveness is bestowed. Many of us are dissatisfied with this explanation, and think that the Scriptures ascribe the remission of sins to Christ's death with an emphasis so peculiar that we ought to consider this as having a special influence in removing punishment, though the Scriptures may not reveal the way in which it contributes to this end." [86]

It has been pointed out that the phrase "many of us" suggests that Channing associated himself with the upholders of the latter view. Certainly such an attitude would be in accord with the principle of stopping "where the Scriptures stop." However this may be, there was, according to Channing, a general agreement among Unitarians that Christ's death was in no sense an appeasement of divine wrath, and that it did not make God "placable or merciful." [87]

The general outlines of Channing's christology are now before us; and, as we review them, we can scarcely fail to be impressed by its self-consistency. You may point, if you will, to a change of emphasis between those passages in which he contrasts the unique authority of Jesus with the unfounded claims of "human" guides and the sermon in *The Perfect Life* in which he stresses the humanity of the Saviour; yet it is very doubtful how much we are to make of this. That it reveals a lessening antipathy toward the Humanitarian theory, we may well conjecture; we have Channing's own word for it that his emotional antipathy did in great measure pass away. To infer, however, that it indicates any change in doctrine would be an unwarranted conclusion. For it is incredible, on the one hand, that Channing ever meant to deny the humanity of Christ—such a denial would be sheer Docetism—while his published writings, on the other hand, give us no reason to suppost that he ever intended to assert that Jesus was *only* human. How illuminating is his own statement in the sermon on The *Imitableness of Christ's Character!*

"I believe him to be a more than human being. In truth, all Christians so believe him. Those who suppose him not to have existed before his birth do not regard him as a mere man,[88] though so reproached. They always separate him by broad distinctions from other men. They consider him as enjoying a communion with God, and as having received gifts, endowments, aids, lights from him, granted to no other, and as having exhibited a spotless purity, which is the highest distinction of heaven. All admit, and joyfully admit, that Jesus Christ, by his greatness and goodness, throws all other human attainments into obscurity." [89]

These words surely make it evident beyond question that for Channing, Jesus was at once man, and more than man. In this sense, obviously we are to interpret that passage in the *Letter on Creeds*[90] in which Jesus is referred to as "not a human but divine Master." Again in the sermon on *Jesus Christ the Brother, Friend, and Saviour* in *The Perfect Life*, where the Master's humanity is so stressed, the theory of his pre-existence—after being referred to as "a doctrine supported apparently[91] by the letter of various texts"—is put on one side as irrelevant to the consideration of the topic in hand—Christ's humanity.

In one respect, indeed, Channing's thought with respect to Jesus clearly underwent a change. In an early period of his life, when still under the influence of Calvinism, he appears to have accepted the theory of the substitutionary atonement—that theory which he was later to denounce so unsparingly. But in other respects his view does not seem to have changed appreciably. We have his own word for it that he was never a Trinitarian. And we have not sufficient ground to conclude that he ever became a simple Humanitarian.

That Jesus was entrusted with a divine mission, that he spoke with divine authority, that in his character men behold a perfect likeness of his heavenly Father—all this Channing firmly believed. "In Christ's words," he affirms, "we hear God speaking; in his miracles we behold God acting; in his character and life we see an unsullied image of God's purity and love. We believe, then, in the divinity of Christ, as this term is often and properly used." [92] And with no less firm a conviction did Channing believe in the potential divinity of man, who has it in him to become all that Christ is. But how is he to become what Christ is? Has Channing a doctrine of grace? What, then, is the relation between the natural and the supernatural, and what is the relation between reason and revelation? To this inquiry we must address ourselves in the following chapter.

## NOTES

1. *Life,* p. 195. n. 1.
2. *Works,* p. 486.
3. To this subject we shall return in the following chapter.
4. *Ibid.,* p. 338. col. 2.
5. See his *Evidences of Christianity,* Part I., *Works,* pp. 198-204.
6. He is here referring to the efforts of the Trinitarians to find textual support for the doctrine of the Trinity.
7. Is this disparaging phrase inconsistent with Channing's own theory of *essential sameness?* It is clear, I think, that it is not; for the words "human passions" seem to refer unmistakably to the doctrine of the corporeality of God, which Channing regards with unaffected horror, and which, as he points out, is involved in the theory of the Incarnation.
8. *Ibid.,* p. 244. col. 1.
9. *Ibid.,* p. 208. col. 2.
10. *Loc. cit.*
11. *Ibid.,* p. 172. col. 2.
12. *Ibid.,* p. 174. col. 2.
13. *Ibid.,* p. 175. col. 1.
14. In July, 1841.
15. *Life,* p. 451.
16. *Ibid.,* p. 371. col. 2. "So entirely do the Scriptures abstain from stating the Trinity," observes Channing, "that when our opponents would insert in into their creeds and doxologies, they are compelled to leave the Bible, and to invent forms of words altogether unsanctioned by Scriptural phraseology. That a doctrine so strange, so liable to misapprehension, so fundamental as this is said to be, and requiring such careful exposition, should be left so undefined and unprotected, to be made out by inference, and to be hunted through distant and detached parts of Scripture,—this is a difficulty which, we think, no ingenuity can explain." (*Ibid.,* p. 372. col. 1.) And more explicitly still Channing succinctly declares, "Believing, then, as I do, that it (i.e. the doctrine of the Trinity) forms no part of Christianity, my allegiance to Jesus Christ calls me openly to withstand it." (*Ibid.,* p. 244. col. 2.)
17. *Ibid.,* p. 374.
18. *Ibid.,* p. 374. "I am aware," concedes Channing, "that these remarks will be met by two or three texts in which Christ is called God, and by a class of passages, not very numerous, in which divine properties are said to be ascribed to him. To these we offer one plain answer. We say that it is one of the most established and obvious principles of criticism, that language is to be explained according to the known properties of the subject to which it is applied. Every man knows that the same words convey very different ideas when used in relation to different beings. Thus, Solomon *built* the temple in

a different manner from the architect whom he employed; and God *repents* differently from man. (Does this imply that Channing was here prepared to concede anything to the theological principle of *analogy?* I think that such an inference would be groundless. The *repentance* of God, Channing would probably have regarded as a metaphor; or he might conceivably have interpreted the phrase as Maimonides would have done, as indicating that God acts *like* a person who had repented, but for other reasons.) Now we maintain that the known properties of Christ, his birth, sufferings, and death, his constant habit of speaking of God as a distinct being from himself, his praying to God, his ascribing to God all his power and offices,—these acknowledged properties of Christ, we say, oblige us to interpret the comparatively few passages which are thought to make him the Supreme God, in a manner consistent with his distinct and inferior nature. It is our duty to explain such texts by the rule which we apply to other texts, in which human beings are called gods, and are said to be partakers of the divine nature, to know and possess all things, and to be filled with all God's fulness. These latter passages we do not hesitate to modify, and restrain, and turn from their most obvious sense, because this sense is opposed to the known properties of the beings to whom they relate; and we maintain that we adhere to the same principle, and use no greater latitude, in explaining, as we do, the passages which are thought to support the Godhead of Christ." *Ibid.*, pp. 374. col. 2.—375. col. 1.

19. *Ibid.*, p. 373.

20. The Nestorian Church regards Jesus Christ as composed of two *persons*, one human and one divine.

21. On *Unitarian Christianity Most Favorable to Piety.*

22. *Ibid.*, p. 395. col. 1.

23. "It is very clear," Channing expressly states, "that love to a being must rest on what we know of him, and not on unknown and unintelligible attributes." *Ibid.*, p. 320. col. 2.

24. "My friends, I have now stated, in general, what knowledge of Christ is most important, and is alone required in order to a true attachment to him. Let me still farther illustrate my views by descending to one or two particulars. Among the various excellences of Jesus, he was distinguished by a benevolence so deep, so invincible, that injury and outrage had no power over it. His kindness towards men was in no degree diminished by their wrong-doing. The only intercession which he offered in his sufferings was for those who at that very moment were wreaking on him their vengeance; and what is more remarkable, he not only prayed for them, but, with an unexampled generosity and candor, urged in their behalf the only extenuation which their conduct would admit. Now, to know Jesus Christ is to understand this attribute of his mind, to understand the strength and triumph of the benevolent principle in this severest trial, to understand the energy with which he then held fast the virtue which he had enjoined. It is to see in the mind of Jesus at that moment a moral grandeur which raised him above all around him. This is to know him. I will suppose now a man to have studied all the controversies about Christ's nature, and to have arrived at the truest notions of his rank in the universe. But this incident in Christ's history, this discovery of his character, has never impressed him; the glory of a philanthropy

which embraces one's enemies has never dawned upon him. With all his right opinions about the Unity or the Trinity, he lives and acts towards others very much as if Jesus had never lived or died. Now I say that such a man does not know Christ. I say that he is a stranger to him. I say that the great truth is hidden from him: that his skill in religious controversy is of little more use to him than would be the learning by rote of a language which he does not understand. He knows the name of Christ, but the excellence which that name imports, and which gives it its chief worth, is to him as an unknown tongue." *Ibid.*, p. 319. col. 2.

25. If it be objected that Channing here crudely travesties orthodoxy, and that his description applies in fact only to Patripassianism, it may be replied that the doctrine of the hypostatic union does logically involve this very consequence. Plainly the orthodox cannot have his cake and eat it too. He cannot reject Nestorianism and escape the consequence of this rejection. *Work,* p. 388. col. 2.

26. *Ibid.,* p. 388. col. 2.

27. Thus in an Episcopal church worshippers commonly bow their heads at the mention of the name of Christ, but not at the mention of those of the Father or the Holy Spirit.

28. "It is indeed possible that this God-man (to use the strange phraseology of Trinitarians) may excite the mind more easily than a purely spiritual divinity; just as a tragedy, addressed to the eye and ear, will interest the multitude more than the contemplation of the most exalted character. But the emotions which are the most easily aroused, are not the profoundest or most enduring. This human love, inspired by a human God, though at first more fervid, cannot grow and spread through the soul, like the reverential attachment which an infinite, spiritual Father awakens. Refined conceptions of God, though more slowly attained, have a more quickening and all-pervading energy, and admit of perpetual accessions of brightness, life, and strength." *Ibid.*, p. 389.

29. *Ibid.,* p. 389. col. 2.

30. *Ibid.,* p. 388. col. 1.

31. *Ibid.,* p. 388. col. 2.

32. *Ibid.,* p. 389. col. 1.

33 "According to all sects, is he not perfect, spotless in virtue, the representative and resplendent image of the moral goodness and rectitude of God? However contending sects may be divided as to other points, they all agree in the moral perfection of his character. All recognise his most glorious peculiarity, his sublime and unsullied goodness. All therefore see in him that which alone deserves love and veneration." (*Works,* p. 318.)

34. See *Works,* pp. 313, 314, 315.

35. In common with the generality of Christians, Channing did not regard the souls of "brutes" as rational beings even in embryo.

36. It is for this reason that Channing so emphatically stresses the *unity* of Christ's personality. If the Trinitarian view be the true one, Christ is not a person in the same sense in which man is a person, inasmuch as he is compounded of two intellects, one human and one divine. But to assert this, is by implication to deny the divinity of man, which is for Channing the πρῶτον ψεῦδος. Moreover the hypostatic union in which these are conjoined is unique, and therefore unsharable by us; hence "our faith is vain."

37. "Not a few," writes Channing, "attach supreme importance to the right decision of the question 'what rank Jesus holds in the universe,—whether he be God, archangel, or man?' Such inquiries it is nowise my wish to discourage; for all truth has its value. But for myself I ask to comprehend the character of Jesus. . . . To understand Christ's rank, I should esteem a privilege; yet I may know this, and be no better or happier for the truth. But to discern the beauty, loveliness, harmony and grandeur of his mind, this is a knowledge which cannot but exert a creative and purifying power on everyone who can attain to it." (*Works,* p. 996. col. 1.)

In like manner, in his sermon entitled *Preaching Christ,* Channing declares, "We place his 'oneness with God,' not in an unintelligible unity of essence, but in unity of mind and heart, in the strength of his love, through which he renounced every separate interest, and identified himself with his Father's designs." (*Works,* p. 394. col. 1.)

"I desire indeed," declares Channing, "to know Christ's rank in the universe; but rank is nothing except as it proves and manifests superior virtue. High station only degrades a being who fills it unworthily. It is the mind which gives dignity to the office, not the office to the mind. All glory is of the soul." (*Works,* p. 318. col. 2.)

38. This was undoubtedly the case during the period, toward the close of his life, when he preached the series of sermons entitled *The Perfect Life.* Yet there seems no reason to suppose that, at any earlier stage of his career, he held a different view. For, as we shall see, it is not the positive content of Humanitarianism, but rather what he takes to be its limitations, to which Channing objects.

39. *Works,* p. 993. col. 1.

40. Lest this assertion be suspected of being an overstatement, I subjoin the following statements of Channing himself. "The Christian minister should often recollect that man, though propense to evil, has yet powers and faculties which may be exalted and refined to angelic glory; that he is called by the gospel to prepare for the community of angels; that he is formed for unlimited progress in intellectual and moral excellence and felicity. He should often recollect that in Jesus Christ our nature has been intimately united with the divine, and that in Jesus it is already enthroned in heaven." (*Works,* p. 332. col. 1.) "The doctrine of the 'Word made flesh' shows us God uniting himself most intimately with our nature, manifesting himself in a human form, for the very end of making us partakers of his own perfection." (*Works,* p. 919. col. 2.)

41. *Works,* p. 993.

42. *Works,* p. 994.

43. See, *Works,* p. 1012.

44. It is not improbable that Channing himself was in agreement with Gallison, to whose opinion he refers (*Works,* p. 621. col. 2.), that the Gospel of John constituted the cornerstone of Unitarianism.

45. Those papers are preserved in the library of the Meadville School of Religion at the University of Chicago. This particular fragment is, I think, of peculiar interest, for it throws light upon an aspect of Channing's thought which his biographer, Chadwick, found perplexing.

46. *Works,* pp. 1007, col. 2—1008, col. 1.
47. See William C. Gannett's, *Life of Ezra Styles Gannett,* pp. 183-184.
48. *Life,* p. 449.
49. See *Works,* pp. 219, 229, 304.
50. "If I regard Jesus," declares Channing," as an august stranger, belonging to an entirely different class of existence from myself, having no common thoughts or feelings with me, and looking down upon me with only such sympathy as I have with an inferior animal, I should regard him with a vague awe; but the immeasurable space between us would place him beyond friendship and affection. But when I feel that all minds form one family, that I have the same nature with Jesus, and that he came to communicate to me, by his teaching, example, and intercession, his own mind, to bring me into communion with what was sublimest, purest, happiest in himself, then I can love him as I love no other being, excepting only him who is the Father alike of Christ and of the Christian." *Works,* p. 315. col. 2.
51. *Works,* p. 313. col. 2.
52. "Jesus respected human nature; he felt it to be his own. This was the greatness of Jesus Christ. He felt, as no other felt, a union of mind with the human race, felt that all had a spark of that same intellectual and immortal flame which dwelt in himself." *Works,* p. 315. col. 2.
53. *Works,* p. 310. col. 1.
54. *Works,* p. 549. col. 1. It is in the same spirit that Channing refers to Washington's "divine energy." (*Works,* p. 328. col. 1.)
55. *Works,* p. 361. col. 2.
    One is inevitably reminded of the words which Mazzini addressed to the authorities of the Roman Church; "I accuse you of having utterly misunderstood the holy soul of Jesus—superior to every other in inspiration and fraternal love—by transforming him, in despite of his sublimest presentments, into an eternal and vulgar tyrant of souls." See Mazzini's *Essays (Everyman* edition), pp. 297-298.
56. "My friends," exclaimed Channing as he concluded his sermon on *The Imitableness of Christ's Character,* "there is no other happiness. Let not the false views of Christianity which prevail in the world seduce you into the belief that Christ can bless you in any other way than by assimilating you to his own virtue, than by breathing into you his own mind. Do not imagine that any faith or love towards Jesus can avail you but that which quickens you to conform yourselves to his spotless purity and unconquerable rectitude. Settle it as an immovable truth, that neither in this world nor in the next can you be happy but in proportion to the sanctity and elevation of your characters. Let no man imagine that through the patronage or protection of Jesus Christ, or any other being, he can find peace or any sincere good but in the growth of an enlightened, firm, disinterested, holy mind. Expect no good from Jesus any farther than you clothe yourselves with his excellence. He can impart to you nothing so precious as himself, as his own mind; and believe me, my hearers, this mind may dwell in you." (*Works,* p. 316. col. 1.)
57. *Works,* p. 1009. col. 2.
58. *Ibid.,* p. 321. col. 2.
59. *Ibid.,* p. 322. col. 1.

60. *Ibid.,* p. 323. col. 1.
61. *Ibid.,* p. 995. col. 2.
62. This may strike the modern reader as a somewhat startling assertion. The pre-occupation of the "historic Jesus," as the critics present him to us, with purely ethical and religious considerations is not infrequently adduced as an evidence of the limitations of the Gospel. But, it must be remembered, Channing's Christ is not the Christ of the critics, but the divine Reason of the Fourth Evangelist. His position, in this respect, will become clearer when we have examined his view of the relation between reason and revelation in the next chapter.
63. *Ibid.,* p. 998. col. 1; *cf.* the famous description of the free mind in the address entitled *Spiritual Freedom. (Ibid.,* pp. 174-175.)
64. *Ibid.,* pp. 998. col. 2.—999. col. 1.
65. *Ibid.,* p. 999. col. 1.
66. *Ibid.,* p. 999. col. 2.
67. *Ibid.,* p. 95. col. 1.
68. *Ibid.,* p. 377. col. 1.
69. *Ibid.,* p. 396. col. 1.
70. "This doctrine (i.e. the traditional theory of the atonement) invests the Saviour with a claim of merit, with a right to the remission of the sins of his followers; and represents God's reception of the penitent as a recompense due to the worth of his Son. And is mercy, which means free and undeserved love, made more manifest, more resplendent, by the introduction of merit and right as the ground of our salvation? Could a surer expedient be invented for obscuring its freeness, and for turning the sinner's gratitude from the sovereign who demands, to the sufferer who offers, full satisfaction for his guilt." (*Ibid.,* p. 396. col. 2.)
71. It is to the Unitarian concept of divine forgiveness that Channing refers when speaking of dedicating a church "to the praise of his free, unbought, un-merited grace." (*Ibid.,* p. 401. col. 1.)
72. *Ibid.,* p. 379. col. 1.
73. *Ibid.,* p. 396. col. 1.
74. "The Trinitarian tells me that, according to his system, we have an infinite substitute; that the Infinite God was pleased to bear our punishment, and consequently that pardon is made sure. But I ask him, Do I understand you? Do you mean, that the Great God, who never changes, whose happiness is the same yesterday, today, and forever, that this Eternal Being really bore the penalty of my sins,—really suffered and died? Every pious man, when pressed by this question, answers, No. What, then, does the doctrine of infinite atonement mean? Why, this; that God took into union with him-self our nature, that is, a human body and soul; and these bore the suffering for our sins; and, through his union with these, God may be said to have borne it himself. Thus, this vaunted system goes out—in words." *Ibid.,* p. 398. col. 1; *cf.* p. 375. col. 2.
75. *Ibid.,* p. 325. col. 1.
76. *Ibid.,* p. 326. col. 2.
77. *Loc. cit.*

78. "I mean not to find fault with this sensibility. . . . Woe to him who has no tears for mortal agony! But in this emotion there is no virtue, no moral worth; and we dishonor Jesus when this is the chief tribute we offer him." (*Ibid.,* p. 324. col. 2.)

79. *Ibid.,* p. 326. col. 2.

80. It has been remarked that the Jesus of the Fourth Gospel, in contradistinction to the Jesus of the Synoptics, exhibits a never-failing calmness and self-possession such as would become the incarnate Logos, and scholars have here detected the influence of Stoicism. In Channing's pre-critical outlook this distinction was naturally blurred. "I have often been struck," he tells us, "by the contrast between the use made of the cross in the pulpit, and the calm, unimpassioned manner in which the sufferings of Jesus are detailed by the Evangelists. These witnesses of Christ's last moments give you in simple language the particulars of that scene, without one remark, one word of emotion; and if you read the Acts and Epistles, you will not find a single instance in which the Apostles strove to make a moving picture of his crucifixion. No; they honored Jesus too much, they felt too deeply the greatness of his character, to be moved as many are by the circumstances of his death. Reverence, admiration, sympathy with his sublime spirit, these swallowed up in a great measure, sympathy with his sufferings. The cross was to them the last crowning manifestation of a celestial mind." (*Ibid.,* p. 325. col. 1.) In all this Channing is, of course, partly right. To the idealizing Christian consciousness the cross rapidly became the supreme symbol of triumph.

81. *Ibid.,* p. 306.

82. *Ibid.,* pp. 326. col. 2.—327. col. 1.

83. *Ibid.,* p. 398. col. 2; *cf.* pp. 403. col. 2.—404. col. 1.

84. *Ibid,* p. 1011. col. 1.

85. "By Christ's blood," asserts Channing, "I understand his spirit, his entire devotion to the cause of human virtue and to the will of God. By his cross I mean his celestial love, I mean the great principles of piety and righteousness in asserting which he died. To be redeemed by his blood is to be redeemed by his goodness." *Ibid.,* p. 1011. col. 2.

86. *Ibid.,* p. 378. col. 2.

87. *Loc. cit.*

88. With the conservative Unitarian Christian this phrase is still anathema.

89. *Ibid.,* pp. 312. col. 2.—313. col. 1.

90. *Ibid.,* p. 486. col. 1.

91. Does the adverb indicate a waning confidence in the theory? Let the psychologist answer. It is worth remarking, however, that a few paragraphs farther on Channing announces "I should say that the greater the redeemer, the stronger was the necessity of his veiling his greatness and of his appearing in the form of a man, and of the lowliest man." *Ibid.,* p. 993. col. 2.

92. *Ibid.,* p. 402. col. 1.

# Chapter Six

# Reason and Revelation,
# Nature and Grace

"If religion be the shipwreck of understanding, we cannot keep too far from it." [1] This sentence, so characteristic of Channing alike in its succinctness, its clarity, and its challenging note, may well be taken as the epitome of his teaching. It is the product of no transitory outburst, for it is to be found in the Baltimore sermon where he is professedly expounding not only his own considered opinions, but also those of the group of Christians to which he belonged; moreover it can be supported almost *ad nauseam* by parallel passages in his writings. In the same tone we hear him exclaim, "Christianity is a rational religion. Were it not so, I should be ashamed to profess it." [2] "I glory in Christianity," he affirms, "because it enlarges, invigorates, exalts my rational nature. If I could not be a Christian without ceasing to be rational, I should not hesitate as to my choice. I feel myself bound to sacrifice to Christianity property, reputation, life; but I ought not to sacrifice to any religion that reason which lifts me above the brute and constitutes me a man. I can conceive no sacrilege greater than to prostrate or renounce the highest faculty which we have derived from God. In so doing we should offer violence to the divinity within us. Christianity wages no war with reason, but is one with it, and is given to be its helper and friend." [3] "He who is compelled to defend his faith, in any particular," urges Channing, "by the plea that human reason is so depraved through the fall as to be an inadequate judge of religion, and that God is honored by our reception of what shocks the intellect, seems to have no defence left against accumulated absurdities. According to these principles, the fanatic who exclaimed, 'I believe, because it is impossible,' had a fair title to canonization. Reason is too godlike a faculty to be insulted with impunity." [4]

Channing thus takes up a position diametrically opposed to that of the Calvinist, whose point of view had been expounded with such brilliant eloquence by his predecessor, Edwards, whose God cannot be approached by the human reason, and for whom religious experience is at once the source of authority and the only access to the divine. Yet, in all this Channing has stated nothing new. He has only reasserted with greater emphasis the doctrine which Locke had already epitomized in his magnificent assertion, "He that takes away reason, to make way for revelation, puts out the light of both." [5] With Locke, then, Channing begins; but with Locke he does not end. As his thinking matures to religious experience he returns, not as to something irrational, but as to a supplement to the logical understanding, at once capable of corroborating, and incapable of contradicting it. Although we cannot hope to trace in detail this intellectual evolution, we must yet note the widening outlook, and the emergence of something akin to the viewpoint of the Transcendentalist. The topic is of peculiar interest at the present day, when we are simultaneously confronted, on the one hand, in the theological world by a reversion to an irrationalism which Channing would have scorned, and, on the other hand, by a wide-spread vogue in the philosophical world of a narrow empiricism which he would equally have condemned.

Let us begin, accordingly, by examining the general view of the relation between reason and revelation which Channing derived from Locke. And, in the first place, we must in fairness take account of Channing's strenuous assertions that he has done his best to clear his mind of every prejudice which might lead him to adopt and defend Christianity from unworthy motives. "I do not affirm the truth of Christianity," he tells us, "because I was so taught before I could inquire, or because I was brought up in a community pledged to this belief. It is not unlikely that my faith and zeal will be traced by some to these sources; and believing such imputations to be groundless, fidelity to the cause of truth binds me to repel them. The circumstance of having been born and educated under Christianity, so far from disposing me to implicit faith, has often been to me the occasion of serious distrust of our religion. On observing how common it is for men of all countries and names, whether Christians, Jews, or Mahometans, to receive the religion of their fathers, I have again and again asked myself whether I too was not a slave, whether I too was not blindly walking in the path of tradition, and yielding myself as passively as others to an hereditary faith. I distrust and fear the power of numbers and of general opinion over my judgment; and few things incite me more to repel a doctrine than intolerant attempts to force it on my understanding. Perhaps my Christian education and connections have inclined me to scepticism, rather than bowed my mind to authority." [6]

The consideration so often urged that religion is an indispensable support to the social order has exercised, Channing reflects, no influence upon himself, since he is convinced that "nothing but truth can be permanently useful." [7] Likewise the charge that his position as a Christian minister is a source of bias, leaves him unmoved. He acknowledges no "peculiar sanctity" in the clerical office, and he fully recognizes that the clergy have frequently been corrupted by the spirit of intolerance and oppression.[8] "I think, then," he declares, "that I come to the examination of Christianity with as few blinding partialities as any man. I indeed claim no exemption from error; I ask no implicit faith in my conclusions; I care not how jealously and thoroughly my arguments are sifted. I only ask that I may not be prejudged as a servile or interested partisan of Christianity. I ask that I may be heard as a friend of truth, desirous to aid my fellow-creatures in determining a question of great and universal concern. I appear as the advocate of Christianity, solely because it approves itself to my calmest reason as a revelation from God, and as the purest, brightest light which He has shed on the human mind. I disdain all other motives. No policy, no vassalage to opinion, no dread of reproach even from the good, no private interest, no desire to uphold a useful superstition, nothing, in short, but a deliberate conviction of the truth of Christianity induces me to appear in its ranks. I should be ashamed of it did I not believe it true." [9]

In this connection Channing insists that he has no intention of reflecting upon the character of unbelievers, or of pronouncing their unbelief a moral offense. "Mere acts of the understanding," he insists, "are neither right nor wrong." [10] One can speak of faith as virtue only if one mean by it the act of the whole man, "not merely the assent of the intellect, but the disposition or temper by which this assent is determined," [11] and the same holds true of unbelief. "The truth is," Channing declares in words which prophetically anticipate the conclusions of our own psychologists, "that the human mind, though divided by our philosophy into many distinct capacities, seldom or never exerts them separately, but generally blends them in one act. Thus, in forming a judgment, it exerts the will and affections, or the moral principles of our nature, as really as the power of thought. Men's passions and interests mix with, and are expressed in, the decisions of the intellect. In the Scriptures, which use language freely, and not with philosophical strictness, faith and unbelief are mental acts of this complex character, or joint products of the understanding and heart; and on this account alone they are objects of approbation or reproof." [12]

From this it follows that the man who accepts Christianity out of deference to popular opinion, or because he regards it as a powerful support of property and wealth, is as morally culpable as the man who rejects it from unworthy motives.[13] "Perhaps," continues Channing, "I ought to go further. Perhaps I ought to say that to reject Christianity under some of its corruptions is rather a virtue than a crime. At the present moment, I would ask whether it is a vice to doubt the truth of Christianity as it is manifested in Spain and Portugal? When a patriot in those benighted countries, who knows Christianity only as a bulwark of despotism, as a rearer of inquisitions, as a stern jailor immuring wretched women in the convent, as an executioner stained and reeking with the blood of the friends of freedom; I say, when the patriot, who sees in our religion the instrument of these crimes and woes, believes and affirms that it is not from God, are we authorized to charge his disbelief on dishonesty and corruption of mind, and to brand him as a culprit? May it not be that the spirit of Christianity in his heart emboldens him to protest with his lips against what bears the name? And if he thus protest, through a deep sympathy with the oppression and sufferings of his race, is he not nearer the kingdom of God than the priest and inquisitor who boastingly and exclusively assume the Christian name?" [14]

In Channing we see, what is not too frequently met with even in our own day, the union of gracious tolerance and burning conviction. To reject Christianity, he has insisted, does not necessarily involve the unbeliever in moral guilt; nevertheless, such rejection constitutes a supreme "calamity." The fact remains that "the unbeliever would gain unspeakably by parting with every possession for the truth which he doubts or rejects." [15] And this truth includes an historic element. Channing is far from sympathizing with those Deists who, repudiating the notion of revelation, would base religion upon the logical understanding alone. In his ears their boasted rationalism does not ring true.

A rational universe is one in which mind is supreme, and matter is its instrument. It thus includes both nature and super-nature. Hence any genuine rationalist, precisely because he is a rationalist, must also be a super-naturalist; and revelation, so far from being at odds with reason, is positively demanded by it.[16]

Like Locke, Channing leaves us in no doubt as to the absolute supremacy of reason, or as to its complete competence to deal with the question of revelation. "I am surer," he affirms, "that my rational nature is from God than that any book is an expression of his will. This light in my own breast is his primary revelation,[17] and all subsequent ones must accord with it, and are, in fact, intended to blend with and brighten it." [18] "Revelation," he explicitly declares, "rests on the authority of reason, because to this faculty it submits the evidences of its truth, and nothing but the approving sentence of reason binds us to receive and obey it. This is a very weighty consideration. Christianity, in placing itself before the tribunal of reason, and in resting its claims on the sanction of this faculty, is one of the chief witnesses to the authority and dignity of our rational nature. That I have ascribed to this faculty its true and proper office may be easily made to appear. I take the New Testament in my hand, and on what ground do I receive its truths as divine? . . . No miraculous voice from heaven assures me that it is God's word, nor does any mysterious voice within my soul command me to believe the supernatural works of Christ.[19] How, then, shall I settle the question of the origin of this religion? I must examine it by the same rational faculties by which other subjects are tried. I must ask what are its evidences, and I must lay them before reason, the only power by which evidence can be weighed. I have not a distinct faculty given me for judging a revelation. I have not two understandings, one for inquiring into God's word and another into his works. As with the same bodily eye I now look on the earth, now on the heavens, so with the same power of reason I examine now nature, now revelation. Reason must collect and weigh the various proofs of Christianity. It must especially compare this system with those great moral convictions which are written by the finger of God on the heart, and which make man a law to himself. A religion subverting these we must not hesitate to reject, be its evidences what they may.[20] A religion, for example, commanding us to hate and injure society, reason must instantly discard, without even waiting to examine its proofs. From these views we learn, not only that it is the province of reason to judge of the truth of Christianity, but, what is still more important, that the rules or tests by which it judges are of its own dictation. The laws which it applies in this case have its origin in itself. No one will pretend that revelation can prescribe the principles by which the question of its own truth should be settled; for, until proved to be true, it has no authority. Reason must prescribe the tests or standards to which a professed revelation from God should be referred; and among these none are more important than that moral law which belongs to the very essence and is the deepest conviction of the rational nature. Revelation, then, rests on reason, and in opposing it would act for its own destruction." [21]

Thus, in company with Locke, Channing differs at once from the Calvinists, who deny the competence of reason in things divine, and from the Thomists, who, while they maintain the supremacy of reason in the field of natural theology, deny its right to adjudicate in the sphere of revelation. For the Englishman and the New Englander alike, reason is supreme always and everywhere.

What does Channing mean by *reason?* He has been good enough to tell us. It is "the highest faculty or energy of the mind." [22] And it has two chief characteristics. One of these is the capacity to grasp universal truths,[23] to frame such notions as those of causality, infinity, the right and the good, and, moreover, to apply these universal principles to particular cases.[24] And, in the second place, "reason is the power which tends and is perpetually striving to reduce our various thoughts to unity or consistency." [25] In other words, it is the principle of coherence, which assures us "that inconsistency is the mark of error," [26] which prompts us to reconcile new facts with former knowledge, which "can allow nothing to stand separate in the mind." "It carries within itself an instinctive consciousness that all things which exist are intimately bound together; and it cannot rest until it has connected whatever we witness with the infinite whole. Reason, according to this view, is the most glorious form or exercise of the intellectual nature. It corresponds to the unity of God and the universe, and seeks to make the soul the image and mirror of this sublime unity." [27]

Locke, it will be remembered, asserts that there are ideas which are "archetypes of the mind's own making, not intended to be the copies of any thing, nor referred to the existency of any thing, as to their originals," [28] and refers us to mathematical and ethical concepts as illustrations of what he means. In a similar vein Channing assures us that "the mind does not receive every thing from abroad.

Its great ideas arise from itself, and by those native lights it reads and comprehends the volumes of nature and revelation. We speak, indeed, of nature and revelation as making known to us an intelligent First Cause: but the ideas of intelligence and causation we derive originally from our own nature. The elements of the idea of God we gather from ourselves. Power, wisdom, love, virtue, beauty, and happiness,—words which contain all that is glorious in the universe and interesting in our existence,—express attributes of the mind, and are understood by us only through consciousness." [29]

How do we, one may reasonably ask, know that these ideas which the human mind somehow fashions for itself correspond to objective reality? This is a question to which Locke returns no satisfactory answer. The problem is that of vindicating the genuineness of *a priori* knowledge, and we shall hereafter inquire whether Channing has given any indications of how he was prepared to deal with it. At present, however, we must take note of the threefold manner in which revelation is related to reason.[30] In the first place it makes use of these "innate" ideas, as we may provisionally term them, which the mind develops from its own resources; it is stated in terms of these, and its validity depends upon their own. In the second place, revelation, as we have seen, appears before reason in the attitude of a plaintiff before a judge in whose court its claims are to be examined. And, in the third place, revelation relies upon reason to function as its interpreter.

This last consideration is of extreme importance. There is no book, Channing informs us, "which demands a more frequent exercise of reason than the Bible." [31] Much of it is written in a highly figurative style. Corporeal attributes are frequently ascribed to God, and these must be understood in a metaphorical sense; otherwise we shall fall into gross absurdity. Historical references are constant, and these relate us "to states of society, to modes of thinking, to controversies in the church, to feelings and usages which have passed away, and without the knowledge of which we are constantly in danger of extending to all times and places what was of temporary and local application." [32] "We find, too," observes Channing, "that some of these books are strongly marked by the genius and character of their respective writers, that the Holy Spirit did not so guide the apostles as to suspend the peculiarities of their minds, and that a knowledge of their feelings, and of the influences under which they were placed, is one of the preparations for understanding their writings." [33] In addition, many of the sayings of Jesus are obviously rhetorical hyperboles, which, not only good sense, but also in many cases ethical considerations, forbid us to take literally. And, lastly, there are numerous verbal contradictions which reason must attempt to reconcile.[34]

What, then, is the conclusion of the whole matter? "From a variety of possible interpretations," says Channing—speaking, not only for himself, but also for his fellow-Unitarians,—"we select that which accords with the nature of the subject and the state of the writer, with the connection of the passage, with the general strain of Scripture, with the known character and will of God, and with the obvious and acknowledged laws of nature. In other words, we believe that God never contradicts in one part of Scripture what He teaches in another; and never contradicts in revelation what He teaches in his works and providence. And we therefore distrust every interpretation which, after deliberate attention, seems repugnant to any established truth. We reason about the Bible precisely as civilians do about the constitution under which we live; who, you know, are accustomed to limit one provision of that venerable instrument by others, and to fix the precise import of its parts by inquiring into its general spirit, into the intentions of its authors, and into the prevalent feelings, impressions, and circumstances of the time when it was framed. Without these principles of interpretation, we frankly acknowledge that we cannot defend the divine authority of the Scriptures. Deny us this latitude, and we must abandon this book to its enemies." [35]

All this is in accordance with Channing's fundamental contention that the Bible is to be interpreted precisely as any other book.[36] Thus far, at least, he anticipates the position of the modern scholar. But his pre-critical approach to the Scriptures renders his outlook very different from that of the liberal of the next generation—from that of Theodore Parker, for example. His notion of inspiration is far more artificial. Natural and revealed religion are still separated by a gap, whereas, for Parker, all religion is *both* natural and revealed. Channing does, however, consider revelation as progressive, in the sense, at least, that the Christian revelation is not only temporally subsequent to the Jewish, but also an intellectual and moral advance upon it.[37] The age-long process has culminated in Christ, who, as the divinely appointed leader, is destined ultimately to bring all humanity under his sway.

Channing is, of course, aware that his relentless insistence that the claims of revelation must be tried by reason is regarded by the orthodox as a frightful error. And he freely admits that the use of reason in

eligion is not without its dangers. But he asks the objector to con-
ider whether the history of the church does not make it abundantly
lear that the renunciation of reason involves one in even greater
langers.[38] He does not question that the detractors of reason have
ieen animated by a worthy motive; they have thought thus to safe-
;uard the claims of revelation. "But truth gains nothing by exaggera-
ion; and Christianity as we have seen, is undermined by nothing
nore effectually than by the sophistry which would bring discredit
in our rational powers."[39] The wise course is also the honest and
:ourageous course; to submit Christianity to the test of reason, and
ee what will happen to it. "If, indeed, irrational doctrines belong to
t," exclaims Channing, "then I have no desire to separate them from
t. . . . Did I think that it was burdened with one irrational doctrine, I
vould say so, and I would leave it, as I found it, with this mill-stone
ound its neck. But I know none such."[40]

Very much in the spirit of Locke, Channing asks the orthodox to
eflect that, if the efficacy of reason be questioned in the sphere of
evelation, it may with equal legitimacy be questioned when it comes
o proving the existence of God. "I am told that I must deny reason.
[ ask, Must I deny it when it teaches me that there is a God? If
;o, the very foundation of religion is destroyed, and I am abandoned
.o utter unbelief."[41] "The truth is, and it ought not to be disguised,
.hat our ultimate reliance is, and must be, on our own reason. Faith
n this power lies at the very foundation of all other faith. No trust
:an be placed in God, if we discredit the faculty by which God is
liscerned."[42] This is an argument which would leave the Calvinist
ind the Thomist both unconvinced; the Calvinist because he believes
.hat there is a better approach to God than through reason, namely,
.hrough the intuition supernaturally imparted to him by divine grace;
ind the Thomist because he is prepared to maintain that the object
iroportionate to the human intellect *secundum statum praesentis vitae*
s being as such, arrived at by abstraction from sense-data,[43] whereas
.he realm of revelation is *supra rationem*. Channing, on the other hand,
ielongs as we shall see, in the Augustinian tradition, according to
vhich the human mind is emphatically *capax Dei*.

There is, however, an argument attributed by Channing to the or-
:hodox, which is of great importance. "We are told that God being
nfinitely wiser than men, his discoveries will surpass human reason.
[n a revelation from such a teacher we ought to expect propositions
vhich we cannot reconcile with one another, and which may seem to

contradict established truths; and it becomes us not to question or explain them away, but to believe and adore, and to submit our weak and carnal reason to the divine word." [44] The presupposition upon which such reasoning is based is clear enough. It is the contention that God and man are not *essentially the same*, that attributes cannot be ascribed to the divine and to human nature in a univocal sense; in other words, it is the product of that very *via negativa* which Channing has repudiated in so unqualified a fashion. It is, therefore, in complete accordance with his own basic conviction that he directs against it a two-fold reply.

In the first place, he urges, "it is impossible that a teacher of infinite wisdom should expose those whom he would teach to infinite error. But if once we admit that propositions which in their literal sense appear plainly repugnant to one another, or to any known truth, are still to be literally understood and received, what possible limit can we set to the belief of contradictions? What shelter can we have from the wildest fanaticism, which can always quote passages that, in their literal and obvious sense, give support to its extravagances? How can the Protestant escape from transubstantiation, a doctrine most clearly taught us, if the submission of reason, now contended for, be a duty? How can we even hold fast the truth of revelation; for if one apparent contradiction may be true, so may another, and the proposition that Christianity is false, though involving inconsistency, may still be a verity." [45]

In the second place, Channing contends that "if God be infinitely wise, He cannot sport with the understandings of his creatures. A wise teacher discovers his wisdom in adapting himself to the capacities of his pupils, not in perplexing them with what is unintelligible, not in distressing them with apparent contradictions, not in filling them with a sceptical distrust of their own powers. An infinitely wise teacher, who knows the precise extent of our minds and the best method of enlightening them, will surpass all other instructors in bringing down truth to our apprehension, and in showing its loveliness and harmony. We ought, indeed, to expect occasional obscurity in such a book as the Bible, which was written for past and future ages as well as for the present. But God's wisdom is a pledge that whatever is necessary for *us*, and necessary for salvation, is revealed too plainly to be mistaken, and too consistently to be questioned, by a sound and upright mind. It is not the mark of wisdom to use an unintelligible phraseology, to communicate what is above our capacities, to confuse,

nd unsettle the intellect by appearances of contradiction. We honor
ur Heavenly Teacher too much to ascribe to him such a revelation.
. revelation is a gift of light. It cannot thicken our darkness and
ultiply our perplexities." [46]

It would be difficult to conceive of a more crushing attack than
hat which Channing thus delivers upon the conservative position; and
is one attack to which orthodox Christianity is peculiarly vulnerable.
udaism and Islam both profess to be revealed religions; yet in the
ase of neither is the believer perplexed to any comparable degree
y unintelligible "mysteries" and dogmas which are "above reason."
'or the Thomist and the Calvinist alike, however, the doctrines of
ne Trinity, the Incarnation, and the Substitutionary Atonement, which
oth esteem of central importance, are "above our capacities"; they
ot only confound the understanding but also shock the moral judg-
nent. It is not, then, permissible to enquire for what conceivable pur-
ose an all-wise intelligence would disclose to the finite mind truths
hich could not fail to appear to it in such a light. Such a revelation
ould only "thicken our darkness and multiply our perplexities." Its
nd, therefore, cannot be enlightenment.

It is important, however, to observe that Channing's argument will
ppear conclusive only to one who accepts the presupposition upon
hich it is based—namely, the theory of *essential sameness*. Channing
s assuming that the divine reason is prepared to vindicate itself before
uman reason, and that it is legitimate to expect it to do so; and
his both the Thomist and the Calvinist would emphatically deny.
According to the doctrine of *analogy*, the divine and the human in-
ellects are incommensurable. Neither man's reason nor his moral judg-
nent is competent to pass upon the content of revelation. And perhaps
he end of revelation is not enlightenment. Perhaps its end is to
rovide us with an opportunity gracefully "to submit our weak and
arnal reason to the divine word."

It is, I repeat, the principle of *essential sameness* which is the ground
f Channing's high estimate of human reason, and which endues it in
is eyes with a sacred, almost with a sacramental, function. The same
aculty which enables man to infer the existence of God, is also
apable of disclosing to him the divine nature; in fact it performs both
asks simultaneously, for one cannot infer *that* God is without at the
ame time inferring *what* he is. "Human reason," insists Channing,
"imperfect though it be, is still the offspring of God, allied to him

intimately, and worthy of its divine Parent. There is no extravagance in calling it, as is sometimes done, 'a beam of the infinite light'; for it involves in its very essence those immutable and everlasting principles of truth and rectitude which constitute the glory of the Divine Mind. It ascends to the sublime idea of God by possessing kindred attributes, and knows him only though its affinity with him. It carries within itself the germ of that spiritual perfection which is the great end of the creation. Is it not, then, truly a 'partaker of a divine nature'? Can we think or speak of it too gratefully or with too much respect? The infinity of God, so far from calling on me to prostrate and annihilate reason, exalts my conception of it. It is my faith in this perfection of the Divine Mind that inspires me with reverence for the human, for they are intimately connected, the latter being a derivation from the former, and endued with the power of approaching its original more and more through eternity. Severed from God, reason would lose its grandeur. In his infinity it has at once a source and a pledge of endless and unbounded improvement. God delights to communicate himself; and therefore his greatness, far from inspiring contempt for human reason, gives it a sacredness and opens before it the most elevating hopes. The error of men is not that they exaggerate, but that they do not know or suspect the worth and dignity of their rational nature." [47]

Pride of reason—if the term *pride* be taken to signify something deplorable and reprehensible—does not manifest itself, urges Channing, in a reverence for the rational nature which is the common endowment of humanity, nor in a profound gratitude to the divine Parent whose gift it is; pride of reason, in an unworthy sense, consists in too high an estimate of one's own intellectual powers, and in a disparagement of, and contempt for, those of others. As such, it is not infrequently found among those very defenders of orthodoxy who fondly regard themselves as untainted by it. For the revelation to which these men appeal is something common to all, its sanctity is recognized by the heretic as well as by the traditionalist. And, in interpreting it, the spokesmen of orthodoxy make us of no other capacity than that very reason which is the birthright of humanity. Yet they presume to force their own views upon their fellows in the name of God himself, and are quick to charge their opponents with an undue reliance upon that very power by the exercise of which they have reached their own conclusions, and by which these conclusions stand or fall.[48]

If, however, Christianity be—as Channing claims that it is—a rational religion, what becomes of the "mysteries of the faith"? In our own day, no less than in his, this phrase is frequently uttered; how often do we hear of "the mystery of the Trinity," or "the mystery of the Incarnation"! To rationalize Christianity, we shall be told, is to excise this essential element, and so to disfigure it beyond recognition. The rationalist, it is contended, forgets that he cannot transcend the limited outlook of the finite human creature, and regard the universe from the standpoint of the infinite Creator. Religion, involves not only man's search for God, but also God's self-disclosure to man. In this self-disclosure we encounter mysteries; they are the expression of the Transcendent; they are not pervious, therefore, to human reason; hence the only proper attitude for man to assume is one of dutiful and reverent acceptance and belief.

To make such a demand, objects Channing, is to ask of man what is psychologically impossible. No one *can* believe a mystery. For what is a mystery? "In the language of Scripture, and in its true sense, it is a secret,—something unknown." [49] What is believed must have some content, but what is unknown has no content—it is a mere blank. There is nothing for the intellect to grasp or for the judgment to affirm. To say this is not to deny that there are unknown truths; it is only to assert that what we do not know we cannot at the same time know or believe.

"I have no disposition," remarks Channing, "to deny the existence of mysteries. Every truth involves them. Every object which falls under our notice, the most common and simple, contains much that we do not know and cannot now penetrate. We know not, for example, what it is which holds together the particles of the meanest stone beneath our feet, nor the manner in which the humblest plant grows. That there are mysteries, secrets, things unknown without number, I should be the last to deny. I only maintain—and in so doing I utter an identical proposition—that what is mysterious, secret, unknown, cannot at the same time be known or an object of faith. . . . For example, my hand is moved by the act of my will. . . . This is a plain fact. The words which convey it are among the most intelligible. But under this fact, which I so well know, lies a great mystery. The *manner* in which the will acts on the hand, or the process which connects them, is altogether unknown. The fact and the mystery, as you see, having nothing in common. The former is so manifest that

I cannot, if I would, withhold from it my faith. Of the latter not even a glimpse is afforded me; not an idea of it has dawned on the mind; and without ideas, there can, of course, be no knowledge or belief. These remarks apply to revelation as well as to nature. The subjects of which revelation treats—God, Christ, human nature, holiness, heaven,—contain infinite mysteries. What is revealed in regard to them is as nothing compared to what remains secret. But 'secret things belong to God,' and the pride of reason is manifested not in declining, but in professing to make them objects of faith. It is the influence of time and of intellectual improvement to bring mysteries to light, both in nature and religion; and just as far as this process goes on, the belief of them becomes possible and right. Thus, the cause of eclipses, which was once a mystery, is now disclosed; and who of us does not believe it? In like manner Christ revealed 'the mysteries of the kingdom of heaven,' or the purposes and methods of God which had been kept secret for ages, in relation to the redemption of the world from sin, death, and woe. Being now revealed, or having ceased to be mysteries, these have become objects of faith, and reason ranks them among its most glorious truths." [50]

Nature and revelation alike thus fall within the province of reason. Christianity is rational through and through; it is "reason in its most perfect form." [51] Revelation presupposes reason, it is addressed to reason, it is judged by reason, and it is vindicated by reason. In language which reminds one of St. Thomas, Channing insists that the occurrence of revelation is something which the theistic rationalist should anticipate *a priori,* so that its absence, rather than its presence, would provide fitting ground for disquiet.[52]

Here, of course, Channing touches upon an issue which is of vital concern to every theistic philosopher. Does not a doctrine of revelation form an essential element in any genuine theism? Can the believer in a personal God actually conceive that the Deity could remain quiescent while man ceaselessly and painfully struggles and stumbles towards him? Must there not inevitably be a divine response to human effort?

To put the matter in this way, it may be said, is to confuse revelation with grace—grace whose function and dignity Edwards has so far exalted above those of inspiration itself. It is one thing to affirm that God aids, sustains, and frequently illumines devout souls which seek after him, and sometimes raises them to a height where they enjoy conscious communion with him; it is another thing to assert that a divinely authenticated teaching has been imparted to the human race as its common possession through the agency of certain individuals who at definite times and in particular places have been empowered to act as the spokesmen of Deity. A religion of grace may be a purely metaphysical religion; revelation carries us into the realm of history.

Now it is quite true that in Channing's writings one can find numerous passages in which the greatest emphasis is laid upon individual illumination. It is an idea which, although present at the outset, becomes more and more prominent as his thinking matures. As we have already seen, human reason constitutes God's primary revelation. Man's reason is "a ray of the Infinite Reason: his conscience is an oracle of the Divinity." [53] To deny this is to deny that God has revealed himself to the heathen, and thus to impugn his universal Fatherhood.[54] Thus Channing speaks with approval of the contention of Fox and his disciples, "that God's illuminating spirit is shed on every soul, not only within the bounds of Christendom, but throughout the whole earth." [55] Furthermore, he assures us, in accents reminiscent of Edwards, that "there is a light to which others are strangers, that visits the inward eye of the man who contends with evil in himself, and is true to his convictions of duty. This is the highest inspiration, surpassing that of the prophets; for the ancient prophet comprehended but imperfectly the revelation with which he was charged, and sometimes shrank from communicating it to the world." [56] And in the same spirit he informs us that "Christians have yet to learn that inspiration, and miracles, and outward dignities are nothing compared with the soul." [57]

Nevertheless there is no contradiction, to Channing's mind, between the belief in divine grace which is as ubiquitous as sunlight, and the faith in an historic revelation—"traditional" revelation, as Locke would say. Christianity is, not only a rational, but also an historic religion. It is the religion which Jesus taught in the early portion of the first century in the land of Palestine, and it constitutes the culmination of a process of divine self-disclosure which began with the origin of the human race.[58] Revelation is, in fact, a form of education to which mankind has been subjected, and is in accordance with the general principle that every mind must learn from other minds more advanced than itself. In the case of revelation, God himself assumes the role of instructor, and immediately illumines a chosen few who in turn become the teachers of humanity at large.[59] This dependence[60] of the many upon the gifted few results in the establishment of relationships of service, attachment, gratitude, and trust among men; and revelation is intended to issue not only in the production of these, but also in the formation of personal relationships between man and God. "We can look on nature," observes Channing, "and not think of the Being whose glory it declares; but God is indissolubly connected with, and indeed is a part of, the idea of revelation. How much nearer does this direct intercourse bring him to the mass of mankind! On this account revelation would seem to me important, were it simply to repeat the teachings of nature. This reiteration of great truths in a less formal style, in kinder, more familiar tones, is peculiarly fitted to awaken the soul to the presence and benignity of the heavenly Parent. I see, then, in revelation a purpose corresponding with that for which human teaching was instituted. Both are designed to bring together the teacher and the taught in pure affections." [61] As all education has futurity in view, so has revelation; but, in this instance, its purview extends beyond this earthly life, and its principal concern is with the life hereafter.[62]

It is not the purpose of revelation, Channing tells us, "to enrich the intellect by teaching philosophy, or to perfect the imagination and taste by furnishing sublime and beautiful models of composition. It was not meant to give sagacity in public life, or skill and invention in common affairs. It was undoubtedly designed to develop all these faculties, but secondarily, and through its influence on a higher principle. It addresses itself primarily, and is especially adapted, to the moral power in man." [63] Revelation is designed to aid man in the struggle against vice, and in the attainment of virtue. "I affirm," writes Channing, "that a broad distinction exists between our moral nature and our other capacities. Conscience is the supreme power within us. Its essence, its grand characteristic, is sovereignty. It speaks with a divine authority. Its office is to command, to rebuke, to reward; and happiness and honor depend on the reverence with which we listen to it. All our other powers become useless, and worse than useless, unless controlled by the principle of duty." [64] The vast importance of the moral issue in the life of man thus "justifies, if it does not demand," the direct intervention of God through the medium of revelation to sustain and invigorate humanity in this terrific combat.[65]

At first, these utterances are perplexing. We have been told that revelation is addressed to reason, and is to be judged by reason. Now it appears that, on the contrary, revelation is addressed to some sort of moral sense, intuitive in character, and that reason has nothing to do with it. We must remember, however, that Channing has protested against the division of the mind into separate faculties, that he has emphasized very strongly the unity of the intellect, and that for him there is no sharp dividing line—any more than there was for Locke—between the logical understanding and intuition, both being activities of the human reason. We cannot, therefore, I think, convict him of any inconsistency here. What he is concerned to stress is the eminently practical character of revelation, and the importance of the moral judgment with regard to it. Undoubtedly, however, there is a sharp division between philosophy and revelation. The latter is, indeed, addressed to reason; but it comes from heaven. It imparts to man knowledge which he could not otherwise attain, and it gives him assurance where human wisdom could only give him an uncertain hope.

What is of chief interest to the modern thinker in Channing's treatment of revelation, and what was clearly of basic importance to himself, is his fundamental contention that a rational universe is a universe under the control of mind—which, for Channing, obviously involves the truth of theism—that it includes both "nature" and "super-nature," and that, consequently, the rationalist cannot avoid being a supernaturalist. From this the occurrence of revelation seems to him inevitably to follow. These *a priori* considerations constitute, in fact, his principal argument; they are familiar to the modern theist, and have lost nothing of their weight.

When we turn, however, to the formal proof which Channing advances in support of the Christian revelation, we enter an atmosphere very different from our own, and breathe the air of another age. The divine origin of Christianity, we are astonished to learn, is made manifest by the fact that nothing can be discovered in the contemporary environment, whether Jewish or pagan, to explain its rise and growth.[66] In the decline of the ancient, classical paganism throughout the Roman empire, Channing sees at work a religious and moral depravity which, he thinks, should have militated against the spread of any new faith. He is aware of the tremendous influence of the Orient, but he regards the cults imported thence as only "grosser and more licentious superstitions," among which he names "the magical arts of Egypt."[67] Greek philosophy constituted, indeed, a "noble effort"; yet, in his judgment, it "did nothing to prepare the way for Christianity."[68] "The most popular systems of philosophy," he remarks, "at the birth of Christianity were the Sceptical and the Epicurean, the former of which turned religion into a jest, denied the possibility of arriving at truth, and cast the mind on an ocean of doubt in regard to every subject of enquiry; whilst the latter placed happiness in ease, inculcated a calm indifference both as to this world and the next, and would have set down the Christian doctrine of self-sacrifice, of suffering for truth and duty, as absolute insanity. Now I ask in what single point do these systems touch Christianity, or what impulse could they have given to its invention?[69] The Stoics, indeed, both preached and practiced the cultivation of virtue, yet the Stoic's pride, his contempt for others, and his insensibility to human suffering, Channing considers, were at so great a variance with Christianity that "our religion might as soon have sprung from Scepticism, and Epicureanism, as from Stoicism." [70] What is even more worthy of note is the lack of sympathy which he displays toward mysticism—the "oriental philosophy," as he terms it —which "though certainly an improvement on the common heathenism, was visionary and mystical, and placed happiness in an intuition or immediate perception of God which was to be gained by contemplation and ecstasies, by emaciation of the body, and desertion of the world." "I need not tell you," he continues, "how infinitely removed was the practical, benevolent spirit of Christianity from this spurious sanctity and profitless enthusiasm." [71]

In these last sentences we seem to hear Locke speaking. Other and kinder references in Channing's works give reason to hope that they do not convey his final judgment either as to Greek philosophy or mysticism. But the assertion that philosophy did nothing to prepare the way for Christianity is indeed remarkable. It is, of course, only fair to remember that by Christianity Channing means the teachings of Jesus, and that many of the doctrines later developed under the influence of Neoplatonism were, in his eyes, not Christian at all. Yet it is significant that he should have been blind in respect to the philosophic background of his own Arianism. We cannot blame him for failing to realize the positive import of the mystery religions, which it has taken the work of so many subsequent scholars to bring out; yet it is strange that he should not have understood how the decay of an old faith breeds the longing for a new, and how sceptical attacks upon human reason provide a fertile soil for the growth of a narrow supernaturalism.

The contrast between Judaism and Christianity, Channing considers, is of so pronounced a nature, and is so well known, that the point need not be labored. On the one hand, we have a religion narrowly national in character, distinguished by a devotion to outward form and ritual, and infused with a spirit of hostility toward, and contempt for, the rest of mankind; on the other hand, we have a religion universal in its appeal, and characterized by inwardness, and a profound spirituality. How, then, he inquires, could the former have given birth to the latter? [72]

This is precisely the question which modern investigators have undertaken to answer. Many of our acutest critics have seen in Jesus a Jewish apocalyptist, who mistakenly looked for the coming of the Last Judgment and the Kingdom of God in the immediate future, and who regarded himself as sent only "to the lost sheep of the house of Israel"; they have regarded the Hellenists, with their leader, Stephen, as the advocates of a more independent attitude with regard to the Jewish Law, and as the ultimate source of missionary activity among the Gentiles; they have stressed the importance of the disharmony between Paul and the church in Jerusalem; and they have emphasized the significance of the mystery religions, and their relation to the spread of Christianity. All this, of course, is foreign to the thought of Channing. Taking the New Testament, as he does, "all of a piece," he is convinced that the purpose of Jesus was to convert all mankind to the worship of the one, true God, and to abolish the distinction between Jew and Gentile.[73] Hence, to him, the contrast between Judaism and primitive Christianity appeared far more pronounced than it does to the man of the twentieth century.

The gospel, Channing tells us, "did not *grow*. The conception which filled the mind of Jesus, of a religion more spiritual, comprehensive, and unworldly than Judaism, and destined to take its place, was not of a gradual formation. We detect no signs of it, and no efforts to realize it, before his time; nor is there an appearance of its having been gradually matured by Jesus himself. Christianity was delivered from the first in its full proportions, in a style of singular freedom and boldness, and without a mark of painful elaboration. This suddenness with which this religion broke forth, this maturity of the system at the very moment of its birth, this absence of gradual development, seems to me a strong mark of its divine original." [74]

Whatever errors may have crept into the text wherein it is recorded, revelation as originally imparted is thus infallible.[75] It is as distinct from the product of the human mind as oil is from water. Hence Channing always envisages the alternative to his own view in terms of Christianity being an "invention of human ingenuity," the product of "fanaticism or imposture." That human and divine co-operation might result in a composite in which their respective contributions are blended is far from his thought. Here he stands with Locke, in opposition to the later Transcendentalists.

Nevertheless there is an aspect of Channing's view which reminds one of the Hegelian outlook which was subsequently to become so popular, for he would undoubtedly have sympathized with the Hegelian conception of Christianity as the "Absolute Religion." Hearken to the language in which he himself describes it. "The more I examine Christianity, the more I am struck with its universality. I see in it a religion made for all regions and all times, for all classes and all stages of society. It is fitted, not to the Asiatic or the European, but to the essential principles of human nature,—to man under the tropical or polar skies, to all descriptions of intellect or condition. It speaks a language which all men need and all can understand; enjoins a virtue which is man's happiness and glory in every age and clime; and ministers consolations and hopes which answer to man's universal lot, —to the sufferings, the fear, and the self-rebuke which cleave to our nature in every outward change. I see in it the light, not of one nation, but of the world; and a light reaching beyond the world, beyond time, to higher modes of existence and to an interminable futurity. Other religions have been intended to meet the exigencies of particular countries or times, and therefore society in its progress has outgrown them; but Christianity meets more and more the wants of the soul in proportion to the advance of our race, and thus proves itself to be eternal truth. After these remarks, may I not claim for Christianity that character of universality which is the highest distinction of reason?" [76]

It does not follow, however, from that fact that the gospel in itself is complete and perfect, that man's appreciation and knowledge of it cannot grow. "It has been the fault of all sects that they have been too anxious to define their religion. They have labored to circumscribe the infinite. Christianity, as it exists in the mind of the true disciple, is not made up of fragments, of separate ideas which he can express in detached propositions. It is a vast and ever-unfolding whole, pervaded by one spirit, each precept and doctrine deriving its vitality from its union with all. . . . From the infinity of Christian truth, of which I have spoken, it follows that our views of it must always be very imperfect, and ought to be continually enlarged. The wisest theologians are children who have caught but faint glimpses of the religion; who have taken but their first lessons; and whose business it is 'to grow in the knowledge of Jesus Christ' " [77]—hence the futility and positive harm of trying to condense the truths of Christianity into creedal propositions.

Whatever theory be held as to the origin of Christianity, it is certain that no sensible man today takes seriously the suggestion that it was the product of conscious "imposture"; consequently Channing's labored arguments to prove the contrary need not detain us. There is, however, one fact in this connection which demands our attention—namely, that the same loathing and contempt for the passion for domination which led him to oppose every form of arbitrary government—autocracy, aristocracy, and unlimited democracy—now causes him to seek to show that Christianity—which, for Channing, be it remembered, is identical with the teachings of Jesus—is free from any such taint; and that so-called Christians, who succumbed to this unworthy motive, have betrayed the spirit of their master. In Judaism, he reminds us, religion and government were intimately related; the Messiah was pictured as a powerful and victorious monarch. In Christianity, however, he insists, the contrary is the case. "Other systems were framed for communities; Christianity approached men as individuals. It proposed not the glory of the state, but the perfection of the individual mind. So far from being contrived to build up political power, Christianity tends to reduce and supplant it, by teaching men to substitute the sway of truth and love for menace and force, by spreading through all ranks a feeling of brotherhood altogether opposed to the spirit of domination, and by establishing principles which nourish self-respect in every human being, and teach the obscurest to look with an undazzled eye on the most powerful of their race." [78]

That Christianity does address itself primarily to the individual rather than to the community is a proposition which few would care to dispute; nevertheless, Channing realizes that he might be asked whether the Founder of the religion was himself entirely devoid of all desire for spiritual domination.[79] His answer, of course, is in the negative. For Channing, as we have seen, Jesus is the great protagonist of freedom, the supreme deliverer from every form of subjection. His reply, therefore, is confident and unequivocal. "I see nothing in Christianity of this enslaving legislation. It has but one aim, which is, not to exalt its teacher, but to improve the disciple; not to fasten Christ's name on mankind, but to breathe into them his spirit of universal love." [80] And what is true of the Master is also true of his disciples.

Channing believes, indeed, that Jesus appointed the Twelve to be "the instruments of propagating his religion," and that they, in turn, "appointed ministers or teachers in the various congregations which they formed"; none the less, with a vigor which would shock alike the Romanist and the high-church Anglican, he roundly affirms that "the New Testament nowhere intimates that these men were to monopolize the privilege of studying their religion or of teaching it to others. Not a single man can claim under Christianity the right to interpret it exclusively, or to impose his interpretation on his brethren. The Christian minister enjoys no nearer access to God, and no promise of more immediate illumination, than other men. He is not intrusted with the Christian records more than they, and by these records it is both their right and their duty to try his instructions. I have here pointed out a noble peculiarity of Christianity. It is the religion of liberty. It is in no degree tainted with the passion for spiritual power. 'Call no man master, for ye are all brethren,' is its free and generous inculcation, and to every form of freedom it is a friend and defence." [81]

We now turn to what Channing esteems one of the most important proofs, if not the most important proof, of the Christian revelation—namely, miracles. Unlike Edwards, who is very much disposed to treat them *de haut en bas,* he, like Locke, holds miracles in high esteem. In the interval between Locke and Channing, Hume had published his famous essay; yet with practical unanimity the New England Unitarians concurred in rejecting his conclusions, and in adhering with unshaken firmness to the position of Locke. How important the issue was in their eyes the reader can realize by recalling the general outburst of denunciation which greeted Theodore Parker's assertion that the belief in miracles is not essential to Christianity. On all sides the daring radical was stigmatized as an infidel—at a further remove from the true faith than the Trinitarians, who, despite their unconscious tritheism, were at least Christians.

In this matter Channing's position was more moderate than that of many. His confirmed and ever-growing mysticism led him to feel, and—as we shall see—at last openly to teach, that man possessed a direct access to God, and was therefore not totally dependent upon any outward revelation nor upon any historic events. Nonetheless he had no desire to minimize the importance of that revelation or of those historic events, or to depreciate one avenue to God as contrasted with the other. Now that miracles were historic events Channing was completely convinced.[82] And it is easy to see why he should have welcomed them as such, for they seemed completely in accord with his conception of a rational universe. The importance of this last consideration can hardly be overrated. In a passage in *The Perfect Life,* which may fairly be taken as the expression of his considered opinion in the latter portion of his life, this aspect of the matter is brought out with characteristic clearness and emphasis.

"I maintain that miracles are most appropriate proofs of a religion which announces the elevation of man to spiritual perfection. For what are miracles? They are the acts and manifestations of a spiritual power in the universe, superior to the powers and laws of matter. And on the existence of such a power, the triumph of our own spiritual nature over death and material influences must depend.

The miracles of Christianity, so far from shocking me, approve themselves at once to my intellect and to my heart. They seem to me among the most reasonable as well as important events in human history. I prize them, not because they satisfy the passion for the wonderful,—though this principle is one of the noble indications of our nature. But I prize them as discovering, in a way which all can comprehend, that there is some real Being mightier than Nature; that there is a mind which *can,* if it will, suspend or reverse the regular operations of the material world; that, of consequence, the power of death is not supreme, and that the mind may ascend to a perfection which Nature cannot give. Christianity, in its miracles and doctrines, is the very charter and pledge which I need of this elevation of the human soul. And on this account I recognize it as the glorious gospel of the blessed God, or as a religion making sure to its sincere disciples the most magnificent good which even Omnipotence can bestow." [83]

In this declaration Channing has touched upon a point which is too easily forgotten. Convinced that, as a matter of fact, miracles have not occurred, the modern liberal has often set out to show why it is better that they should not have occurred—and, sometimes, even that they could not have occurred. Now for the theist who believes in a creative God to affirm the impossibility of miracles is clearly self-contradictory; a God who is powerful enough to create the universe must be powerful enough to produce tremendous effects within it.[84] Granted however, that miracles have not occurred, the theist, on his own premises is justified in maintaining that it *is* better that they should not have occurred; yet it is not clear that it must be obvious to men *why* it is better. There is too much of the *ex post facto* about this kind of argument; the liberal's repudiation of miracles too often smells of sour grapes. For the theist, the question of miracles should surely be one, not of theory, but of fact—in other words, one's conclusion should be arrived at empirically. Glibly to equate a God who can perform miracles with "a God of magic"—as the liberal has sometimes condescended to do—is to forget what magic is.[85] And to assert that no miracle could validate an irrational teaching is to affirm what neither Channing nor Locke would ever have dreamed of denying; for them miracle is a rational authentication of a rational proposition.[86] Whether the notion of miracle is ultimately tenable is a question which we need not attempt to decide, but it is obvious that nothing is gained either for philosophy or theology by making a straw man out of it.

With these observations in mind, let us return once more to Channing's exposition. There is, he admits, a presumption against the truth of the report of any miracle, if that miracle be taken by itself, without regard to the circumstances in which it occurred, or the truth which it might have been intended to validate.[87] The fact that many such reports have been conscious fabrications, or the product of "ignorance and fanaticism," does not, however, settle the question. Indeed, the widespread belief in false miracles is rather indicative of a great need which genuine miracles satisfy.[88] Instead, therefore, of condemning all miracles out of hand, we ought to investigate the attendant circumstances, and the character of the doctrines which they might conceivably be designed to validate. If we do this, Channing urges, we shall at once see how great is the dissimilarity between the reported miracles which are rightly rejected as false, and the actual miracles performed by Christ and his disciples.[89]

Channing is familiar with the objection, still frequently advanced as though it were absolutely conclusive, that the notion of miracle derogates from the perfection of God; that it supposes him to tamper with work, that "it is only the unskilful artist who is obliged to thrust his hand into the machine for the purpose of supplying its defects, and of giving it a new impulse by an immediate agency." To this objection he replies "that it proceeds on false ideas of God and of the creation. God is not an artist, but a moral Parent and Governor; nor is the creation a machine. If it were, it might be urged with greater speciousness that miracles cannot be needed or required. One of the most striking views of the creation is the contrast or opposition of the elements of which it consists. It includes not only matter but mind, —not only lifeless and unconscious masses, but rational beings, free agents; and these are its noblest parts and ultimate objects. The material universe was not framed for itself, but for these. Its order was not appointed for its own sake, but to instruct and improve a higher rank of beings, the intelligent offspring of God; and whenever a departure from this order,—that is, whenever miraculous agency can contribute to the growth and perfection of his intelligent creatures,— it is demanded by his wisdom, goodness, and all his attributes. If the Supreme Being proposed only such ends as mechanism can produce, then He might have framed a machinery so perfect and sure as to need no suspension of its ordinary movements. But He has an incomparably nobler end. His great purpose is to educate, to rescue from evil, to carry forward for ever the free, rational mind or soul; and who that understands what a free mind is, and what a variety of teaching and discipline it requires, will presume to affirm that no lights or aids but such as come to it through an invariable order of nature, are necessary to unfold it?" [90]

A careless reading of these lines might suggest to the humorous cynic that Channing's conception of the divine wisdom and power was almost as limited as that of the author of Judges 1:19.[91] A more careful examination, however, will reveal to us the fact that Channing's basic conviction of the freedom of the human will, which played so large a part in the development of his Arianism, has now caused him to question the possibility of *any* fixed order of nature providing of itself an adequate environment for the development of the soul. "Much of the difficulty," he continues, "in regard to miracles, as I apprehend, would be removed if we were to consider more particularly that the chief distinction of intelligent beings is moral freedom, the power of determining themselves to evil as well as good, and consequently the power of involving themselves in great misery. When God made man, He framed not a machine, but a free being, who was to rise or fall according to his use or abuse of his powers. This capacity, at once the most glorious and the most fearful which we can conceive, shows us how the human race may have come into a condition to which the illumination of nature was inadequate. In truth, the more we consider the freedom of intelligent beings, the more we shall question the possibility of establishing an unchangeable order which will meet fully all their wants; for such beings, having of necessity a wide range of action, may bring themselves into a vast variety of conditions, and of course, may come to need a relief not contained in the resources of nature." [92] In other words, as Channing sees the situation, it is not the limitations of the Creator, but the potentialities of the creature, which necessitate special divine interposition.[93]

In Channing's opinion the human race, before the coming of Christ, had actually entered into a blind alley from which there was no exit. The resources of nature had exhausted themselves in vain.[94] "Philosophy," he tells us, "had done its best, and failed."[95] A divine interposition had, consequently, become indispensable; and it was, accordingly, granted.

One reason why a fixed order of nature must prove itself inadequate is that, while it does reveal to men some of the attributes of God, it also tends to conceal others, and these the most important. The very regularity of nature, although it is, indeed, indicative of the activity of a supreme mind, does not of itself provide an adequate basis for the establishment of personal relationships between God and men. "It reveals him as the Universal Sovereign who provides for the whole or for the general weal, but not, with sufficient clearness, as a tender Father, interested in the individual. I see, in this fixed order, his care of the race, but not his constant, boundless, concern for myself. Nature speaks of a general divinity, not of the friend and benefactor of each living soul. This is a necessary defect attending an inflexible, unvarying administration by general laws; and it seems to require that God, to carry forward the race, should reveal himself by some other manner than by general laws. No conviction is more important to human improvement than that of God's paternal interest in every human being; and how can He communicate this persuasion so effectually as by suspending nature's order, to teach, through an inspired messenger, his paternal love."[96]

Miracles, Channing reminds us, are, from their very nature, rare; for, were they to occur with sufficient frequency, they would be indistinguishable from the general order of nature.[97] There is, thus, something startling about them; and they are, therefore, peculiarly fitted to awaken the sluggish consciousness.[98] There is nothing exciting about mere regularity; the placid uniformity of nature's routine consequently tends to dull the capacity to wonder. Now it is precisely to this sense of wonder that miracles appeal; nor was it unworthy of God to employ them for this end; the potential greatness of the soul thereby aroused to activity abundantly justifying the resort to this extraordinary means.[99]

Moreover, there is a further consideration in view of which divine intervention in the form of miracles should be judged most worthy of a compassionate God. "There is one great point, on which we are deeply concerned to know the truth, and which is yet taught so indistinctly by nature, that men, however disposed to learn, cannot by that light alone obtain full conviction. What, let me ask, is the question in which each man has the deepest interest? It is this: Are we to live again, or is this life all? Does the principle of thought perish with the body, or does it survive? And if it survive, where? how? in what condition? under what law? There is an inward voice which speaks of judgment to come. Will judgment indeed come? and if so, what award may we hope or fear? The future state of man,—this is the great question forced on us by our changing life and by approaching death. I will not say that on this topic nature throws no light. I think it does; and this light continually grows brighter to them whose eyes revelation has couched and made strong to see. But nature alone does not meet our wants. I might prove this by referring you to the ages preceding Christ, when the anxious spirit of man constantly sought to penetrate the gloom beyond the grave,—when imagination and philosophy alike plunged into the future, but found no resting-place. But every man must feel that, left to nature as his only guide, he must wander in doubt as to the life to come. Where but from God himself can I learn my destination? I ask at the mouth of the tomb for intelligence of the departed, and the tomb gives me no reply. I examine the various regions of nature, but I can discover no process for restoring the mouldering body, no sign or track of the spirit's assent to another sphere. I see the need of a power above nature to restore or perpetuate life after death; and if God intended to give assurance of this life, I see not how He can do it but by supernatural teaching,—by a miraculous revelation. Miracles are the appropriate, and would seem to be the only, mode of placing beyond doubt man's future and immortal being; and no miracles can be conceived so peculiarly adapted to this end as the very ones which hold the highest place in Christianity—I mean the resurrection of Lazarus and, still more, the resurrection of Jesus. No man will deny that, of all truths, a future state is most strengthening to virtue and consoling to humanity. Is it, then, unworthy of God to employ miracles for the awakening or the confirmation of this hope? May they not ever be expected if nature, as we have seen, sheds but a faint light on this most interesting of all verities"? [100]

In this passage the importance attached to miracles is certainly tremendous. True enough, it is upon a particular miracle—that of the Resurrection—that Channing's interest is concentrated; yet it is also clear that he does not think of it as standing or falling alone, but as a member of class, and thus as receiving some support from the admission of the genuineness of the other members. The position which he has thus outlined is one which he held in common with the majority of his Unitarian brethren. In the light of his statements one can easily comprehend how utterly subversive of the very foundation of Christianity Theodore Parker's view must have appeared to the men of Channing's generation. It is also necessary to add that the above passage must not be taken as expressing, without qualification, Channing's final position. We shall discover that, in his later writings, he is prepared to appeal both to logical inference and to mystical intuition to substantiate the doctrine of immortality. Never the less miracle remained for him, if not the only, at least an extremely important evidence thereof.[101]

We have now to examine Channing's attitude toward Hume. What is the pith of Hume's contention with regard to miracles? "The argument," Channing tells us, "is briefly this,—'That belief is founded upon and regulated by experience. Now we often experience testimony to be false, but never witness a departure from the laws of nature. That men may deceive us when they testify to miracles, is therefore more accordant with experience than that nature should be irregular; and hence there is a balance of proof against miracles, a presumption so strong as to outweigh the strongest testimony.' " [102] Channing's reply to this argument falls under four heads.

In the first place, he observes, the argument presupposes that nature includes, or can be equated with, the totality of existence—or, to make use of Professor A. E. Taylor's terminology, that there is no such thing as "super-nature"—thence it is inferred that the laws of nature furnish an absolute standard in accordance with which the claim of any statement to credibility is to be tried. If the premise be sound, the argument stands; if it be unsound, the argument falls.[103]

In the second place, Hume's argument, according to Channing, "proves too much, and therefore proves nothing. It proves too much; for if I am to reject the strongest testimony to miracles because testimony has often deceived me, whilst nature's order has never been found to fail, then I ought to reject a miracle, even if I should see it with my own eyes, and if all my senses should attest it; for all my senses have sometimes given false reports, whilst nature has never gone astray; and, therefore, be the circumstances ever so decisive or inconsistent with deception, still I must not believe what I see, and hear, and touch,—what my senses, exercised according to the most deliberate judgment, declare to be true. All this the argument requires; and it proves too much; for disbelief in the case supposed is out of our power, and is instinctively pronounced absurd; and what is more, it would subvert that very order of nature on which the argument rests; for this order of nature is learned only by the exercise of my senses and judgment, and if these fail me in the most unexceptionable circumstances, then their testimony to nature is of little worth." [104]

In the third place, Channing contends that Hume's argument wrongly assumes that the believer in miracles accepts them solely on the strength of human testimony, without submitting that testimony to critical scrutiny. But this is precisely what the intelligent believer does not do. "Testimony," declares Channing, "of itself and immediately proves no facts whatever, not even the most common. Testimony can do nothing more than show us the state of another's mind in regard to a given fact. It can only show us that the testifier has a belief, a conviction, that a certain phenomenon or event has occurred. Here testimony stops: and the reality of the event is to be judged altogether from the degree and nature of this conviction, and the circumstances under which it exists. This conviction is an effect, which must have a cause, and needs to be explained; and if no cause can be found but the real occurrence of the event, then this occurrence is admitted as true. Such is the extent of testimony. Now a man who affirms a miraculous phenomenon or event, may give us just as decisive proofs, by his character and conduct, of the strength and depth of his conviction as if he were affirming a common occurrence. Testimony, then, does just as much in the case of miracles as of common events; that is, it discloses to us the conviction of another's mind. Now this conviction in the case of miracles requires a cause, an explanation, as much as in every other; and if the circumstances be such that it could not have sprung up and been established but by the reality of the alleged miracle, then that great and fundamental principle of human belief, namely, that every effect must have a cause, compels us to admit the miracle." [105]

The point which Channing makes in this passage is excellently illustrated in our own day by contemporary discussions of the problem of the Resurrection. It may safely be said that no informed and intelligent person regards the view that conscious fraud was at the bottom of the belief as meriting serious discussion; and a few would be inclined to take with much greater seriousness the hypothesis that Jesus did not really die, but was merely in a state of "suspended animation," from which in mysterious circumstances he revived only mysteriously to disappear forever. The phenomena experienced by the disciples are almost unaminously admitted to be genuine phenomena. The question at issue is their significance. And every investigator, in blithe disregard of Hume's critique of causality, proceeds at once to look for a cause. If the phenomena were not what the disciples believed them to be, how are they to be accounted for? The effort to answer this question has produced various conjectural psychological reconstructions of what went on in the minds of the disciples. These reconstructions are ingenious and interesting but obviously they can never be put to a direct test, since one cannot cause the event to be repeated. Are they convincing? A man's whole world view is involved in his reply. How Channing would respond, were he alive today, we do not know; but there is no doubt as to what he thought, that the only adequate explanation was in terms of a miraculous event.

In the fourth place, Channing points out that Hume has followed the common procedure of philosophical sceptics, and has directed his argument against the general notion of miracle, rather than against the miracles of Christianity in all their concrete particularity. "And the reason," he adds, "is obvious. Miracles when considered in a general, abstract, manner, that is, when divested of all circumstances, and supposed to occur as disconnected facts, to stand alone in history, to have no explanations or reasons in preceding events, and no influence on those which follow, are indeed open to great objection, as wanton and useless violations of nature's order; and it is accordingly against miracles, considered in this naked, general form that the arguments of infidelity are chiefly urged. But it is great disingenuity to class under this head the miracles of Christianity. They are palpably different. They do not stand alone in history; but are most intimately incorporated with it. They were demanded by the state of the world which preceded them, and they have left deep traces on subsequent ages. In fact, the history of the whole civilized world, since their alleged occurrence, has been swayed and colored by them, and is wholly inexplicable without them. Now such miracles are not to be met, and disposed of by general reasonings, which apply only to insulated, unimportant, uninfluential prodigies." [106]

Channing here makes a point of considerable importance. His protest against every attempt to deal with the question of miracles in a purely *a priori* manner, and his insistence that historical and psychological investigations are necessarily involved, are surely sound. Consider only the problems which arise in connection with the miracles of healing reported in the case of Jesus. How complex is the task of sifting legend from fact, and the study of the manner in which legends originate! Channing's sharp separation of Christian miracles from miracles in general is, of course, bound to impress the twentieth century reader unfavorably. In this Channing was typical of his period.

What of the actual evidence in support of the miracles of Christianity. It consists, Channing informs us, of two varieties, "presumptive" and "direct." [107] With the presumptive we are already familiar. It consists in the extreme importance of the truths miraculously authenticated, which renders such authentication worthy of God. The direct evidence, again, consists of two kinds: the testimony of eye-witnesses, and the effects produced.[108] Channing's relatively uncritical study of the New Testament leads him to conclude that it contains abundant testimony of eye-witnesses, many of them individuals whose names are known.[109] What better testimony could one ask for? The effects produced were the manifold conversions of Jews and pagans to the new faith, and its triumphal progress against all opposition.[110]

The dividing line between miracles and revelation, it will have been observed, is somewhat nebulous. Strictly speaking, miracles are "signs" which authenticate the message imparted through an inspired teacher; whereas the message itself is revelation. Inasmuch, however, as the miracles do manifest the divine intention, they are in a sense, revelatory; and, inasmuch as revelation proceeds from a power above nature, it is, in a sense, miraculous. Accordingly we find Channing asserting that Christianity, "is not only confirmed by miracles, but is in itself, in its very essence, a miraculous religion"; [111] and the character of Christ, he assures us, constitutes the "greatest and most quickening miracle in human history." [112]

The distinction between the natural and the super-natural is of the first importance, and it is a great error ever to confound them; but it is also a great mistake to depreciate nature, as though it had nothing to teach us which is of religious significance. In thoroughly mediaeval fashion Channing thinks of nature as constituting in itself a book of revelation which the Christian must read as well as his Bible. Both proceed from the same source.

"We shall err greatly, if we imagine that his (Christ's) gospel is the only light, that every ray comes to us from a single book, that no splendors issue from God's works and providence, that we have no teacher in religion but the few pages bound up in our Bibles. Jesus Christ came, not only to give us his peculiar teaching, but to introduce us to the imperishable lessons which God forever furnishes in our own and all human experience, and in the laws and movements of the universe. He intends, not that we should hear his voice alone, but that we should open our ears to the countless voices of wisdom, virtue, piety, which now in whispers, now in thunders, issue from the whole of Nature and life. He does not give us a narrow system, and command us to bound inquiry within its limits. He does not prison reason by a rigid, formal creed. He gives us generous principles, which we are to carry out and apply everywhere, and by which we are to interpret all existence. He who studies nothing but the Bible, does not study that book aright. For were it rightly read, it would send him for instruction to every creature that God hath made, and to every event wherein God is acting. The reader has not read aright the Sermon on the Mount, who has not learned to read sermons in the changes of the seasons and in the changes of human history. Wisdom spoke through Jesus as her chief oracle. She beamed forth from the life and lessons of this divine Saviour, with the pure unsullied glory in which She manifests herself in heaven. But Wisdom does not confine herself to one shrine. Her light is not bonded to a single orb. To the humblest that calls she gives her responses. We live amidst a host of teachers of moral and religious truth. Unsought, unpaid, they beset our path. Rejected, they still plead. They begin their ministry with our first breath; and they do not forsake us in the last hour." [113]

The above passage is, indeed, to be found in *The Perfect Life*, but it can be paralleled in Channing's earlier writings; [114] it cannot, therefore, be taken as indicative of any fundamental change in his outlook, although, perhaps, the distinction between the natural and the supernatural has grown somewhat thinner. In words which inevitably remind one of Theodore Parker, Channing asserts that Jesus "creates no new truth; for truth is eternal." "And what is still more important," he continues, "he does not teach truth wholly new to men. The great principles of religion belong to human nature; and they are manifested in all God's works and in his providence. We live in darkness, not because there is no sun of truth shining on and around us. For a spiritual light, brighter than that of noon, pervades our daily life. The cause of our not seeing is in ourselves." [115] When Jesus healed a blind man, he did not create a new light whereby he might see; what he did was to remove an impediment which prevented him from seeing the light that already was.[116] Of such sort also is his spiritual activity: he opens the eyes of the soul to eternal truth.

"But is God," asks Channing, "the infinite and universal Father, made known only by a single voice, heard ages ago on the banks of the Jordan, or by the sea of Tiberias? Is it an unknown tongue that the heavens and earth for ever utter? Is nature's page a blank? Does the human soul report nothing of its Creator? Does conscience announce no authority higher than its own? Does reason discern no trace of an Intelligence, that it cannot comprehend, yet of which it is itself a ray? Does the heart find in the circuits of creation no friend worthy of trust and love? Oh, yes! God is on every side, not only by his essential invisible presence, but by his manifestations of power and perfection. We fail to see him, not from want of light, but from want of spiritual vision." [117]

If such be the case, what, then, precisely is the function of the Christian revelation? "The Christian religion," we are told, "concentrates the truth diffused through the universe, and pours it upon the mind with solar lustre. Still more it heals our blindness by exposing the passions and sins which veil the mind against the light of the spirit, and furnishing the means to remove the films which gather over the inward eye and prevent us from seeing the revelations of Nature." [118]

These passages from *The Perfect Life* certainly do, at their first reading, suggest a change in outlook, and one of no small import. We have previously been told not only that nature and revelation, although distinct, are complimentary, that revelation addresses itself to reason and must be judged by it, but also that revelation provides an illumination which extends the man's mental vision beyond nature, and thus rescues a reason which has exhausted its capacities from an *impasse* into which it has wandered. Now, however, we are informed that the purpose of revelation is to remove a spiritual impediment—the result, it would seem, of a corrupt will—which blinds the soul to the revelations of nature. From this it would appear to follow that the function of revelation is subordinate, that it is infra-natural rather than supernatural, that nature is superior to revelation. Shall we, therefore, conclude that the potential Transcendentalist in Channing is here passing into actuality, that the notion of an inerrant revelation imparted more or less mechanically from without, is fading away, that the idea of immanence is replacing that of transcendence, and that the natural and the supernatural are about to coalesce, as in the thought of Theodore Parker? How, then, shall we explain the fact that the Channing who wrote *The Perfect Life* insists upon the importance of miracles with an earnestness no less emphatic than that of the Channing who wrote the *Evidences of Christianity*? And how shall we account for Channing's differing from Parker precisely over the question of supernaturalism? Has his thought lost all self-consistency, and reduced itself to a hopeless muddle? This may be the right answer, yet it does not appear to be a probable answer. It is clearly our duty to inquire whether it is possible to reconcile these apparently conflicting statements. I believe that it is possible to do so. We shall find, I think, that there is a change in outlook, but a change of subordinate significance, which leaves the main outlines of his thought undisturbed.

The key, I suggest, is to be found in the assertion—the importance of which is stressed—that Jesus does not "teach truth *wholly* new to men." [119] What does this mean? It clearly implies that some portion of the truth which he taught *was* new to men. What, we must accordingly ask, did he teach that was new? We know that Channing believed that Jesus had something to say about his own unique relationship to God, about his own function of intercession, and about his future return in glory to raise the dead and to judge mankind. All this was new. Moreover to these truths unaided human reason could never attain, either by *a priori* speculations or by empirical investigation. Yet they are not the most important truths. What are the truths which Jesus taught that were not new? They were those which the soul derives from the study of nature and of itself—the ideas of God, of goodness, of right, of duty, of the potential divinity of man—these are "the revelations of nature." What is Jesus' function with regard to these? He turns man's attention toward them, he shocks the mind into the consideration of them, he implements them by divine authentication; most of all, in his own moral perfection he provides the assurance that the ideal *is* real, that the ultimate goal which the intellect has envisaged *can* be attained. All this is obviously of the deepest significance. The importance of supernatural revelation is not, therefore, diminished, the uniqueness of Christ is not impugned, by the recognition that nature is also a divine revelation. It is by the aid of revelation that the believer is enabled to interpret the book of nature, and the concordance of the two then becomes clear.

Readers of Dr. Emil Brunner's well-known work, *The Mediator,* will recall that the *bete noire* of this eminent theologian is "universal religion." The phrase plainly suggests some form of philosophic speculation divorced from all that is distinctive of time and place; yet, as he progresses, the reader is astonished to learn that every religion, other than Christianity, is no more than a form of this "universal religion." Two principal reasons are advanced in support of this amazing verdict. Every religion, we are informed, with the exception of Christianity, lacks the element of once-for-allness; that is, it subordinates the historical to the eternal, it points to no single, unrepeatable, event which constitutes the break-through of the eternal into time. Moreover the founders of these religions uniformly point beyond themselves to a higher reality; none of them professes to be more than *primus inter pares*. In Christianity, on the other hand—so Dr. Brunner contends —we have a religion which does center about a single, unrepeatable, terrific event—namely, the Incarnation; and in Christ we have a Founder who does not point beyond himself, but is to be identified with the supreme, self-revealing God.

Now it is interesting to observe that Christianity, as Channing conceives of it, fits into neither of Dr. Brunner's classifications. It does contain an element of once-for-allness. There is only one Christ, one divinely appointed Lord of the human race, he has only once appeared upon earth; his appearance constituted an unrepeatable event, of crucial significance for the entire human race. Yet Christ emphatically points beyond himself to the Father who sent him, "he is nothing to the human race but what he is by God's appointment," [120] he "came into the world not to claim supreme homage for himself, but to carry up the soul to his Father as the only Divine Person, the only Ultimate Object of religious worship." [121] Thus Channing's conception of Christianity, while it clearly meets one of Dr. Brunner's requirements, no less clearly fails to meet the other.

This circumstance directs our attention to the close connection between Channing's Arianism and his view of revelation. The most important truths are those which have to do with God and man— these are the old truths which Christ merely reinforces, although his reinforcement is of vital import; the new truths are those which have to do with Christ and man—with Christ as man's living ideal, and with man as a potential Christ. Each class of truths is important, yet there is no doubt that the former is supremely so.

We have now to inquire in what respect Channing's later writings indicate a change from his earlier viewpoint in regard to revelation. In the first place, we discover that, in *The Perfect Life,* the capacity of human reason to arrive at the truth of immortality is emphasized, rather than depreciated.[122] And, in the second place, we become conscious of an increasing importance attributed to individual inward illumination. This latter development is of such importance as to demand a detailed examination.

That Channing was a man of a profoundly mystical temperament we know full well.[123] In this respect he has more in common with Edwards, among his predecessors, and with the Transcendentalists, among his successors, than with the majority of his contemporaries. Mysticism, as Dean Inge has truly said, is an expression of the spirit of the ages rather than of the spirit of an age, and with the spirit of the eighteenth century it had less in common than with that of many another century. Channing was a child of the eighteenth century, and with its exaltation of reason in opposition to authoritarianism he was in complete sympathy. In this respect his admiration for Locke is in no sense a form of homage to contemporary popularity; it is a genuine manifestation of a consciousness of intellectual kinship. So also is his distaste of unrestrained emotionalism. This, too, was very real. In the field of religion, especially, he deemed it a grave danger; in his eyes it was the expression of an unbalanced and unhealthy mentality, the production of a forced and artificial fervor rather than a genuine piety. There is, he insists, a symmetry and proportion in the soul of the truly religious man, and any disturbance thereof constitutes a spiritual malformation which cannot but impede further development. To this thought he returns again and again.

"I affirm," he writes, "that the great office of religion is to call forth, elevate, and purify the spirit of man, and thus to conform it to its divine original. I know no other way in which religion is to promote our happiness; for I know no happiness but that of a good, wise, upright, firm, powerful, disinterested, elevated character. I look to religion for blessings, because it includes and promotes universal excellence, brings the soul into health and concord, enlarges it, unfolds it in due proportions, and exalts it to the beauty and power for which it was created. It is the office of religion, I repeat once more, to call forth the *whole* spirit of man, the intellect, the conscience, the affections, the will; to awaken energy and holy purpose; to inspire a rational, yet a profound, love of truth and goodness, against which all powers of the universe will be impotent. Did I not hope for this quickening influence from religion, I could not speak of it as the supreme good. For our supreme good is the perfection of our being; and nothing which does not involve and promote this deserves the name." [124]

One reason, in Channing's opinion, why unrestrained emotionalism in religion is so harmful is that it exhausts the vital powers, and is thus productive of subsequent weariness and deadness. "The prevalent error," he observes "always has been, that men have confined their conception of religion too much to its *direct* agencies. They have supposed it to consist chiefly in immediate thoughts of God, in immediate addresses to him, and in fervors of emotion called forth by immediate contemplation of his glory. Now religion so viewed cannot insure our highest happiness. I know, indeed, that these spiritual acts are often the most delightful of which our nature is capable. The pious man, when able to concentrate every energy of mind and heart upon the infinite goodness of his Creator, and to enter by faith and hope into communion with the unseen and everlasting world, has a foretaste of joy unspeakable and full of glory. But I need not tell you that this elevation of thought and feeling is not designed to be the ordinary state of even the most improved human beings. We were plainly not designed for this constant intense action of our spirits towards our Creator. No effort on our part can long sustain it. And were it sustained for a protracted period, it would end in the exhaustion and derangement of our faculties. Besides, there are not a few who seem constitutionally incapacitated for such ardor of religious emotion. If religion insured our happiness, then, only as giving us an immediate enjoyment of God, it would really contribute but little to our well-being,—the greater part of life being necessarily devoted to other duties and engagements, to intercourse with fellow-beings, to toils and relaxations, and to putting forth creative energy on the material world. We cannot live absorbed in the work of adoration. We cannot keep our minds perpetually bent upon one object. And the brighter that object the sooner we are dazzled and exhausted." [125]

We need not, therefore, be astonished to find Channing, in his Baltimore sermon, stressing the importance which he, and his fellow-Unitarians, lay upon the necessity of distinguishing the genuine love of God from "counterfeits." "We think," he announces, "that much which is called piety is worthless. Many have fallen into the error that there can be no excess in feelings which have God for their object: and, distrusting as coldness that self-possession without which virtue and devotion lose all their dignity, they have abandoned themselves to extravagances which have brought contempt on piety. Most certainly, if the love of God be that which often bears its name, the less we have of it the better. If religion be the shipwreck of understanding, we cannot keep too far from it. On this subject we always speak plainly. We cannot sacrifice our reason to the reputation of zeal. We owe it to truth and religion to maintain that fanaticism, partial insanity, sudden impressions, and ungovernable transports are anything rather than piety." [126]

What then is genuine love of God? Channing proceeds to tell us. "We conceive," he continues, "that the true love of God is a moral sentiment, founded on a clear perception, and consisting in a high esteem and veneration of his moral perfections. Thus, it perfectly coincides, and is, in fact, the same thing, with the love of virtue, rectitude, and goodness. You will easily judge, then, what we esteem the surest and only decisive signs of piety. We lay no stress on strong excitements. We esteem him, and him only, a pious man, who practically conforms to God's moral perfections and government; who shows delight in God's benevolence by loving and serving his neighbor; who shows his delight in God's justice by being resolutely upright; his sense of God's purity by regulating his thoughts, imagination, and desires; and whose conversation, business, and domestic life are swayed by a regard to God's presence and authority. In all things else men may deceive themselves. Disordered nerves may give them strange sights, and sounds, and impressions. Texts of Scripture may come to them as from heaven. Their whole souls may be moved, and their confidence in God's favor be undoubting. But in all this there is no religion. The question is, Do they love God's commands, in which his character is fully expressed, and give up to these their habits and passions? Without this, ecstasy is a mockery. One surrender of desire to God's will is worth a thousand transports. We do not judge of the bent of men's minds by their raptures, any more than we judge of the natural direction of a tree during a storm. We rather suspect loud profession, for we have observed that deep feeling is generally noiseless, and least seeks display." [127]

As one reads these sentences one cannot but recall Locke's denunciations of "enthusiasm"; yet, despite profound similarity, there is also a significant difference. The ease with which self-deception may take place is heavily stressed by both writers. Locke, however, admits with seeming reluctance—as it were, against his will—the possibility of an implantation in the mind of an idea of the third class by divine power, and proceeds at once to emphasize the importance of objective verification of means of miracle. In the case of Channing the delineation of such experiences is far more sympathetic.

In the second place, these words explain the tremendous weight laid upon obedience in Channing's works. It is a theme to which he frequently adverts. "God," he insists, "is to be known by obedience, by likeness, by sympathy; that is by moral means, which are open alike to rich and poor." [128] Even the doctrine of immortality, he maintains, has been revealed "wholly as a motive to obedience." [129]

Channing takes pains, however, to guard his conception of obedience from possible misinterpretation. In this he showed a wise foresight; for, in the eyes of too many of the orthodox, any stick was good enough wherewith to beat Unitarians; and, as the latter have actually been accused of conceiving of God as an absolute, undifferentiated monad devoid of all qualities, so they might well have been represented as inculcating a servile, groveling submission to a divine despot, had Channing, their most eminent spokesman, left his conception of un-obedience unelaborated. Knowing what we already know of his view of God, and God's moral attributes, we shall find his explanation in complete harmony therewith.

There is no contradiction, Channing maintains, between conceiving of virtue as "self-dominion," and thinking of it as consisting in obedience to the will of God. "These are perfectly compatible and harmonious views; for genuine obedience to God is the free choice and adoption of a law, the great principle of which our own minds approve, and our own consciences bind on us; which is not an arbitrary injunction, but an emanation and expression of the divine mind; and which is intended throughout to give energy, dignity, and enlargement to our best powers. He, and he only, obeys God virtuously and acceptably, who reverences right, not power; who has chosen rectitude as his supreme rule; who sees and reveres in God the fulness and brightness of moral excellence, and who sees in obedience the progress and perfection of his own nature. That subjection to the Deity, which, we fear, is too common, in which the mind surrenders itself to mere power and will, is any thing but virtue. We fear that it is disloyalty to that moral principle which is ever to be reverenced as God's viceregent in the rational soul." [130]

All this is, of course, quite in accord with the theory of *essential sameness*, and with Channing's view that moral axioms are independent of the divine will. And the same emphasis upon obedience is also to be found, as one would naturally anticipate, in connection with his treatment of love to Jesus. The substitutionary theory of the atonement, he maintains, tends to awaken a sympathy with Christ's physical sufferings, and a gratitude toward him for the benevolence with which he is supposed to have ransomed mankind by his vicarious suffering—to neither of which emotions, as we have seen, does Channing ascribe genuine moral worth. "I know of no feeling more suspicious," he declares, "than the common love to Christ." [131] "The truth is," he assures us, "the love of Christ is but another name for the love of virtue. It is not, as some seem to think, a kind of theological emotion—a mysterious fervor —distinct from moral integrity, from philanthropy, and from our duties to God and our neighbor. We err grievously if we imagine that our salvation is promoted by occasional ardor towards Christ which subsists apart by itself, in the heart—which does not blend with our ordinary feelings and our daily lives. The character of Christ *is* perfect virtue. And consequently attachment to Christ, as I have just said, is but another name for attachment to virtue." [132]

In this spirit, as we have observed, Channing contrasts the "practical, benevolent spirit of Christianity" with the "spurious sanctity" and "profitless enthusiasm" of oriental mysticism.[133] The tendency of the latter, he thinks, is to lose the individual in an incomprehensible Infinite, and this depreciation of the self he regards as the common source of pantheism in philosophy and of despotism in politics.[134] In the somewhat supercilious references to "enthusiasm," which are not infrequent in Channing's works, and in his painstaking effort to show that Jesus was no enthusiast,[135] we discern the influence of the prevalent mentality of the eighteenth century upon his thinking. It is, however, a relatively superficial influence. With the smugness and coldness which one habitually associates with that great period Channing has no sympathy at all.[136] More than once in his writings he reveals an uneasy consciousness that mysticism is something which, in the eyes of his contemporaries [137] is not intellectually respectable, but yet also something which he cannot himself repudiate, but to which he must acknowledge his spiritual allegiance.[138] Yet his reluctance to employ the term *mysticism* to designate his own particular type of spiritual experience cannot be attributed merely to an unwillingness to incur the disapproval or ridicule of his contemporaries. The name *Unitarian* was equally, if not more, disreputable; but the man who boldly adopted it, and practically flaunted it before the world, out of loyalty to Christ and "his truth," was not one to dissemble out of regard for popular prejudice. Some other reason must be found; and that reason, I believe, is easily to be discovered. To Channing, as to many another thinker and writer, mysticism was associated with a pantheism which confounds man with God.[139] If the word is to be used in this sense, Channing was certainly no mystic; but if, on the contrary, one accept Dr. Rufus Jones's definition of it as "religion in its most acute, intense, and living stage," there can be no doubt at all that he was a thorough and confirmed mystic from boyhood to death. And we have seen how large a part his religious experience played in moulding his conception of a uni-personal God. Our present task is to discover how the same experience influenced his conception of human nature and its relation to the divine.

We are already familiar with certain aspects of Channing's outlook upon this problem. We know that, in his view, "all minds are of one family," that the human intelligence is the offspring of the divine. The rational nature of man constitutes, as we have discovered, God's primary revelation.[140] Yet it is not to be considered in abstraction from the physical universe which is its present abode. We have, he tells us, "two great teachers"—"the outward universe," and "the world of thinking, moral beings." [141] That physical nature is also a revelation of God, Channing repeatedly affirms. Its vastness suggests to man the idea of the infinite, in its design and its beauty he beholds the external embodiment of some of the attributes of its Maker.[142] Why, then, is not this revelation also primary in character? The answer would seem to be that it is not so because its function is to turn man's thought inward where alone ultimate certitude is to be found.[143] In a very Cartesian fashion Channing remarks, "We have more evidence that we have souls or spirits than that we have bodies. We are surer that we think, and feel, and will, than that we have solid and extended limbs and organs. Philosophers have said much to disprove the existence of matter and motion, but they have not tried to disprove the existence of thought; for it is by thought they attempt to set aside the reality of material nature." [144] And it is out of acquaintance with his own nature that man develops the idea of God.

Is not all this, it may be asked, very vague and indefinite? Has Channing said anything more than that the whole universe is a revelation of its Creator, a proposition which the vast majority of theists would admit without question? But a revelation which is everywhere in general is nowhere in particular. Has not Channing done with the notion of revelation very much what St. Thomas has done with the notion of illumination—namely, "watered it down" until nothing distinctive is left? One may not unfairly say that, according to St.

Thomas, God illumines man in creating him. And, in like manner, may one not say that, according to Channing, God reveals himself to man by creating him? But is not this empty verbiage? To assert that one can argue from man, or from physical nature, to God is only to affirm what the most rationalistic Deist would concede. Surely revelation, as the Christian uses the word, means something far other than this.

In reply to this imagined critic, there are two considerations which may be stressed. In the first place, the position in which Channing finds himself, as he turns upon his own ego an introspective glance, is very different from that of St. Thomas when he engages in the same form of activity. The latter can reason from his own existence, or that of any other finite entity, to the existence of a Deity, yet of the nature of that *Deus Absconditus* he can form no conception save by employing the indirect, complicated, and miserably inadequate method of analogy. Upon Channing, on the other hand—as we ascertained in the third chapter of this book—the principle of *essential sameness* sheds a flood of light. In studying the human soul, he is studying the image of God, as it were the Deity himself in miniature.[145] Hence Channing's assertion, so often and so forcefully repeated, that "we must start in religion from our own souls." [146]

And, in the second place, it can be pointed out that the criticism is unsound because premature. Channing is here concerned with revelation in its broadest and most general sense, with natural revelation which is bestowed upon all men who will open their eyes to behold it.[147] Yet the capacity to discern more accurately and to see more clearly is one which requires to be cultivated, and which is susceptible of improvement. "If there springs up within you," he writes, "any view of God's word or universe, any sentiment or aspiration which seems to you of a higher order than what you meet abroad, give reverent heed to it; inquire into it earnestly, solemnly. Do not trust it blindly, for it may be an illusion; but it may be the Divinity moving within you, a new revelation, not supernatural, but still most precious, of truth or duty; and if, after inquiry, it so appear, then let no clamor, or scorn, or desertion turn you from it. Be true to your own highest convictions. Intimations from our own souls of something more perfect than others teach, if faithfully followed, give us a consciousness of spiritual force and progress, never experienced by the vulgar of high life or low life, who march, as they are drilled, to the step of their times." [148]

Why is such a revelation not supernatural? Is it because it is unaccompanied by miraculous authentication? Or is it because it is of nature rather than of grace, because it is due to the burgeoning of the soul's own native divinity rather than to a spiritual light illumining it from without. It is difficult, if not impossible, to answer these questions with any exactitude for the reason that it is not easy to determine where we pass from nature to grace—or, in fact, whether we "pass" at all, whether, indeed, it is not with grace that we begin. Like the Calvinist, from whom in certain other respects he differs so profoundly, Channing belongs to the Augustinian tradition rather than to the Aristotelian; and in either case, it is hard to distinguish between "common grace" and "nature."

With justifiable indignation Channing protests against the misrepresentation that Unitarianism has no doctrine of grace. On the contrary, he insists, grace is the very core of the gospel.[149] But what is grace? Grace, Channing tells us, is "unconquerable love," which "waits not for merit to call it forth, but flows out to the most guilty, is the sinner's only hope," and "is fitted to call forth the most devoted gratitude." [150] To this overflowing compassion it appears impossible to set any limits, inasmuch as it expresses itself everywhere. Indeed the natural tends to become absorbed in the supernatural to such a degree that it might plausibly be contended that Channing's entire universe is supernatural. There are, however, degrees of illumination; yet the divine spirit is always and everywhere anxious to impart itself to the soul which is willing to receive it.[151]

Like Locke, who declares that God, "in making the prophet, does not unmake the man," Channing is careful to warn one against the false supposition that divine illumination supersedes the normal human faculties. Milton's doctrine of a "twofold Scripture" comprising the external, written word, and the internal witness of the Holy Spirit, is, he considers, liable to such a misinterpretation. "To this doctrine," observes Channing, "it may be objected, and we think Milton must have felt the objection, that it disparages our faculties, and produces inaction of mind, leading men to expect from a sudden flash from heaven the truth which we are to seek by the right use of our own powers. We imagine that Milton believed that the Holy Spirit works with and by our own understandings, and instead of superseding reason, invigorates and extends it." [152]

Granting the soundness of this criticism we may still ask, however, whether there be any empirical evidence that such an invigoration and enlargement of the natural powers of the intellect by a divine *afflatus* ever takes place. Channing is of the opinion that there is. "The life of the intellect,—" he exclaims, "how mutable it is! There are hours of every day when it droops. Sometimes weeks may pass, and no bright thoughts will visit us. Sadly we feel that the lustre of our intellectual day is dimmed. The light that irradiates the mind does not shine with the steadiness of the sun. The eclipses of that orb we can foretell. Its rising and setting we anticipate. But the sun of the soul rises and sets we know not how. Its radiance fades when we must look and long for its brilliant beams. That sun of the intellect,—what is it? May it not be God, in a more direct sense than we imagine? That glowing splendor, that fervid heat, which sometimes burst upon the soul, and give it new rapidity and reach of thought, new warmth and loftiness of feeling,—whence come they? Are they not irradiations from the Parent mind? Are they not his immediate gift?" [153]

"Books without number," he continues "have been written on the human mind, and many of the laws, according to which its thoughts are associated, have been traced. But the higher workings of the mind —its diviner intuitions, its spiritual conceptions, its apparently self-originated ideas—have never been explained. They come and go, we know not whence or whither. We may give some account of the manner in which a particular train of thought was first suggested to a man of genius. But the life which he breathes through his ideal representation, the hues which he throws round it, the splendor in which he arrays it, the tone of tenderness or sublimity in which he embodies it, the more than lightning speed by which he blends it with remote conceptions, the harmony in which he places it with universal truth, the vital force by which he sends it far and deep to quicken the souls of readers or hearers, and awakes in them new worlds of thought and feeling,—these are inexplicable mysteries. Philosophy cannot reveal their origin or modes of action. They can only be felt by experience. The man of genius himself, in putting forth these powers, is most conscious that he cannot command them. They come not at his bidding; they stay not at his pleasure. If a devout man, he thanks God for these influxes of mental illumination, as peculiar communications of his intellectual energy, and prays that he may be more and more open for the reception of these heavenly gifts." [154]

With the soundness of these psychological observations no one is likely to quarrel; too many men of genius have testified in a similar strain. Yet this passage raises an interesting question. Precisely what is meant by the suggestion that God may be "the sun of the intellect," and that "in a more direct sense than we imagine." Ontologism, as we know, is the term by which Roman Catholic theologians and philosophers designate the theory that every man is naturally endowed with a direct, although confused, awareness of God. If true, this theory is of the first importance; for it then follows that by sufficiently accurate and careful discrimination of one's own mental processes this confused awareness can be clarified, and that the being of God will thereupon become an immediate datum of consciousness. Is this Channing's view? Was he an Ontologist?

I think that we must answer this question in the negative, and for three reasons. In the first place, the experiences thus described, while not limited exclusively to the genius—who doubtless is acquainted with them in their intensest form—nor yet to the professional student, can scarcely be supposed to fall to the lot of the habitually slothful and ignorant; for they clearly presuppose serious mental concentration and effort. In the second place, Channing's insistence upon moral purification as a necessary preparation, which, as we shall see, is most explicit, forbids us to assume that their connection with the character of the experiencing individual is anything but intimate—whereas the awareness which the Ontologist posits is the property of all men, good and bad. And, in the third place, it seems clear that it is by introspection that these influxes are known, and that they are then inferentially ascribed to the Deity as to their cause; whereas the awareness of which the Ontologist speaks is, not inferential, but direct.

These reflections, however, raise in turn yet another question. The Calvinist, as we are aware, attaches fundamental importance to an act of illumination on the part of the Holy Spirit which bestows upon the soul destined for salvation an awareness of God to which he applies the term *intuition*; and yet, at the same time, he denies that the divine Essence, as it is in itself, can be the immediate object of this intuition. The Calvinist, in short, assumes an attitude toward God similar to that which Locke adopts toward the physical universe. Physical objects, Locke concedes, are not known directly; it is only the ideas to which they give rise of which the mind is directly aware. None the less he insists that we have an assurance of the reality of the physical world which "passes under the name of knowledge." In each case an inference is clearly suppressed; and it is suppressed because of a patent unwillingness to acknowledge it, an unwillingness which springs from a consciousness of the great importance which attaches to the said inference, and a consequent desire to represent what is, on the most favorable estimate, a conclusive demonstration as an instance of direct, and consequently indubitable, insight. How is it with Channing? What is the loftiest knowledge of God to which he believes it possible to attain? Is it a direct apprehension of the Deity, or is it also merely inferential?

This is a question easier to ask than to answer; yet, in view of its extreme importance, we must try to extract, if we can, some solution from Channing's descriptions of the higher reaches of the spiritual life. In his case, indeed, the problem is not so crucial as in that of the Calvinist. The latter, proudly professing to disregard all arguments on the ground of the fallibility of human reason, appeals to an "intuition" which, he declares, affords him absolute assurance; yet, upon inspection, this vaunted "intuition" is discovered to be itself no more than an inference, so that he is still left with an argument on his hands. Channing, on the contrary, has no doubt that the divine existence can be established by human reason.[155] Even so, however, if religious experience be capable of providing an empirical confirmation of the reason's speculative achievement by elevating the soul to a height where it enjoys direct acquaintance with the Deity, this is a fact of the greatest significance and a consummation most sincerely to be desired. If, on the other hand, it affords man no more than a reflected vision of the divine glory in his own soul, it provides him only with the basis for another causal argument, which may, indeed, be wholly cogent, but which, if the proofs which Channing has already accepted be sound, is superfluous.

I must frankly admit that I doubt whether, with the evidence available, it is possible to settle this intriguing question beyond dispute. Still, if we can show that the weight of probability inclines on one side or the other, our investigation will not have proved wholly futile. In the first place, then, let us inquire as to the necessary preparations on the part of the soul which aspires to ascend to the highest stage of illumination. "Do you ask," inquires Channing, "by what means this end of entering into living communion with God can be attained? I answer first: Let us each put forth our best force of intellect in gaining clearer and brighter conceptions of the Divine Being. We must concentrate our loftiest powers of thought to this sublime reality. We must not leave to others the duty of thinking for us. We must not be contented to look through others' eyes. We must exercise our own minds with concentrated and continuous energy. One chief source of truth to us, in regard to God, is revelation; and this, accordingly, should claim our most serious and devoted study." [156]

Even more important and more efficacious, however, is the struggle against moral evil in one's own soul.[157] "My belief is," he declares, "that one chief means of acquiring a vivid sense of God's presence is to resist, instantly and resolutely, whatever we feel to be evil in our hearts and lives, and at once to begin in earnest to obey the divine will as it speaks in conscience. You say that you desire a new and nearer knowledge of your Creator. Let this thirst for a higher consciousness of the Infinite Being lead you to oppose whatever you feel to be at war with God's purity, God's truth, and God's righteousness. Just in proportion as you gain a victory over the evil of which you have become aware in yourself, will your spiritual eye be purged for a brighter perception of the Holy One. And this in its turn will strengthen you for a yet more strenuous resistance of sin,—which will prepare you for still more intimate acquaintance with the divine nature and character. This attainment to a knowledge of God and this instant resistance to sin are most intimately and vitally related. Neither can advance beyond the other. For God, as the All-Good, can be known only through our own growing goodness." [158]

The psychologist, or the psychoanalyst, might object that to concentrate upon evil is to make it bulk more large, to absorb one's attention, and thus to augment its appeal and so to frustrate one's own efforts. Yet, fairness bids one remember that Channing is not here speaking of the psychological tactics which it is wise to adopt, but of the moral strategy which should inspire them. It is the moral goal, rather than the means of its attainment which he has in view; and it may well be the case that the most effective way to combat evil is to concentrate upon its opposite.

In so far as the moral ideal is realized, it in turn becomes a means toward a further end—communion with the Divine. "God becomes a real being to us in proportion as his own nature is unfolded within us. To a man who is growing in the likeness of God, faith begins even here to change into vision. He carries within himself a proof of a Deity. He more than believes, he feels the Divine presence;[159] and gradually rises to an intercourse with his Maker, to which it is not irreverent to apply the name of friendship and intimacy." [160]

Channing's loose use of language in these sentences is, indeed, exasperating to one seeking a solution of our problem. Faith is said to change into vision, and belief into feeling—which would seem obviously to imply direct awareness resulting from immediate contact. What, then, is meant by talking of a "proof"? A proof involves inference, a passage from the given to the relatively remote. Clearly one cannot have it both ways. But which way are we to take it?

Let us look at another passage, "There is a light to which others are strangers, that visits the inward eye of the man who contends with the evil in himself, and is true to his convictions of duty. This is the highest inspiration, surpassing that of the prophets; for the ancient prophet comprehended but imperfectly the revelation with which he was charged, and sometimes shrank from communicating it to the world." [161] This is, indeed, strong language. One is irresistibly reminded of Abu Sa'id's "eighth seventh of the Koran." The "highest inspiration surpassing that of the prophets"! Here, if anywhere, should we discern the peak of spiritual experience. Yet, be it noted, Channing does not state that the source of the light is itself visible.

Let us, then, return to *The Perfect Life*, where, after commending intellectual concentration, strenuous resistance to temptation, dedication of the will to God's service, reading of the Scriptures, contemplation of the character of Jesus, and observation of the harmony and beauty in physical nature as effective means of purgation, he continues: "In this spirit look into your own minds, observe what is good and great in the minds of others, and the Infinite Mind will more and more appear to you in his crowning creation, the human soul. And finally, with this purifying purpose of duty, pray for the divine spirit, and you will receive it. A secret influence will aid your efforts after oneness with the Holy One. Peace, silent as dew, will distil on you from heaven. I believe, too, that with such a temper and life, you may enjoy something more than distant communications from the Father of Spirits; that you may be favored with those blessed seasons of universal light and strength, of which good men have often spoken, in which the mind seems warmed by a new flame, and quickened by a new energy from on high, and which, though not miraculous, still bring with them a near consciousness of the Divine Original, and come like the very breath of God upon the soul. Through these various methods, you will ascend by degrees to a living communion with your Creator, which, however low compared with what awaits you in another life, will yet be lofty in contrast with all you could have conceived of in the beginning of your religious course." [162]

Here, again, the powerful influences of God upon the mind are stressed; the soul clearly regards God as the cause of this spiritual warmth and vigor, it believes *that* he is close, even present, to it; yet he is not said to be perceived by it. What, however, is the significance of the injected observation that these impartations are "not miraculous"? What would a miraculous gift of the Spirit be like, and how would it differ from these? Would it be distinguishable because, accompanied by outward, physical manifestations of supernatural order, or by the objectivity and inerrancy of some message announced from on high, divinely protected from any misapprehension or misinterpretation on the part of the receiving subject? Perhaps it would possess both these characteristics. It is to be observed, however, that these experiences would appear closely to resemble that illumination by an inward light which constitutes "the highest inspiration, surpassing that of the prophets." If this suggestion be sound, Channing, despite his profound reverence for miracles, was nearer to Edwards than appears at first sight. Yet it is a suggestion which has much to commend it, for it can find support in his own words. Thus, in his sermon on *Love to Christ,* we find Channing lamenting the fact that many Christians appear to revere Christ more because of the wonders which he performed than because of his perfect virtue. "Christians," he exclaims, "have yet to learn that inspiration, and miracles, and outward dignities are nothing compared with the soul." And in the same vein he declares, "Mere inspiration seems to me a very secondary thing. Suppose the greatest truths in the universe to be revealed supernaturally to a being who should take no interest in them, who should not see and feel their greatness, but should repeat them mechanically, as they were put into his mouth by the Deity. Such a man would be inspired, and would teach the greatest verities, and yet he would be nothing, and would have no claim to reverence." [163]

We may therefore venture, I believe, to conclude that the experiences which Channing is attempting to describe are the most exalted to which he thinks human nature can attain. We must now examine a very important paragraph which is to be found in the last section of his discourse on *The Perfecting Power of Religion* in *The Perfect Life.* It is our misfortune that want of time, as he tells us, had caused him to omit much of what he had previously intended to say, so that we possess only a bare outline of what was to have been a full exposition of his thought upon this most important topic. Even as it stands it is a daring utterance, clearly running counter to what he conceived to be the general opinion and sentiment of his day; and, no doubt, it constituted one of the grounds for the charge of being "too transcendental" which was leveled against him.

"I particularly intended to show," he announces, "that religion is a source of light to the intellect by opening to it the highest order of truths, and thus introducing it to a celestial happiness. On this topic it might not be easy to avoid the charge of mysticism. I believe, however, and I wished to prove that the highest truths are not those which we learn from abroad. No outward teaching can bestow them. They are unfolded from within, by our very progress in the religious life. New ideas of perfection, new convictions of immortality, a new consciousness of God, a new perception of our spiritual nature, come to us as revelations, and open upon us with a splendor which belongs not to this world. Thus we gain the power to look with deeper penetration into human life, as well as into the universe. We read a wider significance in events. We attain to glimpses of the infinite mind and of a future world, which, though we may not be able to define them in human speech, we yet know to correspond to realities. Now this higher wisdom, whereby the intellect anticipates the bright visions which await it in another life, comes only from the growth and dominant interest of the religious principle, by which we became transformed more and more into the likeness of God. So true is it that religion makes intellect a blessing, and an infinite blessing." [164]

Alas that we should lack the full statement of which this paragraph is only an inadequate summary! That it is inspired by the spirit of mysticism is obvious; this is, indeed, boldly avowed; yet we are again confronted with an ambiguous and seemingly contradictory use of words. The phrases "a new consciousness of God," "glimpses of the infinite mind" appear to imply a direct awareness of God; yet, when we are told that these glimpses "correspond to realities," we feel that the veil has not been lifted. What is the reason, one cannot help asking oneself, of this persistent ambiguity? How can Channing remain seemingly indifferent to so vital a question, or confused upon so fundamental a point?

It is true that Channing, again like Edwards, emphatically insists upon the gradual character of the impartation of grace. His reason for so doing is, however, a very different one from that which motivated Edwards; it is a desire to affirm the freedom of the human will to yield to or to resist God's solicitation.[165] Nevertheless, if it be true, as both divines agree, that the process is gradual, it can plausibly be contended that it will necessarily lack the dramatic, breath-taking quality of a single, shattering event. Does this reflection suffice to explain Channing's attitude?

"The light of life," he writes, "is a constant consciousness of divine fellowship. But we should not expect a sudden manifestation of the infinite One to our souls. Gradually we must attain to this serene trust in God's all-protecting care, incessant mercy, and inspiring influence. The blessing will not be less real because it comes upon us gently, according to our spiritual progress. There is no rest for our souls except in this ever-growing communion with the All-Perfect One." [166]

Let it be granted that spiritual progress is gradual; does this get us out of our difficulty? Does it explain how faith, as Channing has said, can *begin* to change into vision? Surely, when vision begins, faith ends. Surely there must be some definite point at which knowledge by description passes over into knowledge by acquaintance. But perhaps this is what Channing is concerned to deny. Perhaps he would insist that knowledge by description is not superseded, but merely supplemented, by knowledge by acquaintance; that conception must continue to order and interpret the data of intuition. This would certainly be in keeping with his insistence that illumination and grace do not supplant, but on the contrary, invigorate and employ the intellect. And, if this contention be sound, faith could gradually pass into vision, and inference into intuition.

With all this in mind, let us look at two additional passages. One is in the Introductory Remarks prefixed by Channing to his collected writings.[167] It runs as follows: "These are great truths, which every honest heart may be assured of. There *is* such a thing as a serene, immovable conviction. Faith is a deep want of the soul. We have faculties for the spiritual as truly as for the outward world. God, the foundation of all existence, may become to the mind the most real of all beings. We can and do see in virtue an everlasting beauty. The distinctions of right and wrong, the obligations of goodness and justice, the divinity of conscience, the moral connection of the present and future life, the greatness of the character of Christ, the ultimate triumphs of truth and love, are to multitudes not probable deductions, but intuitions accompanied with the consciousness of certainty. They shine with the clear, constant brightness of the lights of heaven. The believer feels himself resting on an everlasting foundation. It is to this power of moral or spiritual perception that the following writings are chiefly addressed." [168]

The purport of this passage would seem to be much clearer than that of its predecessors. Our faculties for the spiritual world, whatever they may be, are obviously intended to put us in direct contact with it. The consciousness of God is put upon the same footing as the awareness of goodness and beauty; here, then, we have something which is not inferential but intuitive in character; for by no conceivable process of inference could a man who had no direct awareness of goodness and beauty be made to acknowledge their reality, or even to understand the meaning of the words which signify them.

The second citation is from the *Life,* and the words of Channing's own:

"It is the earnest desire of the pious man, whose heart has been touched by God's good spirit, to feel what he believes, that God is with him; and his attention is often withdrawn from all finite things, that he may bring home this thought with power to his heart.

"The quickness of perception, the sensibility, to which the mind, by use and time, may attain on these subjects, is not easily believed by those who have made no progress in religion. The pious man, whose mind is exercised on God, comes to see him in a peculiar manner. He has a consciousness of his presence which he cannot easily describe or communicate to one who has lived wholly in the world. In scenes which to others are blank and desolate, he feels that he is not alone; and in society where others see only their fellow-beings, a higher presence is revered and perceived. Even when thinking of outward things, there is, if I may so speak, in the breast of a devout man, a latent sense of God; just as, when we are near or in sight of an individual whom we respect, there is a consciousness of him, and a reference to him, even though we are conversing freely with other beings." [169]

The purport of this passage would seem to be quite clear. It is surely a direct contact with God of which Channing is now speaking, that passage from faith to sight to which every mystic aspires.[170] This is, indeed, what we should expect in view of that passionate love of God which Channing so often evinces; for an emotion so intense and rapturous could scarcely be felt by one who was a total stranger to the divine presence. And we shall find our conclusion further substantiated if we recall his strictures upon Trinitarianism as tending to inhibit such an experience by multiplying objects of devotion and scattering the worshiper's attention among them, by "dividing and distracting the mind," [171] instead of concentrating it upon the One,

Infinite Father, with whom, as he tells us, it is possible "to enjoy a communion more tender than human friendship"; [172] and if we consider his antipathy to the doctrine of the Incarnation with its corporeal and external Deity which blinds men to the "unspeakable benefit of the doctrine of a purely spiritual God, that He can be regarded as inhabiting, filling our spiritual nature," so that, "through this union with our minds, He can and does become the object of an intimacy and friendship such as no embodied being can call forth." [173] These are unmistakably the words of a man who believed himself to have been granted the experience of direct contact with Deity, and whose interest in doctrine was the eminently practical one of aiding his fellows to attain to the enjoyment of the same supreme blessing. Here we touch the very heart of Channing's Unitarianism.

It is in his emphasis upon this supersensuous, intuitive, mystical awareness that Channing has most in common with the Transcendentalists. Nevertheless there is a profound dissimilarity. There is in him an intensity of passionate devotion which is lacking in them. And the reason is not far to seek. The trumpets of a monistic idealism were already sounding in the air of Puritan New England, and the blasts increased in volume as the century grew old. Stimulated by the Bhagavadgita and the Upanishads, and yet more powerfully influenced by German idealism, the majority of his younger contemporaries enthusiastically embraced a monistic metaphysics to which the personalistic philosophy of Channing was uncongenial. His ardent love of a uni-personal God, to whom one could feel all the devotion that one person can feel for another, failed to attract men who yearned to immerse themselves in a boundless ocean of impersonal or "superpersonal" Deity. Their piety was of another cast; cosmic rather than personalistic. For this reason, Channing's immediate influence has been least precisely in the field where one would expect to find it greatest.

What is unique in Channing's religious devotion is his emphasis upon the intelligibility of the God whom he adores. By his repudiation of the *Via Negativa,* and by his formulation of the theory of essential sameness, he has placed himself in direct opposition to the Neoplatonic tradition which for so many centuries has so effectually dominated Christian mysticism—a tradition to which the anonymous author of *The Cloud of Unknowing* gave succinct expression in his famous utterance, "By love may He be gotten and holden; but by thought never." [174] It could not be just, assuredly, to assert that the personal element is completely lacking in the piety of orthodox mystics; yet it is the presence of a cosmic, pantheistic urge which finds no response in Channing.[175] It is not that the infinite makes no appeal to him— far from it. In many a passage he dwells with delight upon the infinite actuality of God and the infinite potentialities of the human soul.[176] But the infinite toward which Channing aspires is an infinite Person —the "infinite Father," as he loves to call him. The desire to lose oneself in the supreme, to immerse oneself in an ocean of "boundless being," to experience the dissolution of one's individual identity, to "pass into the Nameless" like Tennyson's Ancient Sage, is something with which he feels no sympathy. The personal relationship, in his view, will never be transcended; it will, on the contrary, become closer, more intimate, more precious, and more satisfying.

There is one point, however, upon which Channing and the orthodox mystics are agreed—namely, that love to God is the deepest and noblest passion which the human heart can feel, and that it constitutes the ultimate τέλος for which man was created. This is affirmed and re affirmed by Channing with the greatest earnestness and empha- sis. Love to God, he declares, is the greatest of virtues, the "true end and happiness of our being," [177] the "profoundest, sublimest, grandest emotion in man." [178] In language which reminds us of Ed- wards, he warns us that fellow human beings will disappoint us by their imperfections, and sometimes their disloyalty.[179] "Love," he observes, "may prove our chief woe, if bestowed unwisely, dispropor- tionately, and on unworthy objects; if confined to beings of imperfect virtue, with whose feelings we cannot always innocently sympathize, whose interests we cannot always righteously promote, who narrow us to themselves instead of breathing universal charity, who are frail, mutable, exposed to suffering, pain, and death." [180] What the soul yearns for is a Being whose character is perfection, whose love is boundless, whose nature is immutable, whose life is everlasting, and who merits and repays the concentrated devotion of the heart.[181] Such a Being is the heavenly Father. "All other beings are as nothing to us, compared with this infinite One." [182] "All other beings, our nearest friends, are far from us, foreign to us, strangers compared to God. Others hold intercourse with us through the body. He is in immediate contact with our souls." [183] And the love for him may become more ardent than that which one feels for parent, child, or friend.[184]

In saying all this Channing has only reiterated what generations of mystically-minded Christians have affirmed. Nevertheless it raises a problem—one to which the majority of mystics have closed their eyes —yet one which presses upon Channing with peculiar force because of the high estimate which he has formed of the human soul. If the love for God be of an intensity such as Channing has depicted, will not all other love pale and fade before it, and at last wither away? Will such concentrated devotion as he has described leave room for any other devotion? Must not the value of human affections be accounted purely extrinsic? Can they be more than rungs of the ladder which must be climbed by him who would view the glory of God; and, when that vision bursts upon the soul, will not the ladder have served its purpose, and may it not be cast down as no longer possessing any worth? [185]

The common teaching is that the creatures are to be loved "for God's sake." This is the doctrine which we find re-stated by Edwards in his *Dissertation on the Nature of True Virtue.* And we hear an echo of it in Channing's assertion that human beings are to be respected and served "for their relationship to the Divinity." [186] Can this indirect relationship justify a high evaluation of human love? Channing, as we have already observed, feels it necessary to stress the "narrowing" effect of human devotion. And, in a similar passage, he solemnly warns us that the "tenderest attachments" may "degenerate more or less into weaknesses and immoralities," by inducing us to sympathize with those we love when engaged in unethical actions or when entertaining evil emotions, by leading us unwisely to praise and pamper them, to show partiality toward them to the hurt of others, and to poison our own minds with jealousy.[187] Such attachments, he continues, can become virtuous only when consecrated by a virtuous and self-denying will.

In all this there is a very Kantian ring. And the inescapable terminus of this way of thinking is, surely, the conclusion that God is, not the supreme, but the *only* legitimate object of love. It is, nevertheless, a conclusion to which Channing is incapable of committing himself. When we turn to the *Note-Book* in which his granddaughter has arranged under various headings brief statements culled from his unpublished writings, we discover there utterances which breathe a very different spirit. "They who fly from love to be devout," he asks, "are they not extinguishing piety?" [188] "Love," he tells us, is "man's glory" [189] "the life of the soul," [190] "the true principle of immortality." [191] "A narrow love," it appears, "is not the true love. We have not penetrated to the Divine in man." [192]  There is, it seems, a love which does not narrow, but expands the soul, which ennobles the lover and desires, not to possess, but to stimulate the moral growth of, the beloved. Clearly such love possesses more than an instrumental value. It is obviously an end in itself.

There is no difficulty about this, it may be said. There is no contradiction in the affirmation that human love is at once an intrinsic and an extrinsic value—extrinsic in so far as it leads the soul onward to the love of the Highest. Yet if the Infinite Being claim all the devotion and then satisfy all the desires of the finite personality, what will there be left to pour out upon other finite beings? Will not God absorb all? There is, I think, a genuine problem here which has escaped the observation of theists in general, perhaps because the objections commonly made to theism presuppose the outlook of a materialistic or naturalistic philosophy.[193]  The difficulty, it would appear, can be solved, if at all, only by showing not only that human love leads on to the love of God, but also that the love of God augments and fosters human love. Such a solution, however, we do not find in the thought of Channing. We can only discriminate the two tendencies, which are—superficially at least—in conflict, and which remain unreconciled.

## NOTES

1. *Ibid.*, p. 381. col. 1. Channing immediately continues: "On this subject we always speak plainly. We cannot sacrifice our reason to the reputation of zeal. We owe it to truth and religion to maintain that fanaticism, partial insanity, sudden impressions, and ungovernable transports are anything rather than piety."
2. *Ibid.*, p. 233. col. 1.
3. *Loc. cit.*, col. 2.
4. *Ibid.*, p. 399. col. 1.
5. *Essay on Human Understanding*, bk. IV. ch. 19. sec. 4.
6. *Ibid.*, p. 189. col. 1.
7. *Loc. cit.*
8. *Ibid.*, p. 189.
9. *Ibid.*, p. 189. col. 2.
10. *Ibid.*, p. 190. col. 1.
11. *Loc. cit.*
12. *Ibid.*, p. 190. col. 1.
13. *Ibid.*, pp. 190-191.
14. *Ibid.*, p. 191.
15. *Ibid.*, p. 192. col. 1.

16. As Locke puts it, "Revelation is natural reason enlarged by a new set of discoveries communicated by God immediately, which reason vouches the truth of, by the testimony and proof it gives that they come from God." *Essay*, bk. IV, ch. XIX, sec. 4.
17. "Reason," says Locke, "is natural revelation." *Loc. cit.*
18. *Works*, p. 338. col. 2.
19. The Calvinistic doctrine of the *testimonium Spiritus Sancti* could hardly be more explicitly repudiated. Channing, as we shall see, partially adumbrates his own theory of illumination, but it is in startling independence of Edwards, with whose views he was well acquainted, and to whom he was, in some ways, so closely akin.
20. *Cf. Locke's Essay*: bk. IV, ch. XVIII, sec. 5.
21. *Works*, pp. 236. col. 2.—237. col. 1.
22. *Ibid.*, p. 234. col. 1.
23. In this respect it resembles the Thomistic intellect which deals with the universal, in contradistinction to sense which is concerned with "singulars."
24. "For example, reason teaches me, as we have seen, that all changes without exception require a cause; and, in conformity to this principle, it prompts me to seek the particular causes of the endless changes and appearances which fall under my observation." *Loc. cit.* col. 2.
25. *Loc. cit.*, col. 2.
26. *Loc. cit.*
27. *Ibid.*, p. 235. col. 1.
28. *Essay*, bk. IV, ch. IV, sec. 5.
29. *Ibid.*, p. 236. col. 1.
30. *Ibid.*, p. 237. col. 1.
31. *Ibid.*, p. 368. col. 2.
32. *Loc. cit.*
33. *Loc. cit.*
34. "Recollect the declarations of Christ, that he came not to send peace but a sword; that unless we eat his flesh and drink his blood we have no life in us; that we must hate father and mother, and pluck out the right eye; and a vast number of passages equally bold and unlimited. Recollect the unqualified manner in which it is said of Christians that they possess all things, know all things, and can do all things. Recollect the verbal contradiction between Paul and James, and the apparent clashing of some parts of Paul's writings with the general doctrines and end of Christianity. I might extend the enumeration indefinitely; and who does not see that we must limit all these passages by the known attributes of God, of Jesus Christ, and of human nature, and by the circumstances under which they were written, so as to give the language a quite different import from what it would require had it been applied to different beings, or used in different connections." *Ibid.*, pp. 368. col. 2—369. col. 1.

"I open the New Testament and my eye lights on this passage: 'If thy right hand offend thee, cut it off and cast it from thee.' Is this language to be interpreted in its plainest and most obvious sense? Then I must mutilate my body, and become a suicide. I look again, and I find Jesus using these words to the Jews: 'Fill ye up the measure of your iniquities.' Am I to interpret this according to the letter or the first ideas which it suggests? Then Jesus commanded his hearers to steep themselves in crime, and was himself a minister of sin. It is only by a deliberate use of reason that we can penetrate beneath the figurative, hyperbolical, and often obscure style of the New Testament, to the real meaning. Let me go to the Bible, dismissing my reason and taking the first impression which the words convey, and there is no absurdity, however gross, into which I shall not fall. I shall ascribe a limited body to God, and unbounded knowledge to man, for I read of God having limbs and of man knowing all things. Nothing is plainer than that I must compare passage with passage, and limit one by another, and especially limit all by those plain and universal principles of reason which are called common-sense, or I shall make revelation the patron of every folly and vice." *Ibid.*, p. 237.

35. *Ibid.*, p. 369. col. 1.

36. "Our leading principle in interpreting Scripture is this, that the Bible is a book written for men, in the the language of men, and that its meaning is to be sought in the same manner as that of other books. We believe that God, when He speaks to the human race, conforms, if we may say so, to the established rules of speaking and writing. How else would the Scriptures avail us more than if communicated in an unknown tongue." *Ibid.*, pp. 367. col. 2—368. col. 1.

37. "We regard the Scriptures as the record of God's sucessive revelations to mankind, and particularly of the last and most perfect revelation of his will by Jesus Christ. Whatever doctrines seem to us to be clearly taught in the Scriptures, we receive without reserve or exception. We do not, however, attach equal importance to all the books in this collection. Our religion, we believe, lies chiefly in the New Testament. The dispensation of Moses, compared with that of Jesus, we consider as adapted to the childhood of the human race, a preparation for a nobler system, and chiefly useful now as serving to confirm and illustrate the Christian Scriptures. Jesus Christ is the only master of Christians, and whatever he taught, either during his personal ministry or by his inspired apostles, we regard as of divine authority, and profess to make the rule of our lives." *Ibid.*, p. 367. col. 2.

38. *Ibid.*, p. 369. col. 2.

39. *Ibid.*, p. 238. col. 1.

40. *Ibid.*, p. 245. col. 2.

41. *Ibid.*, p. 337. col. 1.

42. *Loc. cit.*, col. 2.

43. "Obiectum formale intellectus proprium pro hoc statu unionis animae cum corpore est quidditas rei materialis per phantasiam representatae, non prout est singularis, sed prout est universalis." Gredt's *Elementa Philosophiae Aristelico-Thomisticae*, Vol. I. p. 435.

44. *Ibid.*, p. 370.

45. *Ibid.*, p. 370. "Perhaps," suggests Channing, "I shall be pointed to the many and gross errors into which reason has fallen on almost every subject, and shall be told that here are motives for distrusting and denying it. I reply, first, by asking how we detect these errors? By what power do we learn that reason so often misguides us? Is it not by reason itself? and shall we

renounce it on account of its capacity of rectifying its own wrong judgments? Consider next, that on no subject has reason gone more astray than in the interpretation of the Scriptures; so that if it is to be denied on account of its errors, we must especially debar it from the study of revelation; in other words, we must shut the word of God in despair,—a consequence which, to the Protestant, is a sufficient refutation of the doctrine from which it flows." *Ibid.*, p. 337 col. 2.

46. *Ibid.*, pp. 370. col. 2.—371. col. 1.

47. *Ibid.*, p. 338. col. 1.

48. "Nowhere, I fear, have men manifested such infatuated trust in their own infallibility, such overweening fondness for their own conclusions, such positiveness, such impatience of contradiction, such arrogance towards the advocates of different opinions, as in the interpretation of the Scriptures; and yet these very men, who so idolize their own intellectual powers, profess to humble reason, and consider a criminal reliance on it as almost exclusively chargeable on others." *Ibid.*, p. 239. col. 1.

49. *Ibid.*, p. 339. col. 1.

50. *Ibid.*, p. 339.

51. *Ibid.*, p. 246. col. 1.

52. "Revelation is not at war with nature. Nature prompts us to expect it from the relation which God bears to the human race. The relation of Creator is the most intimate which can subsist; and it leads us to anticipate a free and affectionate intercourse with the creature. That the Universal Father should be bound by a parental interest to his offspring, that He should watch over and assist the progress of beings whom He has enriched with the divine gifts of reason and conscience, is so natural a doctrine, so accordant with his character, that various sects, both philosophical and religious, both anterior and subsequent to Christianity, have believed not only in general revelation, but that God reveals himself to every human soul. When I think of the vast capacities of the human mind, of God's nearness to it and unbounded love towards it, I am disposed to wonder, not that revelations have been made, but that they have not been more variously vouchsafed to the wants of mankind." *Ibid.*, p. 193. col. 2.

53. *Ibid.*, p. 416. col. 1.

54. "Christianity would furnish a weapon against itself, not easily repelled, should it claim the distinction of being the only light vouchsafed by God to men; for, in that case, it would represent a vast majority of the human race as left by their Creator without guidance or hope. I believe, and rejoice to believe, that a ray from heaven descends on the path of every fellow-creature. The heathen, though in darkness as compared with the Christian, has still his light; and it comes from the same source as our own, just as the same sun dispenses, now the faint dawn, and now the perfect day. Let not nature's teaching be disparaged. It is from God as truly as his word. It is sacred, as truly as revelation. Both are manifestations of one infinite mind, and harmonious manifestations; and without this agreement the claims of Christianity could not be sustained." *Ibid.*, p. 238. col. 1.

55. *Ibid.*, p. 164. col. 1.

56. *Ibid.*, pp. 285. col. 2.—286. col. 1.

57. *Ibid.,* p. 321. col. 1.

58. The twentieth-century reader can scarcely fail, *malgré lui,* to be amused by Channing's *naif* assertion that revelation was essential to the survival of the first human beings. "From the necessity of the case, the earliest instruction must have come to human beings from this source. If our race had a beginning (and nothing but the insanity of atheism can doubt this), then its first members, created as they were without human parentage, and having no resource in the experience of fellow-creatures who had preceded them, required an immediate teaching from their Creator; they would have perished without it. Revelation was the very commencement of human history, the foundation of all later knowledge and improvement. It was an essential part of the course of Providence, and must not then be regarded as a discord in God's general system." *Ibid.,* p. 193. col. 2.

59. "The teachings of the wise and good are our chief aids. Were our connection with superior minds broken off, had we no teacher but nature, with its fixed laws, its unvarying revolutions of night and day and seasons, we should remain forever in the ignorance of childhood. Nature is a volume which can be read only by the help of an intelligent interpreter. The great law under which man is placed is that he shall receive illumination and impulse from beings more improved than himself. Now revelation is only an extension of this universal method of carrying forward mankind. In this case God takes on himself the office to which all rational beings are called. He becomes an immediate teacher to a few, communicating to them a higher order of truths than had before been attained, which they in turn are to teach to their race. Here is no new power or element introduced into the system, but simply an enlargement of that agency on which the progress of man chiefly depends." *Ibid.,* p. 194. col. 1.

60. "It is the ordinance of God, and one of his most benevolent laws, that the human race should be carried forward by impulses which originate in a few minds, perhaps in an individual; and in this way the most interesting relations and dependencies of life are framed. When a great truth is to be revealed, it does not flash at once on the race, but dawns and brightens on a superior understanding, from which it is to emanate and to illumine future ages. On the faithfulness of great minds to this awful function, the progress and happiness of men chiefly depend." *Ibid.,* p. 126. col. 1.

61. *Ibid.,* p. 194. col. 2.

62. *Ibid.,* p. 195. col. 1.

63. *Ibid.,* p. 196. col. 1. In this connection it is interesting to observe that he considers that the Corinthian Christians to whom St. Paul wrote "were strongly tempted to assimilate the gospel to the prevelent religions, to blend with it foreign doctrines, to keep the humiliation of its author out of sight, and to teach it as a system of philosophy resting on subtle reasoning rather than on miracles and the authority of God." The apostle was endeavoring "to save them from this danger,—a danger which at present we can hardly estimate." *Ibid.,* p. 335. col. 2.

64. *Ibid.,* p. 196.

65. *Loc. cit.,* col. 2.

66. "I believe Christianity to be true, or to have come from God, because it seems to me impossible to trace it to any other origin. It must have had a cause, and no other adequate cause can be assigned. The incongruity between this religion and all the circumstances amidst which it grew up is so remarkable, that we are compelled to look above and beyond this world for its explanation. When I go back to the origin of Christianity, and place myself in the age and country of its birth, I can find nothing in the opinions of men, or in the state of society, which can account for its beginning or diffusion. There was no power on earth to create or uphold such a system. There was nothing, congenial with it in Judaism, in heathenism, or in the state of society among the most cultvated communities. If you study the religions, governments, and philosophical systems of that age, you will discover in them not even a leaning toward Christianity. It sprung up in opposition to all, making no compromise with human prejudice or passion; and it sprung up, not only superior to all, but possessing at its very beginning a perfection which has been the admiration of ages, and which, instead of being dimmed by time, has come forth more brightly, in proportion to the progress of the human mind." *Ibid.*, p. 204. col. 2.

67. *Ibid.*, p. 205. col. 1.

68. *Loc. cit.*

69. *Loc. cit.*

70. *Loc. cit.*, col. 1.—col. 2.

71. As a matter of fact Channing does, in another connection, call attention to "how nearly the bigot and the sceptic approach." (*Ibid.*, p. 369. col. 2.) And it is, of course, true that scepticism cannot of itself *produce* a religion. Yet it undoubtedly can "prepare the way" for its own antithesis—the acceptance of a belief upon supposedly divine authority—witness Kirkegaard and Barth!

72. *Ibid.*, pp. 205. col. 2.—206. col. 1.

73. "One striking peculiarity in Jesus is the extent, the vastness, of his views. Whilst all around him looked for a Messiah to liberate God's ancient people, whilst to every other Jew, Judea was the exclusive object of pride and hope, Jesus came, declaring himself to be the deliverer and light of the world, and in his whole teaching and life you see a consciousness which never forsakes him, of a relation to the whole human race. This idea of blessing mankind, of spreading a universal religion, was the most magnificent which had ever entered man's mind. All previous religions had been given to particular nations. No conqueror, legislator, philosopher, in the extravagance of ambition, had ever dreamed of subjecting all nations to a common faith.

This conception of a universal religion, intended alike for Jew and Gentile, for all nations and climes, is wholly inexplicable by the circumstances of Jesus. He was a Jew, and the first and deepest and most constant impression on a Jew's mind was that of the superiority conferred on his people and himself by the national religion introduced by Moses. The wall between the Jew and the Gentile seemed to reach to heaven. The abolition of the peculiarity of Moses, the prostration of the temple on Mount Zion, the erection of a new religion, in which all men would meet as brethren, and which would be the common and equal property of Jew and Gentile, these were of all ideas the

last to spring up in Judea, the last for enthusiasm or imposture to originate."
*Ibid.*, p. 227. col. 2.

74. *Ibid.*, p. 206. col. 1.

75. Valuable light is thrown upon this topic by Miss Elizabeth Peabody's report of some remarks addressed by Channing to a group of ladies which deal with the subject before us. "I remember very distinctly," she writes, "the words of one sentence: 'The Scriptures are not themselves revelation, but the *records* of revelation made to men who reported the truths revealed.' Therefore, any narrative or a statement of principles was to be determined 'by using all our powers of understanding in the freest possible manner.' He thought the written words probably never did full justice to the inspired knowledge of the writer, but were to be interpreted by the hope and faith of the reader, which was of kindred origin to the revealed idea. One of the ladies said it was desirable to have some test of inspiration not of this subjective nature. Dr. Channing replied, 'God gives us this desire of certainty to stimulate us to acquire the inward test by self-discipline and prayer. The Hebrew Scriptures taught that though all the people might be prophets, and under certain conditions prophesy [which word, he said, meant to preach according to the Quaker principle, and did not necessarily imply intimation of future events], it remained the duty of the people to judge for themselves as to who was the true and who the lying prophet, and abide the consequences of the decision." *Reminiscences of Rev. William Ellery Channing*, p. 35.

76. *Ibid.*, p. 242. col. 2.

77. *Ibid.*, p. 487. col. 2.

78. *Ibid.*, p. 207. col. 2.

79. "Some may ask, whether its Founder was not instigated by the passion for religious domination,—whether he did not aim to subdue men's minds, to dictate the faith of the world, to make himself the leader of a spreading sect, to stamp his name as a prophet on human history, and thus to secure the prostration of multitudes to his will, more abject and entire than kings and conquerors can achieve." *Ibid.*, p. 208. col. 1.

80. *Loc. cit.*, col. 2.

81. *Ibid.*, p. 209.

82. "That Christianity was received at first on the ground of miracles, and that its first preachers and converts proved the depth and strength of their conviction of these facts by attesting them in suffering and death, we know from the most ancient records which relate to this religion, both Christian and heathen; and, in fact, this conviction can alone explain their adherence to Christianity." *Ibid.*, pp. 230. col. 2.—231. col. 1.

83. *Ibid.*, p. 1002. col. 1.—col. 2.

84. This does not mean that the theist is entitled to maintain that God could violate the laws of logic. St. Thomas himself would be the first to declare that God cannot change the past, for instance, or make two and two equal five. But it is a very different thing to assert that God cannot suspend the operation of a "law" of nature at a particular time and place. Thus Channing observes, "The sceptic tells me that the order of nature is fixed. I ask him, By whom or what is it fixed? By an iron fate?—by an inflexible necessity? Does not nature bear the signature of an intelligent Cause? Does not the very

idea of its order imply an ordaining or disposing Mind? Does not the universe, the more it is explored, bear increasing testimony to a Being superior to itself? Then the order of nature is fixed by a Will which can reverse it. Then a power equal to miracles exists. Then miracles are not incredible." *Ibid.,* pp. 210. col. 2.—211. col. 1.

85. Magic is the establishment of human control over preternatural forces.

86. Thus the doctrine that the bodies of the dead will be raised at the Last Day is one the truth of which obviously cannot be demonstrated *a priori.* Channing and Locke would maintain, however, that it is in accord with reason in the sense of not being *contra rationem,* and that the occurrence of a miracle would provide adequate reason for concluding that he who proclaimed it spoke with divine authority.

87. *Ibid.,* p. 215. col. 1.

88. "I maintain that the multiplicity of false miracles, far from disproving, gives support to those on which Christianity rests; for, first, there is generally some foundation for falsehood, especially when it obtains general belief. The love of truth is an essential principle of human nature; men generally embrace error on account of some precious ingredient of truth mixed with it, and for the time inseparable from it. The universal belief of past ages in miraculous interpositions is to me a presumption that miracles have entered into human history. Will the unbeliever say that it only shows the insatiable thirst of the human mind for the supernatural? I reply, that in this reasoning he furnishes a weapon against himself; for a strong principle in the human mind, impelling men to seek for and to cling to a miraculous agency, affords a presumption that the Author of our being, by whom this thirst for the supernatural was given, intended to furnish objects for it, and to assign it a place in the education of the race." *Loc. cit.,* col. 2.

89. This is a bold assertion. Let us see how Channing tries to make it good. "I say to the sceptic, you affirm nothing but truth in declaring history to abound in false miracles; I agree with you in exploding by far the greater part of the supernatural accounts of which ancient religions boast. But how do we know these to be false? We do not so judge without proofs. We discern in them the marks of delusion. Now I ask you to examine these marks, and then to answer me honestly, whether you find them in the miracles of Christianity. Is there not a broad line between Christ's works and those which we both agree in rejecting? I maintain that there is, and that nothing but ignorance can confound the Christian miracles with the prodigies of heathenism. The contrast between them is so strong as to forbid us to refer them to a common origin. The miracles of superstition carry the brand of falsehood in their own nature, and are disproved by the circumstances under which they were imposed on the multitude. The objects for which they are said to have been wrought are such as do not require or justify divine interposition. Many of them are absurd, childish, or extravagant, and betray a weak intellect or diseased imagination. Many can be explained by natural causes. Many are attested by persons who lived in different countries and ages, and enjoyed no opportunities of enquiring into their truth. We can see the origin of many in the self-interest of those who forged them, and can account for their reception by the condition of

the world. In other words, these spurious miracles were the natural growth of the ignorance, passions, prejudices, and corruptions of the times, and tended to confirm them. Now it is not enough to say, that these various marks of falsehood cannot be found in the Christian miracles. We find them in characters directly the reverse. They were wrought for an end worthy of God; they were wrought in an age of improvement; they are marked by a majesty, beneficence, unostentatious simplicity, and wisdom, which separate them from the dreams of a disordered fancy, or the contrivances of imposture. They can be explained by no interests, passions, or prejudices of men. They are parts of a religion which was singularly at variance with established ideas and expectations, which breathes purity and benevolence, which transcended the improvements of the age, and which thus carries with it the presumption of a divine original. Whence this immense difference between the two classes of miracles? Will you trace both to one source, and that a polluted one? Will you ascribe to one spirit works as different as light and darkness, as earth and heaven? I am not, then, shaken in my faith by the false miracles of other religions. I have no desire to keep them out of sight; I summon them as my witnesses. They show me how naturally superstition and imposture leave the stamp of themselves on their fictions. They show how man, when he aspires to counterfeit God's agency, betrays more signally his impotence and folly. When I place side by side the mighty works of Jesus and the prodigies of heathenism, I see that they can no more be compared with one another than the machinery and mock thunders of the theatre can be likened to the awful and beneficent powers of the universe." *Ibid.*, p. 216. col. 1.—col. 2.

90. *Ibid.*, p. 211. col. 2.—col. 2.

91. "And the Lord was with Judah; and he drove out the inhabitants of the mountain; but could not drive out the inhabitants of the valley, because they had chariots of iron."

92. *Ibid.*, p. 212. col. 1.

93. "I repeat it,—were men mechanical beings, an undeviating order of nature might meet all their wants. They are free beings, who bear a moral relation to God, and as such may need, and are worthy of, a more various and special care than is extended over the irrational creation." *Loc. cit.*

94. "At the introduction of Christianity, the human family were plunged into gross and debasing error, and the light of nature had not served for ages to guide them back to truth." *Loc. cit.*

95. *Loc. cit.*

96. *Loc. cit.*, col. 2.

97. *Ibid.*, p. 214. col. 2.

98. "When the long-repeated and almost monotonous language of creation was not heard, was it unworthy of God to speak with a new and more startling voice? What fitter method was there for rousing those whom nature's quiet regularity could not teach, than to interrupt its usual course." *Ibid.*, p. 213. col. 1.

99. "We are plainly so constituted that the order of nature, the more it is fixed, excites us the less. Our interest is blunted by its ceaseless uniformity. On the contrary, departures from this order powerfully stir the soul, break up its

old and slumbering habits of thought, turn it with a new solicitude to the Almightly Interposer, and prepare it to receive with awe the communications of his will. Was it unworthy of God, who gave us this sensibility to the wonderful, to appeal to it for the recovery of his creatures to himself?" *Ibid.,* pp. 213. col. 2.—214. col. 1. *Cf.* p. 224.

100. *Ibid.,* p. 213. col. 1.—col. 2. The same point is made again, in very similar language, on p. 224. "The natural world contains no provisions or arrangements for reviving the dead. The sun and the rain, which cover the tomb with verdure, send no vital influences to the mouldering body. The researches of science detect no secret process for restoring the lost powers of life. If man is to live again, he is not to live through any known laws of nature, but by a power higher then nature; and how, then, can we be assured of this truth, but by a manifestation of this power, that is, by a miraculous agency, confirming a future life."

101. One must, of course, treat with respect Miss Peabody's assertion in her *Reminiscences* (p. 187) that "Dr. Channing never urged miracles as proofs of Christianity. He said that at the present day they were more apt to produce scepticism than faith; people believed in Christianity, rather than believed in Christianity because of the miracles." It is difficult, however, to reconcile this assertion, not only with the statements quoted above from Channing's published writings, but also with his letter of July 6th, 1841, to Miss Peabody herself *a propos* of Theodore Parker (See her *Reminiscences,* pp. 423-426.). It is, of course, possible, although it is not very likely, that Miss Peabody completely misunderstood Channing. It is also possible, although, I think, even more unlikely in the case of so consistent a thinker as Channing, that he had temporarily abandoned a position to which he later returned. To speculate in any detailed fashion as to how the two points of view might conceivably have been reconciled in the mind of Channing would be to indulge in baseless conjecture. It may not be amiss, to conclude, however, that his conception of rational universe might well have seemed to him to carry it with the acceptance of Christianity *plus* miracles.

102. *Works,* p. 224. col. 2.

103. "This argument affirms that the credibility of facts or statements is to be decided by their accordance with the established order of nature, and by this standard only. Now, if nature comprehended all existences and all powers, this position might be admitted. But, if there is a Being higher than nature, the origin of all of its powers and motions, and whose character falls under our notice and experience as truly as the creation, then there is an additional standard to which facts and statements are to be referred; and works which violate nature's order will still be credible, if they agree with the known properties and attributes of its Author; because for such works we can assign an adequate cause and sufficient reasons, and these are the qualities and conditions on which credibility depends. *Ibid.,* pp. 224. col. 2.—225. col. 1.

104. *Ibid.,* p. 225. col. 1.

105. *Ibid.,* p. 225. col. 1.—col. 2.

106. *Ibid.,* pp. 225. col. 2.—226. col. 1.

107. *Ibid.,* p. 216. col. 2.

108. *Ibid.*, p. 217. col. 1.
109. "We have, first, the most unexceptionable testimony, nothing less than that of contemporaries and eye-witnesses, of the companions of Jesus, and the first propagators of his religion. We have the testimony of men who could not have been deceived as to the facts which they report; who bore their witness amidst perils and persecutions; who bore it on the very spot where their Master lived and died; who had nothing to gain, and everything to lose, if their testimony were false; whose writings breathe the sincerest love of virtue and of mankind; and who at last sealed their attestation with their blood. More unexceptionable witnesses to facts cannot be produced or conceived." *Loc. cit.*
110. "If Jesus Christ and his apostles were indeed sent and empowered by God, and wrought miracles in attestation of their mission, then the establishment of Christianity is explained. Suppose then, on the other hand, to have been insane enthusiasts or selfish impostors, left to meet the whole strength of human opposition, with nothing but their own power, or rather their own weakness, and you have no cause for the stupendous effect I have described. Such men could no more have changed the face of the world than they could have turned back rivers to their sources, sunk mountains into valleys, or raised valleys to the skies. Christianity, then, has not only the evidence of unexceptionable witnesses, but that of effects,—a proof which will grow stronger by comparing its progress with that of other religions such as Mahomitanism, which sprang from human passions, and were advanced by human power." *Ibid.*, p. 218. col. 1.—col. 2.
111. *Ibid.*, p. 221. col. 1.
112. *Ibid.*, p. 250. col. 2.
113. *Ibid.*, p. 940.
114. Compare the following sentences from *Christianity a Rational Religion*: "Revelation, we must remember, is not our earliest teacher. Man is not born with the single power of reading God's word, and sent immediately to that guide. His eyes open first on another volume,—that of the creation. Long before he can read the Bible he looks round on the earth and sky. He reads the countenances of his friends, and hears and understands their voices. He looks, too, by degrees, within himself, and acquires some ideas of his own soul. Thus his first school is that of nature and reason, and this is necessary to prepare him for a communication from heaven. Revelation does not find the mind a blank, a void, prepared to receive unresistingly whatever may be offered; but finds it in possession of various knowledge from nature and experience, and, still more, in possession of great principles, fundamental truths, moral ideas, which are derived from itself, and which are germs of all its future improvement." *Ibid.*, pp. 235. col. 2.—236. col. 1.
115. *Ibid.*, p. 939. col. 1.
116. *Loc. cit.*
117. *Loc. cit.*, col. 1.—col. 2.
118. *Ibid.*, pp. 939. col. 2.—940. col. 1.
119. Italics mine.
120. *Ibid.*, p. 379. col. 1.
121. *Ibid.*, p. 385. col. 1.

122. "The future world is in no way laid open to the senses. But the idea of it is one of the most universally recognized among men. The thought of immortal life preceded Jesus. We meet glimmerings of it even in the darkest and most barbarous times. The germ of this great truth is in our nature; in the conscience, that includes as one of its elements a presentiment of retribution; in the reason, that beholds in the present an incomplete destiny, needing to be continued for the fulfilment of its end: in the thirst for happiness, that is too deep to be satisfied on earth, but opens into aspiration towards an infinitely blessed Being; in the love of moral goodness and beauty, which in proportion as it is cultivated awakens the ideal of spotless virtue and a desire of community with the All-Perfect One. The voice of our whole nature indeed, properly interpreted, is a cry after-existence. The restless activity of life is but a pressing forward towards a fulness of good not to be found on earth, and indicates our destination for a state more brightly beautiful than we can now conceive. Heaven is in truth revealed to us in every pure affection of the human heart, and in every wise and beneficent action, that uplifts the soul in adoration and gratitude. For heaven is only purity, wisdom, benevolence, joy, peace, in their perfected form. This immortal life may be said to surround us perpetually." *Ibid.*, p. 939. col. 2.

"Are we not surrounded by signs of an infinite mind, and may we not be sure that such a mind must have unfathomable counsels, and must intend to bestow imaginable good? Can we believe that human nature was framed by such a being for no higher spiritual development than we now witness on this planet? Is there not, in the very incompleteness and mysteriousness of man's present existence, a proof that we do not yet behold the end for which he is destined; that the infinite Father has revealed but a minute portion of his scheme of boundless mercy; that we may trust for infinitely richer manifestations than we have experienced of his exhaustless grace." *Ibid.*, p. 961. col. 2.

123. We have seen that the central doctrine of *essential sameness,* and the cognate doctrine of the divinity of man, acquire their supreme importance for Channing because they constitute the theoretical expression of his experience of communion with God.

124. *Ibid.*, p. 985. col. 1. "I am satisfied," he observes elsewhere, "that one cause of the limited sway of religion is the narrow conception formed of its function. That religion is a universal principle,—spreading its influence through the whole being, developing every power to a fulness which it could not otherwise attain, diffusing inspiration through the intellect, as well as the conscience and the will, taking under its purifying rule the appetites and passions as well as the affections, imparting fresh interest to common existence, exhalting and expanding practical energy, refining and adorning social manners, adding cheerfulness as well as purity to friendly intercourse, and blessing us only by this universally enlivening agency,—this is a truth not yet understood as it should be. Hence to many, religion, instead of being thought of as comprehending whatever is good, wise, energetic, beautiful, great, and happy in human nature, is a word of doubtful import,—especially suggesting notions of retraint, repression, narrowness of thought, exclusive feeling, and habitual gloom." *Ibid.*, p. 988. col. 1. *Cf.* pp. 399. col. 2.—400. col. 1.

125. *Ibid.*, pp. 988. col. 2.—999. col. 1.

126. *Ibid.*, pp. 380. col. 2.—381. col. 1.

127. *Ibid.*, p. 381. col. 1. "Better be cold," exclaims Channing, "than affect to feel. In truth, nothing is so cold as an assumed, noisy enthusiasm. Its best emblem is the northern blast of winter which freezes as it roars." *Ibid.*, p. 265. col. 2.

128. *Ibid.*, p. 81. col. 1. "Moral discipline is much more important than a merely intellectual one, for gaining just apprehensions of the Supreme Being. I beg you to consider this. To know God we must have within ourselves something congenial to him. No outward light, not the teachings of hosts of angels, could give a bad man bright conceptions of God." *Ibid.*, p. 937. col. 1. "No outward teaching can bring us to a vision of the Divine Being. The soul must join with intellectual effort a moral operation upon itself." *Loc. cit.* col. 2.

129. *Ibid.*, p. 1010. col. 1. "To believe in immortality is to believe in the everlasting triumph and growth of virtue, and under this conviction to choose it as our supreme good." *Loc. cit.*, col. 2.

130. *Ibid.*, p. 552. col. 2.

131. *Ibid.*, p. 327. col. 1. "There is undoubtedly," concedes Channing, "much of fervent feeling towards him in the Christian world." But, he continues, "let me speak plainly. I do it from no uncharitableness. I do it only to warn my fellow-Christians. The greater part of this affection to Jesus seems to me of very doubtful worth. In many cases, it is an irregular fervor, which impairs the force and soundness of the mind, and which is substituted for obedience to his precepts, for the virtues which ennoble the soul. Much of what is called love to Christ I certainly do not desire you or myself to possess. I know of no sentiment which needs more to be cleared from error and abuse, and I therefore feel myself bound to show you some of its corruptions." *Ibid.*, p. 324. col. 2.

132. *Ibid.*, pp. 1009. col. 2.—1010. col. 1. The last two sentences correct any impression that Channing is, for the moment, dreaming of a "Christianity without Christ." This would be utterly alien to his spirit. "There is no such thing," he declares, "as Christianity without Christ. We cannot know it separately from him. It is not a book which Jesus wrote. It is his conversation, his character, his history, his life, his death, his resurrection. He pervades it throughout. In loving him, we love his religion; and a just interest in this cannot be awakened, but by contemplating it as it shone forth in himself." *Ibid.*, p. 323. col. 1.

133. *Ibid.*, p. 205. col. 2.

134. *Ibid.*, p. 3. col. 2.

135. *Ibid.*, pp. 305-306.

136. Thus, in his Baltimore sermon, after giving full expression to the Unitarian "dread" of a showy religion, he thinks it necessary to warn his hearers that self-control is not to be identified with coldness. "We think it no part of piety," he asserts, "to publish its fervors, but prefer a delicacy in regard to these secrets of the soul; and hence, to those persons who think that religion is to be worn conspicuously and spoken of passionately, we may seem cold and dead, when perhaps, were the heart uncovered, it might be seen to be 'alive to God' as truly as their own." *Ibid.*, p. 405. col. 2.

137. For contemporary criticism of Channing as an "enthusiast" and "visionary," see, *Works*, p. 929. col. 2.
138. He is sensitive to "the charge of mysticism" (See, *Works*, p. 992. col. 1). Thus, in speaking of the spiritual nature of man, in connection with the doctrine of immortality, he exclaims, "Whoever discerns truly and feels deeply this greatness of humanity, this relation of the soul to God, must, indeed, pass for an enthusiast in the present day; for our state of society is, in a great degree, a denial of the higher rights, claims, and destinies of a human being" (*Ibid.*, pp. 586. col. 2.—587. col. 1). In this utterance mystical, ethical, and social interests are blended.
139. *Ibid.*, p. 616. col. 2. *Cf. Ibid.*, p. 3.
140. *Ibid.*, p. 338. col. 2.
141. *Ibid.*, p. 940. col. 1.
142. *Ibid.*, pp. 933. col. 2.—944. col. 1.
143. That this was, possibly in an unusual degree, Channing's own experience appears from Miss Peabody's *Reminiscences*. See pp. 128-129.
144. *Works*, p. 360. col. 1.
145. Let us again recall Channing's emphatic words. "The divine attributes are first developed in ourselves, and thence transferred to our Creator. The idea of God, sublime and awful as it is, is the idea of our own spiritual nature, purified and enlarged to infinity. In ourselves are the elements of the Divinity. God, then, does not sustain a figurative resemblance to man. It is the resemblance of a parent to a child, the likeness of a kindred nature." *Ibid.*, p. 293.
146. *Ibid.*, p. 6. col. 2.
147. It is characteristic of his period that Channing should think it worth while to stress the fact that religion is not "a human contrivance, an invention for selfish ends." The charge is one still occasionally reiterated in Marxist circles; it may be well, therefore, to cite Channing's rejoinder. "You tell me, my sceptical friend, that religion is the contrivance of the priest. How came the priest into being? What gave him his power? Why was it that the ancient legislator professed to receive his laws from the gods? The fact is a striking one, that the earliest guides and leaders of the human race looked to the heavens for security and strength to earthly institutions, that they were compelled to speak to men in a higher name than man's. Religion was an earlier bond and a deeper foundation of society than government. It was the root of civilization. It has founded the mightiest empires; and yet men question whether religion be an element, a principle of human nature!" *Ibid.*, p. 410.
148. *Ibid.*, p. 24. col. 2.
149. "We always and earnestly maintain that no human virtue, no human obedience, can give a legal claim, a right by merit, to the life and immortality brought to light by Christ. We see and mourn over the deficiencies, broken resolutions, and mixed motives of the best men. We always affirm that God's grace, benignity, free kindness, is needed by the most advanced Christians, and that to this alone we owe the promise in the gospel, of full remission and everlasting happiness to the penitent. None speak of mercy more constantly than we." *Ibid.*, p. 404. col. 1.—col. 2.

150. *Ibid.*, p. 395. col. 2.
151. "The doctrine of grace, as it is termed, reveals the Infinite Father imparting his Holy Spirit—the best gift he can impart—to the humblest human being who implores it." *Ibid.*, p. 919. col. 2. *Cf.* p. 417. col. 2.
152. *Ibid.*, pp. 517. col. 2.—518. col. 1.
153. *Ibid.*, p. 970. col. 1.—col. 2.
154. *Ibid.*, p. 970. col. 2.
155. His frequent references to the order of nature as a manifestation of the divine intelligence indicate that he accepted the argument from design as well as the Lockian formulation of the *argumentum ex contingentia mundi.*
156. *Ibid.*, p. 936. col. 1. In this connection Channing adds that he has in mind the Christian revelation which contains more exalted conceptions of God than are to be found in many parts of the Old Testament. But nature, he continues, and the human soul, should also receive our attention, since we cannot comprehend God aright "if we do not go beyond revelation, and take lessons in religion from all that we observe, enjoy, and suffer." *Ibid.*, p. 936. col. 2.
157. *Ibid.*, pp. 937. col. 2.—938. col. 1.
158. *Ibid.*, p. 958. col. 2.
159. Is this phrase an echo of Edwards', "not only argues, but sees."? *Cf.* above p. 17.
160. *Works.*, p. 292. col. 1.
161. *Ibid.*, pp. 285. col. 2.—286. col. 1. It is, perhaps, significant that this passage is taken from a sermon preached at the ordination of the Rev. John Sullivan Dwight as pastor of the Second Congregational Church of Northampton; for Northampton had been the scene of Edwards' ministry, and an admiring reference to Edwards precedes this citation. The phrase "a light to which all others are strangers" is reminiscent of Edwards' "supernatural light in the soul" and of his "ideas, or sensations of mind, which are different from all that can be in the minds of natural men"; and the inspiration "surpassing that of the prophets" recalls Edwards' exaltation of divine grace, to which salvation is promised, over inspiration which is cast out, "as it were to dogs and swine." (See, above p. 57.) There seems to be a genuine echo of Edwards in this passage.
162. *Ibid.*, pp. 937. col. 2.—938. col. 1.
163. *Ibid.*, p. 321. col. 1.—col. 2. Here, again, we may perhaps detect the influence of Edwards' "dogs and swine."
164. *Ibid.*, pp. 991. col. 2.—992. col. 2.
165. See *Life*, pp. 226-227.
166. *Works*, p. 958. col. 1.
167. *Ibid.*, p. 11. col. 1.—col. 2.
168. *Ibid.*, p. 11. col. 1.—col. 2.
169. *Life*, p. 227.
170. This conclusion is borne out by Channing's remark, in another connection, that "the human mind, by cultivation of pious sentiments, may be, and often has been, raised to an intimate union with the Divine Being, to a vivid feeling of his presence, to an habitual discernment of him in his works and providence." *Ibid.*, p. 245.

171  *Works,* pp. 372. col. 2.; 387. col. 2.—388. col. 1.; 391. col. 2.

172. *Ibid.,* p. 400. col. 1.

173. *Ibid.,* p. 389. col. 2.

174. Ch. 6.

175. The doctrine of the Undifferentiated Godhead, as developed by Eckhart and Ruysbroek, is only the logical outcome of this same tendency. The dogma of the Trinity, as Channing so clearly saw, is an obstacle that must be evaded, surmounted, or destroyed by the soul that yearns for God. One way of evasion is to dissociate one's practical piety from one's theology, to think of God as a Person when one prays to him, and to be a Trinitarian only, as it were, *officially.* Another way is to concentrate upon the God-Man, and to disregard in great measure the other Persons of the Trinity. Many mystics have sought by one or other of these ways to escape the difficulty. If, however, the dogma be taken seriously, the result is practical tritheism; hence the constant temptation for philosophically and pantheistically inclined mystics to subordinate the Trinity to the Unity, and, by making the latter the goal of the religious life, to surmount the obstacle.

176  See *Works,* pp. 294. col. 2.—295; 933. col. 2.—934. col. 1.; 966. col. 1.

177. *Ibid.,* p. 380. col. 2.; *cf.* p. 974. col. 2.

178. *Ibid.,* p. 999. col. 2. Human love and even the love of nature, constitute, Channing considers, a preparation for this end. *Ibid.,* p. 573.

179. *Ibid.,* p. 960. col. 1. *Cf.* Edwards' treatment of the same theme in his *Dissertation on the Nature of True Virtue.*

180. *Ibid.,* p. 573. col. 2.

181. *Loc. cit., cf.* p. 387 and p. 400.

182. *Ibid.,* p. 966. col. 1.

183. *Ibid.,* p. 417. col. 2.

184. *Ibid.,* p. 935. col. 2.; *cf.* pp. 957. col. 2.; 988. col. 1.; 999. col. 2.

185. This is the conclusion which has been clearly enunciated by the Persian mystic, Jami:

> "Even from earthly love the face avert not,
> Since to the Real it may serve to raise thee.
> Eer A, B, C are rightly apprehended,
> How canst thou con the pages of the Koran?
> A sage (so heard I), unto whom a student
> Came craving counsel on the course before him,
> Said, 'If thy steps be strangers to love's pathways,
> Depart, learn love, and then return before me!
> For, shouldst thou fear to drink wine from Form's flagon,
> Thou canst not drain the draught of the Ideal.
> But yet beware! Be not by Form belated:
> Strive rather with all speed the bridge to traverse.
> If to the bourne thou fain wouldst bear the baggage,
> Upon the bridge let not thy footsteps linger.' "

Quoted by Professor R. A. Nicholson in his *Mystics of Islam,* p. 110.

186. *Ibid.,* p. 421. col. 1.

187. *Ibid.,* p. 344. col. 2.

188. *Note-Book,* p. 47.

189. *Ibid.,* p. 43.

190. *Ibid.*, p. 45.
191. *Ibid.*, p. 44.
192. *Ibid.*, p. 45.
193. See my article on *McTaggart's Contribution to the Philosophy of Religion*, in *Philosophy*, July, 1931.

# Chapter Seven

# Salvation

The term *salvation* is an unhappy one, and is used by theologians in default of a better. Its original significance is negative, and it is therefore unsuited to designate the attainment of the supreme, positive good. Miss Peabody assures us that Channing preferred the word *perfection*.[1] "Salvation by Christ," she reports him to have said, "means perfection by understanding Christ; and the word perfection more surely awakens the mind to do its own part."[2] Such a definition is in keeping with Channing's strenuous emphasis upon the freedom of the will. In his own writings, however, we find a more elaborate, and evidently a carefully considered, statement of what he understood by salvation, and with this we shall begin our investigation of the subject.

"Salvation is a sublime doctrine. But what does it mean? According to the Scriptures, salvation is to be rescued from moral evil, from error and sin, from the diseases of the mind, and to be restored to inward truth, piety, and virtue. Consequently, salvation and Christian obedience are one and the same. Nor, indeed, can salvation be anything else. I know but one salvation for a sick man, and that is to give him *health*. So I know but one salvation for a bad man, and that is to make him truly, thoroughly conscientiously *good*, to break the chains of his evil habits, to raise him to the dignity and peace of a truly religious life. An intelligent and moral being is saved and blessed just as far as he chooses freely—fully—what is good, great, and god-like; as he adopts for his rule the will of God. I therefore repeat it. Salvation and virtue are but different aspects of the same supreme good."[3]

Here, again, we have the familiar stress upon freedom of choice. But what is even more impressive about this passage is the stoical outlook which inspires it. This is, indeed, one of the most prominent characteristics of Channing's thought.[4] "Perfection of mind is our only happiness," it alone yields "enduring gratification."[5] Even the delight which one experiences in the contemplation of physical nature is due to its being an objectification of mind; "natural beauty is an image or emblem of harmonious qualities of the mind. It is a type of spiritual beauty."[6]

Is not this too extreme? we may ask. Happiness may always accompany virtue—it may even be correctly defined as the pleasure which accompanies virtue, in contradistinction to the pleasure which accompanies vice—yet surely it is a feeling or an emotion distinct in itself. Is not something more than simple virtue, then, an essential element in perfection? As a matter of fact, a glimpse into Channing's heaven will assure us that it is a state of intense bliss. We must not, therefore, interpret his language too literally. Joy and peace are the concomitants of moral progress, even though they be fused with and transfigured by it.

To affirm the perfectibility of the human soul is to presuppose the truth of the doctrine of immortality; hence the tremendous importance which this doctrine possessed for Channing, and which it must possess for everyone who shares his conviction. The suggestion that an adequate substitute for it can be found in the assurance of the continuance of the race Channing dismisses[7] as based upon an utterly superficial estimate of the value of the individual.[8] In his earlier writings, as we have had occasion to observe, Channing is content to appeal to the resurrection of Jesus as the sufficient—and the only—guarantee of immortality. The soul is not naturally immortal; its continued existence is dependent upon the will of God. Nature, then, can proffer no assurance of a life hereafter; God alone can reveal to man his destiny. Such a revelation must be miraculous in character and the requisite miracle has been provided in Jesus' resurrection.[9]

In *The Perfect Life*, however, we discover a significant change in outlook. Although the importance of the great miracle is there nowhere depreciated, yet the belief in immortality is said to be rooted in human nature, and the rational character of the conviction is given the fullest emphasis.[10] It is evident, indeed, that the doctrine follows as a necessary consequence from Channing's conception of a rational universe;[11] and the various considerations which he advances in its support merely illumine this salient fact from various points of view.[12] In man's unquenchable zest for knowledge, in his tendency to project his hopes and interests beyond the span of this life, in his ability to form the conceptions of a life to come, of God, and of duty, in his capacity for communion with God, in his thirst for moral improvement and his power of forming ideals which surpass all that he has yet achieved, in his love of beauty and of the vastness of nature, and in his power to conceive of a greater beauty than any of which he has yet had sensuous experience, in his capacity for self-sacrifice and for martyrdom, in the courage and magnanimity with which he faces the dissolution of the body and which so often renders the hour of death "an hour of peculiar glory," in his enjoyment of activity, growth, and improvement, Channing sees the indications of immortality.

If this be a doctrine full of consolation for the good, it is also one full of menace for the wicked. God's love for men is far removed from sentimentality, it is not "an instinctive tenderness, which cannot inflict pain," it is directed by boundless wisdom, and its very genuineness renders it inevitable that the Creator will shrink from inflicting no pain upon his creatures which may prove remedial.[13]

Sin is "voluntary wrong-doing." [14] In the spirit of Locke, and in company with all his fellow-Unitarians, Channing totally rejects the notion of inherited guilt. Man, he observes, is the creature of God, not of Adam.[15] The soul proceeds from its Creator free from any transmitted moral infection, and with unrealized potentialities both for good and evil. As in the case of most indeterminists, Channing's belief in the freedom of the will rests upon an ineradicable conviction that without it there could be no such thing as moral obligation rather than upon any formal argument.[16] Edwards' work on the subject, in his opinion "gives no great or elevated thoughts; but, as a specimen of logical acuteness and controversial power, it certainly ranks in the very highest class of metaphysical writings"; [17] yet, "happily it is a demonstration which no man believes, which the whole consciousness contradicts." [18]

Sin is the worst of all evils.[19] The vigor with which Channing insists upon this fact clearly exonerates him from the charge of hedonism. "To do wrong," he asserts, "is more pernicious than to incur all the calamities which nature or human malice can heap upon us"; and this is a truth which reason and revelation unite to inculcate.[20] None the less it is also true that, in the majority of instances, sin brings most other evils in its train.[21] Such, however, is by no means invariably the case; frequently the ill-doer attains his object, and his wickedness is the means to his success. There is a providential design in this. Were sin always followed by calamity, men would be dragooned into outwardly virtuous behavior which would have no moral worth. If he is to come to love the good for its own sake, man must learn to disabuse himself of the notion that loyalty to it always pays, or that he may never be called upon to suffer for it.[22]

The Scriptures, however, clearly reveal that in the life to come suffering for sin will be far more intense than in this life.[23] As a believer in free will Channing is justified in maintaining that such punishment is not merely remedial but also retributive; that there is an inherent fitness in wickedness receiving its proportionate recompense.[24] Nothing, he considers, is more irrational than the view that suffering for sin is confined to this earth.[25] Such a theory, he contends, outrageously exaggerates the importance of death, and utterly disregards the causal connections between past, present, and future mental states, and the continuity of moral development. Death is only the dissociation of soul and body, a dissociation which is followed by the dissolution and corruption of the latter. What is there in this which could conceivably produce such a tremendous transformation, which could nullify the influence of one's past life and negate the consequences of previous choices and actions, and which could suddenly turn a bad man into a good one? Moral progress is a gradual affair. One cannot by a single bound leap to perfection, one must advance by constant struggle, by battling against temptations and by continuously drilling oneself into conformity to the ideal.[26] This, as we have seen, is what Christ did, and what every soul must do if it is to progress. "Why," he asks, "are we placed in a state of discipline, exposed to temptation, encompassed with suffering, if, without discipline, and by a sovereign act of omnipotence, we are all of us, be our present characters what they may, soon and suddenly to be made perfect in virtue and perfect in happiness?" [27]

To this pertinent question it is difficult to conceive of a satisfactory answer being returned by one who shares Channing's theistic and voluntaristic presuppositions. It is obvious, therefore, he concludes, that souls will enter the next life with the same natures with which they left this life, for, after all, they *are* their natures. Reason and Scripture [28] alike assure us that in this life man determines his future destiny. But the environment which will encompass him hereafter will be very different from that which he has known here. Here there are manifold opportunities for diversion and amusement, for escape, for self-forgetfulness. "There the evil mind will be exposed to its own terrible agency, and nothing, nothing will interfere between the transgressor and his own awakened conscience." [29]

Moreover the Scriptures indicate that hereafter the soul will be provided with some sort of body.[30] This Channing believes to be a rational supposition, for he considers it highly improbable that, in a universe in which it appears to be a general law that change and improvement are gradual, the soul should enter immediately into a purely spiritual state of existence.[31] Even in this world, however, the power of the mind over the body is a manifest and impressive fact; and the disorder of the latter frequently results from that of the former. Channing writes:

I believe that, in the future state, the mind will have this power of conforming its outward frame to itself incomparably more than here. We must never forget that in that world mind or character is to exert an all-powerful sway: and, accordingly, it is rational to believe that the corrupt and deformed mind, which wants moral goodness, or a spirit of concord with God and with the universe, will create for itself, as its fit dwelling, a deformed body, which will also want concord or harmony with all things around it. Suppose this to exist, and the whole creation which now amuses may become an instrument of suffering, fixing the soul with a more harrowing consciousness on itself. You know that even now, in consequence of certain derangements of the nervous system, the beautiful light gives acute pain, and sounds which once delighted us become shrill and distressing. How often this excessive irritableness of the body has its origin in moral disorders, perhaps few of us suspect. I apprehend, indeed, that we should all be amazed were we to learn to what extent the body is continually incapacitated for enjoyment, and made susceptible of suffering, by sins of the heart and life. That delicate part of our organization on which sensibility, pain, and pleasure depend, is, I believe, peculiarly alive to the touch of moral evil. How easily, then, may the mind hereafter frame the future body according to itself, so that, in proportion to its vice, it will receive, through its organs and senses, impressions of gloom which it will feel to be the natural productions of its own depravity, and which will in this way give a terrible energy to conscience! For myself, I see no need of a local hell for the sinner after death. When I reflect how, in the present world, a guilty mind has power to deform the countenance, to undermine health, to poison pleasure, to turn prosperity into a curse, I can easily understand how, in the world to come, sin, working without obstruction according to its own nature, should spread the gloom of a dungeon over the whole creation, and wherever it goes should turn the universe into a hell.[32]

How long will these sufferings endure? Will they ultimately effectuate the reclamation and reformation of the sinner? Or will they terminate in his annihilation? Revelation, Channing concludes, provides no definite answers to these questions; accordingly, in compliance with his own principle of stopping "where the Scriptures stop," he declines to indulge in idle speculation with regard to them.[33] But it is clear that the notion of an unending hell does not enter his purview, any more than it does that of Locke. The guilt of any being, he observes, can only be proportionate to his nature and powers.[34] No finite being, therefore, is capable of receiving infinite guilt, or of deserving infinite punishment.

Virtue, like vice, is the product of genuinely free choice.[35] This is, of course, the familiar position of the indeterminist, and to Channing, as we have previously observed, it carries with it the consequence that no feelings, however desirable in themselves, possess any moral worth when divorced from moral purpose.[36] Such being the case, does it not follow, we may ask, that man must work out his salvation by his own efforts? And must he not be fully competent to do so? Freedom of choice surely presupposes the ability to act.[37] In other words, are we not forced to conclude that Channing's position is that of the uncompromising Pelagian whose motto is, "If I ought, I can"? There is nothing startling in this suggestion. He who had the hardihood to deny the deity of Christ would shrink from championing no lesser heresy did he believe that truth was on its side. Yet, if this be the case, how are we to account for Channing's exaltation of Unitarianism as *par excellence* the religion of grace?[38]

The truth of the matter appears to be that Channing's doctrine is identical with that of the Semi-Pelagians. The Augustinian and Calvinistic theory of irresistible grace he indignantly repudiates.[39] But this does not mean that he regards the human soul as utterly impervious to divine influence, or that he thinks of man as left wholly to his own resources so that he must sink or swim without assistance from above. On the contrary, the grace of God, in Channing's opinion, is absolutely essential to moral and spiritual progress; [40] it is freely proffered, even to the undeserving,[41] but it must be sought for,[42] and it is never a substitute for the individual's own effort. The perfection of the soul is a joint enterprise on the part of God and man, and neither party can prosecute it sucessfully without the cooperation of the other.

So far, although we have observed that Channing's theory of salvation is, from the orthodox standpoint, heretical—which was, of course, a foregone conclusion—we have discovered in it nothing profoundly original. Yet original it is, and if we are adequately to appreciate that originality, we must contrast it with the orthodox doctrine. From the latter point of view man is not only a creature, but a fallen creature, tainted with inherited guilt. Human nature, moreover, is radically other than the divine nature; so much the doctrine of degrees of being renders indisputable. Every creature, even the most exalted archangel, is nearer non-being, than pure Being; the gap between the divine and the human is infinite. That gap can be crossed only by the Infinite itself; only so can man be raised from his fallen state, and his salvation be accomplished through union with the Deity. This divine influx is imparted to man through the Incarnation. Fallen man, by contemplating his own ruined nature, can attain no adequate idea of his Creator. The negative Theology and the *Analogia Entis* are rooted in this inherent incapacity. By uniting himself to Christ, however, man attains the status of adopted sonship, his inherited guilt is washed away, and his transformation into the divine likeness has begun.

In Channing's eyes, however, this doctrine is a ghastly travesty of the actual situation. Man is the child of God by nature and that nature is uncontaminated by any fall; the statement that he was created in the image of God is literal truth, and is to be taken with the utmost seriousness. "God," declares Channing, "is more than Creator. To create is not to be a Father in the highest sense of that term. He created the mountain, the plant, the insect, but we do not call him their father. We do not call the artist the father of the statue which he models, nor the mechanician the father of the machine he contrives. It is the distinction of a father that he communicates an existence like his own. The father gives being to the child, and the very idea of the child is, that he bears the image as well as receives existence from the power of the parent. God is the Father, because He brings into life minds, spirits, partaking of energies kindred to his own attributes. Accordingly the Scripture teaches us that God made man in his own image, after his own likeness. Here is the ground of his paternal relation to the human race, and hence He is called in an especial sense the Father of those who make it the labor of life to conform themselves more and more to their divine original." [43]

What is implied by the notion of divine Fatherhood? In the first place, it implies that God loves the kindred minds which he has created "with an energy like that with which He upholds the universe." In the second place, it implies that "It is his chief purpose in creating and governing the universe to educate, train, form, and ennoble the rational and moral being to whom He has given birth." In the third place, it implies authority which is exercised to awaken in man the recognition of duty and to encourage him to perform it.[44] But there is something more. "When I call God the Father," writes Channing, "I understand that He communicates himself, his own spirit, what is most glorious in his own nature, to his rational offspring,—a doctrine almost overwhelming by its grandeur, but yet true, and the very truth which shines most clearly from the Christian Scriptures. It belongs to a parent to breathe into the child whatever is best and loftiest in his own soul, and for this end a good father seeks every approach to the mind of the child. Such a father is God. He has created us not only to partake of his works, but to be 'partakers of a divine nature'; not only to receive his gifts, but to receive himself. As He is a pure spirit, He has an access to the minds of his children not enjoyed by human parents. He pervades, penetrates our souls. All other beings, our nearest friends, are far from us, foreign to us, strangers compared with God. Others hold intercourse with us through the body. He is in immediate contact with our souls. We do not discern him because He is too near, too inward, too deep to be recognized by our present imperfect consciousness. And He is thus near, not only to discern, but to act, to influence, to give his spirit, to communicate to us divinity. This is the great paternal gift of God." [45]

The thoughts thus expressed are not only in harmony with, they directly follow from, the great principle of essential sameness. This is the very charter of man's salvation. And his status of divine sonship man owes to the Father alone, not to Christ. The mediatorial work of Christ is subsequent to, and is based upon, the establishment of this fundamental relationship. For this sonship is largely potential. It is true that man does not need to put on a new nature, but only to grow into the fulness of the nature which is already in him in germ; that to become truly human is to become truly divine. Nevertheless it is also true that such growth involves pain, effort, tension, conflict; and it is also true that sin is so terrible because of the very glory of the potentialities which it can blight, and of the nature which it can deface, corrupt, and ruin. The function of Christ is to give men hope by revealing to them in his own person what they may become. And they can become what Christ is only because they are potentially what he is actually. In the essential sameness of their nature and his lies the ground of this hope.

All this is as intelligible as it is unorthodox. But we must now turn to the consideration of a phase of Channing's thought where, at first sight at least, it appears to be involved in hopeless contradiction. The progress of the soul, we are told, is never to end. Again and again and again the same thought is reiterated in different words.[46] "We are to approach God for ever by a brighter vision, an intenser love, a freer communion and a larger participation of his spirit and his life!"[47] To approach God for ever! But are we never to reach him? Is there no ultimate attainment, no final victory? Is a progress which never ends, which never arrives at its goal, really progress at all? Is it, in fact, conceivable? Does not the very finitude of the creature impose a limit which cannot be overpassed?

Channing, as we have seen,[48] was prepared even to affirm the infinitude of the rational creature in respect to its potentiality for moral improvement, and not altogether without warrant. There would seem to be no contradiction between infinity in one aspect or dimension and finitude in another. If man be immortal, his duration is at least infinite *a parte post*. And perhaps the notion that he may learn forever[49] is not indefensible, since what one may fairly be said to know need not be perpetually before the mind. But does the same hold true of moral and spiritual improvement? Is there no utmost degree of integrity or loyalty which is expressive of the entire personality, no fulness of self-dedication which cannot be surpassed, no depth of devotion which is ultimate? To some, at least, the notion of endless moral progress will appear meaningless.

Clearly we have here to do with that "temporalizing of the chain of being" which Professor Lovejoy has expounded to us,[50] and which was so characteristic of the eighteenth century. And no doubt Channing's attitude was affected by Locke's identification of eternity with unending time. We may conjecture, not without a certain amount of plausibility, that he would not have been wholly averse to the Roycean doctrine which includes the endless temporal progress of the finite personality within the infinite specious present of the Deity.[51] But, however this may be, we cannot blind our eyes to the fact that Channing's view appears to be wholly incompatible with the idea of a final and complete achievement, the attainment of an ultimate goal, to which the great theistic religions, Christianity, Islam, and Judaism—in their philosophical manifestations—have attached supreme importance, with that *Visio Dei* which sweeps the soul of the beholder out of time and into "the fathomless abyss that is the being of God, and that shall never more be disturbed by Him or any creature." [52]

It would be useless to deny that many contemporary theists would unhesitatingly pronounce in favor of Channing's theory. A state of timeless repose, it is often said, would be utterly sterile, intolerably boring, an eternity of unmitigated *ennui*. But, as McTaggart has so acutely pointed out,[53] these criticisms are beside the mark, for they are the result of an imaginative picture of the final perfection in terms of stagnation at a lower level at which latent capacities still remain undeveloped and unrealized. In the Beatific Vision the noblest capacities of the soul would all be actualized. Far from being a condition of boredom, it would be one of sublime exhilaration and profoundest enjoyment. Such a state cannot be imagined, but it can be conceived—it has been conceived; and the conception involves no contradictions. In comparison with it Channing's doctrine will appear to many minds pale and devitalized; man is always being saved but his salvation is never accomplished, he is always being perfected, yet he never becomes perfect.

Furthermore, the whole theory seems flatly to contradict Channing's christology. For Channing, as we have seen, Christ is perfect. Yet he was not always so; it is impossible that he should always have been so. For perfection is not ready-made; it must be fought for; and the fight must take place in time. Through struggle in time, therefore, Christ attained perfection; and his victory is extolled as the most splendid promise to his followers that the heart of man could desire, in that it assures them that what he is they may become. The Christian, we are told, can propose to himself no lower goal without renouncing his discipleship. But then, as the French say, "of two things one." Either perfection can be attained in time, in which case there is an ultimate goal, and progress is not endless; or else, progress is endless, and then Christ is still progressing, in which case he is not yet perfect but steadily advancing toward a perfection which he will never reach. He is ahead of us upon the road, but he has not yet arrived. And, if he have not arrived, he is not the spotless image of the divine perfection. But, to say this, is to contradict Channing's repeated and most solemn affirmations that he is the perfect image of the perfect God, the divine exemplar whose supreme achievment is the ground of human hope.

Clearly something is wrong with the theory as it is presented to us, but it is not easy to say what it is. The contradiction is so blatant that it appears incredible that it should have escaped Channing's notice, and that he should not in some manner have resolved it for himself, but he has not communicated to us an account of how he accomplished this feat. In the same paragraph he confronts us with mutually incompatible assertions. "Is it true," he asks, "that man's chief happiness consists in animated pursuit, in consciousness of improvement,—that, when his advancement is most swift and sure, this principle prompts him to press forward? Is not *perfection*, then, the end of his being? Is he not made to advance, to ascend, forever?" [54] "Jesus Christ," he again affirms, "thought nothing worthy of his notice but the soul of man; and the whole tone of his gospel is, that the soul is capable of all that is great and excellent, that it may become the image of God, that it may ascend to the glory and purity of angels. It is constantly his doctrine, that man is appointed to join the society of heaven, and that he will there shine as the sun, that he will exchange his present imperfection for spotless purity. As in the child we view the future man, so in man we are taught by the gospel to view the germ of the future angel. We are taught that there is no height of excellence in the universe to which the human mind in the progress of eternity may not attain. These are views which have little to interest him who never reflects on his inward nature, who only feels that he has a body and organs of sense, and who thinks the highest happiness is to be found in the gratifications of the brute. But there are those who feel conscious of the heavenly principle within them, who, at the sight of distinguished virtue, pant to attain to its resemblance, who kindle at the thought of a boundless progression, of a never-ending ascent towards God." [55]

In these two passages we find presented in bizarre juxtaposition the incompatible notions of unending progress and of the attainment of perfection. How is this psychologically possible? Did Channing not see the contradiction in what he had just written and which was staring him in the face, or did he see it, and did he also see something else which he expected us to see, in the light of which these two antithetical affirmations can be reconciled? If so, what is it? Obviously the contradiction cannot be banished while both the assertions stand; one of them must be modified. But which shall it be? One suggestion which will undoubtedly occur to the reader is that we are taking him too literally when he speaks of endless progress, that he is contemplating a goal so remote that it appears to be at an infinite distance while it is not really so, and that, consequently, when he speaks of progress toward it as going on forever, he is merely employing the forceful language of rhetoric. As a matter of fact there is one passage in his writings of which the opening sentences suggest that this is the correct interpretation, and we follow happily along until we arrive at the conclusion which once more disillusions us. It is, therefore, worth citing *in extenso*.

> Human nature is indeed at present in a very imperfect stage of its development. But I do not therefore distrust that perfection is its end. For an end, from its very nature, is something to be attained through inferior degrees. We cannot begin with the end. We cannot argue that a being is not destined for a good, because he does not instantly reach it. We begin as children, and yet are created for maturity. So we begin life imperfect in our intellectual and moral powers, and yet are destined to wisdom and virtue. The philosopher, whose discoveries now dazzle us, could not once discern between his right hand and his left. And the energies of an adoring seraph were once probably wrapped up in a germ as humble as the mind of a human infant. We are to read God's end in our inherent tendencies, not in our first attainments. With godlike capacities, it matters little what rank we hold at the outset, if only the spirit be awakened in us to fulfill its destiny. To him who has entered an interminable path, with impulses which are carrying him onward to perfection, of what importance is it where he first plants his step? The future is all his own.[56]

All goes smoothly enough until we reach the adjective *interminable* in the last sentence but one. Did this passage stand alone, I should be inclined to interpret it in accordance with the hypothesis which we are now considering. But it does not stand alone,[57] and, in view of Channing's repeated assertions that spiritual progress is endless, I feel reluctantly compelled to abandon the proposed solution.

What other possibility is there? Readers of the late A. E. Taylor's *Faith of a Moralist* will recall the distinction which that thinker endeavors to draw between "progress toward fruition" and "progress in fruition." I am not sure that this distinction is tenable, or even that it makes sense, but let us see if we can make sense of it, and, if so, whether it throws any light upon Channing's meaning. Perhaps an illustration may help us. Two individuals, strangers to each other, meet and discover that they are mentally and spiritually akin. Quickly they are drawn together in the bonds of one of those rare and intimate friendships of which the relationships of David and Jonathan and Damon and Pythias are the classical instances in Hebrew and Hellenic literature. The connection is all that could be desired. Each feels that the other is his veritable *alter ego*. Yet, as the years pass, should we not be justified in saying that even so ideal a relationship becomes ever closer and more precious? Let us now turn to the relation between the soul and God as Channing conceives it. To the child God is a being mysterious and remote, known only by hearsay and conceived with difficulty. As he grows to maturity the man learns to think of God more worthily, and by a process of inference to assure himself of his existence. As he advances in his spiritual progress, he becomes directly conscious of the divine presence, at first fitfully and doubtfully, then at last clearly and with full assurance. As he progresses, in this life or another, God, as Channing says, becomes "the most real of all beings." The will of the creature has become completely in harmony with that of the Creator; communion is direct, constant, and transfiguring. May we not now say that perfection has been attained? Yet surely, this is not the end. The fellowship will continue to grow ever closer and more intimate.

How does Channing's christology appear in the light of such a view? Is it possible that he thought of Christ's will as wholly at one with that of God, of Christ's knowledge of the Father as complete and comprehensive, and in this sense was prepared to affirm his perfection, yet would not have denied that even to him further progress was possible. It does seem to me that he may have believed this, or at least something very like it, although I should not venture positively to affirm it. The point is of importance, for "the temporalizing of the chain of being" does appear at first glance to be wholly incompatible with the ancient conception of salvation as an ultimate and final achievement which is clearly expressive of some deep-seated need of the human spirit. It is obvious that Channing sought to reconcile both points of view, and, in default of any adequate exposition of his own, I have felt it incumbent upon me to offer the reader the most plausible conjecture which I can frame as to what Channing's attitude may have been. But I shall not quarrel with him if he do not find it entirely satisfactory, for I do not find it so myself.

We pass next to yet another phase of Channing's thought which, if not involved in actual self-contradiction, is certainly not free from difficulty and obscurity. Again, the point is of importance; and the importance I feel compelled to stress. The worker in the field of the philosophy of religion is, at the outset, most concerned with points of view antithetical to his own, and rightly so; for, unless he can refute the objections of opponents and make good the premises from which he is to proceed, he is entitled to advance no further. He can benefit neither himself nor his fellow-man by rearing a castle in the air. The importance of his subject—and, surely, upon any interpretation there is no subject the importance of which equals his—focuses his attention upon the foundations of his structure. It is the materialist and the naturalist whom he has constantly in mind as he develops his system. But, as his work progresses, and reveals to his inspection no signs of collapsing, a feeling of increasing security is apt to spring up in his mind. This is a dangerous delusion. For it is by his conception of man's ultimate destiny, which is the vital nerve of the whole religious enterprise, that his work will finally be judged. And, as he thinks worthily or unworthily of this, will he succeed or fail. Accordingly he ought to be peculiarly sensitive to criticisms proceeding from positions similar to his own, for these will contain more of truth, and will, therefore, be all the more likely to prove damaging.

Now it has been urged by the atheistic idealist, McTaggart, that the fundamental defect of theism is that it sets, and must set, a low value upon human love. The point of the criticism will not be duly appreciated until the distinction be grasped between love and benevolence. Benevolence is basically volitional in character; it does not, indeed, exclude emotion, but that emotion is of an impersonal variety. Theists of all faiths and in all ages have concurred in emphasizing the value of benevolence. When it comes, however, to personal affection and devotion, such as engages the whole personality, theists have habitually told us that this in its purest and intensest form belongs to God alone, that the creatures are to be loved "for God's sake" [58] rather than for themselves. In no Christian thinker is this characteristic more pronounced than in Channing's predecessor, Edwards. Love, Edwards maintains, should be proportionate to its object. God, the Supreme Good, alone deserves the fulness of one's love; to bestow this upon any finite being would be idolatry. In opposition to this view McTaggart contends that love, *as such,* regardless of its object, is the supreme good.

All judgments of value, like judgments with respect to sense-data, are ultimate, and there is no place for argument. It is open to the theist flatly to deny the validity of McTaggart's value-judgment, and deny it he will, if he adhere to the orthodox tradition. Channing, however, although as convinced and enthusiastic a theist as ever lived, was emphatically not of the orthodox tradition. What, we must inquire, was his position in regard to this issue. True enough, we cannot blame him if he did not anticipate a criticism which would not be advanced until more than a century after his death; yet we must seek to discover, if we can, any indications of what his attitude toward it would have been.

In the first place, then, we must take account of numerous passages in which Channing speaks quite in the spirit of the conventional Christian philosopher or theologian as regards the unique and ultimate intensity of devotion which the soul can and should feel toward God. Some of these passages the reader may recall, but there are others which have not been cited.[59] "We may cherish," asserts Channing, "a reverence and attachment to him (God) more profound and devoted than the affections with which we embrace parent, and child, and dearest human friends"; [60] we "sometimes enjoy communion with him more tender than human friendship," [61] "such as no embodied being can call forth." [62] All this is in the familiar strain of traditional piety. And it is evident whither such a piety, if no counter influence assert itself, will ultimately tend. Carried away by such rapturous transports the soul may at last find itself in the condition of the renowned Rabi'a, who was too much taken up with loving God to love or hate anyone else.

Yet we may also discover in Channing's writings statements of a very different tenor, and these are chiefly to be found in that *Note-Book* composed of pithy extracts culled by his devoted granddaughter from his unpublished papers. "They who fly from love to be devout, are they not extinguishing piety?" [63] "Is not perfect love perfect happiness? Is not love heaven?" [64] "When our friends die, in proportion as we loved them, we die with them—we go with them." [65] "We cannot enjoy a friend here. If we are to meet it is beyond the grave." [66]

Utterances such as these certainly suggest, indeed they directly imply, that human love is an ultimate good in itself; that human affections do not merely constitute the rungs of a ladder which the soul ascends toward the love of God, and which, having been mounted, may henceforth be disregarded. How can the rights of human relationships be safeguarded against the tremendous claims of the Deity? Only, I think, by showing that, so far from conflicting, these relationships are mutually implicatory, and that each strengthens and invigorates the other. Is there any evidence that Channing actually regarded them in this light? I think that there is some, but that it is not conclusive, inasmuch as it must be weighed against other assertions of a different tenor. It is noteworthy that Channing insists, apparently with the earnestness of intense conviction, that the good "form new, holier, stronger ties above." [67] "If we have ever known the enjoyments of friendship, of entire confidence, of co-operation in honorable and successful labors with those we love, we can comprehend something of the felicity of a world where souls, refined from selfishness, open as the day, thirsting for new truth and virtue, indued with new power of enjoying the beauty and grandeur of the universe, allied in the noblest works of benevolence, and continually discovering new mysteries of the Creator's power and goodness, communicate themselves to one another with the freedom of perfect love. The closest attachments of this life are cold, distant, stranger-like, compared with theirs." [68] Moreover the blessed also remember and regard with stranger affection those whom they have left on earth. "They love human nature as never before, and human friends are prized as above all price." [69] It is noteworthy also that Channing does not make these assertions upon the authority of revelation, his appeal is to reason; and the reason given for this increased love of their beloved is the greater nearness of the blessed to Christ and to God. From all this we might well conclude that, in Channing's opinion, love for God can and does stimulate and intensify human love.

Yet there are other affirmations which give us pause. "Let us not think of the departed as looking on us with earthly, partial affections. They love us more than ever, but with a refined and spiritual love. They have now but one wish for us, which is, that we may fit ourselves to join them in their mansions of benevolence and piety. Their spiritual vision penetrates to our souls. Could we hear their voice, it would not be an utterance of personal attachment so much as a quickening call to greater effort, to more resolute self-denial, to a wider charity, to a meeker endurance, a more filial obedience of the will of God. Nor must we think of them as appropriated to ourselves. They are breathing now an atmosphere of divine benevolence. They are charged with a higher mission than when they trod the earth. And this thought of the enlargement of their love should enlarge ours, and carry us beyond selfish regards to a benevolence akin to that with which they are inspired." [70]

This sounds suspiciously like what McTaggart means by benevolence; indeed Channing's repeated use of this very word in the passage just cited is significant. Does he mean by it personal affection purified from all taint of selfishness, or does he mean impersonal affection, universal good-will? No definite answer to this question seems possible. I do not believe, therefore, that we can formulate a plausible hypothesis as to how Channing would have answered McTaggart's criticism had he been confronted by it. And yet this is, I believe, the most crucial of all the objections which can be made to theism.[71]

We have now to face a kindred difficulty—one which follows from the fundamental principle that "all minds are of one family." [72] By the phrase "all minds" is plainly meant "all rational minds," for, with characteristic Christian ontological snobbishness, Channing leaves the animals out of account. That there are spiritual beings superior to man Channing has no doubt.[73] The fact, as he considers it, is "plainly revealed in Scripture.[74] Yet, however exalted they may be, they constitute with human minds a single family. It is because of this consubstantiality of nature that Channing would not "shrink before an archangel." [75] But what of the divine mind itself? It is the parent of the family. It is numerically other than any one of them, and it is also the Creator of all of them. There is no question of the soul ever at any future instant however remote "becoming God"; for one individual cannot become another, nor can creature become creator any more than convex can become concave or black become white. The principle of essential sameness, therefore, leaves Channing's theism unendangered.

How will matters stand, however, if we reject the doctrine of creation? It is founded upon revelation, but, once the inerrancy of Scripture be questioned, it must fight for its life in the arena of debate. It has been imported into philosophy by the theologians, but what if the philosophers return it to them? Man cannot render the notion of creation intelligible, we are told, because he is himself a creature. But ought he, then, to talk about it? Is there any excuse for darkening counsel by the introduction of the unintelligible? Personally, I do not think that there is, but I do not intend to argue the question. I wish merely to inquire whether it is only the doctrine of creation that keeps Channing's system from collapsing into an atheistic pluralism.

There remains the distinction between the infinite and the finite. But Channing has discovered "traces of infinity" [76] in the human mind

—in its boundless capacities for moral and intellectual improvement. Conceive these realized, and what befalls? They will never become realized *in toto*, it may be answered, since time knows no termination and progress will be endless. But can we be sure that time is ultimately real? And, granted that it be so, as progress continues will the universe not be tending, if only tangentially, towards a state in which the heavenly monarchy will become transformed into a divine republic? We seem perilously close to a world view not so very remote from that of the Jaina and Sankhya philosophies. One recalls the theistic pluralism of Howison, with his infinitely infinite God surrounded by his entourage of finite-infinite spirits, each of which is progressing towards the goal of becoming a perfect mirror of one of the limitless number of facets of the divine immensity. Can a theistic pluralism be saved by replacing the doctrine of a creative God by the theory of God as a final cause? To reply in any adequate fashion to this question would require one to write a treatise on metaphysics. Yet merely to ask the question will make one realize clearly that only a single step will take one from Channing to Howison.

We have already glanced briefly into Channing's heaven. There, as we have already seen, spirits enjoy constant and intimate communion with God, with Christ, and with one another. A second glance reveals that heaven is not "a stationary community." "I think of it," writes Channing, "as a world of stupendous plans and efforts for its own improvement. I think of it as a society passing through successive stages of development, virtue, knowledge, power by the energy of its own members. Celestial genius is always active to explore the great laws of creation and the everlasting principles of the mind, to disclose the beautiful in the universe, and to discover the means by which every soul may be carried forward. In that world, as in this, there are diversities of intellect, and the highest minds find their happiness and progress in elevating the less improved. There the work of education, which began here, goes on without end; and a diviner philosophy than is taught on earth reveals the spirit to itself, and awakens it to earnest, joyful effort for its own perfection.

"And not only," continues Channing, "will they who are born into heaven enter a society full of life and action for its own development. Heaven has connection with other worlds. Its inhabitants are God's messengers through the creation. They have great trusts. In the progress of their endless being, they may have the care of other worlds. But I pause, lest to those unused to such speculations

I seem to exceed the bounds of calm anticipation. What I have spoken seems to me to rest on God's word and the laws of the mind, and these laws are everlasting." [77]

The thoroughly temporal character of Channing's heaven thus becomes fully apparent. What we most miss is a discussion of the problem of time, and its relations to the notion of salvation, or *perfectification,* if I may be permitted to coin such a term. This deficiency might, conceivably, have been remedied, at least in some measure, had Channing been able to complete his *Treatise on Man;* yet as to this it is vain to speculate. None the less the writings which he has left us contain profound insights which deserve our gratitude. By his rejection of the doctrine of original sin, and his noble vindication of the "free, unbought, unmerited" character of divine grace and forgiveness, he was enabled to render the theory of a substitutionary atonement as unnecessary as it is morally revolting; and, in like manner, his doctrine of the essential sameness of man and God rendered otiose the dogma of the Incarnation, a dogma which he has given cogent reasons for esteeming as spiritually harmful as it is irrational. The kinship of man and God, the impossibility of conceiving of either apart from the other, this is the great idea which inspires at once his theology, his anthropology, his christology, his soteriology, his philosophy of politics, and his doctrine of salvation. No devoted altruist ever framed a nobler apology for his devotion to his race than did he in the impressive words with which we shall terminate this chapter, words which it is good to reread at the present day:

"I do and I must reverence human nature. Neither the sneers of a worldly scepticism nor the groans of a gloomy theology disturb my faith in its godlike powers and tendencies. I know how it is despised, how it has been oppressed, how civil and religious establishments have for ages conspired to crush it. I know its history. I shut my eyes on none of its weaknesses and crimes. I understand the proofs by which despotism demonstrates that man is a wild beast, in want of a master, and only safe in chains. But injured, trampled on, and scorned as our nature is, I still turn to it with intense sympathy and strong hope. The signatures of its origin and its end are impressed too deeply to be ever wholly effaced. I bless it for its kind affections, for its strong and tended love. I honor it for its struggles against oppression, for its growth and progress under the weight of so many chains and prejudices, for its achievements in science and art, and still more, for its examples of heroic and saintly virtue. These are marks of a divine origin and the pledges of a celestial inheritance; and I thank God that my own lot is bound up with that of the human race." [78]

## NOTES

1. *Reminiscences*, p. 154.
2. *Loc. cit.*
3. *Works*, p. 1010. col. 2.
4. "My belief," he informs us, "is that the supreme good of an intelligent and moral being is the perfection of its nature. Nothing gives what is worthy of being considered happiness, and nothing is of enduring benefit, unless it exalts us to that excellence for which God designs us." *Ibid.*, p. 984. "Perfect goodness," he writes, "is the supreme good,—may I not say *the only good?* We often hear, indeed, of the rewards of virtue, as if they were something separate from virtue, and virtue was but the means. But I am sure that virtue itself is worth more than all outward rewards; its truest recompense is found in *itself,* in its own growing vigor, in its own native peace, in the harmony which it establishes between our souls and God, in the sympathy and friendship by which it identifies us with the universe." *Ibid.*, p. 1012.
5. *Ibid.*, p. 1003.
6. *Ibid.*, pp. 1003. col. 2.—1004. col. 1.
7. *Ibid.*, p. 963. col. 1. "In every human mind he (God) sees powers kindred to his own,—the elements of angelic glory and happiness. These bind the Heavenly Father's love indissolubly to every single soul. And these divine elements authorize a trust utterly unlike that which springs from superficial views of man's transitory existence." *Loc. cit.*
8. *Loc. cit.* It is significant that the Nazis possessed sufficient philosophical penetration to see that their cult of the German race could only seem preposterous nonsense to the believer in immortality, and accordingly placed the doctrine upon their index.
9. *Ibid.*, p. 213. It is interesting to observe that in this passage, which I have briefly summarized above, the resurrection of Lazarus is coupled with that of Jesus, although the latter is, of course, stated to be the more important. This is, indeed, amazing, since it is obvious that they fall under entirely different categories. The resurrection of Lazarus, like the restoration of the dead to life by Elijah or Elisha, would constitute an extraordinary event, of a supernatural character indeed, but one from which no general conclusion could be drawn. The resurrection of Jesus, on the other hand, is of unique significance because it is the resurrection of the Messiah, and because of the promise that his disciples will be similarly resuscitated. It constitutes, therefore, a *guarantee,* whereas these other events do not. Elsewhere in Channing's writings it alone is appealed to. See pp. 324, 358, 359, 381. (See above, p. 327.)
10. *Ibid.*, pp. 979-984.
11. This fundamental contention has recently been re-stated by the Rev. John Haynes Holmes in his Ingersol Lecture entitled *The Affirmation of Immortality.*

12. The section just cited in *The Perfect Life* should be compared with a fragment preserved in his nephew's biography (pp. 244-249), where Channing's fullest reflections upon this topic will be found.
13. *Ibid.,* pp. 396. col. 1.; 376. col. 2.—377. col. 1.; 1004. col. 2.
14. *Ibid.,* p. 348. col. 1.
15. *Ibid.,* p. 341. col. 1.
16. "We all of us feel that virtue is not something adopted from necessity, something to which feeling impels us, something which comes to us from constitution, or accident, or outward condition; but that it has its origin in our moral freedom, that it consists in moral energy." *Ibid.,* p. 345. col. 2.
17. *Ibid.,* p. 128. col. 2.
18. *Ibid.,* p. 4. col. 2.
19. *Ibid.,* pp. 196. col. 2.—348. col. 1.
20. *Ibid.,* p. 348. *Cf.* p. 1012. col. 2.
21. *Ibid.,* pp. 349. col. 2.—350. col. 2.; 688. col. 2.
22. "The present world," asserts Channing, "is a state for the formation of character. It is meant to be a state of trial, where we are to act freely, to have opportunities of wrong as well as right action, and to become virtuous amidst temptation. Now such a purpose requires that sin, or wrong-doing, should not regularly and infallibly produce its full and immediate punishment. For suppose, my hearers, that at the very instant of a bad purpose or a bad deed a sore and awful penalty were unfailingly to light upon you: would this be consistent with trial? would you have moral freedom? would you not live under compulsion? Who would do wrong if judgment were to come like lightning after every evil deed? In such a world fear would suspend our liberty and supersede conscience. Accordingly, sin, though, as we have seen, it produces great misery, is still left to compass many of its objects, often to prosper, often to gain." *Ibid.,* p. 351. col. 2.
23. *Loc. cit.*
24. "Retribution is the claim of our moral nature." *Ibid.,* p. 933. col. 1.
25. *Ibid.,* pp. 350. col. 2.—351. It is probable, as the compilers of the index to his *Works* evidently believe, that Channing here makes reference to the primitive form of Universalism which was committed to this doctrine, and which was then disseminating itself in New England. It is possible, however, that he had also in mind the Calvinistic doctrine of justification by faith alone, according to which a sincere death-bed repentence will admit a dying villain to the bliss of paradise.
26. "To suppose moral goodness breathed from abroad into the guilty mind, just as health may be imparted to a sick body, is to overlook the distinction between corporeal and intellectual natures, and to degrade a free being into a machine." *Ibid.,* p. 351. col. 1.
27. *Ibid.,* p. 351.
28. *Ibid.,* p. 352. col. 1.
29. *Loc. cit.*
30. *Ibid.,* p. 352. col. 2.
31. *Loc. cit.* This statement carries with it the important implication that in due course the soul, as it advances, will be freed from its connection with a body, and will enjoy a purely spiritual immortality.

32. *Ibid.,* pp. 352. col. 2—353. col. 1.
33. *Ibid.,* p. 353. col. 2.
34. *Ibid.,* pp. 379. col. 1.; 403. col. 2.
35. "The very idea of virtue is, that it is a free act, the product or result of the mind's self-determining power. It is not good feeling, infused by nature or caught by sympathy; nor is it good conduct into which all have slidden through imitation, or which has been forced upon us by another's will." *Ibid.,* p. 552. col. 1.
36. For a discussion of this subject, in a very Kantian spirit indeed, see *Works,* pp. 343-345.
37. *Ibid.,* p. 460. col. 1.
38. *Ibid.,* pp. 395. col. 2.—396. col. 1.
39. "We believe that no dispositions infused into us without our own moral activity are of the nature of virtue, and therefore we reject the doctrine of irresistible divine influence on the human mind, moulding it into goodness as marble is hewn into a statute." *Ibid.,* p. 380. col. 1.
40. "We always and earnestly maintain that no human virtue, no human obedience, can give a legal claim, a right by merit, to the life and immortality brought to light by Christ. We see and mourn over the deficiencies, broken resolutions, and mixed motives of the best men. We always affirm that God's grace, benignity, free kindness, is needed by the most advanced Christians, and that to this alone we owe the promise in the gospel, of full remission and everlasting happiness to the penitent." (*Ibid.,* p. 404.)
41. *Cf. Ibid.,* p. 401, where divine grace is stated to be "free, unbought, unmerited."
42. "Prayer is a proper and appointed acknowledgment of our dependence, an essential means and branch of piety; and they who neglect it have no reason to hope the protection which they will not implore." (*Ibid.,* p. 686. col. 1.) The immediate reference here is, indeed, to providential succour in physical danger rather than to spiritual guidance and assistance, yet it is plain that the same principle applies to both.
43. *Ibid.,* p. 415. col. 2.
44. *Ibid.,* pp. 416. col. 2.—417. col. 1.
45. *Ibid.,* p. 417.
46. *Cf. Ibid.,* pp. 293. col. 1.; 314. col. 1.; 425. col. 1.; 550. col. 1.; 934. col. 1.; 982. col. 1.; 987. col. 2.; 1000. col. 1.; 1001. col. 1.
47. *Ibid.,* p. 965. col. 2.
48. *Ibid.,* pp. 204. col. 2. 295. col. 1.
49. *Ibid.,* p. 990. col. 2.
50. *The Great Chain of Being,* ch. IX.
51. It is interesting to observe that, *a propos* of the difficulty of reconciling divine foreknowledge with human freedom, Channing saw fit to remark, "It is probable that much of the obscurity arises from our applying to God the same kind of foreknowledge as men possess by their acquaintance with causes, and from our supposing the Supreme Being to bear the same relation to time as man." (*Ibid.,* p. 488. col. 2.) Is this suggestion, one may ask, inconsistent with the principle of essential sameness? I do not think so. Human inference, as Descartes pointed out, consists of a series of intuitions or awarenesses held together in memory. An omniscient mind, especially if its relation

to time were different from man's, and if it could survey all reality as present in a single glance, would be incapable of inference. But it would still be aware in the same sense in which man is aware of what is directly presented to him. The difference, so far as knowing is concerned, would be *accidental* and not *essential*.

52. *Cf.* Ruysbroeck's *The Book of the Twelve Bequines* (tr. by John Francis), p. 100.
53. *The Nature of Existence,* vol. II, p. 436. n. 1.
54. *Life,* p. 248.
55. *Ibid.,* pp. 249-250.
56. *Works,* pp. 964. col. 2.—965. col. 1.
57. Thus, in the next paragraph but one, we are told that "God appoints all changes as the means of a spiritual growth which is never to cease," that we are "to approach God forever."
58. In this spirit Channing exhorts his hearers, "Worship God within these walls, as universally, impartially good to his human offspring; and go forth to breathe the same spirit." (*Ibid.,* p. 421. col. 1.)
59. *Cf. Ibid.* pp. 380. col. 2.; 411. col. 1.; 935. col. 1.; 966. col. 1.; 999. col. 2.
60. *Ibid.,* p. 935. col. 2.
61. *Ibid.,* p. 400. col. 1.
62. *Ibid.,* p. 389. col. 2.
63. *Notebook,* p. 47.
64. *Ibid.,* p. 45.
65. *Ibid.,* p. 42.
66. *Ibid.,* p. 43.
67. *Ibid.,* p. 363. col. 1.
68. *Ibid.,* p. 365. col. 1.
69. *Ibid.,* p. 363. col. 1.
70. *Ibid.,* pp. 363. col. 2.—364. col. 1.
71. See p. 384. n. 1
72 This assertion is, of course, only a restatement of the principle of essential sameness.
73. He not infrequently refers to them. *Cf. Ibid.,* pp. 360. col. 1.; 944. col. 2.; 957. col. 1.; 965. col. 1.
74. *Ibid.,* p. 1019. col. 2.
75. *Ibid.,* p. 994. col. 1.
76. *Ibid.,* p. 294. col. 2.
77. *Ibid.,* pp. 365. col. 2.—366. col. 1. It is probable, Channing believes, that the blessed are aware of what passes in this world, and such knowledge will inevitably lead them to sympathize with human sufferings, yet their more extended vision, and their fuller knowledge of the divine purpose, will save them from being thereby involved in misery.
78. *Ibid.,* p. 299. col. 1.

# PART THREE

# Conclusion

Chapter Eight

# Conclusion

The reader of the foregoing chapters cannot fail to have been impressed by the thoroughly personalistic character of Channing's thought. And this observation will naturally lead him to raise the following questions: What was the nature of Channing's cosmology? Was it dualistic or idealistic? And, in particular, what was his attitude toward the philosophy of Berkeley, whose works, as we know, he had scrupulously examined? [1] Unfortunately his published writings afford all too few and all too brief indications of his thoughts upon these subjects; but, happily, the initial chapters of his unfinished *Treatise on Man* which still survive among his unpublished papers provide us with precious additional information.

With the last question, in mind we may turn first to the essay on *The Writings of Milton,* where the name of Berkeley appears in connection with an illuminating comment upon the great puritan's view of matter as "an efflux of the Deity." "These speculations of Milton," observes Channing, "will be received in this age with more favor, or with less aversion, than in his own; for, from the time of Locke, the discussions of philosophers have tended to unsettle our notions of matter, and no man is hardy enough now to say what it is, or what it may not be. The idealism of Berkeley, though it has never organized a sect, has yet sensibly influenced the modes of thinking among metaphysicians: and the coincidence of this system with the theory of certain Hindoo philosophers may lead us to suspect that it contains some great latent truth, of which the European and Hindoo intellect, so generally at variance, have caught a glimpse. Matter is indeed a

Proteus, which escapes us at the moment we hope to seize it. Priestley was anxious to make the soul material; but for this purpose he was obliged to change matter from a substance into a power, that is into no matter at all; so that he destroyed in attempting to diffuse it. We have thrown out these remarks to rescue Milton's memory from the imputation, which he was the last man to deserve, of irreverence towards God; for of this some will deem him guilty in tracing matter to the Deity as its fountain. Matter, which seems to common people so intelligible, is still wrapped in mystery. We know it only by its relation to mind, or as an assemblage of powers[2] to awaken certain sensations. Of its relation to God we may be said to know nothing. Perhaps, as knowledge advances, we shall discover that the Creator is bound to his works by stronger and more intimate ties than we now imagine. We do not, then, quarrel with such suggestions as Milton's, though we cannot but wonder at the earnestness with which he follows out such doubtful speculations." [3]

In the above passage we find a sympathetic attitude toward idealism combined with a hesitancy to accept it, based, apparently, upon the conviction that the proofs advanced in support of it are inadequate. In *The Perfect Life,* however, the idealistic thesis is again stated, only to meet with an explicit, if qualified, rejection. "From the very dawn of philosophy there have been schools which have held that the material universe has no existence but in the mind that thinks it. I am far from assenting to these speculations. But I recur to them with pleasure, as indicating how readily the soul passes above matter, and as manifesting man's consciousness of the grandeur of his spiritual nature. Let me add that, whilst rejecting this doctrine as a whole, I receive an important part of it as undoubtedly true. I do not say that the world exists in our thoughts *only.* But I do say that it derives its most interesting properties from the mind which contemplates it. For example, the forms of outward objects have doubtless actual existence, but they owe their beauty—that mysterious charm—to thoughts and feelings which we blend with them, and of which they are but the reflected image." [4]

Although, at first blush, this may appear an amazing doctrine when held by a man who insisted as explicitly and earnestly as did Channing upon the objectivity of moral values, our amazement ceases when we reflect that it is the logical consequence of the subjectivity of secondary qualities involved in the epistemological dualism of Locke. Let us, therefore, turn to *The Treatise on Man,* where, if anywhere, we may hope to discover Channing's final view of the matter. To accomplish this we must grasp the successive stages of his thought as he unfolds them before us in order that we may see in its proper perspective the conclusion to which he would lead us.

The first of the eight completed chapters deals with sensation. There we discover, possibly to our astonishment, that "we have no authority whatever for ascribing sensation to the body, as its cause. The body is the occasion, not the cause." It is probable that the immediate source of this distinction is Price's *Review of the Principal Questions in Morals* [5] where it is applied in the mental realm, but beyond Price, as he himself indicates,[6] it may be traced, as every student of philosophy knows, to Malebranche; nor does the trail end there, for the roots of the doctrine are to be found in St. Augustine, and possibly also in the theologians of Islam.[7]

"The distinction which I have laid down between occasion and cause," remarks Channing, "is one with which we are all familiar. A miller lifts a sluice and his wheels begin to turn, but the motion of the sluice is not the power which turns his wheel. It is the occasion. Its motion only gives liberty to the stream to act. I open my eye and I see, nor can I see without this action of the lids. But this action is not the cause of vision. It is the occasion. It admits the light, nor is the light its cause. Its single office is to give a certain impulse to the retina or nerves.

"Nor is this affection of nerves the cause. It is only the occasion of sight. Philosophers now conceive that the movement and vibration of the nerve excites galvanic action. Electricity is disengaged and should this theory prove true, future observers will find electricity to be but an occasion of something more remote and subtle, and we have every reason to think that when we shall reach the last material agent, we shall not discover a proper cause, a productive power, but must ascribe the connection between it and thought to the immediate ever present energy of God."

Why is this conclusion inescapable? "There is," answers Channing, "of necessity a proportion between the cause and the effect. A cause cannot produce all effects indifferently, but those to which its own nature adapts it. This we cannot help believing. That an agent should produce something which is in no respect allied to itself, which is of a different and far higher order, shocks this fundamental conviction." These sentences remind us of the Augustinian view that matter is unable to act upon mind because of the superior "nobility" of the latter.

But, again, the immediate source is doubtless Price,[8] whose theory that, while the senses acquaint one with contiguity and succession, reason reveals the presence of a necessary connection is accepted by Channing.

"Immediate antecedence," he urges, "is not the essence of a cause. The presence of two sounds or two colors to the mind is followed immediately by the perceptions of agreement or disagreement among them. But can two colors, blue and green, be considered as the causes of the idea of difference? Do they create a thought which has nothing in common with them, which is not a sensation, and which is so general as to be recognized in all successions of thought. The senses are the occasions, the appointed condition of all intellectual action. Without them we should not think or will. But thought, will, affection are entirely different from agitations of a nerve, and immeasurably superior to them and require a very different cause." [9]

If all this is reminiscent of Malebranche, what follows is strongly suggestive of the influence of Leibnitz. "I incline much," Channing tells us, "to the doctrine that sensations may be considered as existing in the mind, at the first moment of its creation, and as becoming objects of consciousness by the impressions made on the senses from abroad. The mind may possess what it is not conscious of.[10] Of the countless thoughts which form its [endowment] how few are present to it at any given moment. It sometimes happens that an impression received in childhood, after having disappeared for a long life, will revive in old age. The occasion only was wanting, and so when the occasion of sensation appears, these spring forth into conscious life."

Obviously we are not far from the notion of a monadology; not far also, perhaps, from that of a pre-established harmony, inasmuch as all souls are provided at their creation with sensations appropriate to every future occasion, yet clearly the souls will not be windowless, since they can at least respond to the occasions and are capable of genuine activity.

The body—leaving on one side, for the moment, the question of its ultimate status—the body has also an important function to fulfill. So far from producing sensations, it restrains them, it is to be conceived of as "repressing rather than creating feeling and intelligence." The soul, Channing assures us, is "essentially active," it is "an unbounded force seeking perpetual and indefinite expansion, and if left to itself, it would break out into a chaos of sensation, thought, affection, and will." The body is designed to limit this spontaneous but chaotic activity. "By union with the body, the soul's activity is not created but confined. According to the present constitution of things it sees and hears only when the eye and ear are impressed from abroad. Without this or some restraining organism, sensation(s) of sight and hearing would break forth like torrents from within itself. The body is a prison as the instinctive wisdom of all ages, has taught, curbing the soul's action, except in particular directions and under particular conditions."

If, however, the body is powerless to produce sensations, how, one wonders, can it inhibit them? The connection, Channing admits, is "mysterious," and it seems plain that the only ultimate explanation must be the correlating activity of God. In other words, we are not far from the position of Cordemoy. But even in man's present state the will is not wholly powerless to augment the wealth of sensation. By the concentrating of attention sensations which would otherwise be unperceived are brought before the consciousness, as in the case of the painter who learns to discriminate between shades of color where the unstrained eye can perceive no distinction, or in the case of a savage who can follow a trail imperceptible to a civilized man. Moreover the soul is in large measure independent of the senses, as is evident from the fact that persons deprived of the use of one, or even of most, of their sense-organs may yet develop an intellectual life of high quality in defiance of their impediments.

It is highly improbable, Channing considers, that the five types of sensation of which man is now possessed are the only types contained in the universe. Those which he is to develop hereafter, we must suppose, are already created but latent within the depths of his unconscious. Those that he now enjoys must be peculiarly suited to his present condition—a topic which in Channing's opinion, merits an examination which it has not yet received. Thus sight obviously ministers to the intellect and sound to the emotions.

The impressions of sight and touch occasion the formation idea of space. No one, Channing assumes, will think that they *cause* it, for space is vastly different from sensation, it has neither color nor taste nor smell, it is, "necessary, immutable and infinite," whereas they are "finite and changeable." In like manner sound occasions the perception of time, or continuous succession.

But what of matter? How do men become aware of it? And how do they conceive of it? One conceives of it, replies Channing, as substance. "By substance we understand that which lies beneath the properties, attributes, phenomena of matter or mind, and in which they inhere." But how do we penetrate beneath phenomena to grasp this underlying reality? "Is it by the eye, the taste, by sound, by touch, that this mysterious essence is made known? Do we rank among our sensations this universal truth, that all properties, phenomena must have beneath them a subject, substance, being in which they inhere? This is plainly a universal truth of reason. It belongs to our highest intellectual power. It has nothing to do with the senses. Without senses we should hold it, for it is revealed to us just as clearly by the properties or energies of the soul, as by the properties of matter. Thus the fundamental idea of matter is of spiritual origin. It belongs to our highest nature, so that the material universe is strictly revealed to us by our own souls." [11]

The primary properties of matter are "extension, solidity, mobility." But these are nothing other than "the relations of the unknown subject, called matter to space. Thus by the extension of matter we mean that the unknown substance fills or occupies a portion of space. By solidity is meant that the matter occupying a portion of space excludes all other matter from the same. By mobility is meant that a portion of matter may occupy successively different portions of space or pass from one to the other. By vis inertia is meant the resistance which matter makes to being moved from the sphere it occupies and the reverse. Thus the essential attributes of matter are its relations to space." Yet space is very different from matter. Matter acts on the senses, whereas space does not act upon them. "Space is not solid, is not movable, has no inertia or resistance, nor has it extension in the sense in which this is ascribed for matter is extended as it fills or occupies space, and surely space does not fill or occupy itself. And not only does space thus want the attributes of matter. It is directly opposed. Space is necessarily continuous, for its contiguous portions cannot be separated from each other, whilst matter is separable. Space exists by necessity, for we cannot conceive of its non-existence or annihilation, but we can conceive of matter as destroyed. Space is indefinite, i.e., no limits can be assigned to it, but matter is bounded. How different, how opposite the ideas of matter and space." As the result of these reflections Channing arrives at the conclusion that "the essential properties of matter are its relations to that which differs essentially from itself, and the idea of which is of purely intellectual origin, and consequently our conceptions of matter are to be traced chiefly to the same origin. It is a creation of our own minds."

What, then, of the secondary properties of matter? In truth these are not properties of matter at all; they are affections of the mind. Matter has the power of exciting them; thus it is related not only to space but to minds. But what do we mean by power? Power is not something which can be discerned by the senses, as Hume rightly remarked, and on that very ground he was compelled to deny the existence of any such idea. "In this denial the philosopher gave a striking proof of his preference of theory to truth, for of all ideas perhaps the most common, that which enters most largely into combination with others, that which gives most of life and interest to the world of thought is that of power; but the ground of his denial that power is an object of either of the five senses is plain. Its origin is higher. It is an idea of the understanding or reason." Once more we reach the conclusion that "the world around us is much more the creature of the mind, than the mind of the world."

At this point Channing interjects the observation that "whether the unknown subject, called matter, possesses power or be only the sphere within which our higher power acts, whether indeed, there be such a subject or anything more than the creative Power acting within certain spaces—these are questions open to discussion and perhaps not be settled with our present means of knowledge." Thus we behold Channing standing at the intersection of three ways; one of which, did he decide to follow it, would lead him toward Malebranche, a second toward Berkeley, and the third toward Kant. Before we proceed, however, it will be well to remark that by referring to matter, after he has enumerated its ostensible qualities as an unknown subject, Channing reveals that he has fallen into the common error of those who criticise the notion of substance. If we know the characteristics of a substance, we know what the substance is. *Whether* there be substances or not is disputable, but, *if* there be substances, they are not characteristics. They *possess* characteristics. It is only in terms of the characteristics which it possesses that the substance can be described; and, once these have been enumerated, to complain that it is still "unknown" is to demand that it have another nature than the nature that it has—which is a meaningless requirement.

Channing now continues with his critique of the notion of matter. Like Bradley, he finds a contradiction in the notion of infinite divisibility which dissipates it "into nothing." Nor can he render intelligible the notion of one particle of matter putting another in motion. If the particles do not touch, which he takes as proved, then the one which impels the other must act where it is not, "at which the mind revolts." The difficulty remains, he thinks, even if the interval be eliminated, and if the particles actually touch. "Still more," and this, one suspects, is the crucial point, "the difficulty of conceiving of power as existing apart from intelligence is great, and grows on us as we are accustomed to reflection." Matter is assumed to be inert. How, then, can one reconcile inertness with self-movement, or with action upon another on the part of any particle? The senses reveal change and motion, but not force. Perhaps matter is only a "sign" of force, perhaps it is nothing but force. Yet what is force—"the divine energy manifested within a given space, by the phenomenon of resistance, motion, etc."?

"According to these views," concludes Channing, "matter which seems to some the only reality vanishes, and nothing is left us in the outward world but the infinitely diversified agency of the creator. Matter and God become one, and Spirit which seems to many a shadow is the only existence distinct from the Divinity. But I attach no importance to speculations of this character. The essences of things are hidden from us in darkness yet impenetrable. Of matter we know nothing beyond a few relations. What it is, neither the senses nor the reason teach us, but one thing is plain. Our great ideas of it have their origin in our own intellectual nature. Its powers, laws, and glories are revealed by the light which beams from our own souls."

The dogmatic agnosticism of these last lines is quite astonishing. All agnosticism, one reflects, is dogmatic. True enough, but why should Channing, the persistent and undaunted rationalist thus succumb to its allurements? It is not because of the development of any seemingly insoluble antinomies, for the argument, as the reader will have observed, leads straight in one direction. Channing has advanced to the very threshold of idealism, and then refused to enter. Why? Because of some lingering fondness for dualism? It is not apparent. Because of a fear of pantheism? That is not apparent either, and would, moreover, be wholly groundless. Because of any theological considerations? [12] Channing is not the man to be restrained by these, nor is it obvious what these could be. The reason, perhaps, may be his confused conception of substance—the unknown something, the thing-in-itself behind phenomena. Hence his outlook upon the external universe is very similar to that of Kant. Or, even more probably, the influence of Price, whose argument and conclusion are similar to his own, was the deciding factor.

When he turns to the examination of the self, however, all seems to become light. The experience of introspection wherein the individual becomes aware of himself is, he tells us, "not to be described." It cannot be put into words. "The 'I' cannot be analysed. There is nothing more simple into which it can be resolved; of course there is no room for definition in the case. Philosophy may teach us how the idea springs up, how it becomes associated with acts of the mind, etc., but the idea or feeling itself is primitive, uncompounded, and could a man exist without it, we could in no way reveal it to him."

It is neither a sensation nor an idea of reflection. That it is not the first is obvious, for it is clear that the self is other than the body. "I may lose limb after limb," remarks Channing, "and in a certain time shall change every particle of my present frame, but I, myself, shall be unmutilated, and uncompounded, undivided whole, the same person as at the present moment. My body is mine, not myself." [13] Again, ideas of reflection acquaint us with "operations, thoughts, feelings, powers, acts of the mind." But the "I" is none of these. "It is that which thinks, acts, feels, and is plainly distinguished by us from all these mental modifications." Here Channing is at one with Descartes, who also was able to discriminate between "the thing that thinks" and the thinking which the thing is doing.

There is a third class of ideas, Channing tells us, beside those of sensation and reflection—the Ideas of Reason or understanding which include those "of time, space, substance, cause, right, deity, etc." [14] But all these the mind can view as distinct from itself; moreover the awareness of them always follows upon "a sensation or act of reflection." But the self is known immediately and independently of everything else. Nor is it compounded out of a multiplicity of sensations and reflections which are referred "to a common subject." The whole self is present in each sensation and act of reflection. Thus we do not infer the existence of the "I." "I recognize myself in each separate desire or feeling of yesterday. I need no comparison or bringing together of different states or acts of my mind to help me to the idea of the 'I.' I feel it in each act. I must perceive myself in each of the sensations, or no comparison of them would give rise to the consciousness. When it is said, that by self we mean only the subject of various thoughts or feelings, it should be considered that most of these feelings are brought to the mind by the memory. But the memory recognizes the 'I' in each of its acts." "Each recollection includes as part of itself the oneness of the doer of the recollected act, with the being who remembers it. Identity is not a deduction, not founded on bringing together various actions in which we discern one subject, but is involved in each act of memory."

Here we have an extremely interesting anticipation of the argument adumbrated by Lord Russell in his *Problems of Philosophy,* and developed in such detail by McTaggart.[15] The self thus grasped is, like the Leibnitzian self, a simple unity. Its nature is complex, but it is not itself complex.[16] "It can be divided into no elements. I have indeed a great variety of thoughts and feelings, but I, who think and feel, am a simple unity. This infinite diversity of mental affections meets in one point, myself. In accordance with this, self is revealed as something permanent. Our thoughts and sensations indeed are changing, and often fleet through the mind with the speed of lightning. But the I is the same."

How does such self-knowledge initially come about? Channing is inclined to reject Cousin's theory that self-consciousness arises in connection with an act of volition. It is not certain, Channing thinks, that it arises in connection with any mental phenomenon or idea of reflection, it is conceivable that attention should become directed immediately upon the "I." But, on the supposition that such is not the case, it is evident, he contends, that the mental phenomena upon which attention is directed by the will must become known prior to the act of will which has directed the attention upon them. None the less consciousness of will is most important, being closely linked to that of activity and power. It is thus that the self recognizes its own capacities, and comes to know itself as a free agent. And this becomes enhanced when moral ideas enter upon the scene, and the soul experiences the feelings of obligation, aspiration, and remorse.

The principle features of Channing's world-view are now before us, and into its more extended details we must refrain from following him. It is clear, as we look back over the path we have traversed, that his greatness lies in the realm of theology and the philosophy of religion. There his insight is characterized by remarkable penetration, his grasp is sure, his arguments are clearly formulated, and are admirably, and often eloquently, stated. His thought in this field is remarkably well integrated. The principle of essential sameness binds it together like a hoop of iron. Moreover reason and religious experience are blended with a sense of fitness and equity which, I confess, impresses me as well-nigh incomparable. And, above all, the man's transparent honesty and intellectual courage make one love him. One never feels that Channing is trying to persuade one of anything of the truth of which he is not himself convinced, or that he could ever find himself in the wrong and not acknowledge it. His moral enthusiasm is always genuine, and, therefore, never palls; and his emotions, when aroused, sometimes carry him to lofty heights of eloquence.

Moreover it is in this field, where his chief interests lay and his main work was done, that we can gauge his real ability. In the related fields of ethics and the philosophy of politics much the same may be said, although, had he been able to spend more time there, he would probably have elaborated his views in more detailed and systematic fashion. As we approached the periphery of his thought, we noted various "loose ends" which were never tied together. His treatment of the self is admirable, his philosophy of nature inadequate, his vacilation between dualism and idealism regrettable. It is sad to reflect that had his life-span and health permitted him to complete his *Treatise on Man* his entire system would in all likelihood have become as tightly integrated as is his philosophy of religion.[17]

Theism, as Channing presents it, possesses a peculiar charm. The clouds and mists with which the negative theology and the *analogia entis* shroud the weakness of orthodoxy vanish away. Yet, the ensuing clarity is itself a danger, since the foe can the better determine where to direct his attacks. Thus the problem of evil confronts Channing with especial menace, since he is unable to take cover behind the smoke-screen of analogous predication. But his thesis of indeterminism, granted that it can be sustained, enables him to make a defense which is plausible—so far as it goes. It is in the nature of perfection, he maintains, that it can never be a free gift but must always be fought for; and where there is fighting, there must be pain and suffering. It is a philosophy of "no cross, no crown." All this may be true, yet is it all the truth? So much suffering seems to make for imperfection. Channing's God is limited by the laws of logic and by the free will of man. But must there not be other limitations, if the sufferings that result in putrification rather than in purification and the woes that beset the animal kingdom are to be accounted for? In this respect we may regret that Channing was not a mere vigorous pioneer.

Nevertheless, if the theistic hypothesis is to be vindicated in the face of its enemies, has not Channing clearly indicated the way in which it must be done? A personal God, one in the sense in which man is one, good in the sense in which man is good, loving in the sense in which man loves—his attributes essentially the same though the degree be exempt from limitation—here is a being who can be under stood, and *because* understood, can be loved. No nobler apology for any religion was ever framed, no more optimistic affirmation was ever uttered, than the sentence in which Channing expressed the substance of his faith—"there is no good too vast for us to anticipate for the universe or for ourselves from such a Father as we believe in."

## NOTES

1. *Life*, p. 34.
2. *Cf.* Mill's "permanent possibilities of sensation."
3. *Works*, pp. 514. col. 2.—515. col. 1.
4. *Ibid.*, p. 981. col. 2. *Cf. Ibid.*, p. 248. col. 1.
5. See Professor D. Daiches Raphael's edition: pp. XII, 25n, 26, 183n.
6. *Ibid.*, p. 25n.
7. The occasionalism of the *Mutakallimun* was known to, and criticized by, St. Thomas Aquinas. (See my *Conception of God in the Philosophy of Aquinas*, pp. 448-468.) Of this Malebranche must surely have been aware, but whether there is any evidence for his own thought having been affected by this knowledge I cannot say.
8. *Ibid.*, pp. 25-27.
9. This, Channing considers, is the true interpretation of Locke. "It has been the custom of late to find much fault with Mr. Locke as the author of the sensual philosophy on account of the high rank he has given to sensation as the [immediate cause] in explaining the origin of our ideas. But he plainly means only that sensation is the occasion, not the productive cause. When he traces the idea of space to the senses, he does not mean that space falls under any of these, that it can be seen, handled, tested, heard and touched, or that the idea of it is included as a part in any of the mental affections, which properly are called sensations. He means that by the exercise of the senses this idea springs up to us, or becomes present to consciousness. His simple object was to show the way in which ideas come to us, to trace them back to their first manifestation, to give us their history, not to unfold their cause, nor did he dream of confounding under one head all which owe their birth to the same circumstances."
10. This recognition of the unconscious may we not safely ascribe to the influence of Leibnitz?
11. For Price's treatment of space, time, and substance see the *Review*, pp. 23-24. It will be observed that Channing follows his lead in making the knowledge of them intuitive, but elaborates upon his treatment by connecting the

        awareness of space with sight and touch, that of time with sound, and that of substance—though in a somewhat different fashion—with self-awareness.

12. Malebranche, it will be recalled, accepts the reality of the physical world because he thinks it is implied by Scripture, and because of the Incarnation. Neither of these considerations disuaded Berkeley, and certainly the latter would not have influenced Channing!

13. Hence a man can *own* his body.

14. See Price's *Review,* Ch. I.

15. McTaggart's argument is to be found in his article on *Personality* in *Hastings Encyclopedia of Ethics and Religion,* and also in the chapter entitled *Spirit* in the second volume of *The Nature of the Existence.* No appeal to memory is made by McTaggart, but he contends that, when such a judgment is made as for example, "I am aware of equality" the "I" which makes the judgment identifies itself with the "I" which is aware of equality, and that such identification cannot possibly be the result for inference—for reasons far too detailed to be here summarized—but must be grasped intuitively.

16. In this respect, interestingly enough, it differs from the self in the philosophy of McTaggart.

17. Even there his doctrine of salvation suffers from the fact that closely related problems in the realm of metaphysics were accorded no adequate treatment.

# Index

# INDEX

## J.

Jami, 253
Javenel, 3
Jeanne d'Arc, 174
Johnson, Dr., 30
Jones, Rufus, 89, 223
Judaism, 193, 200-201

## K.

Kant (Kantian), 58 (n. 46), 73, 105, 107, 237, 287, 289
Koran, 9

## L.

Laboring class, elevation of, 143 (n. 91)
Lagrange, R. Garrigou-. See Garrigou-Lagrange, R.
Lecerf, M., 7-8, 43
Leibniz, 284, 292 (n. 10)
Liberalism (liberal, liberals), 18, 23-24; Channing as outstanding liberal, 21, 54
Locke, John, 14, 29-60, 105, 107, 110, 113, 129, 135, 149, 184, 187-89, 191, 197, 200, 202, 204, 206, 220, 225, 227, 260, 263, 282, 292 (n. 9)
Love: in general, 169-70; set free by Christ, 169-70; toward God and man, 220; toward God, 236-38, 268-71
Lovejoy, Arthur O., 263
Luther, Martin, 5

## M.

McTaggart, John E., 35, 264, 268-69, 271, 290, 293 (n. 15)
Maimonides, 72, 95 (n. 67), 177
Malebranche, 283-84, 287, 293 (n. 12)
Man, Channing's doctrine of: 97-148; elevation of soul in, 101; free will of, 100; greatness of, related to God, 99-100; immortality of, 104-108, 136-37; soul of man as source of his knowledge of God, 100; *summum bonum* for, 103-104
Matter, 286-88
Mazzini, 140 (n. 36), 147 (n. 164), 180
Melancthon, Philip, 5
Milton, 100, 225, 281-82
Mind, human, 226-27

Miracle(s); Channing's doctrine of, 204-13, 245-46 (n. 88), 246-47 (n. 99), 248 (n. 110; Locke's doctrine of, 46-48
Mohammed, 47
Monadology, 284
Montefiore, Claude, 171, 173
Montesquieu, 127
Mysticism (mystic, mystical), 9, 89, 99, 200, 218, 222-23, 232, 234-37, 251 (n. 138)

## N.

Nature (human), 273
Nature (natural), 187, 199, 213-14, 291
Neo-Platonism, 200, 235
Nestorianism, 156, 172. See also Trinity, Trinitarianism
New Testament, 19, 49, 151. See also Bible, Scriptures
Nicholson, R. A., 9
Nominalism, 56 (n. 9)
Norton, Andrews, 160

## O.

Occam's Razor, 150. See also Unitarianism, razor
Ontology (ontologism, ontologist), 44, 227
Orthodoxy, 21-22

## P.

Pantheism (pantheistic), 97, 99, 136, 138 (n. 13), 236, 288
Parker, Theodore, 23-24, 52, 64, 151, 153, 166, 190, 204, 210, 214, 216
Patripassianism, 155
Patterson, Robert L., 254 (n. 193), 292 (n. 7)
Paul of Samosata, 23, 50
Peabody, Elizabeth, 244, 247, 255
Peake, A. S., 27 (n. 62)
Perfection (perfectibility), 255-57
Personalism (personalistic), 155
Plato (Platonic), 52, 91
Plotinus, 52
Pratt, James B., 89
Prayer, 276 (n. 42)
Price, 52, 283-84, 289, 292 (n. 11)
Priestley, Joseph, 65, 282
Progress, endless moral, 263-67
Property, 109-10, 141 (n. 55)